"Sustainable investing isn't just for socia ... become one of the fastest growing parts of the wealth management industry, and the extraordinary array of contributors to this volume explain why. If Homo sapiens is to survive to the next millennium, the species will have to put these ideas into practice sooner rather than later."

Andrew Lo, MIT Sloan School of Management

"This is an engaging book encompassing a wealth of knowledge for anyone interested in sustainable investing: from the experienced investor who wants to better understand the field of sustainable investing to the intellectually curious business leader who wants to learn more about what it is and how it can be practiced."

George Serafeim, Harvard Business School

"This impressive book shows why market transformation is imperative and how business and finance can build a safe and liveable future."

Dr. Herbert Diess, CEO Volkswagen AG

"This book argues convincingly that sustainable investing is becoming mainstream, as increasing numbers of asset owners, investment managers and companies take steps toward addressing longer-term challenges facing businesses and society. The question is not whether these commitments are welcome – they are – but whether they will be anywhere near enough to address our climate crisis and accomplish the Just Transition so necessary in the decade ahead."

Al Gore and David Blood, Generation Investment Management

"As the global Zeitgeist has shifted, the vision of a sustainable future is within reach. The investment universe will play a big role in implementing ESG into the fabric of the economic system. This insightful book shows that we already have the ideas and, yes, the means to get it done."

Asoka Wöhrmann, CEO DWS

Sustainable Investing

This book tells the story of how the convergence between corporate sustainability and sustainable investing is now becoming a major force driving systemic market changes. The idea and practice of corporate sustainability is no longer a niche movement. Investors are increasingly paying attention to sustainability factors in their analysis and decision-making, thus reinforcing market transformation.

In this book, high-level practitioners and academic thought leaders, including contributions from John Ruggie, Fiona Reynolds, Johan Rockström, and Paul Polman, explain the forces behind these developments. The contributors highlight (a) that systemic market change is influenced by various contextual factors that impact how sustainable investing is perceived and practiced; (b) that the integration of ESG factors in investment decisions is impacting markets on a large scale and hence changes practices of major market players (e.g. pension funds); and (c) that technology and the increasing datafication of sustainability act as further accelerators of such change.

The book goes beyond standard economic theory approaches to sustainable investing and emphasizes that capitalism founded on more real-world (complex) economics and cooperation can strengthen ESG integration. Aimed at both investment professionals and academics, this book gives the reader access to more practitioner-relevant information and it also discusses implementation issues. The reader will gain insights into how "mainstream" financial actors relate to sustainable investing.

Herman Bril joined the United Nations Joint Staff Pension Fund (UNJSPF) in New York as Director of the Office of Investment Management in June of 2016. He has over 25 years of experience in international financial institutions in multiple countries.

Georg Kell is Chairman of Arabesque, an ESG Quant fund manager that uses self-learning quantitative models and big data to assess the performance and sustainability of globally listed companies. Georg is the founding Director of the United Nations Global Compact.

Andreas Rasche is Professor of Business in Society at the Centre for Sustainability at Copenhagen Business School (CBS) and also acts as the Associate Dean for the CBS MBA program. He is Visiting Professor at the Stockholm School of Economics.

Sustainable Investing

A Path to a New Horizon

Edited by

Herman Bril,
Georg Kell and
Andreas Rasche

Routledge
Taylor & Francis Group

LONDON AND NEW YORK

First published 2021
by Routledge
2 Park Square, Milton Park, Abingdon, Oxon OX14 4RN

and by Routledge
52 Vanderbilt Avenue, New York, NY 10017

Routledge is an imprint of the Taylor & Francis Group, an informa business

British Library Cataloguing-in-Publication Data
A catalogue record for this book is available from the British Library

Library of Congress Cataloging-in-Publication Data
Names: Bril, Herman, 1967- editor. | Kell, Georg, editor. | Rasche,
Andreas, editor.
Title: Sustainable investing : a path to a new horizon / edited by Herman
Bril, Georg Kell, and Andreas Rasche.
Description: First Edition. | New York : Routledge, 2020. | Includes
bibliographical references and index.
Identifiers: LCCN 2020011506 (print) | LCCN 2020011507 (ebook) | ISBN
9780367367336 (hardback) | ISBN 9780367367350 (paperback) | ISBN
9780429351044 (ebook)
Subjects: LCSH: Investments–Environmental aspects. | Investments–Social
aspects. | Social responsibility of business. | Investment analysis.
Classification: LCC HG4515.13 .S87 2020 (print) | LCC HG4515.13
(ebook) |
DDC 332.6–dc23
LC record available at https://lccn.loc.gov/2020011506
LC ebook record available at https://lccn.loc.gov/2020011507

ISBN: 978-0-367-36733-6 (hbk)
ISBN: 978-0-367-36735-0 (pbk)
ISBN: 978-0-429-35104-4 (ebk)

Typeset in Minion
by Swales & Willis, Exeter, Devon, UK

Contents

Figures

Tables

Boxes

Boxes

Abbreviations

4IR	Fourth Industrial Revolution
5IR	Fifth Industrial Revolution
AI	Artificial Intelligence
ACGA	Asian Corporate Governance Association
APG	Algemene Pensioen Groep
AUM	Assets Under Management
BCG	Boston Consulting Group
BR	Business Roundtable
CAPM	Capital Asset Pricing Model
CAS	Complex Adaptive System
CalPERS	California Public Employees' Retirement System
CDP	Carbon Disclosure Project
CDSB	Climate Disclosure Standards Board
CEO	Chief Executive Officer
CERCLA	Comprehensive Environmental Response, Compensation and Liability Act
CFA	Chartered Financial Analyst
CFO	Chief Financial Officer
CGE	Computable General Equilibrium
CLSA	Credit Lyonnais Securities Asia
CMIP	Climate Model Intercomparison Project
CNPC	China National Petroleum Corporation
CO_2	Carbon Dioxide
CO_e	Carbon Dioxide Equivalent
COP	Convention on Climate Change
CRIO	Chief Responsible Investment Officer
CSR	Corporate Social Responsibility

CVaR	Climate Value-at-Risk
DDM	Dividend Discount Modelling
EC	European Commission
EMH	Efficient Market Hypothesis
EP	Equator Principles
EPFI	Equator Principle Finance Institution
ESG	Environmental, Social, Governance
EU	European Union
FCA	Financial Conduct Authority
FI	Financial Institution
fintechs	Financial Technology
GABV	Global Alliance for Banking on Values
GAI	Governance and Accountability Institute
GDP	Gross Domestic Product
GHG	Greenhouse Gas
GIIN	Global Impact Investing Network
GIZ	Gaesong Industrial Zone
GRI	Global Reporting Initiative
GSIA	Global Sustainable Investment Alliance
GPS	Global Positioning System
GVA	Gross Value Added
HLEG	High-Level Expert Group
IAM	Integrated Assessment Models
IEA	International Energy Agency
IFAC	International Federation of Accountants
IFC	International Finance Corporation
IIASA	International Institute for Applied Systems Analysis
IIGCC	Institutional Investors Group on Climate Change
IMF	International Monetary Fund
IP	Internet Protocol
IPCC	Intergovernmental Panel on Climate Change
IPR	Inevitable Policy Response
IRRC	International Integrated Reporting Council
LGBTQ	Lesbian, Gay, Bisexual, Transgender, Queer
MDGs	Millennium Development Goals
MSCI	Morgan Stanley Capital International
MIT	Massachusetts Institute of Technology
MPT	Modern Portfolio Theory
MVO	Mean Variance Optimization
NGO	Non-Governmental Organization
NLP	Natural Language Processing
NPV	Net Present Value

OCED	Organization for Economic Co-operation and Development
PIK	Potsdam Institute for Climate Impact Research
PRB	Principles for Responsible Banking
PRI	Principles for Responsible Investment
PSI	Principles for Sustainable Insurance
SASB	Sustainability Accounting Standards Board
S-BMI	Sustainable Business Model Innovation
SBTI	Science Based Targets Initiative
SCC	Social Cost of Carbon
SDGs	Sustainable Development Goals
SRI	Socially Responsible Investment
STIR	Spending, Transition, Impact, and Resource Availability
S&P	Standard & Poor's
TEG	Technical Expert Group
TFCD	Task Force on Climate-Related Financial Disclosures
TNC	Transnational Corporation
TSI	Total Societal Impact
TSR	Total Shareholder Return
UK	United Kingdom
US	United States
USD	US Dollar
UN	United Nations
UNCTAD	United Nations Conference on Trade and Development
UNEP	United Nations Environmental Programme
UNEP FI	United Nations Environmental Programme Finance Initiative
UNFCCC	United Nations Framework Convention on Climate Change
UNGC	United Nations Global Compact
VaR	Value at Risk
VUCA	Volatile, Uncertain, Complex, and Ambiguous
WBCSD	World Business Council for Sustainable Development
WEF	World Economic Forum
WHO	World Health Organization
WRI	World Resources Institute
WWF	World Wide Fund for Nature

Contributors

Keith Ambachtsheer has been named "Top 30 Difference-Maker" by P&I, the "Globe's #1 Knowledge Broker in Institutional Investing" and "Top 10 Influential Academic in Institutional Investing" by aiCIO, in the "Top Pension 40" by II, "Outstanding Industry Contributor" by IPE, the Lilywhite Award recipient by EBRI, the "Professional Excellence" and "James Vertin" Awards recipient by the CFA Institute, the McArthur Industry Pioneer Award recipient by IMCA, and the Hirtle-Callghan Award for Investment Leadership. He is Adjunct Professor of Finance, Rotman School of Management, University of Toronto, and Director Emeritus of its International Centre for Pension Management. He is a member of the Melbourne-Mercer Global Pension Index Advisory Council, the CFA Institute's Future of Finance Advisory Council, the Georgetown University Center for Retirement Initiatives Scholars Council, and the Advisory Council of the Tobacco Free Portfolios initiative. He is also a co-founder of KPA Advisory Services and of CEM Benchmarking Inc.

Almut Beringer, Full Professor Environment and Sustainability, is a researcher at the Potsdam Institute for Climate Impact Research. Her research areas are human–nature relations, conservation psychology, and religions and sustainable development. Almut has applied the Planetary Boundaries concept in theology, pioneered research into the moral psychological foundation of environmental ethics, and was instrumental in researching and implementing sustainable development in the higher education sector. Her work in climate change, biodiversity conservation, and nature protection spans science, university, NGOs, and public administration.

Helga Birgden is Partner, Mercer's Global Leader, Responsible Investment. Helga has more than 20 years' experience advising global pension funds, sovereign wealth funds, endowments, and insurers on responsible investment. She has prepared economic and policy advice for multilateral institutions on ESG and climate change, including multilateral institutions such as the International Finance Corporation, World Bank Group, G20, Development Banks and United Nations programs. Over the last decade Helga has been a leader in Mercer's global climate change studies 2011, 2015, and 2019 *Investing in a Time of Climate Change* and *The Sequel*. She lives off the grid (solar and wind).

Patrick Bolton is the Barbara and David Zalaznick Professor of Business at Columbia University and visiting Professor at Imperial College London. He is a Co-Director of the Center for Contracts and Economic Organization at the Columbia Law School, a past President of the American Finance Association, a Fellow of the Econometric Society (elected 1993), the American Academy of Arts and Sciences (elected 2009), and a Corresponding Fellow of the British Academy (elected 2013).

Herman Bril joined the UNJSPF in New York as Director of the Office of Investment Management in June 2016. With 25+ years of experience in international financial institutions in multiple countries, Mr. Bril possesses broad-level expertise encompassing asset management, sustainable investing, pension funds, development finance, investment banking, derivatives trading, and treasury. Before joining the UNJSPF, he served as Group CFO and Managing Director at Cardano in London. Prior to Cardano, Mr. Bril was Senior Vice President, Head of Treasury and Capital Management at Aegon NV, and Head of Asset Management and Chief Investment Officer of Syntrus Achmea Asset Management. He started his career as a fixed-income derivative trader for ABN AMRO, Dresdner Bank and Deutsche Bank in Amsterdam, Frankfurt, and London. Mr. Bril graduated from the Free University in Amsterdam with a master's in Economics. Additionally, he graduated from INSEAD, where he earned a diploma in Consulting and Coaching for Change. Mr. Bril completed a master's degree in Studies in Sustainability Leadership from the University of Cambridge.

Mark Carney is the Governor of the Bank of England and Chair of the Monetary Policy Committee, Financial Policy Committee and the Board of the Prudential Regulation Authority. His appointment as Governor was approved by Her Majesty the Queen on 26 November 2012. The Governor joined the Bank on 1 July 2013. In addition to his duties as Governor of the Bank of England, Mark Carney also served as First Vice-Chair of the

European Systemic Risk Board. He is a member of the Group of Thirty and the Foundation Board of the World Economic Forum. Mark Carney was Chair of the Financial Stability Board from 2011 to 2018. Mark Carney was appointed as the UN Special Envoy for Climate Action and Finance on 1 December 2019, and Prime Minister Johnson's Finance Adviser for COP26 on 16 January 2020. Mark Carney was born in Fort Smith, Northwest Territories, Canada in 1965. He received a bachelor's degree in Economics from Harvard University in 1988. He went on to receive a master's degree in Economics in 1993 and a doctorate in Economics in 1995, both from Oxford University. After a 13-year career with Goldman Sachs in its London, Tokyo, New York, and Toronto offices, Mark Carney was appointed Deputy Governor of the Bank of Canada in August 2003. In November 2004, he left the Bank of Canada to become Senior Associate Deputy Minister of Finance. He held this position until his appointment as Governor of the Bank of Canada on 1 February 2008. Mark Carney served as Governor of the Bank of Canada and Chairman of its Board of Directors until 1 June 2013.

Beatrice Crona (Associate Professor) is executive director of the Global Economic Dynamics and the Biosphere program at the Royal Swedish Academy of Sciences, Stockholm. She has pioneered research efforts focused on examining links between the financial sector and the biosphere, and also leads research designed to inform a transition to a sustainable and health-promoting food system. Professor Crona is Deputy Science Director at the Stockholm Resilience Centre, Stockholm University.

Jacob Davidson joined Bridgewater in 2016 and has focused on developing Bridgewater's approach to sustainable investing. As a member of Bridgewater's Investment Associate program, he has researched macroeconomics, global financial markets, and portfolio construction. Jacob received a BA in Political Science and Middle Eastern Studies from Columbia University.

Nathan Fabian is the Chief Responsible Investment Officer at the Principles for Responsible Investment. He directs and oversees PRI's Investment Practices, Active Ownership, Policy and Research, ESG, Climate Change, and SDG activities. Nathan is also the Rapporteur for the Taxonomy Group of the EU Technical Expert Group on Sustainable Finance. He was an Observer on the EU High Level Expert Group on Sustainable Finance and part of the Secretariat for the UK Green Finance Taskforce. Prior to the PRI, Nathan was the CEO of the Investor Group on Climate Change (IGCC) Australia/New Zealand. Previous roles include Head of ESG Research at Regnan; founding Partner of Full Corp Partners; and Corporate Governance Policy Advisor in the Australian Parliament. He has also worked as a senior change management consultant for Arthur Andersen and as a market analyst at Krone. Nathan holds an M.A. in International Relations from the University of New South Wales, a B.Bus. from the University of Newcastle (Australia), and is a Vincent Fairfax Fellow in ethics and leadership.

Owen Gaffney is an Anthropocene analyst and writer at the Potsdam Institute for Climate Impact Research and Stockholm Resilience Centre. He is a senior fellow at Future Earth and a fellow at the Edmund Hillary Foundation, New Zealand. He holds a faculty position at Singularity University, Mountain View, California. He publishes analysis and commentary on global sustainability policy, earth system science, technological innovation, and the media. His background is in astronautic engineering and journalism.

Daniel Hochman joined Bridgewater in 2011 and heads Sustainable Investing and ESG Research. He is a nine-year member of Bridgewater's Investment Associate program, researching macroeconomics, global financial markets, portfolio construction, and institutional investing. Daniel received an AB in History from Dartmouth College. In 2019, he was named to *Forbes* 30 Under 30 list in Finance.

Karen Karniol-Tambour joined Bridgewater in 2006 and heads Investment Research. She oversees teams of investors developing systematic insights on global markets and economies and is a regular author of Bridgewater's *Daily Observations*, with a focus on fixed income, monetary and fiscal policy, money and credit flows, and portfolio construction. Karen received her AB from Princeton's Woodrow Wilson School of Public and International Affairs with a Certificate in Finance. She is an Atlantic Council Millennium Fellow and serves on the Board of Seeds of Peace, a nonprofit cultivating young leaders to transform conflict in the Middle East and South Asia. She was included in *Fortune*'s 40 Under 40 most influential leaders in business.

Georg Kell is Chairman of Arabesque, an ESG Quant fund manager that uses self-learning quantitative models and big data to assess the performance and sustainability of globally listed companies. Arabesque was launched in 2013 following a management buyout from Barclays Bank. Georg is the founding Director of the United Nations Global Compact, the world's largest voluntary corporate sustainability initiative with over 9,000 corporate signatories in more than 160 countries. Georg helped to establish the UN Global Compact as the foremost platform for the development, implementation, and disclosure of responsible and sustainable corporate policies and practices. In a career of more than 25 years at the United Nations, he also oversaw the conception and launch of the Global Compact's sister initiatives, the

Principles for Responsible Investment (PRI), the Principles for Responsible Management Education (PRME), and the Sustainable Stock Exchanges (SSE). Georg started his career as a research fellow in engineering at the Fraunhofer Institute in Berlin. He then worked as a financial analyst in various countries in Africa and Asia before joining the United Nations in 1987. Georg holds advanced degrees in economics and engineering from the Technical University of Berlin.

Daniel Klingenfeld is an expert on energy and climate policy issues and Head of the Directors' Staff at the Potsdam Institute for Climate Impact Research (PIK). Daniel Klingenfeld has been working at PIK since 2009, initially as a research analyst for the director at the German Advisory Council on Global Change to the Federal Government (WBGU). His doctoral thesis was published in the series Studies on International Environmental Policy. Dr. Klingenfeld holds further degrees from the Kennedy School at Harvard University (Master in Public Policy) and ESCP Europe (M.Sc. in Management).

Theo Kocken is Professor of Risk Management at VU University Amsterdam and extraordinary professor at NWU University (South Africa). He founded the Anglo-Dutch pension investment and risk management firm Cardano in 2000 and is chairman of the Cardano Development Foundation, aiming to improve risk solutions in frontier markets. Before founding Cardano, he was head of Market Risk at ING Bank and Rabobank. He has a master in Econometrics and received his Ph.D. at VU University Amsterdam. Over the past 25 years he has published many books and articles on risk management and produced the documentary "Boom Bust Boom" on endogenous financial instability.

Brian Kreiter is the Chief Operating Officer of Bridgewater Associates, responsible for delivering the company's strategic plan, as well as overseeing critical Finance, Talent, and Business Intelligence functions. In addition, Brian co-leads the company's Sustainable Investing efforts. Prior to joining Bridgewater, Brian was a management consultant with McKinsey & Company, where he served clients across several industries and worked on the launch of the firm's Social Sector Office. In 1998, Brian co-founded LIFT, a nonprofit organization that empowers families to break the cycle of poverty across the United States. Brian has since been involved with a broad array of endeavors across the social and private sectors connected to his interest in creating meaningful opportunities for those in need.

Simon Levin is the James S. McDonnell Distinguished University Professor in Ecology and Evolutionary Biology and the Director of the Center for BioComplexity in the Princeton Environmental Institute, at Princeton University. He holds a B.A. in Mathematics from Johns Hopkins University and a Ph.D. in Mathematics from the University of Maryland, College Park. Levin has won the Heineken Prize for Environmental Sciences, Kyoto Prize in Basic Sciences, Margalef Prize for Ecology, the Ecological Society of America's MacArthur and Eminent Ecologist Awards, Tyler Prize for Environmental Achievement, and the 2014 National Medal of Science.

Ania Levina is a Project Leader at the Boston Consulting Group and ambassador to the BCG Henderson Institute. Prior to BCG, Ania completed her Ph.D. in Organic Chemistry at Harvard University, and received her Bachelor of Science from MIT.

Stefan Lundbergh is Director of Cardano Imagine. In his past he held various positions at APG in the Netherlands and Skandia Life Insurance Company in Sweden. He holds a Ph.D. from Stockholm School of Economics. Stefan is a frequent speaker and writer in the field of behavioral investing and pension design. He headed a review of the Swedish premium pension system in 2017 and has been a non-executive board member of the Fourth Swedish National Pension Fund (AP4).

Ashby Monk is the Executive Director and Research Director of Stanford University's Global Projects Center. He is also the Co-founder, President and Board member of RCI, a technology company serving long-term investors that's in closed-beta. He is also Co-founder and Chairman of Long Game, a company that uses short-term incentives to help people make long-term financial plans.

Mark Moody-Stuart is Chairman of the Global Compact Foundation, and a director of Saudi Aramco. He was Chairman of the Royal Dutch/Shell Group (1998–2001), of Anglo American plc (2002–09), Hermes Equity Ownership Services and Innovative Vector Control Consortium (IVCC). After a doctorate in geology, he worked for Shell, living in Holland, Spain, Oman, Brunei, Australia, Nigeria, Turkey, Malaysia, and the UK. He is a former director of Accenture and HSBC, Chairman of the FTSE ESG Advisory Committee (2014–19), Honorary Co-Chairman of the International Tax and Investment Center, and author of *Responsible Leadership: Lessons from the front line of sustainability and ethics.*

Paul Polman is Co-founder and Chair of IMAGINE, an activist corporation and foundation that promotes implementation of the global goals through transformational leadership. He is also Chair of the International Chamber of Commerce and the B Team, and Vice-Chair of the UN Global Compact. As CEO of Unilever (2009–18), Paul demonstrated that a long-term, multi-stakeholder model goes hand-in-hand with excellent financial performance. He was appointed by then United Nations Secretary-General Ban Ki-moon to the High-Level Panel that developed the UN's Sustainable Development Goals, and he remains an active SDG Advocate, working with global organizations and across industries to make the case for the 2030 development agenda.

Marcel Prins is COO at APG Asset Management and responsible for Operations, Technology, Innovation and Procurement. He is member of the advisory board of Euronext Netherlands and Business Intelligence and Smart Service (BISS) Institute and Chairman of two EMEA client advisory boards of global custodian banks. Marcel joined APG in 2011 when he left ABN Amro, where he was Managing Director Operations International, providing services to the various international businesses in 17 countries. Prior to this position Marcel was COO Merchant Banking and Head of Operations at Fortis Bank Nederland. Marcel holds a B.ICT in Information and Communication Technology.

Andreas Rasche is Professor of Business in Society at the Centre for Corporate Sustainability at Copenhagen Business School (CBS) and acts as the Associate Dean for the CBS MBA program. He is Visiting Professor at the Stockholm School of Economics. He has authored more than 40 academic articles in international top journals and published various cases on topics related to corporate sustainability. He authored and edited numerous well-known books, such as: *The United Nations Global Compact: Achievements, Trends, and Challenges, Building the Responsible Enterprise,* and *Corporate Social Responsibility: Strategy, Communication, Governance.* He is Associate Editor of *Business Ethics Quarterly.*

Martin Reeves is a Managing Director and Senior Partner in the San Francisco office of the Boston Consulting Group and Chairman of the BCG Henderson Institute, BCG's think tank on business strategy. Mr. Reeves is also author of *Your Strategy Needs a Strategy,* which deals with choosing and executing the right approach in today's complex and dynamic business environment. Mr. Reeves holds a triple first-class MA degree in natural sciences from Cambridge University and an MBA from Cranfield School of Management. He also studied Japanese at Osaka University of Foreign Studies and biophysics at the University of Tokyo.

Fiona Reynolds is the CEO of the Principles for Responsible Investment (PRI). Appointed in 2013, Fiona has 25 years' experience in the financial services and pension sector. Fiona joined PRI from the Australian Institute of Superannuation Trustees (AIST), where she spent seven years as the CEO. Fiona serves on the Board of the UN Global Compact, is a member of the International Integrated Reporting Council (IIRC), the Global Advisory Council on Stranded Assets at Oxford University, the UN Business for Peace Steering Committee, the Global Steering Committee for the Investor Agenda, and the Steering Committee for Climate Action 100+. Fiona has been a member of the UK Government Green Finance Taskforce and is currently on the Advisory Board for the UK Green Finance Centre.

Johan Rockström (Professor) is director of the Potsdam Institute for Climate Impact Research in Germany. He is co-founder of the Stockholm Resilience Centre. Dr. Rockström's research focuses on global sustainability and Earth resilience. His work on global sustainability issues has gained him international recognition and, in 2009, he led an international team of academics who advanced the planetary boundaries framework for sustainable development in the Anthropocene.

Dane Rook is a Research Engineer in Stanford University's Global Projects Center, where he explores applications of advanced technologies to problems in long-term investing. Previously, he worked as a quantitative analyst at Kensho, an AI startup that was acquired by S&P. Earlier, he worked in investment banking at JPMorgan. Dane earned his doctorate from Oxford University as a Clarendon Scholar, and also holds degrees from the University of Cambridge and the University of Michigan. He is an advisor to several fintech startups in the US and Europe.

John Gerard Ruggie is the Berthold Beitz Research Professor in Human Rights and International Affairs at Harvard's Kennedy School of Government. Ruggie introduced the concepts of international regimes, epistemic communities, and embedded liberalism into the international relations field. His most recent book, *Just Business: Multinational Corporations and Human Rights*, has been translated into Chinese, Japanese, Korean, Portuguese, and Spanish. A fellow of the American Academy of Arts and Sciences, Ruggie is also a recipient of a Guggenheim Fellowship. From 1997 to 2001, Ruggie served as United Nations Assistant Secretary-General for Strategic Planning, a post created specifically for him by then Secretary-General Kofi Annan. He was one of the architects of the United Nations Global Compact and the Millennium Development Goals. In 2005, he was appointed as the UN Secretary-General's Special Representative for Business and Human Rights.

In that capacity, he developed the UN Guiding Principles on Business and Human Rights, which the UN Human Rights Council endorsed unanimously in 2011 and which serves as the global standard.

Frédéric Samama is Head of Responsible Investment at Amundi. He is the founder of the SWF Research Initiative and co-edited a book on long-term investing alongside Patrick Bolton and Nobel Prize Laureate Joseph Stiglitz; he has also published numerous papers on green finance. Formerly, he oversaw Corporate Equity Derivatives within Credit Agricole Corporate Investment Banking in New York and Paris. During his tenure, he developed and implemented the first international leveraged employee share purchase program, a technology now widely used among French companies. Over recent years, his action has been focused on climate change with a mix of financial innovation, research, and policymaking recommendations, being an advisor of governments, central banks, sovereign wealth funds or policymakers on the topic.

Omar Selim is the founder and Chief Executive Officer of Arabesque. Omar has 20 years' experience in international banking, having held senior positions at UBS, Morgan Stanley and Credit Suisse. He joined Barclays Bank in 2004, where he was responsible for a multi-billion-dollar revenue budget and over a thousand staff. In 2012, he initiated a values-based asset management project at Barclays, originating the concept and developing it into Arabesque. Established independently in 2013, Arabesque today is a global financial and research group providing investment and data solutions through advanced sustainability and AI capabilities. Through its group of companies, Arabesque leverages cutting-edge technology and research to deliver a new approach to sustainable finance. Omar holds an M.S. in Finance from the University of Fribourg (Switzerland).

Carsten Stendevad has held leadership positions at various global financial institutions over the past 20 years, and is a recognized thought leader in the sustainable investment community. He is currently a senior executive at Bridgewater Associates (a global leader in institutional portfolio management), and also serves as an advisor to the Investment Strategies Committee at GIC (Singapore's Sovereign Wealth Fund) and board member at Novo Holding (the investment arm of Novo Nordisk Foundation, the world's largest charitable endowment). Previously, he was the CEO of ATP (Denmark's national pension plan), a managing director in Citigroup's Investment Banking division in New York with global responsibility for Citi's corporate finance advisory team, and a consultant in McKinsey's financial institutions practice and a co-founder of their International Development practice. He served on the Danish Committee for Corporate Governance, where he chaired the working group tasked with developing a Danish Stewardship Code for institutional investors. He also served on the steering committee for the Blended Finance Taskforce, which aims to increase mainstream private investments for the UN Sustainable Development Goals. Carsten holds a B.Sc. and M.Sc. in Economics from the University of Copenhagen, as well as a Master of Public Policy from the Harvard Kennedy School of Government.

Rory Sullivan is CEO of Chronos Sustainability, Visiting Professor in Practice at the Grantham Research Institute at the London School of Economics, and Strategic Advisor to the Principles for Responsible Investment. He is an internationally recognized expert on responsible investment and climate change, with over 30 years' experience in these and related areas. He is the author/editor of eight books and of many papers and reports on responsible investment, climate change, and related issues, including *Valuing Corporate Responsibility: How Investors Really Use Corporate Responsibility Information* (2011) and *Responsible Investment* (2006).

Halla Tómasdóttir is the CEO of The B Team. Having started her leadership career in corporate America working for Mars and PepsiCo, she later joined the founding team of Reykjavik University, was the first female CEO of the Iceland Chamber of Commerce, and co-founded an ESG-focused investment firm. She has served on for-profit boards in education, healthcare, finance, and consumer products and was the runner-up in Iceland's presidential elections in 2016.

Eric Usher heads the UN Environment Programme Finance Initiative, UNEP FI, which over the years has established some of the most important sustainability oriented frameworks within the finance industry, including the Principles for Responsible Investment, the Principles for Sustainable Insurance, and in 2019 the Principles for Responsible Banking. Prior to UNEP FI, Mr. Usher has worked for over 25 years on the low-carbon sectors and financial sector development across emerging markets. During 2011, Mr. Usher worked on the establishment of the Green Climate Fund and led efforts to create its Private Sector Facility. Earlier in his career, Eric ran a solar rural electrification company based in Morocco.

Foreword

Mark Carney

The catastrophic impacts of climate change will be felt beyond the traditional horizons of businesses, financial regulators, and politicians. By the time climate change becomes a clear and present danger, it could be too late to avoid widespread environmental and economic destruction.

This "Tragedy of the Horizon" appeared inevitable—until recently.

Rising public pressure, led by younger generations, is feeding a growing awareness of the looming climate crisis. When combined with government action and private innovation, this is leading to major changes in the financial system, increasing the prospect of a transition to a net-zero economy.

A more sustainable financial system is being built. It is funding the private sector innovation, it has the potential to amplify the effectiveness of the government climate policies, and it could accelerate the transition to a net-zero economy.

But the task is large, the window of opportunity is short, and the risks are existential.

Changes in climate policies, new technologies, and growing physical risks will prompt reassessments of the values of virtually every financial asset. Firms that align their business models with the transition will be rewarded handsomely. Those that fail will cease to exist.

The changes required are enormous. To get on track for net zero by 2050, carbon emissions will have to be cut in half from 2010 levels over the next decade. This will require a massive reallocation of capital, creating unprecedented risks and opportunities. As one example, investment in the energy sector will need to be $3.5 trillion each year to achieve this goal.

To bring climate risks and resilience into the heart of financial decision-making, climate disclosure must be comprehensive, climate risk management must be transformed, and sustainable investing must go mainstream. Growing expertise in sustainable investing will shape these developments and, as a result, realize the benefits from one of the greatest commercial opportunities of our time.

A few years ago, catalyzed by the G20 economies and established by the private sector, the Task Force on Climate-related Financial Disclosures (TCFD) developed the go-to recommendations for climate-related financial disclosure.

Since then, there has been a step change in both the demand and supply of climate reporting.

The demand is now enormous. Current supporters control balance sheets totaling over $138 trillion and include the world's top banks, asset managers, pension funds, insurers, credit rating agencies, accounting firms, and shareholder advisory services. The supply of disclosure is responding: four-fifths of the top 1,100 G20 companies now disclose climate-related financial risks in line with some of the TCFD recommendations.

Financial practitioners are increasingly focusing on the most decision-useful disclosures around emissions, the resilience of companies' strategies for their reductions, and the governance of these initiatives. Authorities are looking for pathways to make these disclosures mandatory.

Of course, for the market to understand where the risks and opportunities lie, disclosures need to go beyond the static to the strategic. Indeed, the nature of climate risks—given their breadth, magnitude, and foreseeable nature—mean the biggest challenge will be to assess the resilience of firms' strategies to transition risks.

This is easier said than done. Scenario analysis is a new and complex practice. And most of the off-the-shelf climate scenarios (such as the IEA and IPCC publications) are intended for policy or research, not business analysis.

But experience is growing and best practice reveals common characteristics of good scenario analysis:

- using multiple climate-related scenarios to assess strategic resilience;
- describing assumptions and parameters specific to the company;
- identifying potential impacts of climate-related risks or opportunities; and
- disclosing potential strategic resilience under different climate-related scenarios.

One example of such risk analysis is stress testing. The Bank of England is the first regulator to stress test its financial system against different climate pathways, including the catastrophic business-as-usual scenario and the ideal—but still challenging—transition to net zero by 2050, as well as the late policy action—or climate Minsky moment—scenario. It has made those scenarios public for others to use and adapt as they see fit. This open-source approach to climate scenarios will be important to developing the discipline.

Climate stress tests focus on sizing risks and evaluating the strategies of banks and insurers rather than testing firms' capital adequacy. They are longer term, stretching out to 2050, as it is a common horizon to achieve net zero. And they show whether and how major financial firms expect to adjust their business models, and what the collective impact of these responses could be on the wider economy.

Increasingly, banks will need to determine how their borrowers are managing current and future climate-related risks and opportunities. These assessments will reveal:

- which firms have strategies for the transition to a net-zero economy;
- which are gambling on new technologies or government inaction; and
- which haven't yet thought through the risks and opportunities.

Stress tests and scenario analysis will size the exposures of financial firms and the financial system to climate risk, reveal the challenges to business models and the implications for the provision of financial services, and help develop and mainstream cutting-edge risk management techniques. New concepts, such as Climate VaR and stranded asset sensitivities, could become increasingly commonplace.

But the risks from climate change are only half the story. The transformation to a low-carbon economy will also bring enormous opportunities. As I noted, energy infrastructure investments could double to $3.5 trillion every year for decades. There will be huge opportunities for new technologies, from advanced materials to carbon capture, AI, and reinventing protein.

Investments of this scale cannot be financed in niche markets. So, although they are important catalysts, specialist investments like green bonds and transition bonds will not be sufficient to finance the transition to a low-carbon future. Indeed, such securities accounted for only 3% of global bond issuance in 2018.

To date, approaches to measuring and managing the financial implications of climate change have been inadequate, such as carbon footprints (which are not forward-looking), divestments (which only focus on the most carbon-intensive sectors), green investments (which are challenging to bring to scale and often overlook transition sectors) or shareholder engagement (with results that are difficult to measure).

For sustainable investment to go truly mainstream, it needs to do more than exclude incorrigibly brown industries and finance new, deep-green technologies. Sustainable investing must catalyze and support all companies that are working to shift from brown to green. We need approaches which capture

"Fifty Shades of Green." The mainstreaming of such strategies and the tools to pursue them are essential.

That will require forming judgments about transition pathways in different sectors and the effectiveness of company strategies relative to both techno-logical possibilities, the strategies of their competitors, the rapidly evolving expectations of their clients, and the evolution of climate regulation.

Promising options include the development of transition indices com-posed of corporations in high-carbon sectors that have adopted low-carbon strategies, and estimates of the "warming potential" of portfolios.

Such a forward-looking measure can help asset owners and managers understand the transition pathway of their assets and develop strategies to align financial flows toward the Paris Agreement target.

And they could have a number of ancillary benefits. They will signal to governments the transition path of the economy, and therefore the effective-ness of their policies. They can empower consumers, giving them more choice in how to invest their savings and pensions. No longer will they be limited to a choice between risk and return, but also a choice in how best to support the transition.

With our citizens demanding climate action, it is becoming essential for asset owners to disclose the extent to which their clients' money is being invested in line with their values.

****

Sustainable Investing: A Path to a New Horizon presents a unique combina-tion of contributions from academics and practitioners, bringing the theory and practice together, through a range of voices.

In the first part of the book, existing theory is reset, as the reader is brought up to date with recent developments. Current and emerging investing prac-tices are discussed, with practitioners exploring the levers for institutional investors. The authors then move onto new frontiers, exploring how big data and artificial intelligence can reshape investing practices. And consistent with the imperative to mainstream sustainable finance, the book empowers the reader with practical steps to accelerate change.

This book demonstrates steps finance professionals can take to build a virtuous circle of better management of climate risks by banks and insur-ers, better pricing of transition risks and opportunities by investors, better decisions by policymakers, and ultimately a smoother transition to a net zero-carbon economy for all. It represents an important advance towards building the skills needed to bring us to a new horizon that is both more sus-tainable and more prosperous.

Sustainable investing

A path to a new horizon

Herman Bril, Georg Kell, and Andreas Rasche

A CHANGING CONTEXT FOR SUSTAINABLE INVESTING

This book tells the story of how the convergence between corporate sustainability and sustainable investing is now becoming a major force driving systemic market changes. The idea and practice of corporate sustainability is no longer a niche movement. It is now on the agenda of the boardrooms of leading corporations on all continents. At the same time, investors are increasingly paying attention to sustainability factors in their analysis and decision-making, thus reinforcing market transformation. This book discusses the link between sustainability and investment practices—a link which is increasingly discussed under the Environment, Social, Governance (ESG) label. Although a number of terms and definitions populate the broader field of sustainable investing (see the overview by the Institute of International Finance, 2019), we follow the Principles of Responsible Investment (PRI) and see such investing as an approach "to incorporate ESG factors in investment decisions and active ownership" (PRI, 2019). Some of the chapters in this volume even move beyond sustainable investment in the narrow sense, for instance by highlighting the role of banking (Chapter 8 by Eric Usher).

Sustainable investing is not about philanthropy or giving up returns. The value of investments is not only determined by short-term profits but influenced by many long-term global drivers, including technology, natural resources and the environment, geopolitics, the inter-dependencies of globalization, shifts in social norms, inequality, and demographics (see e.g., McAfee, 2019). One important implication of considering these drivers is that we need to rethink how externalities impact systemic risks and the long-term financial implications they may have. Considering these drivers is also essential to ensure the long-term viability of investments, because investors should strive to avoid risks that may compromise long-term economic value. Colin Mayer (2018, p. 132) recently summarized this as follows: "The survival of firms depends as much as we do on the maintenance not only of physical and financial capital but also of natural, human, and social capital."

Sustainable investing not only needs to cope with these drivers; it also needs to do so in an increasingly volatile, uncertain, complex, and ambiguous (VUCA) business context. Managing in such a VUCA business context has profound consequences for how to approach sustainable investing. Consider these two examples: (1) In a complex world, the volume and nature of information can be overwhelming, making predictions and assessments more difficult. However, assessments of firms' ESG performance are necessary even when our knowledge about what exactly drives relevant ESG attributes is still rather limited. It is therefore not surprising that research shows divergence of companies' ESG ratings (Berg, Koelbel, and Rigobon, 2019). (2) In an ambiguous world, causal relationships are often unclear, for instance because no precedent cases or reliable information exist (Bennet and Lemoine, 2014). For the world of finance—which is to a large degree based on understandings of cause and effect relationships—this is surprising, maybe even upsetting.

This book is about managing sustainable investing in a such a VUCA world. We have invited high-level academics and practitioners to reflect on four key themes, which constitute the four main part of this book. First, we have asked a group of contributors to reflect on the changing context of sustainable investing (Part I). These discussions clearly touch upon the relevance of a VUCA business context for ESG, but they also reach beyond it, for instance by challenging deeply embedded theoretical assumptions (e.g., the efficient market hypothesis) that may impede further progress. Second, we have asked a group of contributors to reflect on how to rethink sustainable finance (including both investing and lending) against this changing business context (Part II). These contributions also explore the role that corporate leadership has to play when it comes to ESG investing. Third, we also asked a group of scholars and practitioners to discuss the emerging link between sustainable investing, technology, and (big) data (Part III). These contributions show how alternative data sources, algorithms, and artificial intelligence can reshape the practices attached to sustainable investing (e.g., risk assessments) and drive transparency. Finally, we also asked some contributors to reflect on the future of ESG and sustainable investing (Part IV). What can drive future change in the field? How can relevant debates be mainstreamed, also when looking at organizational requirements for asset owners and investment managers?

We do not claim that this book contains all the answers to the multiple questions which are thrown up in the four parts. But we are positive that the contributions contain vital lessons on future debates in the field of sustainable investing, including the contextual conditions shaping future ESG practices and the role of technology and data. The remainder of this opening chapter discusses two key aspects that were critical while developing this book. The first aspect relates to the need to *challenge traditional assumptions*, both in theory and in practice (see "Challenging traditional assumptions"). We debate the role of some theoretical assumptions that underlie traditional management theory and investment thinking. Our main aim is to show that future progress in the ESG field will depend on challenging and critically debating some of these assumptions. The second aspect relates to the need to consider more closely what *drives and impedes progress in sustainable investing* ("Drivers of and challenges for sustainable investing"). We identify a number of drivers that support the further uptake of sustainable investing (e.g., the perceived importance of planetary boundaries and the increasing availability of ESG data). However, we also show that these drivers can possibly impede further progress in the field, if businesses and policymakers do not manage them correctly.

CHALLENGING TRADITIONAL ASSUMPTIONS

Efficient financial markets

Traditional management and investment thinking has been rather linear and is mostly based on the neoclassical economic ideology, which itself is grounded in unrealistic rational homo-economicus assumptions (see, e.g., Ghoshal, 2005). The financial crisis of 2008 showed the fallibility of this traditional school of thinking. This led to renewed interest in behavioral economics, complexity economics, evolutionary economics, and ecological economics. A number of well-known scholars denounced the efficient markets hypothesis, which is one of the most influential ideas underpinning finance and economics. At the heart of this hypothesis is the idea that market prices include all relevant information in a rational manner (Fama, 1970). Behavioral economics criticized this hypothesis for its lack of empirical support (Kahneman and Tversky, 1979). Are financial markets rational and efficient, as traditional economists would claim, or irrational and inefficient, as some behavioral economists would argue? This debate goes to the heart of debates around ESG and sustainable investing, as it influences our very understanding of how investors and markets behave.

Andrew Lo's work integrated both theories in the so-called *Adaptive Markets Hypothesis* (Lo, 2004, 2017), which is influenced substantially by ideas from evolutionary psychology. This new hypothesis claims that markets can indeed be efficient when the environment is stable. But, in times of instability investors resort to instinctive reactions, which have been shaped over the course of human evolution. In other words: "Markets do look efficient under certain circumstances, namely, when investors have had a chance to adapt to existing business conditions, and those conditions remain relatively stable over a long enough period of time" (Lo, 2017, p. 3). The VUCA business context, which was mentioned above, influences the possibility of these adaptation processes and thereby affects how long investors need to adapt.

The *Adaptive Market Hypothesis* also influences our thinking about sustainable investing. It shows that investors have to reach beyond traditional economic data when analyzing their business environment, for instance to calculate market volatility and risk premia. Simon Levin, Martin Reeves, and Ania Levina (Chapter 2) follow this line of thinking and propose a number of principles that can shape the future of business and sustainable investing. Their arguments, which are based on nested complex adaptive systems theory as well as considerations around systems robustness and longevity, highlight the need to consider the broader, planetary context when evaluating risks and opportunities. Detecting risks that are not local in character, but rather stem from the instability of the planetary system in which businesses are embedded (e.g., related to climate change and biodiversity), creates significant future challenges for managing ESG.

Short-termism

It is no secret that much of the business world is based on short-term thinking. Business objectives are often short-term and so are the resulting incentives and performance metrics (see Levin et al., Chapter 2). In 2015, Mark Carney, Governor of the Bank of England, gave a famous speech on the need to break the *Tragedy of the Horizon* when dealing with the impacts of climate change. Carney (2015, p. 4) argued:

> We don't need an army of actuaries to tell us that the catastrophic impacts of climate change will be felt beyond the traditional horizons of most actors— imposing a cost on future generations that the current generation has no direct incentive to fix.

In other words, the time horizon of important actors—such as business leaders, investors, and policymakers—is too short, so that once "climate change becomes a defining issue for financial stability, it may already be too late."

This book was inspired by Carney's reflections on the *Tragedy of the Horizon*. We believe that sustainable investing can only progress once we address this *Tragedy*. What the contributors of this volume try to do is to chart what Carney (2019) in a later speech called "a path to a New Horizon." Such a path refers to those steps that we can take to break with those problems that are attached to the *Tragedy of the Horizon*. Paul Polman and Halla Tómasdóttir (Chapter 10) address the problem of short-termism directly. They discuss what corporations can do to move financial markets to longer-term thinking. They highlight that firms need to first of all focus on the broader stakeholder network in which they are embedded—a network that reaches beyond a sole focus on investors. They also discuss the need to escape from quarterly reporting—a step that was taken successfully by Unilever in 2009.

A recent survey by FCLTGlobal (2019) revealed that global corporations are less long-term-oriented than they were before the 2007/08 financial crisis. One key driver of this lack of long-term orientation is an overdistribution of capital in the form of buybacks and dividends. Firms that tend to return money to shareholders instead of safeguarding the money for other uses (e.g., long-term investments) generated lower returns on invested capital. Interestingly, the study also finds that the existence of many ESG controversies in a company can impede long-term value creation. By contrast, a diversified board (in terms of gender and age) contributed to higher long-term value creation. What these results show is that a path to a new horizon can take many shapes. One key ambition of this book is to explore some of them.

Division of labor among societal actors

Much of traditional research on business and finance still assumes that there is a rather clear division of labor among different societal actors. Governments define the legal rules of the game (e.g., regarding property and contractual rights) and also enforce these rules. Businesses employ people, obey the law, and pay taxes. Civil society acts as a base of values for society. Of course, this picture is simplifying. However, it still underlies some of our thinking about how markets, firms, and civil society actors interact. There is need for a paradigm change so that we create a robust conceptual foundation for understanding corporations' role in global society. John Ruggie's call to finally let go of Milton Friedman (Chapter 9) is a case in point. As Ruggie observes: "ESG investing already has been and is likely to become even more of a factor in reinforcing the construction of a broader social conception of the public corporation."

Sustainable investing not only operates in a VUCA business context; this context is to a large degree the outcome of changes in the division of labor among societal actors. German philosopher Jürgen Habermas (2001) once argued that a traditional division of labor among societal actors reaches its limits under a "postnational constellation"—that is, a situation in which the steering capacity of state authorities remains limited because social and economic activities reach beyond the territorially bound national or regional jurisdiction (see also Rasche, 2015). In other words, we face gaps in governing (global) business activities—gaps which are unlikely to be closed by inter-governmental action alone. Such governance gaps are by no means a recent phenomenon; they have been part of the debate for many years. What is new, however, is that we need to start thinking about how the existence of these gaps enables and constrains sustainable investing.

Sustainable investing is affected by this post-national constellation in a number of ways. First, some of the problems that ESG practices try to address result from governance gaps and failures. On the global level, topics like climate change or water sustainability deal with common pool resources and therefore require truly global coordination. Sustainable investing is one way to work towards such coordination. Financial markets are knowing few borders; they are a global phenomenon operating at an enormous scale and scope. This makes them a strong actor that can acknowledge and address problems that reach beyond the nation state. Financial markets can coordinate and command resources across borders, and it is this flexibility that allows sustainable investing to make a contribution to address some of the problems ESG is concerned with. Second, and relatedly, sustainable investing is based on an institutional infrastructure that relies to a large degree on voluntary initiatives and standards (e.g., the PRI, TCFD, SASB). Such a "soft law" approach not only enhances the flexibility and pace of solution-finding, it also increases the legitimacy attached to ESG practices. Legitimacy in a post-national constellation relies on interactions among a broad set of stakeholders (Scherer, Rasche, Palazzo, and Spicer, 2016). A number of the voluntary ESG initiatives are based on such multi-stakeholder thinking where businesses together with governments and civil society actors engage in solution-finding.

Lack of systems thinking

Traditional business and finance thinking is rather linear. We usually look for cause-and-effect relationships that are based on linear causality. Higher investments in sustainable forest management should yield more sustainable forests. Such linear thinking has a long tradition in business and management. It reduces problems into manageable parts and relies on actors' ability to control and predict outcomes. There is nothing wrong with approaching *some* management problems this way. However, when it comes to sustainability, an overly linear approach to problem-solving reduces our awareness of how interdependent social and environmental problems are. Some of the core concepts underlying systems thinking hold important lessons for sustainable investing (Williams, Kennedy, Philipp, and Whiteman, 2017).

Social, ecological, and economic systems are interconnected. Organizations (including businesses, regulators, and investors) are agents in these systems and have to recognize that we cannot work towards sustainability based on a silo mentality. What occurs as a solution to one sustainability issue can emerge as a problem in the context of another issue. For instance, the SDGs have been criticized for not sufficiently acknowledging synergies and trade-offs among the 17 Goals (see, e.g., Reyers et al., 2017). As the overarching ambition is to reach all 17 SDGs simultaneously, there is need to know more about inter-linkages among the Goals. For instance, Spaiser, Ranganathan, Swain, and Sumpter's (2017) empirical research noted trade-offs between Goals that are related to economic and social development and some Goals that highlight environmental sustainability. On the other hand, it is also possible to iden-tify targets that work synergistically towards achieving multiple SDGs (see, e.g., Dörgo, Sebestyén, and Abonyi, 2018). Investors have to acknowledge the interconnected nature of sustainability problems, both in their thinking and in their products.

DRIVERS OF AND CHALLENGES FOR SUSTAINABLE INVESTING

Sustainable investing has undergone tremendous growth in recent years. It now reflects a major force in some of the key financial markets around the globe. The Global Sustainable Investment Alliance (GSIA) estimates that sustainable investing assets in the five major markets (i.e., Europe, the United States, Japan, Canada, and Australia and New Zealand) account for $30.7 trillion in the beginning of 2018 (GSIA, 2018). This reflects a 34% increase in the last two years. The growth in assets applying some form of ESG approach is also visible in the impressive growth of signatories of the PRI. The initiative started out with 63 participants in 2006, while it unites more than 2,300 signatories today (see also Chapter 5 by Fiona Reynolds and Nathan Fabian).

Sustainable investing is growing but the implementation is a journey and not the flip of a switch. The challenge lies in the practical implementation. It requires leadership, a culture of innovation, and perhaps most impor-tantly, effective engagement with all stakeholders. This is not always easy in a growing tribal world that seems to struggle to agree on anything. To better understand what drives the sustainable investing agenda, we briefly review some key issues that have supported growth in recent years. We also show that there is need to critically reflect on these drivers, as they can potentially also impede future growth and the dissemination of sustainable investing.

Data and technology

Technology and alternative data are playing a key role in reshaping sustainable investing, spurring market transformation away from industrial-era concepts towards future-fit models. Technology can open up new opportunities for finance to come to grips with the dawning reality of planetary and societal boundaries. The contributors in this book discuss different ways in which technology enables sustainable investing (see in particular Chapters 12, 13, and 14). For instance, Helga Birgden (Chapter 13) discusses some of the results and challenges that occur when investors consider climate risk. Her discussion shows that it is possible for major global investors to use shared climate scenario and stress-testing tools as well as integrated assessment models to take investment action.

While data and technology unlock growth in sustainable investing, there are also a number of challenges that need to be overcome. Ashby Monk, Marcel Prins, and Dane Rook (Chapter 14) emphasize that alternative data needs to be used responsibly. They uncover two main ways in which data can be used to exploit investors—detection and manipulation. Detection refers to other parties uncovering what data sources an investor uses to make sustainable investment decisions (e.g., because the digital footprint of the investor can be revealed). Manipulation includes more direct exploitation of an investor, for instance by altering or even fabricating data that is used for decision-making. This type of exploitation can expose investors to new types of risk (including the risk of making ill-informed decisions). Monk et al. suggest different strategies to cope with exploitation (e.g., to camouflage what sustainability data is being used by an organization), and they summarize these strategies through a novel concept: data defense.

Another problem attached to sustainability data is rater divergence. Even if sustainability data is fully reliable, there are still different ways to use this data in order to assess a firm's ESG performance. One key problem that has received research attention recently is the divergence of ESG ratings (Berg et al., 2019; Doyle, 2018; State Street Global Advisors, 2019). One company can simultaneously receive significantly different scores from different ratings agencies. Berg et al. (2019) show that some of this divergence is due to differences in the underlying methodology. Divergence can emerge because raters use different indicators to measure the same ESG attributes. For instance, corruption can be measured in a number of ways (e.g., fines paid or cases solved). Divergence can also emerge because raters include different attributes in their assessment. Rater A may include board diversity into an assessment, while Rater B may not consider this category at all. Doyle (2018) also shows that ESG ratings are subject to a number of biases, for instance related to company size (higher market-cap firms tend to receive better ratings than peers) and also geographic location (European firms tend to receive higher ratings than US peers). All of this is *not* to suggest that we do not need ESG ratings. Rather, it shows that we still have a long way to go to standardize ratings in a way that they become more comparable.

Supporting policy environment

One key driver behind the growth of sustainable investing is the rising involvement of regulators. Market players today acknowledge that robust policies and standards matter to ratchet up ESG practices. Systems-wide change, without which we cannot address planetary problems like climate change, requires that we define new rules of the game and develop different incentive structures. The regulatory environment for sustainable investing compromises many actors and approaches, ranging from direct governmental interventions to voluntary standards. Consider the following example. In March 2018, the European Commission released an *Action Plan for Financing Sustainable Growth* (COM(2018) 97). The Plan contained suggestions in three main areas: (1) reorienting capital flows towards a more sustainable economy, (2) mainstreaming sustainability into risk management, and (3) fostering transparency and long-termism. The Action Plan served as a ground for a number of legislative proposals, including a proposal for the establishment of a framework to facilitate sustainable investment (COM(2018) 353). The proposal aims most of all at the creation of an EU classification system for sustainability activities (a so-called "taxonomy"). Such a taxonomy aims to answer a simple, yet enormously complex, question: What counts as sustainable economic activity? Answering this question is an essential enabler to channel further investments into sustainable activities (e.g., because it provides a secure basis for defining what counts as a "sustainable" financial product).

While governments are becoming increasingly active in the sustainable investment field, we have also seen the proliferation of a number of voluntary (often multi-stakeholder) initiatives. Take the example of the Global Reporting Initiative (GRI). Ever since its launch in 2000, the GRI has worked towards making social and environmental disclosures more robust and comparable. More recently, the Task Force on Climate-Related Financial Disclosures (TCFD) started to develop voluntary climate-related risk disclosures which consider transition risks as much as physical and liability risks (TCFD, 2019). As a consequence of these (and other) initiatives, the incentives for companies to disclose ESG information has increased. As the supply and demand for ESG disclosures increases and as disclosure frameworks themselves become more robust, investors can use the information as input to their decision-making and benchmarking.

The universe of policy frameworks and regulations that relate to sustainable investment is enormous (de Bakker, Rasche, and Ponte, 2019). On the one hand, this is an opportunity, as it shows that regulators, market actors, and other stakeholders are interested in defining standards and best practices which level the playing field. On the other hand, the simultaneous existence of multiple ESG-related voluntary frameworks with similar aims (e.g., disclosing relevant information) can also be problematic. The discussion around the divergency of ESG ratings as well as the recent Action Plan by the European Commission show that we still lack common standards for measuring and benchmarking sustainability-related information. Prior research on voluntary sustainability standards has shown that the existence of too many—often competing, or at least strongly overlapping—initiatives can impede progress (Fransen, Kolk, and Rivera-Santos, 2019). We therefore need more collaboration and interaction among initiatives that exist in the universe of sustainable investing, so that reliable and objective global benchmarks for ESG are produced.

Changing perception of planetary sustainability problems

It goes without saying that we have known about various sustainability problems for a long time. In 1962, Rachel Carson's (1962) seminal work *Silent Spring* already pointed to some of the negative effects that humans have on the natural world, especially related to the use of pesticides. In 1968, a study by the Stanford Research Institute noted: "If the earth's temperature increases significantly, a number of events might be expected to occur, including the melting of the Antarctic ice cap, a rise in sea levels, warming of the oceans, and an increase in photosynthesis" (Robinson and Robbins, 1968, p. 108). So, what has changed? Why do we consider ESG issues such as climate change, loss of biodiversity, or human rights as increasingly inevitable and material parts of financial decision-making today?

First, we have more scientific evidence than ever to objectively back claims regarding sustainability problems. Consider climate science: By now, nearly all climate scientists (97%) support the fact that climate change is anthropogenic (Cook et al., 2016). The fact-based and objective nature of claims related to sustainability problems has influenced the perception of these problems by business leaders, policymakers, and investors. Early discussions around corporate social responsibility (CSR) viewed at least some social and environmental problems as discretionary (Rasche, Morsing, and Moon, 2017). However, the emerging scientific consensus on a number of sustainability issues together with increasing evidence about the positive relationship between addressing ESG issues and firms' financial performance (Friede, Busch, and Bassen, 2015; Kotsantonis and Bufalari, 2019) have changed this picture. ESG is viewed as risk and opportunity management and is therefore a natural part of doing business (and not a discretionary activity). By now, investors make clear connections between risk modelling and sustainability problems. For instance, a recent BlackRock study assessed the exposure to climate risk for over 250 publicly listed US companies (e.g., based on plant locations and property). The study concludes that climate risks are currently underpriced and that climate-resilient firms trade at a premium (BlackRock, 2019, p. 3). As companies move towards adopting science-based targets to battle climate change (Trexler and Schendler, 2015), it becomes clear that the scientific foundations on which ESG claims and practices rest are strong and forceful.

Second, the urgency that is attached to some sustainability issues has also put them on the radar of financial decision-makers. By now, there is broad agreement that a number of sustainability issues do not just require some sort of action; they require urgent and coordinated action. For instance, Rockström et al.'s (2009) research has identified and quantified nine planetary boundaries—that is, "boundaries that define the safe operating space for humanity with respect to the Earth system" (p. 472). Three of these boundaries have already been transgressed (i.e., climate change, rate of biodiversity loss, and the nitrogen cycle), creating irreversible damage to Earth-system processes. Another four boundaries will soon be approached (i.e., global freshwater use, change in land use, ocean acidification, and interferences with the global phosphorous cycle). The *New York Times* just recently argued relating to climate change: "Few thought it would arrive so quickly. Now we're facing consequences once viewed as fringe scenarios" (Linden, 2019). Furthermore, scholarly work has shown that a number of Earth systems are likely to exceed "tipping points" which then create irreversible and cascading effects (Lenton et al., 2019). Evidence from this stream of research suggests that we are in a state of planetary emergence, where "both the risk and the urgency of the situation are acute" (Lenton et al., 2019, p. 595).

The message that this (and other) research has is simple: business-as-usual and conventional economic growth do not work anymore. A recent report by the Stockholm Resilience Centre suggests that if we stick to the business-as-usual scenario (i.e., a world without extraordinary policy efforts), we won't achieve the SDGs—neither by 2030, nor even by 2050. In such a scenario, "[t]here is high risk for pushing the Earth's life supporting systems beyond irreversible trigger-points by 2050" (Randers et al., 2018, p. 7). Alternative scenarios rely on transformational policies and changes in the way investments are being made (e.g., to finance the growth of renewables). The urgency of problems combined with risk and opportunity considerations create a world in which ignoring sustainable investing becomes dangerous, both for the planet and for profit.

Third, as a result of increased scientific consensus and higher levels of urgency, many sustainability issues have moved into the public domain.

Theoretically speaking, issue lifecycle theory suggests that not all ESG issues that seem objectively important are also necessarily perceived as such by relevant stakeholders (Waddock and Rasche, 2012; see also Mahon and Waddock, 1992). The perception of ESG issues evolves over time as societal expectations are changing and policy frameworks as well as business practices are adapted to environmental circumstances. For instance, trigger events such as the Fukushima nuclear catastrophe have altered some governments' energy policies, which in turn has influenced the context in which ESG risk and opportunities are evaluated. Societal expectations also change because some issues become more enduring, pervasive, and increase in intensity (see above). Media coverage and the promotion of issues by trusted decision-makers influence these dynamics. Sustainable investing is important in this context, because it can help close the gap between what stakeholders expect vis-à-vis certain ESG issues and what businesses are actually doing in support of these issues.

NEW HORIZONS

The contributors of this book agree that a path to a new horizon, as envisioned by Mark Carney (2019), is necessary, possible, and timely. This path looks different depending on what issues, problems, and solutions we focus on. The chapters that are collected in this volume outline a number of ways for thinking about how this path could look, ranging from considerations about whether we actually have the right theoretical tools at hand to think about new horizons (e.g., Chapters 2 and 3) to discussions about rethinking established ESG practices (e.g., Chapter 7) and pushing the boundaries of the debate through technology and alternative forms of data (e.g., Chapters 12, 13, and 14).

Businesses and financial institutions can only thrive if they secure long-term profitability and positive investment returns, which is the basic premise of markets and capitalism. However, this requires simultaneously managing the short and the long term, dealing with ever-changing (disruptive) competition and considering possible material impact from a variety of interconnected ESG factors. We hope that this book will improve our knowledge about how sustainable investing can support such a balancing act.

REFERENCES

Bennet, N. and Lemoine, G. J. (2014). *What VUCA Really Means for You.* Available at: https://hbr.org/2014/01/what-vuca-really-means-for-you (Accessed: 4 November 2019).

Berg, F., Koelbel, J. F., and Rigobon, R. (2019). *Aggregate Confusion: The Divergence of ESG Ratings (MIT Sloan School Working Paper 5822-19).* Cambridge, MA: MIT.

BlackRock. (2019). *Getting Physical: Scenario Analysis for Assessing Climate-Related Risks.* Available at: www.blackrock.com/ch/individual/en/insights/physical-climate-risks (Accessed: 5 February 2020).

Carney, M. (2015). *Breaking the Tragedy of the Horizon—Climate Change and Financial Stability*. Available at: www.bankofengland.co.uk/-/media/boe/files/speech/2015/breaking-the-tragedy-of-the-horizon-climate-change-and-financial-stability.pdf (Accessed: 5 February 2020).

Carney, M. (2019). *A New Horizon*. Available at: www.bankofengland.co.uk/speech/2019/mark-carney-speech-at-european-commission-high-level-conference-brussels (Accessed: 5 February 2020).

Carson, R. (1962). *Silent Spring*. Boston: Houghton Mifflin.

Cook, J., Oreskes, N., Doran, P. T., Anderegg, W. R. L., Verheggen, B., Maibach, E. W., ... Rice, K. (2016). 'Consensus on consensus: A synthesis of consensus estimates on human-caused global warming'. *Environmental Research Letters*, 11(4), p. 048002.

de Bakker, F. G. A., Rasche, A., and Ponte, S. (2019). 'Multi-stakeholder initiatives on sustainability: A cross-disciplinary review and research agenda for business ethics'. *Business Ethics Quarterly*, 29(3), pp. 343–383.

Dörgo, G., Sebestyén, V., and Abonyi, J. (2018). 'Evaluating the interconnectedness of the sustainable development goals based on the causality analysis of sustainability indicators'. *Sustainability*, 10(10), pp. 1–26.

Doyle, T. M. (2018). *Ratings that Don't Rate: The Subjective World of ESG Ratings Agencies*. Available at: http://accf.org/2018/07/19/ratings-that-dont-rate-the-subjective-world-of-esg-ratings-agencies (Accessed: 5 February 2020).

Fama, E. (1970). 'Efficient capital markets: A review of theory and empirical work'. *Journal of Finance*, 25, pp. 383–417.

FCLTGlobal. (2019). *Predicting Long-Term Success: For Corporations and Investors Worldwide*. Available at: www.fcltglobal.org/research/reports/article/predicting-long-term-success (Accessed: 5 February 2020).

Fransen, L., Kolk, A., and Rivera-Santos, M. (2019). 'The multiplicity of international corporate social responsibility standards implications for global value chain governance'. *Multinational Business Review*, 27(4), pp. 397–426.

Friede, G., Busch, T., and Bassen, A. (2015). 'ESG and financial performance: Aggregated evidence from more than 2000 empirical studies'. *Journal of Sustainable Finance and Investment*, 5(4), pp. 210–233.

Ghoshal, S. (2005). 'Bad management theories are destroying good management practice's'. *Academy of Management Learning and Education*, 4(1), pp. 75–91.

Global Sustainable Investment Alliance (GSIA). (2018). *2018 Global Sustainable Investment Review*. Available at: www.gsi-alliance.org/wp-content/uploads/2019/03/GSIR_Review2018.3.28.pdf (Accessed: 5 February 2020).

Habermas, J. (2001). *The Postnational Constellation*. Cambridge, MA: MIT Press.

Institute of International Finance. (2019). *The Case for Simplifying Sustainable Investment Terminology*. Available at: www.iif.com/Portals/0/Files/content/Regulatory/IIF%20SFWG%20-%20Growing%20Sustainable%20Finance.pdf (Accessed: 21 November 2019).

Kahneman, D. and Tversky, A. (1979). 'Prospect theory: An analysis of decision under risk'. *Econometrica*, 47, pp. 263–291.

Kotsantonis, S. and Bufalari, V. (2019). *Do Sustainable Banks Outperform? Driving Value Creation through ESG Practices*. Available at: www.eib.org/attachments/documents/sustainable-banks.pdf (Accessed: 5 February 2020).

Lenton, T. M., Rockström, J., Gaffney, O., Rahmstorf, S., Richardson, K., Steffen, W., and Schellnhuber, H. J. (2019). 'Climate tipping points: Too risky to bet against'. *Nature*, 575, pp. 591–595.

Linden, E. (2019). *How Scientists Got Climate Change So Wrong*. Available at: www.nytimes.com/2019/11/08/opinion/sunday/science-climate-change.html (Accessed: 5 February 2020).

Lo, A. W. (2004). 'The adaptive markets hypothesis'. *Journal of Portfolio Management*, 30, pp. 15–29.

Lo, A. W. (2017). *Adaptive Markets: Financial Evolution at the Speed of Thought*. Princeton, NJ: Princeton University Press.

Mahon, J. F. and Waddock, S. A. (1992). 'Strategic issues management: An integration of issue life cycle perspectives'. *Business and Society*, 31(1), pp. 19–32.

Mayer, C. (2018). *Prosperity: Better Business Makes the Greater Good.* Oxford et al.: Oxford University Press.

McAfee, A. (2019). *More from Less: The Surprising Story of How We Learned to Prosper Using Fewer Resources.* New York: Scribner.

Principles for Responsible Investment (PRI). (2019). *What is Responsible Investment.* Available at: www.unpri.org/pri/an-introduction-to-responsible-investment/what-is-responsible-investment (Accessed: 21 November 2019).

Randers, J., Rockström, J., Stoknes, P. E., Golüke, U., Collste, D., and Cornell, S. (2018). *Transformation Is Feasible: How to Achieve the Sustainable Development Goals within Planetary Boundaries.* Stockholm: Stockholm Resilience Centre.

Rasche, A. (2015). 'The corporation as a political actor—European and North American perspectives'. *European Management Journal, 33*(1), pp. 4–8.

Rasche, A., Morsing, M., and Moon, J. (2017). *Corporate Social Responsibility: Strategy, Communication, Governance.* Cambridge: Cambridge University Press.

Reyers, B., Stafford-Smith, M., Erb, K.-H., Scholes, R. J., and Selomane, O. (2017). 'Essential variables help to focus sustainable development goals monitoring'. *Current Opinion in Environmental Sustainability, 26*, pp. 97–105.

Robinson, E. and Robbins, R. C. (1968). *Source, Abundance, and Fate of Gaseous Atmospheric Pollutants.* Stanford Research Institute (SRI) Project PR-6755. Palo Alto, CA: Stanford University.

Rockström, J., Steffen, W., Noone, K., Persson, A., Chapin, F. S., Lambin, E. F., ... Foley, J. A. (2009). 'A safe operating space for humanity'. *Nature, 461*, pp. 472–475.

Scherer, A. G., Rasche, A., Palazzo, G., and Spicer, A. (2016). 'Managing for political corporate social responsibility: New challenges and directions for PCSR 2.0'. *Journal of Management Studies, 53*(3), pp. 273–298.

Spaiser, V., Ranganathan, S., Swain, R. B., and Sumpter, D. J. T. (2017). 'The sustainable development oxymoron: Quantifying and modelling the incompatibility of sustainable development goals'. *International Journal of Sustainable Development and World Ecology, 24*(6), pp. 457–470.

State Street Global Advisors. (2019). *Into the Mainstream: ESG at the Tipping Point (Research Report on ESG).* Boston, MA: State Street Global Advisors.

Task Force on Climate-Related Financial Disclosures (TCFD). (2019). '2019 Status Report'. Available at: www.fsb-tcfd.org/wp-content/uploads/2019/06/2019-TCFD-Status-Report-FINAL-053119.pdf (Accessed: 5 February 2020).

Trexler, M. and Schendler, A. (2015). 'Science-based carbon targets for the corporate world: The ultimate sustainability commitment, or a costly distraction?'. *Journal of Industrial Ecology, 19*(6), pp. 931–933.

Waddock, S. and Rasche, A. (2012). *Building the Responsible Enterprise: Where Vision and Values Add Value.* Palo Alto, CA: Stanford University Press.

Williams, A., Kennedy, S., Philipp, F., and Whiteman, G. (2017). 'Systems thinking: A review of sustainability management research'. *Journal of Cleaner Production, 148*, pp. 866–881.

PART I

The changing context of sustainable investing

PART 1

2

Business and sustainability, from the firm to the biosphere

Simon Levin, Martin Reeves, and Ania Levina

TRADITIONAL GAME OF BUSINESS: LOCAL, SHORT-TERM, FINANCIAL RETURN-MAXIMIZATION

Historically, businesses, including financial institutions, have operated like isolated, short-term return-maximization machines. They have focused on maximizing short-term financial gains, often at the expense of their own enduring success and the collective robustness and sustainability of their eco-systems, society, and the planet more broadly. This myopia is often driven by the incentives of top business executives that overweight the near term, the unwavering demands of Wall Street for consistent short-term returns, and a mentality of "limited liability" that assumes any collateral impacts are the responsibility of other social actors (Young, Woods, and Reeves, 2019).

The timescales that executives focus on when pricing the future and making decisions are relatively short compared with the optimal ones for society. For example, CEOs typically focus on maximizing business performance and total shareholder return (TSR) during their tenure, which has been declining: median CEO tenure has fallen from six years in 2013 to five years in 2017 (Marcec, 2018).[1] Moreover, during their tenure, CEO bonuses are commonly linked to short-term performance metrics (McClure, 2019), leading Paul Polman, the former CEO of the British–Dutch conglomerate Unilever, to recently declare in the *Atlantic* that "too many CEOs play the quarterly game and manage their businesses accordingly" (quoted in Semuels, 2016). Society more broadly, on the other hand, should value the survival and sustainability of the environment on the timescale of multiple generations.

The company-by-company, short-term, return-maximization game of business is further reinforced by the pressure for efficiency and quarterly earnings from Wall Street, to which business is accountable. The short-termism of the financial sector is apparent from the tax laws, which define "long-term" investors as holding stocks for more than one year (IRS, 2019); the decrease in stock holding time over the last 50 years (Fiske, 2016; Sadoff, 2018; World Bank Group, 2019);[2] and investors' demand that publicly listed companies report on their performance each quarter. To address finance's hunger for immediate returns, many public companies are focused on enhancing their quarterly reports by investing in share buy-backs (2018 was an all-time high year for corporate stock buy-backs (Pisani, 2018)) to boost their current financial metrics, instead of reinvesting in future sustainable growth. In an op-ed for the *Wall Street Journal*, Warren Buffet, head of Berkshire Hathaway Inc., and James Dimon, head of JPMorgan Chase & Co, urged companies to abandon the practice of forecasting their quarterly performance, since it forces excessive short-term focus: "In our experience, quarterly earnings guidance often leads to an unhealthy focus on short-term profits at the expense of long-term strategy, growth and sustainability" (Dimon and Buffet, 2018).

CORPORATE CAPITALISM HAS PROVEN TO BE AN ADAPTABLE AND RESILIENT SYSTEM

While the current model of business as an isolated, short-term return-maximization machine is being increasingly called into question, we must acknowledge that corporate capitalism has proven to be a very resilient and adaptive system with many accomplishments. Corporate capitalism has so far proven more enduring than other systems (e.g., centrally planned economies). Among its many achievements are the creation of massive wealth, lifting millions out of poverty, increases in quality and expectancy of life, and continuous innovation to support this.

Throughout its history, capitalism has shown tremendous flexibility, as is evident from its ability to adapt at various inflection points (Figure 2.1). State regulation of business took off in response to the speculation that led to the South Sea bubble of 1720, when the Bubble Act was passed requiring all corporations to obtain a state charter. The 19th century saw financial unpredictability around the world, which led to the liberalization of incorporation and the passing of limited liability laws to encourage more people to start businesses by protecting their personal assets.

With the onset of the Great Depression in 1929, more regulations for stock markets and protections for investors were put in place, including deposit insurance. After the turmoil of the 1960s and 1970s, a number of laws were passed to democratize credit—in other words, to give access to credit to a

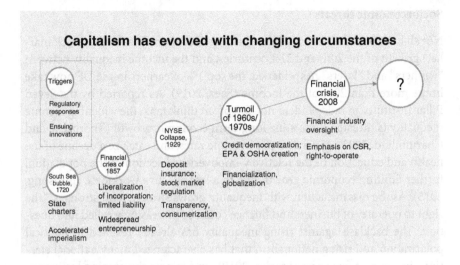

FIGURE 2.1 Capitalism has proven its evolvability in response to changing circumstances

Sources: BCG Henderson Institute analysis

larger segment of the population and protect vulnerable groups from abusive credit practices. Moreover, in the 1970s the Environmental Protection Agency and Occupational Safety and Health Administration were established, to reduce the externalization of environmental costs and to enforce safe employment practices.

The most recent financial crisis of 2008 led to public outrage, the creation of movements like Occupy Wall Street, and another wave of regulation for finance. The public eye and the focus of many business leaders have turned to questions of corporate responsibility and the right of business and finance to operate in society. Perhaps now is the time for capitalism to evolve again in response to the changing context of business today: the pressure of climate change and growing socioeconomic issues.

SIGNS THAT THE CURRENT MODEL OF BUSINESS IS NO LONGER WORKING

Over the last few decades, we have witnessed a number of major developments, which fundamentally change the context in which businesses and financial markets operate, and which potentially undermine "the right to operate." Socioeconomic threats and the growing risks to the sustainability of the broader earth system suggest that the traditional model of business has reached an inflection point requiring radical action.

Socioeconomic threats

Not all have benefited equally from the overall economic (as well as stock market) growth of the 20th and 21st centuries, and the income inequality between "winners" and "losers" has widened: the top 1% of earners in the US now take home more than 20% of the income (Saez, 2019). As reported by the Seven Pillar Institute, an independent not-for-profit think tank, the widening income inequality is threatening to stifle long-term economic growth (Thorbecke and Charumilind, 2002); generate a rise in crime rates; and catalyze a decline of the health and education of the relatively impoverished section of the population, further limiting economic growth due to a less effective workforce (Birdsong, 2015). As the dissatisfaction with inequality grows stronger and stronger, "the right to operate" of business and finance could be increasingly called into question. The backlash against rising inequality has already resulted in political polarization and rising nationalism that has characterized many national elections in the past few years (Snyder, 2019), and is now threatening businesses through tensions in international trade (Coke-Hamilton, 2019).

Rising income inequality is mirrored in the widening gap in trust in business, NGOs, governments, and media between the less trusting mass population and the more informed stakeholders.[3] According to the Edelman Trust Barometer, while the trust index overall moved up by a few points in 2019, the trust gap returned to record highs previously seen in 2017 (16-point gap), signaling a further divide between different segments of society (Edelman, 2019). The trust gap is yet another symptom of social division, which is threatening the sustainability of the business environment.

Further exacerbating social stress in the US, and in the world more broadly, are the symptoms of the backlash against technology and globalization, and the resulting rise of protectionism, which are no longer merely theoretical considerations and are starting to impact business (Reeves, Kell, and Hassan, 2018). New developments in automation and AI are widely seen as threats to the future of work rather than opportunities, and the ability of technology to drive progress and economic growth is being increasingly questioned by a significant fraction of the workforce.

The decline in growth threatens to exacerbate distrust, dissatisfaction, and animosity among different layers of the population, putting even more strain on the already weakened socioeconomic fabric that supports our society and, consequently, business and finance. Business leaders broadly are starting to recognize that corporate capitalism as it is today is not meeting broader societal needs: in the 2019 Fortune 500 CEO survey, 71% of respondents agreed that "capitalism is not in crisis, but would benefit from some tweaking to better serve society" (Murray, 2019). In response to the growing inequality and political polarization, Ray Dalio, the founder of one of the top hedge-funds, called for capitalism to "evolve or die" (Dalio, 2019).

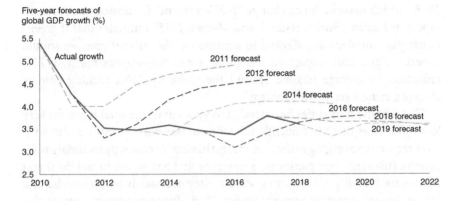

FIGURE 2.2 Global economic growth is trending down

Source: BCG Henderson Institute analysis; IMF projections from fall outlooks of each year, except 2019 (from April outlook)

Ever-closer risks to the sustainability of the earth system

Since its initiation about a decade ago by the Stockholm Resilience Center, planetary boundaries research has identified nine processes that are essential to the sustainability and resilience of the earth system, and has shown that a number of these processes are already compromised to the level of medium and high risks of potentially catastrophic environmental changes (Stockholm Resilience Centre, 2015).

We have now witnessed the kind of events that climate change can generate, including extreme weather like devastating hurricanes, flooding, droughts, wildfires, and heatwaves. The recent heatwave that gripped Europe in summer 2019 has also created significant melting of Greenland's ice sheet, which contributes to the rising sea level and could eventually put a vast number of people and key economic centers at risk of flooding (McKenzie, 2019). Flooding will in turn create migration pressure from at-risk areas to more elevated locations, likely intensifying tensions between nations. In another self-perpetuating cycle, increasing global temperatures is causing the warming of the permafrost (Berwyn, 2019), which in turn contributes to further global warming through release of methane into the atmosphere. Furthermore, there is widening recognition that climate change is putting the global food system at risk by diluting crop yields, lowering their nutritional content, and spreading destructive pests and diseases (IPCC, 2019). The World Health Organization reports that climate change is already impacting human health, both directly (e.g., effects of extreme weather events) and indirectly (e.g., deterioration in air and water quality) (WHO, 2018).

The current rate of CO_2 concentration rise implies that we could cross the 1.5°C global temperature increase threshold in as little as 10 years (Tollefson,

2018), which makes climate change "NPV-relevant" for businesses. A recent report in *Nature* (Burke, Hsiang, and Miguel, 2015) estimates that if greenhouse gas emissions are allowed to continue at the current rate, we should expect a significant impact on the global economy—approximately a 20% reduction in average income around the globe by 2100, making climate change a critical *economic* problem.

Historically, companies have tended to view environmental issues on very long timescales that were outside the scope of business operations. But such risks are now converging to the present and having increasingly material implications. Insurance companies are among the first businesses to feel the threat to the sustainability of the earth system as they necessarily take a broader and longer-term perspective on risks (Jergler, 2018). Insurance consumers are also starting to see the effects of climate change on their experiences: one of the authors of this chapter has recently had difficulties obtaining flood insurance on the East Coast of the US and fire insurance following a move to the West Coast of the US. Insurance companies are in a "hot seat" when it comes to climate change since global warming can lead to correlated risks, resembling a car accident that everybody is part of and consequently posing financial risk to insurers who are no longer able to diversify risk. In a recent example, due to the struggle of the current program to keep up with flood claims (flooding in the US has surged in recent years (McNeill and Nelson, 2014)), the Federal Emergency Management Agency has announced a reform to the National Flood Insurance Program to prevent it from collapsing (Flavelle, 2019).

Financial businesses are not the only ones affected: it is becoming increasingly clear that climate change could be a threat to supply chains and operations. In 2018 company reports to CDP (formerly Carbon Disclosure Project) on the risks of climate change, 215 of the world's 500 largest companies reported approximately $1 trillion at risk, with the expectation for over half of these risks to materialize within *five years* or earlier (CDP, 2018; Plumer, 2019), bringing them firmly into the present. One of the financial regulators in the US Commodity Futures Trading Commission compared the risks of climate change to the US financial markets with those of the 2008 financial crisis.

> If climate change causes more volatile frequent and extreme weather events, we are going to have a scenario where these large providers of financial products—mortgages, home insurance, pensions—cannot shift risk away from their portfolios … it's abundantly clear that climate change poses financial risk to the stability of the financial system.
>
> (Davenport, 2019)

These socioeconomic and environmental threats come at a time when businesses are already facing unprecedented levels of uncertainty and risk, due to technological evolution and its impact on business models and competition.

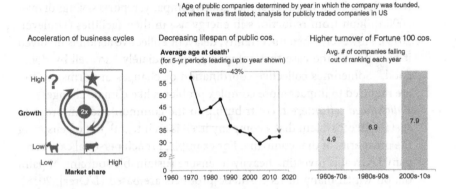

FIGURE 2.3 Businesses are facing unprecedented levels of uncertainty and volatility
Source: BCG Henderson Institute analysis; S&P Global; Fortune

The lifespan of listed public companies is shrinking; the winners in business are changing ever more rapidly, as evidenced by increased turnover of the Fortune 100 over time; and companies are moving through the different quadrants of the growth share matrix almost twice as fast as they did around 20 years ago. The eroding sustainability of the socioeconomic fiber and the broader earth system is exacerbating the challenge of sustaining business models and companies.

The inadequacy of the "isolated, short-term return-maximization machine" approach was predicted more than 2,000 years ago by Aristotle, who distinguished between two kinds of economics: (1) *Chrematistike* (wealth maximization as an end itself) and (2) *Oikonomia* (the art of managing a household). Aristotle believed that using maximization as a goal in itself would likely undermine society, as we are seeing now, and proposed that *Oikonomia*, with its focus on the higher purpose of shared prosperity, would be a superior model for the long-term survival of the "family"—that is, both business and the society more broadly. We used natural language processing techniques to divide companies into *Chrematistike* and *Oikonomia* orientation and were able to show that the latter are already generating superior long-term returns and growth (Reeves, Dierksmeier, and Chittaro, 2018).

Businesses therefore need to take action in their own individual and long-term self-interest to create a more sustainable model. There are multiple levels at which companies should optimize self-interest while contributing to the common good:

- *Narrow self-interest*: optimizing for the self-interest of individual companies only. It is relatively easy for companies to address their own inefficient use of natural resources, for example, since it leads to direct cost reductions. Unilever, a consumer goods company, reports savings of over €600 million from reductions in energy use in their facilities (Unilever, 2019). However, when uncertainty, delay, or collective action is involved it may not be the case that companies immediately "do well by doing good." Sometimes collective coordination or changes in norms or laws are required to impact more complex problems like climate change.

- *Enlightened self-interest*: contributing to the common good in order to sustain an ecosystem that a company itself is an integral part of, ensuring the prosperity of that company. For example, French personal care company L'Oreal is investing heavily to ensure sustainable sourcing of palm oil, on which many of its cosmetic products are based (L'Oréal, 2018). Acting in the common interest requires going beyond local maximization of individual company benefits and may require cooperative leadership, collective coordination, or regulatory action.

- *Pro-social behavior*: contributing to the common good, because that is the right thing to do, even in the absence of easily quantifiable, collective financial benefit. For example, Bill Gates, Gordon Moore, and Warren Buffett's current engagement in philanthropy cannot be explained by the need to maintain reputation or ecosystem health; they are engaging in pro-social behavior. A variant on this idea is doing the right thing in the absence of definitive proof. If we were to wait for definitive and detailed causal evidence for complex phenomena like climate change, our actions may come too late, necessitating therefore prudence and pro-social behavior.

Given the elevated risks and potentially catastrophic consequences mentioned above, companies and financial institutions will need to place more emphasis on enlightened self-interest and pro-social behaviors, while relying only on the belief that individual companies will "do well by doing good" will not be enough to meet the challenges facing corporate capitalism.

EFFORTS TOWARDS A BETTER SOLUTION

There have been many efforts to shift business strategy from the traditional "isolated, short-term financial return-maximization machine" approach to a more enlightened approach. The United Nations Global Compact was established in 2000 to help businesses adopt sustainable and socially responsible practices, and its efforts have led to the widespread recognition of the UN Sustainable Development Goals. In the 2018 UN Global Compact Progress Report survey, 80% of Global Compact members reported that they are taking actions to advance the Sustainable Development Goals (UN, 2018).

The awareness of environmental, social, and governance (ESG) topics and pressure to address them is now being reinforced by the broader public, rather than only through organizations like Global Compact. Goldman Sachs analysis shows that Twitter posts on ESG topics grew almost 20 times between 2010 and 2018 and are becoming more "trendable" (Bingham et al., 2018). The workforce is putting more pressure on employers to address ESG issues: responsible business practices are an important deciding factor for millennials when choosing an employer and 67% of employees expect employers will join them in taking action on social issues (Cone Communications, 2016; Edelman, 2019).

Driven at least in part by these pressures from the workforce and the public, many companies are attempting to clarify their social "purpose" and integrating broader considerations into their core business strategy. After historically being on the sidelines, corporate sustainability and corporate social responsibility functions are being integrated more into core business activity. As a result, an increasing number of companies are building emission controls, decarbonization and other ESG goals into their business strategies. The most progressive companies are seeking ways to gain competitive advantage by differentiating themselves on environmental and societal dimensions: for example, Rothy's, a footwear company that makes shoes out of recycled plastic bottles, has now captured the hearts and pockets of women in America's urban centers, bringing in over $140 million in revenue in 2018 only two years after its launch (Stock, 2018). We expect to see further growth of such "ethical premium" goods, for which consumers pay a premium for an ethical or ecological benefit.

A number of prominent companies have made visible moves to signal their commitment to sustainable strategy. Korean conglomerate SK Group developed a methodology to quantify the company's contribution to society and said it will evaluate employees in part on social value created (Jun-suk, 2019). IBM CEO and the Business Roundtable urged Congress to pass a bill protecting the LGBTQ community from a range of discriminations in areas such as employment and housing credit (Fried, 2019). Nordic companies in particular consistently outperform the rest of the world on ESG metrics and seem to have mastered the art of *Oikonomia* to protect their own sustainability by promoting the sustainability of the broader systems on which this depends (Beal et al., 2019). And in a statement signed by nearly 200 prominent CEOs in August 2019, the Business Roundtable declared that companies "share a fundamental commitment to *all* of our stakeholders," including, but not limited to, shareholders (Business Roundtable, 2019).

While the financial sector has not abandoned demands for quarterly reporting, many investors now expect companies to report on ESG metrics and are eager to integrate ESG into their decision-making. Sixty percent of executives in publicly traded companies believe that sustainability is important to investors (Unruh et al., 2016). The rise in passive index investing, in which investors hold stocks for long periods, has created incentives for investors to be more attentive to the long-term sustainable performance of their holdings (Stein, 2018). There has been a push by institutional shareholders (e.g., Blackrock and Vanguard) to consider diversity and other ESG goals as a means of improving sustainable financial performance (Brown, 2019). As an example, the California Public Employees' Retirement System (CalPERS) is examining its circa $180 billion portfolio for ESG factors in an effort to address climate change, corporate board diversity, and executive pay of the companies it is invested in (Frampton, 2019). In an even more aggressive move, some funds are divesting their holdings in coal and oil stocks (Gilblom, 2019). Moody's Corporation recently acquired Four Twenty Seven, Inc., one of the pioneers in assessing risks and economic impacts of climate change, with the intention to incorporate climate impacts into credit ratings, signaling an important mindset shift in how the financial industry addresses such issues, which have traditionally fallen outside their purview (Bershidsky, 2019). The Climate Action 100+ investor initiative, for which more than 300 investors with more than $33 trillion under management have already signed up, aims to ensure that the world's largest greenhouse gas emitters take necessary action against climate change (Climate Action 100, 2019). Overall, the advancement of ESG investing has resulted in $31 trillion in global active and passive "sustainable" investments (GSI Alliance, 2018; Kell, 2018a).

Critical for evaluating the sustainability of businesses, ESG data and metrics have significantly improved in both their availability and quality. In efforts to promote disclosure, task forces like the Bloomberg/Carney TFCD[4] have been created to help companies report on climate risks to their businesses. Big data and machine learning techniques allow for development of new ways to assess risks which are not traditionally accounted for. New tools are under development to better measure the sustainability performance of companies: for example, Arabesque Partners has developed S-Ray, a tool that helps understand a company's value to society, and is developing a "Celsius score" to evaluate the climate impact of companies (Arabesque, 2019; Kell, 2018b); Truvalue Labs developed innovative solutions to analyze ESG data (Truvalue Labs, 2019); and a group of 16 large insurers and reinsurers is partnering to develop tools and indicators to develop scenarios and measure climate-related risks in their portfolios (UNEP FI, 2018). With the development of practical tools and standards, the "integrated reporting" of financial and ESG metrics is gradually becoming less of an aspirational goal and more of a realistic prospect. Goldman Sachs' GS SUSTAIN framework integrates analysis of financial strength, strategic positioning, and ESG performance to ensure that analysis of companies is holistic, and not purely focused on financials (Goldman Sachs, 2019).

With the development of better metrics, significant efforts have also been undertaken to identify *material* ESG factors—those most likely to have an impact on the operational performance or sustainability of a *specific* business, and therefore, ensure better alignment between financial and broader goals. The Sustainability Accounting Standards Board (SASB) has developed a set of widely recognized ESG materiality standards tailored to individual industries (SASB, 2018). For example, material factors for oil and gas exploration include greenhouse emissions and air quality, while for healthcare delivery, material factors include access and affordability, data security, and consumer protection.

Mounting evidence that performance on ESG metrics influences financial performance helps justify investing and participating in such initiatives. Stocks of sustainable companies tend to outperform their less sustainable counterparts by 4.8% annually (Eccles, Ioannou, and Serafeim, 2014). First-time corporate social responsibility (CSR)-disclosing firms with superior CSR performance enjoy a lower cost of equity capital (Dhaliwal et al., 2014). ESG performance has also been shown to have positive impact on profit margins (Beal et al., 2017). Overall, companies that employ a total societal impact (TSI) lens—considering social and environmental impacts in addition to financials—were shown to have superior valuations and profit margins (Ibid).

...BUT IN TOTAL SUCH EFFORTS ARE STILL INSUFFICIENT

Despite all of the well-intentioned moves and positive changes outlined above, there has been very limited aggregate progress on major planetary issues, such as plastic pollution of oceans, CO_2 emissions, and global warming (Rubel et al., 2019). The Intergovernmental Panel on Climate Change (IPCC) forecasts that global temperatures will rise by 2.5 to 10 degrees Fahrenheit (1.4 to 5.6°C) over the next century (NASA, 2019). UN Environment's *Sixth Global Environment Outlook* highlights the consequences of not addressing climate change more robustly, including increasing environmental pressure on agricultural and food systems, escalating global clean water scarcity and millions of premature deaths from ambient air pollution (due to burning of fossil fuel) in the next few decades (UN Environment, 2019). In 2017, the US announced that it would withdraw from the Paris Agreement, thereby undermining the first functional (albeit imperfect) global climate change agreement, exacerbating the gap between current efforts and the efforts that will be required.

We typically expect governments to address issues affecting the common good, but they will likely not be able to address such challenges on their own. Their resources are becoming more limited as public wealth declines in developed countries (Reeves, Kell, and Hassan, 2018). Furthermore, political polarization limits opportunities for public action, and the collaboration between nations is weakened in an increasingly nationalistic environment. Businesses therefore need to become a major part of the solution.

But for businesses, too, many challenges still remain. For instance, leaders need to learn how to balance multiple timescales in creating strategy: CEOs are traditionally driven by shorter-term financial metrics, while ESG-driven strategy requires a longer-term perspective. As a result, it remains challenging to fully integrate sustainability considerations into strategy and business models. In BCG's 2016 survey, 90% of executives see sustainability as important, but only 60% reported having a sustainable strategy in place (Kiron et al., 2017). Leadership attitudes also need to progress. According to the 2019 Fortune 500 CEO survey, only about 40% of the Fortune 500 CEO respondents believe that "their company should actively seek ways to address major social problems as part of their core business strategy" (Murray, 2019).

WHY ARE CLIMATE CHANGE AND OTHER SOCIAL AND ENVIRONMENTAL ISSUES SO CHALLENGING TO TACKLE?

Despite the many efforts described, meaningful progress on key issues facing humanity today, like climate change, plastics pollution, and inequality, remains woefully elusive. The disjunction between the benefits and costs of taking action, the long delay between actions and reward, as well as the necessity of wide-ranging collective action make such challenges particularly tough to tackle.

Addressing climate and socioeconomic issues is complicated by the disjunction of benefits and costs, where benefits don't necessarily accrue to those who act—as well as an intergenerational manifestation of the same problem. Since today's actions will have costs or benefits that accrue over long timescales, subsequent generations might have to pay for our mistakes or benefit from our sacrifices. To address this mismatch, there is currently no easy "toolkit" to think about longer timescales or the broader context. Further exacerbating the temporal separation of costs and benefits is the paradox of hyperbolic discounting, which refers to people's tendency to succumb to the temptation of short-term satisfaction and forfeit long-term benefits—i.e., what is rational at one point in time appears not to be later. This is due to the coexistence of multiple discount rates, which leads to logical inconsistencies. Just like most of us fail at dieting by falling prey to the temptations of desserts and baked goods, we could "burn the planet" by adopting financially rational short-term solutions now at the expense of future generations (Kell, 2019).

In order to truly shift the needle on the toughest issues that business and society face today, collective action and coordination are needed among many independent agents, including individuals, businesses, financial institutions, NGOs, and governments. Coordination becomes extremely challenging when many heterogeneous agents are involved, especially when they lack the full knowledge of each other's intentions. These are problems of the commons, in which the perceived or even real utilities of individual agents do not necessarily align with the collective optimum. Moreover, we also need to account for the context in which these various agents operate, which can be very different. Curtailing coal mining in developed countries and in India have very different economic, political, and historic contexts. In the book *The Person and the Situation*, authors Lee Ross and Richard E. Nisbett show that the context of the situation significantly affects how we act and think (Ross and Nisbett, 2011). While we tend to focus on the overall problem and the actors, the *context* of each actor is often critical, impeding even communication, let alone common solution identification.

A recent report in *Nature Ecology & Evolution* highlights the additional risks associated with the increasing concentration of power in the hands of a few transnational corporations (TNCs) (Folke et al., 2019). Because of their now enormous scale and influence (80% of profits globally are attributed to roughly 10% of corporations), TNCs can now either accelerate or severely hinder progress on sustainability issues, further exacerbating the riskiness of the situation, and underlining the importance of the role of corporations (The Economist, 2016).

The challenges outlined above continue to perplex leading researchers globally, so perhaps it isn't surprising that the decision-making practices of business and finance today are not yet equipped to deal with such issues, especially given the historical dominance of the short-term, local, profit-maximization, and shareholder-centric model of business.

PARADIGM SHIFT IS NEEDED

The biggest challenges for business currently lie not in profit maximization, but rather in addressing the unprecedented risk and unpredictability stemming from changes in the natural and socioeconomic environment. Generally we tend to think of issues like climate change and socioeconomic tensions to be in the purview of governments; however, the private sector has a critical role to play now—therefore we here focus on how business and finance can help address these challenges. A paradigm shift in how both businesses and financial markets operate is needed, inspired by the new thinking from systems science, ecology, and biology more generally. Some helpful perspectives include, we propose: a "biological" view of businesses as *complex adaptive systems* nested within the broader society and environment; thinking on effective systems leverage points; and the recent scientific finding that bottom–up collectives, represented by small coalitions, can be surprisingly effective in taking action on issues like climate change.

Businesses as complex adaptive systems

In our previous work, we have argued that businesses, like biological systems, are complex adaptive systems (CASes), in which interactions among individual agents at small scales give rise to emergent patterns and processes that in turn feed back to affect individual behaviors and interactions (Reeves, Levin, and Ueda, 2016, 2017). Hence, in CASes, seemingly small local events and interactions among individual agents (employees, business units, and the whole company) can cascade and significantly reshape the entire system; in response, individual agents will then adapt to the changes in the system through feedback loops that can further change and reshape the system. As a result, the system continuously changes in often unpredictable ways through cycles of "emergence" and "feedback." For example, when wolves were reintroduced into Yellowstone National Park, they had cascading effects on not only their immediate prey but on the trees, riverbanks, and river flow (Reeves, Levin, and Ueda, 2017). Applying CAS thinking to business makes it apparent that business can be neither fully predicted nor controlled. However, currently our managerial approaches are mainly based on the belief that both are possible. Given the inherent unpredictability of business, comfortable and familiar traditional managerial approaches, focused on meticulous planning and efficiency optimization, are inadequate to address the unprecedented uncertainty and risk that businesses are facing today.

Within the CAS framework, "mechanical management" is especially insufficient to address the complex long-term societal and environmental challenges that threaten the stability of businesses and financial markets. The modern generation of business leaders needs to move away from a "mechanical" managerial approach, which focuses on deterministic engineering of desired outcomes, in favor of a "biological" approach to business problems, which directly acknowledges and addresses the underlying uncertainty and complexity of business problems. Adoption of adaptive "biological management" will allow for a shift from a short-term, local, financial focus to long-term robustness for the whole system and give businesses a chance to address the broader challenges facing them today.

Businesses as nested complex adaptive systems

Moreover, businesses and financial markets do not function in isolation. Like many other complex adaptive systems, businesses exist as parts of broader nested systems (Reeves, Levin, and Ueda, 2016). In biological systems, a population is a CAS, nested in a broader natural ecosystem, which in turn is nested in the environment overall. Similarly, companies are complex adaptive systems embedded within local and global markets, which in turn are nested in the broader system of societies and ultimately the natural environment.

As in CASes described above, in nested systems also, local interactions can lead to emergence and feedback loops that can result in unpredictable events and changes that propagate between levels to the whole system. Events in any

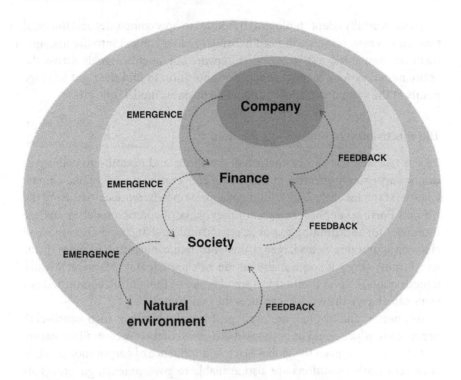

FIGURE 2.4 Businesses and financial institutions are nested within the broader complex adaptive system of society and natural environment

Source: BCG Henderson Institute

part of the nested system may relatively quickly cascade to its other parts. For example, the introduction of European rabbits to Australia led to many devastating unintended consequences to the Australian ecology, including the loss of many plant species and erosion. Similarly, the impacts of climate change are now threatening companies' bottom lines (e.g., the rise in global temperatures is putting pressure on Alphabet to increase resources going into cooling of its data centers) (Plumer, 2019).

In order to survive and prosper in the new context, businesses need to learn how to manage the inevitable conflicts between levels of the complex nested system, which will inescapably involve sacrificing some self-interest for the benefit of the whole, and through this, address long-term self-interest. Our analysis of company language as being self-interest focused vs. broader focus on system (using NLP) confirms that companies that have broader focus on the whole system perform better in the long run (Reeves, Dierksmeier, and Chittaro, 2018). While an excessive focus on efficiencies can produce short-term gains, it can also destabilize the business environment and society in the long run (Martin, 2019).

To successfully adapt "biological thinking" to how companies and financial markets operate, leaders will need to bring broader context into the management of companies, use "purpose" to ensure alignment of goals across the entire nested system, facilitate adaptive innovation to find the right leverage points in the system and apply sustainable business model innovation.

The effectiveness of bottom–up solutions

Recent research has shown that small coalitions and bottom–up collectives can be surprisingly effective in deepening cooperation on issues like climate change (Hannam et al., 2017). Joint collaboration between scientists from the US and Portugal applied an evolutionary-game-theoretic model to analyze incentives for contributing to public goods, finding that cooperation in small club configurations yields larger co-benefits than cooperation in more inclusive forums (even if some members do not participate). Margaret Mead's famous quote, "Never doubt that a small group of thoughtful, committed citizens can change the world," captures the insight well.

Businesses and capital are well positioned to adopt such small-club approaches, which could be both feasible because of their decentralized nature and also effective given the global reach and influence of corporations. While such cooperative solutions are also available to governments, governments tend to be largely national in their focus, and different countries, especially today, have misaligned incentives. Businesses can help align incentives across borders using their global reach. And effective collective action is enabled most by the actors wielding the biggest levers—which today are often global businesses and institutional capital. The adage "from those to whom much has been given, much is required" seems apt.

TOWARDS A NEW PARADIGM FOR BUSINESS: SUGGESTED PRINCIPLES

Accordingly, we suggest some principles for a new paradigm leveraging these perspectives (see Figure 2.5):

(1) Make corporations part of the solution

Very often collective global challenges are regarded as beyond the purview of business executives and left for governments and global NGOs to solve. However, because of unprecedented external environmental shifts (e.g., climate change) and internal workforce cultural shifts (e.g., mistrust of business; millennials demanding employers to adopt responsible business practices), companies and financial institutions are forced for the first time to question

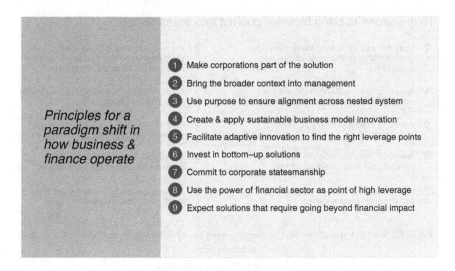

FIGURE 2.5 Principles to implement a paradigm shift in how business and finance
currently operate
Source: BCG Henderson Institute

their short-term return-maximization approach and search for a new strategic paradigm. Companies, and especially financial institutions, have an
important role to play in addressing today's climate and societal challenges.

(2) Bring the broader context into management

In order to address the unprecedented environmental and societal issues that
threaten business prosperity, business strategy needs to consider the whole
nested system, not just local issues and interests. The broader context needs
to become an integral part of management of organizations. Businesses and
financial institutions need to invest in evaluating the effectiveness of their ESG
efforts. In turn, governments can further encourage holism by aligning what
we measure and regulate with what we value as a society, and facilitating the
right sort of cooperation among competitors when it is in the common good.

Broader system considerations should also be included in risk analyses and
built into financial models and projections. In order to detect the risks stemming from instability of the broader nested system, businesses and finance
need to pay attention to the negative feedback from government, society,
and environment more broadly (e.g., the regulatory and societal backlash
Facebook is experiencing over concerns that the company has failed to protect user data) (Hendrickson and Galstn, 2019). Explicitly accounting for
such risks in financials will help businesses to simultaneously balance both
financial and sustainability goals.

10 questions to bring broader context into management

? Does our purpose lead to sustainable value creation? Is our self-interest aligned with social value?

? Are we measuring the long-term competiveness of the business? Have we balanced the present and the future?

? Are we "on purpose" and, if not, are we taking corrective action accordingly?

? Where does our business model fail first as a result of ESG-related risks?

? Are those actions sufficient in impact and speed?

? How will we address this weakness with sustainable business model innovation?

? Are we defining the boundary of what we measure and manage appropriately?

? Do we have the right collective action platforms to addres pressing problems?

? Are other stakeholders reresented in or part of our strategy process?

? Are we exercising corporate statesmanship to effect external change?

FIGURE 2.6 Key questions that strategists need to ask to bring the broader context into management

Source: BCG Henderson Institute

Doing so effectively also requires expanding the timescales of business. A typical annual planning timeframe creates blindness to the decade-long timeframes within which planetary issues may evolve. To bring broader context into management, leaders need to ask broader questions, outlined in Figure 2.6, as part of the strategy formulation processes.

(3) Use the concept of "purpose" to ensure alignment across nested systems

As discussed in previous sections, CASes often react unpredictably to interventions. The right approach for intervention is rarely obvious due to feedback loops and non-obvious cause-and-effect relationships. As a result, indirect, rather than direct, managerial approaches often work better in nested CAS systems and are likely to be more effective in addressing the complex challenges businesses face today. Indirect approaches address the context and the incentives which shape it, rather than trying to directly engineer the outcome. One such approach is a clear statement of purpose—the intersection of a company's aspirations, capabilities and its contribution to society—which can ensure that strategies and tactics promote coherence between the different levels of company, society, and planet. In a 2018 survey across 28 countries, about 80% of people said they expect CEOs to be personally visible in sharing the company's purpose, and around 75% want CEOs to discuss how their company benefits society (Edelman, 2019).

To ensure that purpose is effectively pursued, a company's vision, business model, strategy, planning, budgeting, performance management, and incentives need to be consilient (Wilson, 1998). Today's ESG measures are a start, yet non-financial reporting largely remains focused on compliance, rather than sustainable advantage. Both businesses and finance need to embrace metrics that create the connection between a company's purpose, its business model, and its societal impact—its "full business value" (Young, Woods, and Reeves, 2019).

(4) Create and apply the discipline of sustainable business model innovation

The shift in mindset from the self-focused maximization of short-term returns to long-term success and robustness of the whole nested system will require businesses and financial institutions to transform themselves through what we call sustainable business model innovation (S-BMI) (Ibid). While traditional business model innovation aims to create competitive advantage through reengineering the company's customer value proposition and operating model, S-BMI takes a broader view for the purpose of ensuring sustainable performance: it embodies biological thinking and takes into account a broader set of stakeholders, the larger socio-environmental context, extended time horizons for sustaining advantage, the limits, resilience, and externalities of current business models, the entire lifecycle of products, and key system leverage points (BCG, 2019a). In contrast, traditional approaches to sustainability are generally insufficient in a number of ways—they often aim to "do no harm" rather than "do the ultimate good," they under-emphasize the role of innovation, and they do not take a system-wide perspective.

In other words, S-BMI involves recasting the relationship between a company and its broader environment. A handful of companies are already implementing a number of S-BMI typologies today, all of which carry the potential to have a positive effect on both financial returns and benefits to society. These include:

- *"Own the origins,"* which allows to compete and stand out through evaluation and optimization of "social value" of inputs to production process, products, and services (e.g., pursuing clean energy, minimizing waste, fair trade, inclusive and empowering work practices).
- *"Own the whole cycle"* creates competitive advantage through creation of societal impact though the whole product lifecycle (e.g., design for circularity and recyclability, creating offerings to be shared rather than owned).
- *"Expand social value"* model expands the "social value" of products and services along five dimensions: environmental sustainability, customer wellbeing, ethical content, societal enablement, and access and inclusion.

- *"Expand the chains"* expands value chain and overlay with other industries' value chains to expand the reach of societal impact for products and services of all parties, while simultaneously mitigating the risks of doing so (e.g., use of the broad reach of a consumer product's distribution system to provide payments and financial services to small merchants).
- *"Energize the brand"* model allows companies to compete by digitizing, promoting, and monetizing the social value embedded in products and services along the whole value chain. This data can be used to rethink and re-evaluate brand experience, differentiation of the offering, investor engagement, and potentially new businesses.
- *"Re-localize and regionalize,"* which provides competitive advantage through contracting and reconnecting global value chains to bring societal benefits closer to home markets (e.g., building brands that better express local tastes and values).
- *"Build across sectors,"* which allows companies to compete by designing models that include public and social sectors to improve the company's business and societal position (e.g., working alongside NGOs to improve agricultural capacity of small farmers so they become the sources of agricultural inputs to the agro-processing value chain) (Young, Woods, and Reeves, 2019).

(5) Facilitate adaptive innovation to find the right leverage points

Companies often take the same approach for sustainability as they do for strategy: top–down, deliberate planning. But this approach is likely to be inadequate, and innovation is required. Moreover, making a shift to "societal needs-in" strategy in the complex adaptive systems of business and society will require leaders to find the link between local behavior and global impact and to find the right leverage point to effect global change, realizing that "leverage points [are] not necessarily found where the problems arise" (Mandl, 2019). Given the inherent unpredictability of the nested CAS, leaders will need to experiment rather than rely on deduction and planning. Leaders will need to look beyond financial levers, and beyond short-term efficiency and returns to find the right levers to foster sustainability by embracing key principles of biological management that foster adaptive innovation, especially heterogeneity and modularity (Reeves, Levin, and Ueda, 2016).

Finding leverage points in any system will first require a clear understanding of how it is structured and organized, how it evolves, and interdependencies between different elements (Mandl, 2019). Crucially, this involves engaging with stakeholders on the periphery—those who have been excluded or lack access—who often see the world differently and can provoke important insights for how to create value for the broader system. Companies will then need to develop a portfolio of experiments, smaller bets, monitor changes in the environment, and continuously scale up the most promising experiments to push on the right leverage points at the right time (BCG, 2019b). Leaders should take action, tinker, and get their hands dirty. Finance can play a critical role in monitoring the aggregate progress of such experimentation.

(6) Invest in bottom–up solutions

Elinor Ostrom's research on self-organization in fisheries also showed that communal management is an effective way to prevent the "Tragedy of the Commons"—depletion of a scarce shared resource (Ostrom, 2009). While top–down centralized government regulations are hard to bring about, and often fail to prevent overfishing, rules for managing the fisheries and sanctions for violations developed and enforced by local communities can be very effective in long-term stock preservation and fishing yield maintenance. In a separate recent study, evolutionary-game-theoretic analysis indicates the importance of a building blocks approach to substantially deepen cooperation on complex issues (e.g., climate change) (Hannam et al., 2017). Bottom–up approaches are also a lot more feasible in many cases, since the scale of coordination required is more tractable. Taking a lesson from these findings, business leaders should invest time and effort into forming targeted industry-level agreements which are more feasible and effective than larger all-inclusive collaborations to promote communal management to reach sustainability goals.

(7) Commit to corporate statesmanship

Governments alone might not be able to address climate and socioeconomic issues that society is currently facing due to the magnitude of challenges, the divisiveness of contemporary politics, and declining global cooperation. Corporations and financial institutions need to step up to the challenge. We define corporate statesmanship as actions, especially by a company's CEO, to intervene in public affairs to foster collective action in support of the common good, beyond the scope of their narrow self-interest (Reeves, Kell, and Hassan, 2018). This requires a shift in mindset for corporate leaders, who must consider the health of not only their organizations but the systems in which they are embedded. Businesses should engage in corporate statesmanship by acting in the interest of the common good, rather than being solely motivated by self-interest. Farsighted leaders should build coalitions within their industry to find and scale new solutions to broader challenges. Sustainability goals should be adjusted to the specific circumstances of each industry. For example, a pharmaceutical company and a power plant would need very different goals that truly capture the unique value added and points of highest risk to the sustainability for each business.

(8) Use the power of financial sector as point of high leverage

Over time, the financial system has demonstrated power to effect meaningful societal and commercial innovation through its oversight of business, access to capital, ability to visualize broad trends and institute new metrics, and unique capacity to serve as a connection between different layers of the nested CAS. Finance can serve as a multiplier because all businesses depend on financial institutions and markets in multiple ways, including issuing debt, raising equity, rating credit worthiness, analysis of performance, and so on (Dunn, 2019). Furthermore, internally, CFOs are usually the second most powerful people in companies and have more power to bring about fundamental change than the head of corporate affairs. Finance can also deploy capital to make a difference, and can use capital to promote the right goals. Finance can potentially promote holism through comprehensive metrics and help visualize issues that may be currently invisible or unmanaged. Finance can serve as a connecting function between different layers and players of the nested system. Since financial institutions (FIs) and insurers depend on the financial health of their many customer companies, system-wide stability and sustainability are crucial to them, providing a strong incentive to innovate. Financial institutions therefore possess incredible power to help move the needle on the big challenges facing society today, and should use this power for good.

(9) Expect that some solutions will require going beyond financial impact

In evolution, "winning" means surviving to play another round of an infinite game (Slobodkin, 1964). Without survival, performance is irrelevant. And this may require companies to focus on what is of value, rather than only that which can be easily quantified. We should expect therefore that not all solutions will be reducible to quantitative metrics and financial payoffs. At the highest level, the norms and values that guide a complex system are critical to survival. We need therefore to reinforce the notion that at least in part, an ethical revolution in business is necessary. A healthy economy and a healthy planet are inseparable.

NOTES

1   According to the same report, average CEO tenure is weighted by the few long-standing CEOs, but has, nevertheless, also dropped, but less dramatically: from 7.5 to 7.2 years.
2   Different sources show declining holding periods, although the exact numbers vary.
3   According the definition by the 19th annual Edelman Trust Barometer, informed public meets the following criteria: aged 25–64; college-educated; in top 25% of household income per age group in each market; report significant media consumption and engagement in public policy and business news.
4   Task Force on Climate-Related Financial Disclosures.

REFERENCES

Arabesque (2019) *S-Ray. Explore the Sustainability of the World's Biggest Companies* [Online]. Available at: https://arabesque.com/s-ray/ (Accessed: 5 December 2019).

BCG (2019a) *Business Model Innovation* [Online]. Available at: www.bcg.com/en-us/capabilities/strategy/business-model-innovation.aspx (Accessed: 16 December 2019).

BCG (2019b) *Adaptive Strategy* [Online]. Available at: www.bcg.com/publications/collections/your-strategy-needs-strategy/adaptive.aspx (Accessed: 16 December 2019).

Beal, D., Eccles, R., Hansell, G., Lesser, R., Unnikrishnan, S., Woods, W., and Young, D. (2017) 'Total Societal Impact: A New Lens for Strategy', *BCG.com* (27 October) [Online]. Available at: www.bcg.com/en-us/publications/2017/total-societal-impact-new-lens-strategy.aspx (Accessed: 5 December 2019).

Beal, D., Lind, F., Young, D., Pollmann-Larsen, M., Alagiah-Glomseth, A., and Lundestad, I. (2019) *What Companies Can Learn from World Leaders in Societal Impact* [Online]. Available at: www.bcg.com/en-us/publications/2019/world-leaders-social-impact.aspx (Accessed: 5 December 2019).

Bershidsky, L. (2019) 'Moody's Catches on to Climate Risk Mispricing', *Bloomberg News* (25 July) [Online]. Available at: www.bloomberg.com/opinion/articles/2019-07-25/moody-s-links-with-four-twenty-seven-to-price-climate-risk (Accessed: 5 December 2019).

Berwyn, B. (2019) 'Permafrost is Warming around the Globe, Study Shows. That's a Problem for Climate Change', *Insideclimate News* (16 January) [Online]. Available at: https://insideclimate-news.org/news/16012019/permafrost-thaw-climate-change-temperature-data-arctic-antarcti-ca-mountains-study (Accessed: 23 November 2019).

Bingham, R.D., Tylenda, E., Scott-Gall, H., Vilburn, C., and Wilson-Otto, G. (2018) *A Revolution Rising – From Low Chatter to Loud Roar* [Online]. Available at: www.goldmansachs.com/insights/pages/new-energy-landscape-folder/esg-revolution-rising/report.pdf (Accessed: 5 December 2019).

Birdsong, N. (2015) *The Consequences of Economic Inequality* [Online]. Available at: https://sevenpil-larsinstitute.org/consequences-economic-inequality/ (Accessed: 23 November 2019).

Brown, P. (2019) 'Institutional Investors Turn Up Pressure on Companies to Embrace Diversity', *Corporate Compliance Insights* (29 March) [Online]. Available at: www.corporatecomplian-ceinsights.com/institutional-investors-turn-up-pressure-on-companies-to-embrace-diversity/ (Accessed: 5 December 2019).

Burke, M., Hsiang, S.M., and Miguel, E. (2015) 'Global Non-linear Effect of Temperature on Economic Production', *Nature*, 527(7577), pp. 235–239.

Business Roundtable (2019) *Statement on the Purpose of a Corporation* [Online]. Available at: https://opportunity.businessroundtable.org/wp-content/uploads/2019/08/Business-Roundtable-Statement-on-the-Purpose-of-a-Corporation-with-Signatures.pdf (Accessed: 5 December 2019).

CDP (2018) *Major Risk or Rosy Opportunity. Are Companies Ready for Climate Change?* [Online]. Available at: www.cdp.net/en/research/global-reports/global-climate-change-report-2018/cli-mate-report-risks-and-opportunities (Accessed: 23 November 2019).

Climate Action 100 (2019) *Global Investors Driving Business Transition* [Online]. Available at: www.climateaction100.org/ (Accessed: 5 December 2019).

Coke-Hamilton, P. (2019) 'How Trade Wars Pose a Threat to the Global Economy', *World Economic Forum* (7 February) [Online]. Available at: www.weforum.org/agenda/2019/02/how-trade-war-diverts-the-world-unctad-tariff/ (Accessed: 23 November 2019).

Cone Communications (2016) *Millennial Employee Engagement Study* [Online]. Available at: www.conecomm.com/research-blog/2016-millennial-employee-engagement-study (Accessed: 5 December 2019).

Dalio, R. (2019) *Why and How Capitalism Needs to Be Reformed* [Online]. Available at: www.linkedin.com/pulse/why-how-capitalism-needs-reformed-parts-1-2-ray-dalio/ (Accessed: 23 November 2019).

Davenport, C. (2019) 'Climate Change Poses Major Risks to Financial Markets, Regulator Warns', *The New York Times* (11 June) [Online]. Available at: www.nytimes.com/2019/06/11/climate/climate-financial-market-risk.html (Accessed: 23 November 2019).

Dhaliwal, D., Li, O.Z., Tsang, A., and Yang, Y.G. (2014) 'Corporate Social Responsibility Disclosure and the Cost of Equity Capital: The Roles of Stakeholder Orientation and Financial Transparency', *Journal of Accounting and Public Policy*, *33*(4) [Online]. Available at: https://doi.org/10.1016/j.jaccpubpol.2014.04.006 (Accessed: 5 December 2019).

Dimon, J. and Buffet, E.W. (2018) 'Short-Termism Is Harming the Economy', *Wall Street Journal* (6 June) [Online]. Available at: www.wsj.com/articles/short-termism-is-harming-the-economy-1528336801 (Accessed: 23 November 2019).

Dunn, K. (2019) 'Central Banks Are the World's Newest Climate Change Activists', *Fortune* (26 April) [Online]. Available at: https://fortune.com/2019/04/26/climate-change-central-banks/?utm_source=fortune.com&utm_medium=email&utm_campaign=ceo-daily&utm_content=2019042610am (Accessed: 16 December 2019).

Eccles, R.G., Ioannou, I., and Serafeim, G. (2014) 'The Impact of Corporate Sustainability on Organizational Processes and Performance', *Management Science*, *60*(11), pp. 2835–2857.

Edelman (2019) *Edelman Trust Barometer* [Online]. Available at: www.edelman.com/trust-barometer (Accessed: 23 November 2019).

Fiske, W. (2016) 'Mark Warner Says Average Holding Time for Stocks has Fallen to Four Months', *Politifact Virginia* (6 July) [Online]. Available at: www.politifact.com/virginia/statements/2016/jul/06/mark-warner/mark-warner-says-average-holding-time-stocks-has-f/ (Accessed: 23 November 2019).

Flavelle, C. (2019) 'Government Overhaul of National Flood Insurance Cheered by Climate Resilience Experts', *Insurance Journal* (18 March) [Online]. Available at: www.insurancejournal.com/news/national/2019/03/18/520933.htm (Accessed: 23 November 2019).

Folke, C., Österblom, H., Jouffray, J.B., Lambin, E.F., Adger, W.N., Scheffer, M., Crona, B.I., Nyström, M., Levin, S.A., Carpenter, S.R., and Anderies, J.M. (2019) 'Transnational Corporations and the Challenge of Biosphere Stewardship', *Nature Ecology & Evolution*, *3*(10), pp. 1396–1403.

Frampton, M. (2019) 'New Alaska Permanent Fund Chief to Head CIO Podcast', *Chief Investment Officer* (22 April) [Online]. Available at: www.ai-cio.com/news/new-alaska-permanent-fund-chief-head-cio-podcast/ (Accessed: 5 December 2019).

Fried, I. (2019) 'IBM CEO, Business Group Call on Congress to Pass LGBT Rights Bill', *AXIOS* (7 March) [Online]. Available at: www.axios.com/ibm-chief-1551972283-d2868b8c-7681-4b18-aca6-f265f416e988.html (Accessed: 5 December 2019).

Gilblom, K. (2019) 'Big Money Starts to Dump Stocks That Pose Climate Risks', *Bloomberg News* (7 August) [Online]. Available at: www.bloomberg.com/news/articles/2019-08-07/big-money-starts-to-dump-stocks-that-pose-climate-risks (Accessed: 5 December 2019).

Goldman Sachs (2019) *Environmental Market Opportunities. Global Investment Research* [Online]. Available at: www.goldmansachs.com/citizenship/environmental-stewardship/market-opportunities/global-investment-research/ (Accessed: 5 December 2019).

GSI Alliance (2018) *Global Sustainable Investment Review 2018* [Online]. Available at: www.gsi-alliance.org/wp-content/uploads/2019/03/GSIR_Review2018.3.28.pdf (Accessed: 5 December 2019).

Hannam, P.M., Vasconcelos, V.V., Levin, S.A., and Pacheco, J.M. (2017) 'Incomplete Cooperation and Co-benefits: Deepening Climate Cooperation with a Proliferation of Small Agreements', *Climatic Change*, *144*(1) [online]. Available at: https://doi.org/10.1007/s10584-015-1511-2 (Accessed: 16 December 2019: ().

Hendrickson, C. and Galstn, W.A. (2019) *Big Tech Threats: Making Sense of the Backlash against Online Platforms* [Online]. Available at: www.brookings.edu/research/big-tech-threats-making-sense-of-the-backlash-against-online-platforms/ (Accessed: 16 December 2019).

IPCC (2019), *Climate Change and Land: An IPCC Special Report on Climate Change, Desertification, Land Degradation, Sustainable Land Management, Food Security, and Greenhouse Gas Fluxes in Terrestrial Ecosystems* [Online]. Available at: www.ipcc.ch/report/srccl/ (Accessed: 23 November 2019).

IRS (2019) *Topic No. 409 Capital Gains and Losses* [Online]. Available at: www.irs.gov/taxtopics/tc409 (Accessed: 23 November 2019).

Jergler, D. (2018) 'Report Outlines Climate Change Risks Faced by Insurance Sector', *Insurance Journal* (23 August) [Online]. Available at: www.insurancejournal.com/news/national/2018/08/23/499027.htm (Accessed: 23 November 2019).

Jun-suk, Y. (2019) 'SK Group Comes Up with Way to Measure Firm's Social Contribution', *Korea Herald* (21 May) [Online]. Available at: www.koreaherald.com/view.php?ud=20190521000647 (Accessed: 5 December 2019).

Kell, G. (2018a) 'The Remarkable Rise of ESG', *Forbes* (11 July) [Online]. Available at: www.forbes.com/sites/georgkell/2018/07/11/the-remarkable-rise-of-esg/#ccaa35a16951 (Accessed: 5 December 2019).

Kell, G. (2018b) 'Time To Step Up Climate Action', *Forbes* (26 November) [Online]. Available at: www.forbes.com/sites/georgkell/2018/11/26/time-to-step-up-climate-action/#4b6fbb6e6113 (Accessed: 5 December 2019).

Kell, G. (2019) 'It Still Makes Financial Sens to Burn the Globe', *Barron's* (21 March) [Online]. Available at: www.barrons.com/articles/climate-change-is-still-too-cheap-esg-investing-51553104880 (Accessed: 16 December 2019).

Kiron, D., Unruh, G., Kruschwitz, N., Reeves, M., Rubel, H., and Meyer Zum, F.A. (2017) 'Corporate Sustainability at a Crossroads. Progress Toward Our Common Future in Uncertain Times', *MIT Sloan Management Review* (23 May) [Online]. Available at: https://sloanreview.mit.edu/projects/corporate-sustainability-at-a-crossroads/ (Accessed: 5 December 2019).

L'Oréal (2018) *L'Oréal Takes Palm Oil Sustainable Sourcing One Step Beyond* [Online]. Available at: www.loreal.com/sharing-beauty-with-all-innovating/achieving-zero-deforestation/l%E2%80%99or%C3%A9al-takes-palm-oil-sustainable-sourcing-one-step-beyond (Accessed: 5 December 2019).

Mandl, C. (2019) *Managing Complexity in Social Systems. Leverage Points for Policy and Strategy.* Cham: Springer Nature Switzerland AG.

Marcec, D. (2018) *CEO Tenure Rates* [Online]. Available at: https://corpgov.law.harvard.edu/2018/02/12/ceo-tenure-rates/ (Accessed: 23 November 2019).

Martin, R. (2019) 'The High Price of Efficiency', *Harvard Business Review* (January/February) [Online]. Available at: https://hbr.org/2019/01/rethinking-efficiency#the-high-price-of-efficiency (Accessed: 16 December 2019).

McClure, B. (2019) *A Guide to CEO Compensation* [Online]. Investopedia. Available at: www.investopedia.com/managing-wealth/guide-ceo-compensation/ (Accessed: 23 November 2019).

McKenzie, S. (2019) 'Greenland is Melting in a Heatwave. That's Everyone's Problem', *CNN* (31 July) [Online]. Available at: www.cnn.com/2019/07/31/europe/greenland-heatwave-climate-crisis-intl/index.html (Accessed: 23 November 2019).

McNeill, R. and Nelson, D.J. (2014) 'Coastal Flooding has Surged in US', *Scientific American* (10 July) [Online]. Available at: www.scientificamerican.com/article/coastal-flooding-has-surged-in-u-s/ (Accessed: 23 November 2019).

Murray, A. (2019) 'The 2019 Fortune 500 CEO Survey Results Are In', *Fortune* (16 May) [Online]. Available at: https://fortune.com/2019/05/16/fortune-500-2019-ceo-survey/ (Accessed: 23 November 2019).

NASA (2019) *The Effects of Climate Change* [Online]. Available at: https://climate.nasa.gov/effects/ (Accessed: 5 December 2019).

Ostrom, E. (2009) 'A General Framework for Analyzing Sustainability of Social-ecological Systems', *Science, 325*(5939), pp. 419–422.

Pisani, B. (2018) 'Stock Buybacks Hit a Record $1.1 trillion, and the Year's Not Over', *CNBC Trader Talk* (18 December) [Online]. Available at: www.cnbc.com/2018/12/18/stock-buybacks-hit-a-record-1point1-trillion-and-the-years-not-over.html (Accessed: 23 November 2019).

Plumer, B. (2019) 'Companies See Climate Change Hitting Their Bottom Lines in the Next 5 Years', *New York Times* (4 June) [Online]. Available at: www.nytimes.com/2019/06/04/climate/companies-climate-change-financial-impact.htm (Accessed: 23 November 2019).

Reeves, M., Dierksmeier, C., and Chittaro, C. (2018) *The Humanization of the Corporation* [Online]. Available at: www.bcg.com/en-us/publications/2018/humanization-corporation.aspx (Accessed: 5 December 2019).

Reeves, M., Kell, G., and Hassan, F. (2018) 'The Case for Corporate Statesmanship', *BCG.com* (1 March) [Online]. Available at: www.bcg.com/en-us/publications/2018/case-corporate-statesmanship.aspx (Accessed: 16 December 2019).

Reeves, M., Levin, S., and Ueda, D. (2016) 'The Biology of Corporate Survival', *Harvard Business Review* (January–February) [Online]. Available at: https://hbr.org/2016/01/the-biology-of-corporate-survival (Accessed: 16 December 2019).

Reeves, M., Levin, S., and Ueda, D. (2017) 'Think Biologically: Messy Management for a Complex World', *BCG.com* (18 July) [Online]. Available at: www.bcg.com/en-us/publications/2017/think-biologically-messy-management-for-complex-world.aspx (Accessed: 16 December 2019).

Ross, L. and Nisbett, R. (2011) *The Person and the Situation: Perspectives of Social Psychology*. London: Pinter & Martin Publishers.

Rubel, H., Jung, U., Follette, C., Meyer Zum Felde, A., Appathurai, S., and Benedi Díaz, M. (2019) 'A Circular Solution to Plastic Waste', *BCG.com* (15 July) [Online]. Available at: www.bcg.com/publications/2019/plastic-waste-circular-solution.aspx (Accessed: 5 December 2019).

Sadoff (2018) *The Major Trends* [Online]. Available at: www.sadoffinvestments.com/media/1106/1118sim.pdf (Accessed: 23 November 2019).

Saez, E. (2019) *Striking It Richer: The Evolution of Top Incomes in the United States (Updated with 2017 Final Estimates)* [Online]. Available at: https://eml.berkeley.edu/~saez/saez-UStopincomes-2017.pdf (Accessed: 23 November 2019).

SASB (2018) *Standards Overview* [Online]. Available at: www.sasb.org/standards-overview/ (Accessed: 5 December 2019).

Semuels, A. (2016) 'How to Stop Short-Term Thinking in America's Companies', *The Atlantic* (23 December) [Online]. Available at: www.theatlantic.com/business/archive/2016/12/short-term-thinking/511874/ (Accessed: 23 November 2019).

Slobodkin, L. (1964) 'The Strategy of Evolution', *American Scientist*, 52(3). Available at: www.jstor.org/stable/27839075 (Accessed: 16 December 2019).

Snyder, J. (2019) 'The Broken Bargain. How Nationalism Came Back', *Foreign Affairs* (March/April 2019) [Online]. Available at: www.foreignaffairs.com/articles/world/2019-02-12/broken-bargain (Accessed: 23 November 2019).

Stein, C. (2018) 'Shift From Active to Passive Approaches Tipping Point 2019', *Bloomberg News* (31 December) [Online]. Available at: www.bloomberg.com/news/articles/2018-12-31/shift-from-active-to-passive-approaches-tipping-point-in-2019 (Accessed: 5 December 2019).

Stock, K. (2018) 'Instagram-Popular Shoemaker Rothy's Expected to Post $140 million in Revenue', *Bloomberg Businessweek* (17 December) [Online]. Available at: www.bloomberg.com/news/articles/2018-12-17/rothy-s-hits-its-stride-with-35m-from-goldman-sachs (Accessed: 5 December 2019).

Stockholm Resilience Centre (2015) *The Nine Planetary Boundaries* [Online]. Available at: www.stockholmresilience.org/research/planetary-boundaries/planetary-boundaries/about-the-research/the-nine-planetary-boundaries.html (Accessed: 23 November 2019).

The Economist (2016) 'The Rise of the Superstars', *The Economist* (15 September) [Online]. Available at: www.economist.com/special-report/2016/09/15/the-rise-of-the-superstars (Accessed: 16 December 2019).

Thorbecke, E. and Charumilind, C. (2002) 'Economic Inequality and Its Socioeconomic Impact', *World Development*, 30(9), pp. 1477–1482.

Tollefson, J. (2018) 'IPCC says Limiting Global Warming to 1.5°C Will Require Drastic Action', *Nature News* (8 October) [Online]. Available at: www.nature.com/articles/d41586-018-06876-2 (Accessed: 23 November 2019).

Truvalue Labs (2019) *Raising the Bar on ESG Data Integration* [Online]. Available at: https://insights.truvaluelabs.com/wp_raisingbaresgdataint_offer (Accessed: 5 December 2019).

UN (2018) *UN Global Compact Progress Report 2018* [Online]. Available at: www.unglobalcompact.org/library/5637 (Accessed: 5 December 2019).

UN Environment (2019) *Global Environment Outlook 6* [Online]. Available at: www.unenvironment. org/resources/global-environment-outlook-6 (Accessed: 5 December 2019).

UNEP FI (2018) *UNEP FI Working with 16 Global Insurers to Better Understand Risk & Implement TFCD Recommendations* [Online]. Available at: www.unepfi.org/news/industries/insurance/ unep-fi-working-with-16-global-insurers-to-better-understand-risk-implement-tcfd-recom-mendations/ (Accessed: 5 December 2019).

Unilever (2019) *About Our Strategy* [Online]. Available at: www.unilever.com/sustainable-living/ our-strategy/about-our-strategy/ (Accessed: 5 December 2019).

Unruh, G., Kiron, D., Kruschwitz, N., Reeves, M., Rubel, H., and Meyer Zum Felde, A. (2016) 'Investing for a Sustainable Future', *MIT Sloan Management Review* (11 May) [Online]. Available at: https://sloanreview.mit.edu/projects/investing-for-a-sustainable-future/ (Accessed: 5 December 2019).

WHO (2018) *COP24 Special Report. Health and Climate Change* [Online]. Available at: https:// apps.who.int/iris/bitstream/handle/10665/276405/9789241514972-eng.pdf?sequence=1&isAl-lowed=y (Accessed: 23 November 2019).

Wilson, E.O. (1998) *Consilience: The Unity of Knowledge.* New York: Random House.

World Bank Group (2019) *Stock Turnover Ratio Data* [Online]. Available at: https://data.worldbank. org/indicator/CM.MKT.TRNR?locations=US&view=chart (Accessed: 23 November 2019).

Young, D., Woods, W., and Reeves, M. (2019) *Optimize for Both Social and Business Value* [Online]. Available at: www.bcg.com/publications/2019/optimize-social-business-value.aspx (Accessed: 23 November 2019).

3

Renewing markets from within

How businesses and the investment community can drive transformational change

Georg Kell and Andreas Rasche

INTRODUCTION

Sustainable investing does not exist in a vacuum. Its emergence and diffusion were impacted by a number of events and historical development. This chapter takes this historic context seriously. It starts with a review of how the corporate (social) responsibility movement matured and started to converge with sustainability concerns, and then discusses how the increasing uptake of responsibility and sustainability concerns impacted the investment community. We work out a number of drivers that have enabled the increasing cross-fertilization of corporate sustainability and sustainable investing, such as concerns for how "material" ESG issues impact firms' financial bottom line.

Once we understand that corporate sustainability and sustainable investing are intertwined in a number of ways, we need to ask whether (corporate) sustainability is just a fleeting trend or whether it can be seen as a lasting building block for market transformation. If sustainable investing is to transform markets from within, there is a need to show that sustainable business practices are here to stay. We approach this discussion by highlighting four "forces" that have shaped (and will further shape) the sustainability agenda: (1) technological changes, (2) constraints put upon us by the natural environment (i.e., planetary boundaries), (3) (international) politics and social norms, as well as (4) the increasing blurring of boundaries between the public and private sphere. We discuss why, once we consider these forces, there is no reason to believe that sustainability in general, and corporate sustainability as well as sustainable investing in particular, are fleeting trends. Rather, we highlight that sustainable investing has the power to renew markets from within—i.e., to kick off transformational processes which could help to address some of the grand challenges that humanity faces. However, we also discuss a number of factors that have to be addressed on the corporate (e.g., development of future-fit business models) and investment (e.g., improving the quality of ESG data) side for such transformational changes to happen.

LOOKING BACK: CORPORATE RESPONSIBILITY MEETS SUSTAINABLE INVESTING

Corporate responsibility has gone global

The role of business in society evolved over centuries. The central question of who and what corporations should be responsible for has given rise to countless debates and social and legal actions; it has shaped modern capitalism and the meaning and practice of corporate responsibility in society (for a review of corporate responsibility in the US, see Carroll, Lipartito, Post and Werhane, 2012). Corporate responsibility is a dynamic concept which is continuously reacting to shifting societal expectations and regulatory changes. In the past, the notion and practice of corporate responsibility was different for each region and economy (Kell, 2017; Schwalbach and Klink, 2012). But about two decades ago, as corporations were expanding their global value chain in an era of liberalization, the launch of the United Nations Global Compact (UNGC) in June 2000 by former United Nations Secretary General Kofi Annan planted the seeds of change and triggered a global movement of corporate responsibility—a movement which is increasingly referred to as corporate sustainability.[1]

Mr. Annan made the case that power and responsibility cannot be separated. He urged corporations to embrace ten universal principles based on international frameworks endorsed by governments, such as the Universal Declaration of Human Rights, the International Labour Organization's (ILO) Fundamental Principles and Rights at Work, the Rio Declaration on Sustainable Development, and the UN Convention against Corruption. These universal principles were designed to inform corporate strategy and operations to "give globalization a human face" (UN Global Compact, 2020). From China to Argentina, from South Africa to Iceland, the UNGC built local networks to advance the practice of the principles through learning, dialogue, and partnerships. The movement has grown from initially 50 corporations in the year 2000 to over 10,000 by 2020 (UN Global Compact, 2020).

The UNGC laid the foundation for the UN Sustainable Development Goals (SDGs) which were introduced by the United Nations in 2015. It also helped to build several other initiatives, including the Principles for

Responsible Investment (PRI) and the Sustainable Stock Exchange Initiative (SSE). Other initiatives coincided with the growth of the UNGC, notably the Global Reporting Initiative (GRI), which grew in parallel and which tackles the issue of corporate disclosure.

The corporate responsibility movement brought about massive incremental changes impacting corporate strategies, operations, and stakeholder engagement. Over time, these changes have added up to improvements for workers, the environment, and communities (Det Norske Veritas and UN Global Compact, 2015; Eccles, Ioannou and Serafeim, 2014). Issues such as emission reductions, water management, women's empowerment, human rights in the supply chain, and action against corruption, which used to be regarded as irrelevant or as externalities, became mainstream agenda items of corporate boards, strategies, and practices. The growth of corporate responsibility was supported by government action (Knudsen and Moon, 2017) and the projection of global rules for global markets, based on managed interdependence and informed by the historical experiences of the post-World War II era. For corporations who embraced corporate responsibility, it not only became a moral imperative and a pathway to protect against costly mistakes while building brand value, it also became an incentive to improve performance in a race to the top to ease access to markets.

Sustainable investing is catching up

Historically speaking, the corporate responsibility and (sustainable/responsible) investment movements were not overly intertwined. Mainstream investing traditionally paid little attention to environmental and social issues, with the notable exception of niche actors such as faith-based and ethical investors, often referred to as "socially responsible investment" (SRI). SRI's main approach was not to invest in certain industries and products, such as tobacco, alcohol, and arms (Schueth, 2003). The disconnect between corporate responsibility and investing was frequently recognized as a major barrier, holding corporations back from doing more on environmental stewardship, social inclusion, and clean business (see, e.g., Accenture and UN Global Compact, 2015). This started to change in 2004 when UN Secretary General Kofi Annan invited major asset owners to join an initiative entitled "Who Cares Wins," which coined the term "ESG" (environmental, social, and governance) (UN Global Compact, 2004), and then launched the PRI at the New York Stock Exchange in 2005.

The idea that ESG factors have material relevance and that it is therefore prudent for investors to integrate such factors into their analyses and decision-making was in principle well understood. During the first decade of this century, asset owners, managers, and service providers began to explore ESG issues,[2] but actual practices were slow to change. As the chase for short-term returns accelerated in the run up to the financial crisis of 2007/08, financialization became a goal in itself. The devastating impact of the financial crisis led to a loss of trust from which the industry has yet to fully recover. Central banks had to step in. This created a new era of low interest rates through financial easing. In the aftermath of the financial crisis, the financial industry in the Western world was struggling to survive, fending off heavy regulation. The PRI continued to grow and an increasing number of actors, including stock exchanges, started paying attention to ESG integration. In 2009, UN Secretary Ban Ki-moon launched the Sustainable Stock Exchange initiative at the United Nations. However, progress on ESG integration into mainstream finance was still slow.

Morality meets materiality

So, what gave ESG integration a major push? We suggest that the increasing acknowledgment of the materiality of ESG factors acted as a game changer. Practitioners have long understood that ESG factors reflect good management practices that are a proxy for corporate survival and long-term financial success. It was not difficult to make this case when corporations were entangled in major crises situations. The costs of getting it wrong could be measured (Thomas, Schermerhorn and Dienhart, 2004). There was clear evidence that neglecting environmental stewardship, good workplace and supply chain practices, or ignoring the corrosive effect of corruption, were not a winning strategy. Numerous corporate crises situations gave strength to the corporate responsibility movement, as corporations shared and mainstreamed the learnings of their journey. Examples include mainstreaming of environmental stewardship practices by Dow Chemical and their legacy burden stemming from the Bhopal accident, and the integrity drive by Siemens in the wake of their corruption crisis.

But while it was easy to learn from mistakes and to make the case that corporate responsibility is also an insurance against disasters, it was far more difficult to make the case for the benefits of responsible and sustainable corporate behavior in the absence of a crisis. The emergence of empirical evidence that sustainability and financial performance go hand in hand was a game changer (Kell, 2018),[3] as well as by progress made by data framework providers, notably the GRI and the Carbon Disclosure Project (CDP). Several studies have summarized the discussion of the link between firms' financial and their social/environmental performance (see, e.g., Clark, Feiner and Viehs, 2015; Friede, Busch and Bassen, 2015).

As perceptions about the financial relevance of ESG factors, which traditionally were not accounted for, began to shift, the notion of "fiduciary duty" started changing as well. During the early days of ESG, trustees of pension funds would frequently make the point that their fiduciary duty was to maximize returns and that they could therefore not integrate ESG factors. This argument got turned around as evidence was mounting that ignoring ESG factors has financial implications and that it is therefore the fiduciary duty of trustees to integrate ESG factors into analyses and decision-making. This shift of attitudes was documented in several landmark studies initiated by PRI and UNEP-FI and endorsed by former US Vice President Al Gore (see UN PRI, 2017; PRI, 2020).

The convergence of moral imperatives, such as respecting human rights and upholding high ethical standards in countries that suffer from governance gaps, and a focus on the financial relevance of ESG factors, such as costing emissions, is now providing a new basis for evaluating corporate performance. Two camps have frequently struggled over definitions and boundaries of sustainability themes across the communities that advocate corporate disclosure and accounting for ESG factors: (1) those who advocate that only strict materiality criteria should be applied in relevant analyses and (2) those who see a narrow materiality concept as insufficient and therefore advocate a principled approach based on norms. These debates are inconclusive and will continue, and ultimately reflect the shifting boundaries of the societal consensus. But irrespective of the shifting nature of these debates, the fundamental relationship between moral imperatives and materiality is mutually reinforcing and strong, as demonstrated by Figure 3.1. The analysis[4] underlying this figure suggests that compliance with the ten principles of the UN Global Compact is closely related with participants' ESG performance based on sector-specific, material ESG factors. Morality and materiality are

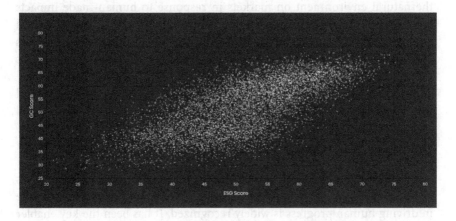

FIGURE 3.1 Scatterplot: correlation between ESG and GC scores

Source: Arabesque

not mutually exclusive concepts. They reinforce each other. As common sense suggests, corporations with strong values and high ethical standards are often also strong on ESG performance.

SUSTAINABILITY: A FLEETING PHENOMENON OR A BUILDING BLOCK FOR MARKET TRANSFORMATION?

The emerging relationship between what is nowadays coined corporate sustainability and sustainable investing holds the promise of renewing capitalism from within, leading to smarter, healthier, and more inclusive outcomes. As concepts and practices of sustainability continue to grow and are involving an ever-greater number of market actors, while spreading across their supporting ecosystem and governing institutions, the question remains whether sustainability is just a fleeting trend or whether it is becoming a mainstream force for good. This question is especially relevant as the post-World War II era of managed interdependence and the rules-based system has started giving way to a new system where economic nationalism and new rivalries play a greater role in shaping investment and trade flows. Will the idea and practice of corporate and financial sustainability fall victim to these trends, as market players are seeking political protection and global norms and shared values of humanity are taking a backseat?

To answer this question, it is helpful to have a closer look at the long-term and systemic forces behind the sustainability movement, beyond short-term cycles of stakeholder pressure or country-specific regulatory changes. Based on our experience over the past three decades, it is clear that the most fundamental forces that drive the sustainability agenda are (1) technology, which powers transparency, efficiency, and innovation, (2) constraints imposed by the natural environment on markets in response to human-made impacts on the natural environment, (3) policy changes at global, national, and sub-national levels and changing social norms, and (4) a blurring of the lines between public and private interests. A closer look at these four forces shows that their momentum has been growing over time. This suggests that sustainability issues are not a fleeting trend but are rather becoming the new normal for market actors.

The first force: technology

Technological change is irreversible. Government action can support its creation, but it cannot reverse its diffusion. Technology's fundamental role in driving human progress is widely recognized. It has been the key enabler behind the transparency movement that has fueled the sustainability reporting movement. Technological advances are also a key driver of business models that are aligned with circularity (Ellen MacArthur Foundation, 2015). For instance, the increasing use of radio frequency identification helps firms to track material flows and hence supports the implementation of value recovery systems (e.g., reuse or remanufacture; Pagoropoulos, Pigosso and McAloone, 2017).

Technological change is enabling investors to analyze massive data sets to better assess corporate ESG performance and to offer additional insights into risk and opportunity analysis for all asset classes. For instance, the Arabesque S-Ray® data machine processes over 150 million data points daily, a number that will increase in the near future, as new data sources are onboarded (Arabesque, 2020). Declining costs for data processing and the dramatic increase of data availability, combined with rapid progress in machine learning and artificial intelligence, suggest that a more fundamental transformation will happen within the near future where sustainability information will be a critical raw material for making core business decisions. Technological change is also likely to disrupt financial markets, as more cost-effective and superior solutions will replace traditional functions across a wide spectrum of activities.

A defining feature of our time is that technology no longer just moves in long-term cycles as is commonly perceived. Its pace of change is accelerating and so is its disruptive and creative impact across all sectors of the economy (see, for example, the dramatic increase of patents in artificial intelligence; WIPO, 2019). For many corporations, this means that path-dependent developments will no longer be an option. Often, radical shifts are required to keep pace with technological changes. An example for this is the current transition in the mobility sector where e-mobility, combined with digitalization and information services, defines an entirely new business environment. Similar trends can be observed in the energy sector, where declining costs of renewable energy and smarter energy management are now competing with established actors.

Digital technologies, smart analytics, and artificial intelligence are of particular importance for the sustainability movement. Besides enabling ever more precise measurements, they also help to improve efficiency across all economic activities. By some estimates, greenhouse gas emissions could be reduced by over 1.3 gigatons by introducing measures such as smarter transport and energy systems to the "business as usual" scenario (GESI, 2019). Beyond efficiency improvements, the pipeline of inventions has been steadily filling across the globe as entry barriers have been falling. The ecosystem for innovation has both broadened and deepened, including in areas such as advanced materials, automation, robotics, and quantum computing (Portincaso, de la Tour and Soussan, 2019). The development of such technologies often addresses big societal and environmental concerns and will undoubtedly play a critical role in shaping the sustainability agenda.

The second force: planetary boundaries

Environmental concerns have long been key drivers behind the sustainability movement. Many landmark events and publications have shaped this movement. Rachel Carson's (1962) *Silent Spring* is often cited as the wake-up call that ignited the environmental movement. In 1987, the World Commission on Environment and Development published the widely cited report *Our Common Future*. The same year saw the adoption of the "Montreal Protocol," which reversed the depletion of the ozone layer. This protocol was a high point in international cooperation and the first universally ratified treaty in the history of the UN. In 1992, a major conference in Rio de Janeiro, the so-called "Earth Conference," established general principles, such as "the polluter pays" (UN, 1992), and laid the basis for climate negotiations, the protection of biodiversity, and the reversal of desertification.

Although many governments and corporations have made progress in terms of pollution reduction, environmental stewardship, protection of habitat and resource efficiency, research shows that essential earth-system processes are pushed to their limits, or, in some cases, have already crossed these limits. Research on planetary boundaries has quantified these boundaries. According to Rockström et al. (2009, p. 474):

> [t]he boundaries we propose represent a new approach to defining biophysical productions for human development. For the first time, we are trying to quantify the safe limits outside of which the Earth system cannot continue to function in a stable, Holocene-like state.

Three of these boundaries are already crossed (i.e., with regard to climate change, biodiversity loss, and the nitrogen cycle), while the other processes remain under intense pressure.

But we are just beginning to understand what it means to live in an era where humans have become a geophysical force. In *The Climate of History*, Dipesh Chakrabarty (2009, p. 201) writes: "The anthropogenic explanations of climate change spell the collapse of the age-old humanist distinction between natural history and human history." This has fundamental implications for markets. Major transitions will be required from corporations and finance to move away from traditional approaches and methods of valuations. Societies are no longer the only context that shapes the framework conditions for market players. The natural environment is now becoming the defining framework within which societies and markets must establish a new relationship. We will have to come to grips with the necessity of reducing the human impact on the natural environment, while at the same

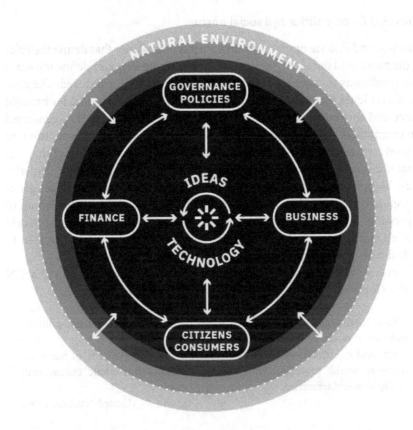

FIGURE 3.2 Market interdependencies embedded into the natural environment
Source: Georg Kell

time learning to adapt to the consequences of a rapidly changing natural environment. Figure 3.2 depicts these relationships; it shows that markets, society, and relevant governance choices are embedded into (and hence constrained by) the natural environment.

The implications are profound and will shape markets and societies for generations to come. The long-term and irreversible effects on nature are reinforced by the fact that the human footprint tends to have a long-term impact. Carbon, once released into the atmosphere, depletes only slowly, and other impacts, such as plastic in the soil and water, have even longer half-lives. The theories and beliefs of the industrial era will need to be replaced as our ideas about markets and societies will need to be reimagined (see also Lo, 2017). There is no doubt: the boundaries set by the natural environment, besides technology, are a long-term, systemic, and irreversible force that is changing the framework conditions of markets and societies.

The third force: politics and social norms

Business and finance operate within political boundaries that define the rules of the game, and the access to markets. These boundaries also define the space and conditions to compete and how best practices can be diffused. The classic liberal ideas that supported markets over the past seven decades brought peace and enormous economic prosperity. At the same time, they generated environmental degradation and accentuated inequality and exclusion in markets where policymakers failed to offset disruptions. The system that was created over 70 years ago was based on the idea that peace and prosperity must be built on the pillars of shared rules and managed interdependence as well as on liberal ideas such as respect for human rights and freedom of expression. Multilateral organizations such as the United Nations, the World Trade Organization, and the Bretton Woods organizations were created to embed rules that govern markets and related social norms.

Already two decades ago, when inviting corporations to join the UN Global Compact, former UN Secretary General Kofi Annan warned:

> History teaches us that an imbalance between the economic, social and political realms can never be sustained for very long. [...] the global economy will be fragile and vulnerable—vulnerable to backlash from all the 'isms' of our post-cold-war world: protectionism; populism; nationalism; ethnic chauvinism; fanaticism; and terrorism.
>
> (United Nations, 1999)

Kofi Annan's warning turned out to be a prophecy come true. Today, the liberal experiment is facing strong headwinds as economic power has migrated from the West to the East and given rise to new geostrategic rivalry, while the rise of nationalism and populism has eroded the rule-based approach to economic integration. Politics and power have reclaimed supremacy over markets in a fragmenting landscape, where old and new ideas struggle with each other, and where assumptions about a fair level playing field and trust in public institutions no longer hold. Nationalism and the retreat from multilateralism also plays out on the Internet, which is the engine of globalization. Initially perceived as a liberating technology that connects in an unfettered global public sphere that fosters transparency, the Internet is now the subject of state control in a growing number of countries. This raises the spectrum of digital nationalism and the splintering of the Internet along national spheres of influence (Kapur, 2019). The liberal dream to build a rule-based and integrated global market, where competition leads to a race to the top, has crashed. The dark forces it could not contain are now roaring back. Politics trumps markets again and in some places of the world the lessons of history are being forgotten. For corporations and finance, this means that political considerations have moved up on the agenda and are influencing investment and location decisions, also through the prism of political risks.

Will this changing landscape slow down the sustainability movement? At the multilateral level, this is arguably already occurring. The retreat of the US from the Paris Climate Accord has certainly slowed down progress and is setting an example for other countries not to meet their voluntary obligations. Government support is essential. But it is not the only force that is shaping market behavior. Technological change will continue to drive transparency, digitalization, and low-carbon innovations. And natural boundaries will increasingly put a premium on low-carbon solutions and practices that support social inclusion. Moreover, climate change does not respect political spheres of influence, nor does it have a political color. The search for solutions is here to stay and will intensify, irrespective of political swings. Nature cannot be fooled.

There is a silver lining across the spectrum of troubling political developments. Young people all over the world are pushing for changing social norms. People are increasingly able to express their personal values and preferences through the Internet, whether they live in democratic or autocratic systems. In our modern age, where "individualization"[5] is a defining characteristic across all cultures and political regimes, the young, digitalized generation can set changes into motion at the speed of light. As awareness about environmental and social ills is growing, young people are speaking up and are putting pressure on decision-makers and markets with their lifestyle choices. The amazing rise of the "Fridays for Future" movement, started in Sweden by 16-year-old Greta Thunberg, has arguably done more for climate action within one year than dozens of voluntary initiatives accomplished over decades.

The long march through the institutions during the second half of the last century that modernized our current system took several decades. In today's digitalized world, new trends and the expression of changing values unfold much more quickly. We can observe this by the impact of health and food lifestyle choices, by the growing importance of sharing and caring over ownership, by changed social norms such as highlighted by the #MeToo movement, and by the growing tendency to invest money in such a way that it aligns with one's values.[6]

The fourth force: the growing overlap between public and private interests

There is a fundamental blurring of lines between public and private interests which traditionally were more clearly separated, with the former having a monopoly on security issues and a broad mandate to foster prosperity, while the latter was primarily seen as maximizing profits while striving for growth.

Some time ago, John Ruggie (2004) already pointed out that the global public domain is being reconstituted. The "public" sphere, which was traditionally concerned with the actions of sovereign states, is increasingly complemented by a system in which state *and* non-state actors are concerned with the production of (global) public goods.

Rapid technological change and the commercialization of science gives the private sector a clear lead over the public sector, which is lagging behind trying to define and secure public interests. Public goods, such as air quality and access to clean water, have an increasingly private character. Businesses and investing are both major sources of the degradation of such goods, but are also essential partners when it comes to solutions. Investing and workplace decisions are shaping social conditions with growing implications for social welfare, as their reach and influence is growing. Business has long understood that public and private interests overlap. The emergence and wide adoption of stakeholder-based concepts (Freeman, 1984), such as "creating shared value" (Porter and Kramer, 2011) and "corporate purpose" (Reiman, 2013), are expressions of positioning corporations in such a way that profit and public good stewardship go hand in hand. Investors have less of a track record in advancing public goods as part of their core strategy. But with the adoption of the SDGs, the entry barriers for alignment with public goods have significantly been lowered.

Taken together, the four forces make sustainability in general and sustainable investing in particular important building blocks of future market transformation. It is not always easy to distinguish these forces, neither "in practice" nor "in theory." Often, the forces overlap and mutually influence each other, for instance when technological changes enable new solutions to sustainability problems which then are diffused through public and private governance mechanisms.

MARKET TRANSITION ON THE MOVE

If market transformation is given (due to the forces described above), we need to better understand how businesses and investing are adapting to these fundamental changes. Path-dependent and incremental changes are no longer an assurance to thrive in the future. The mechanical and compartmentalized concepts that worked well in the past no longer suffice to navigate the future. We can neither understand businesses as mechanical organizations nor can we assume that (financial) markets are efficient and fully rational (see, e.g., Lo, 2017). Leading business consultancies are already introducing concepts of evolutionary biology, such as "agility" (Accenture, 2020) and "resilience" (Reeves and Levin, 2017), to find new ways to frame strategies and organizational change in order to be better prepared to navigate uncertainty. In the following sections, we take a closer look at how exactly businesses (as organizations) and investing (as a practice) need to change.

Business transformation

There are many ways to look at needed organizational change in the light of the forces that are redefining market frameworks. A fitting way could be to frame transformation as a journey from the "industrial era" towards something that could be labeled "future-fit" (see Figure 3.3). We know where we are coming from. We can describe corporate functions as they have evolved over decades. We do not know exactly what it means to be future-fit. But we can already identify the key properties of a future-fit organization based on the direction of changes. Two pathways stand out in particular: *decarbonization* and *digitalization*. They capture the essence of technological changes and the growing imperative to transition towards a carbon-constrained world. They are also deeply connected with each other. Radical decarbonization efforts almost always require technology shifts, and new technologies and innovations are in the end the only pathways to tackle climate change.

Corporations are at different stages when it comes to managing corporate sustainability (Rangan, Chase and Karim, 2015). Many are still holding on to industrial-era paradigms, trying to extend the life span of business models that are still profitable in this transition period. Others are moving ahead faster by shifting technologies—the electrification of mobility and the spread of smart grid systems are examples of technology shifts—away from fossil fuels towards clean sources of energy. Some companies also abandon classic government-affairs concepts that are based on the notion of the industrial era where the

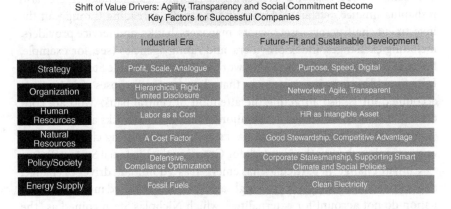

FIGURE 3.3 Driving market transformation

Source: Georg Kell

private sector "optimized compliance." Rather, these firms take a proactive role in shaping policy changes that support future-fit business models. An example is VW CEO Herbert Diess advocating a carbon tax (Krogh, 2019).

The transition towards future-fit business models requires all classic corporate functions to reframe strategies and operations. Consider the example of environmental management. The classic view that natural resources are a cost factor, the negative externalities of which could largely be socialized, led to incremental efficiency improvements without solving underlying problems, such as emission growth, loss of biodiversity, and plastic pollution. As public pressure and looming regulatory changes to tackle such problems are bound to intensify, corporations have started to elevate decarbonization and emission measurements as strategic imperatives (Science Based Targets, 2020) and redesigned processes along the "circular economy" model are starting to take shape (Rutqvist, 2015).

The transition towards future-fit business models is moving slowly, including in key sectors, such as energy, which accounts for over two-thirds of all emissions that cause global warming (Kell, 2019). But as the factors that drive the transformation are gaining momentum, one can anticipate that faster and deeper changes are bound to happen. With finance now catching up on the urgency to integrate ESG factors into valuations, and with governments, driven by rapidly changing norms and the pressure coming from the younger generation, are responding more robustly to the climate crisis, it is clear that decarbonization and digitalization are bound to become new paradigms for the corporate world at large.

Sustainable investing: in search of new valuations

The same forces that are propelling corporate transformation are also reshaping finance. Sustainable investing is rapidly spreading throughout the investment chain across asset owners, managers, banks, and service providers, including exchanges, index providers, and rating agencies (see, for example, the NASDAQ Sustainable Bond Network and the Sustainable Stock Exchange Initiative). The growing awareness that climate change poses risks not yet accounted for is also attracting the attention of central banks who are concerned that sudden changes in valuations could lead to shocks and instability (Carney, 2015). Dozens of central banks are now monitoring climate change as a systemic risk (e.g., the Network for Greening the Financial System[7]).

Climate change, in particular, has emerged as a dominant driver of change, as the financial industry is increasingly aware that established methods of valuation do not account for externalities, which Nicholas Stern coined as "the biggest market failure" (Stern, 2006). Traditional economic theory, which suggests that price signals reflect all available information, isn't helpful so long as the unknown full costs of climate change-related risks are not accounted for. In the short run, it still makes financial sense to burn the globe, although it is known that the costs of dealing with the consequence will increase in the future. There are also inter-generational dilemmas in the way future costs and benefits are discounted, as most current practices are biased towards short-term profit maximization, at the expense of future generations (for a discussion on this fundamental dilemma, see Stern, 2006).

As societies are only slowly moving to the pricing of externalities, especially of carbon emissions, and as climate science is itself an exploration of the unknown, financial markets are left to their own devices to square up to the dilemma of how to price climate risks. The impediments for sustainable investing are significant, as summarized, for example, in a recent report by a coalition of CEOs of financial institutions, the "Finance Leadership Coalition" (Bloomberg, 2019), which concludes that proven investment models are not replicated at scale and that available solutions are not yet profitable. The obvious conclusion is that until and unless emissions are priced sufficiently, a massive transition towards low-carbon or "net-zero-carbon" practices will not happen on a scale needed to stay within the goals of the Paris Agreement.

Operating in a context of rapidly changing regulatory environments, technological advances, societal pressure, and new insights coming from climate science, a growing number of financial actors are taking first steps to prepare for the transition towards low-carbon economies. A major catalyst in this regard has been provided by the Task Force on Climate-related Financial Disclosure (TCFD), an initiative started in 2015 by the G20. While many other disclosure frameworks have failed to gain traction, the TCFD framework stands a good chance to succeed. Designed for investors, it not only puts the spotlight on performance indicators and targets that are designed to measure the status quo, it also contains metrics to assess future strategies for corporations to deal with climate risks and to govern these risks. To deal with the uncertainty of future risks—both physical risks and so-called transition risks (regulatory and technology changes)—the TCFD framework asks market actors, both investors and corporations, to undertake scenario planning (TCFD, 2019). The forward-looking perspective of the TCFD and its simplicity regarding the core metric is already acting as an important bridge between finance and corporations and is catalyzing many new approaches.

The way out of the ESG data jungle

Despite two decades of progressive voluntary disclosure and promising new approaches, such as the TCFD, ESG data is still incoherent and has many gaps. Measurement methodologies and disclosure standards vary greatly. Rating agencies, which try to provide uniform assessments, often rely on outdated information, using opaque methodologies and have their own biases when constructing scores (Berg, Koelbel and Rigobon, 2019). Past efforts to establish clear criteria for rating agencies, such as undertaken by the Global Initiative for Sustainability Ratings (GISR), failed, largely because the small but rapidly growing market of information providers was too dynamic and not mature enough to forge quality standards. The CEO of Arabesque S-Ray®, Andreas Feiner, describes the current status of ESG data as being at the same level as financial accounting was before the financial crash of 1928. It took financial accounting many decades to establish uniform measurements.

The broad scope of ESG factors and differing views about their financial relevance at different points in time across different regions suggest that there is a growing premium on smart data analytics using real-time corporate raw data combined with relevant unstructured data, which has the flexibility to adopt to new insights and changing contexts. Rapid advances in technology and declining costs of processing massive amounts of information will undoubtedly improve the quality of ESG ratings in the future. At some point, regulators at national levels will have to set standards and define disclosure methodologies, especially in the area of Green House Gas emissions. Incremental progress made through voluntary disclosure is inadequate and current climate rating practices to estimate emissions prevents investors from accurately managing risks, as they cannot differentiate companies that are taking a lead and disclose emissions and those that are not. Moreover, proprietary data that is locked up behind paywalls does not allow for public scrutiny. New tools such as the Arabesque Temperature score[8] can help to bridge the gap by focusing on corporate disclosed and publicly available data and reveal that major polluters do not yet disclose relevant emissions.

THE WAY AHEAD

We cannot predict the future, but we can learn from the past. And we should have enough common sense to know that we can create the future we want if only we can mobilize the will to do so. The following concluding reflections may help to serve as guideposts in the quest for market solutions that serve people and planet.

1. The rise of sustainable investing, largely driven by growing awareness about climate change risks, is now for the first time converging with corporate-driven transformations in search of low-carbon and socially acceptable business practices. ESG investing is already relocating capital away from laggards towards better performers across all industries and asset classes on a very large scale, thus helping to accelerate market transformations through changes in cost of capital and valuations.

As methods of measurement and smarter interpretations are bound to improve over time, such market-led changes will gain further momentum, and at some point, ESG integration will be mainstreamed across all economic activities. But for the business case for decarbonization to be firmly established, policymakers will need to lead by example, putting a price on carbon and aligning fiscal policies accordingly. There is also an urgent need to create more awareness among citizens at large that their consumption behavior and their choices are not the only leverage they have to express their values. Now that technology enables smarter investment choices, people can express their values and preferences with their money and demand that the pension schemes they are participating in do so likewise.

2. Climate science is continuously discovering new insights. The scientific community works largely for the public good. To ensure that climate science informs decision-making more directly and without the lengthy lags usually associated with political interpretations of scientific findings, there is now a premium on building bridges between economists, financial analysts, and climate scientists. Many scenario models are now being constructed to deal with uncertainties. Committed business and finance leaders should ensure that best practices are made publicly available to ensure more widespread uptake.

3. The climate crisis is undoubtedly one of the biggest challenges that humanity is facing. But it is not the only one. The fragmenting political landscape and the rise of economic nationalism pose a threat to peace and stability, while the age-old scourge of corruption continues to destroy development opportunities for the poor. Markets cannot thrive in failing societies and best practices cannot easily be diffused in a protectionist environment. As multilateralism and universal values of humanity are coming under assault, business and finance leaders have choices to make. Their voices and influence can go a long way. Enlightened business and finance leaders need to make their voices heard now. Supporting the universal principles of the UN Global Compact and the UN SDGs is one way to do so. Another option is to more forcefully shape public debate that serves public interests and market transformation than corporate statesmen can (Reeves, Kell and Hassan, 2018).

4. The race is on to establish the business case for decarbonization, while securing a predictable and rule-based policy environment that ensures socially cohesive outcomes. The convergence between corporate responsibility/sustainability and sustainable investing now offers scalable market-led solutions to go mainstream. Winning over policymakers and citizens to embrace the big market transformation can be a powerful pathway to ensure a smooth transition into the future. We have the

choice between a fragmented and divided world where survival of the fittest is defined by wealth and geography and the destiny of the rest is left to chaos, or we can collaborate and realize that in the end we have no choice but to survive together.

5. Accelerating technological change offers new opportunities to produce socially acceptable outcomes while decarbonizing markets. But this will only happen to the extent that innovations are designed and introduced with a purpose that goes beyond profit maximization. The way regulators will redesign industrial policies and the speed at which new social norms will demand future-fit innovations will greatly shape the future of technology and the way it is part of the solution.

6. With a few notable exceptions, such as the countries of Northern Europe, governments have so far avoided playing a constructive role in shaping market transformation. They still stick with industrial policies such as subsidizing fossil fuel consumption. And most are failing to invest sufficiently in equal access to opportunities through education and training to build the competencies and skills required to master the future. Rejuvenating policymaking and industrial policies is now becoming an urgent priority across all regions of the world.

Change is inevitable. We know with scientific certainty that nature will force our hands, prepared or not. It is inevitable that policymakers will have to respond more robustly at some point in the not so distant future. How will policymakers react once they are forced to? The prospect of a world divided by wealth and carbon walls may not be the only possible outcome. An anecdote that took place at the 1985 Geneva Summit at the peak of the Cold War may give hope for the future. During a private conversation overheard only by their interpreters, President Reagan and General Secretary Gorbachev agreed without hesitation that they would cooperate if the world were to be invaded by aliens (Lewis, 2015). Later, President Reagan gave a speech in which he recounted this incident and stressed the common bonds of humanity. The obvious point here is the climate crisis may well at some point be seen as our common enemy and planetary stewardship may become the universal calling.

NOTES

1   We use the term "corporate responsibility" to designate the historical context of this discussion. Nowadays, most practitioners use the term "corporate sustainability," also to show the integration of environmental issues into the original debate around firms' societal responsibilities. We use the term corporate sustainability in this chapter, unless we make reference to the historic context of the movement. See Bansal and Song (2017) for a discussion of the differences between the responsibility and sustainability discourses, and their increasing convergence.

2   For the early diffusion of ESG concepts, see the IFC's report "Future Proof? Outcomes of the Who Cares Wins Initiative 2004–2008" (IFC, 2009).

3　See also the discussions related to integrated reporting (https://integratedreporting.org) as well as the resources provided by the Sustainable Accounting Standards Board (www.sasb.org).

4　The analysis was conducted by Arabesque. More information on the methodology underlying this assessment can be found here: https://arabesque.com/docs/sray/SRay_Methodology.pdf. See also Arabesque (2020).

5　For a good description of the sociological phenomenon of "individualization," see Zuboff (2019),

6　See, for instance, MSCI's (2017) study of ESG investing among millennials. The study finds that 67% of millennials see ESG investing as a way to express their values, while 90% want to direct their allocations into responsible investments.

7　For further information, see: www.ngfs.net/en

8　This score uses a firm's emissions intensity ratio (i.e., the greenhouse gas emissions that a company emits per unit of economic value added) and translates this into a Celsius degree temperature. This score represents the increase in global temperature if every other company on the globe would behave like this firm.

REFERENCES

Accenture (2020). *Competitive Agility*. Available at: www.accenture.com/us-en/insights/competitive-agility-index (Accessed: 6 January 2020).

Accenture and UN Global Compact (2015). *The United Nations Global Compact-Accenture CEO Study*. Available at: www.unglobalcompact.org/docs/issues_doc/Environment/climate/UN-Global-Compact-Accenture-CEO-Study-A-Call-to-Climate-Action-Full.pdf (Accessed: 8 January 2020).

Arabesque (2020). *S-Ray*. Available at: https://arabesque.com/s-ray/ (Accessed: 6 January 2020).

Bansal, P. and Song, H.-C. (2017). 'Similar but Not the Same: Differentiating Corporate Responsibility from Sustainability'. *Academy of Management Annals*, *11*(1), pp. 105–149.

Berg, F., Koelbel, J.F., and Rigobon, R. (2019). *"Aggregate Confusion": The Divergence of ESG Ratings (MIT Sloan School Working Paper 5822-19)*. Cambridge, MA: MIT.

Bloomberg (2019). *Financing the Low-Carbon Future: A Private Sector View on Mobilizing Climate Change*. Available at: https://data.bloomberglp.com/company/sites/55/2019/09/Financing-the-Low-Carbon-Future_CFLI-Full-Report_September-2019.pdf (Accessed: 6 January 2020).

Carney, M. (2015). *Breaking the Tragedy of the Horizon—Climate Change and Financial Stability*. Available at: www.bankofengland.co.uk/speech/2015/breaking-the-tragedy-of-the-horizon-climate-change-and-financial-stability (Accessed: 6 January 2020).

Carroll, A.B., Lipartito, K.J., Post, J.E., and Werhane, P.H. (2012). *Corporate Responsibility: The American Experience*. Cambridge/New York: Cambridge University Press.

Carson, R. (1962). *Silent Spring*. Boston: Houghton Mifflin.

Chakrabarty, D. (2009). 'The Climate of History: Four Theses'. *Critical Inquiry*, *35*(2), pp. 197–222.

Clark, G.L., Feiner, A., and Viehs, M. (2015). *From the Stockholder to the Stakeholder: How Sustainability Can Drive Financial Outperformance*. Oxford: University of Oxford & Arabesque Partners.

Det Norske Veritas (DNV) and UN Global Compact (2015). *Impact: Transforming Business, Changing the World: The United Nations Global Compact*. New York, NY: United Nations Global Compact Office.

Eccles, R., Ioannou, I., and Serafeim, G. (2014). 'The Impact of Corporate Sustainability on Organizational Processes and Performanc'e'. *Management Science*, *60*(11), pp. 2835–2857.

Ellen MacArthur Foundation (2015). *Towards a Circular Economy: Economic and Business Rationale for an Accelerated Transition*. Cowes: The Ellen MacArthur Foundation.

Freeman, R.E. (1984). *Strategic Management: A Stakeholder Approach*. Boston: Pitman.

Friede, G., Busch, T., and Bassen, A. (2015). 'ESG and Financial Performance: Aggregated Evidence from More than 2000 Empirical Studies'. *Journal of Sustainable Finance and Investment*, *5*(4), pp. 210–233.

Global Enabling Sustainability Initiative (GeSI) (2019). *Digital with Purpose*. Available at: https://gesi.org/research/gesi-digital-with-purpose-summary (Accessed: 10 January 2020).

International Finance Corporation (IFC) (2009). *Future Proof? Outcomes of the Who Cares Wins Initiative 2004-2008.* Available at: www.ifc.org/wps/wcm/connect/0df4f760-a4e4-4cdf-8a2a-acb-f605753da/p_SI_WCW08_report_WEB.pdf?MOD=AJPERES&CACHEID=ROOTWORK-SPACE-0df4f760-a4e4-4cdf-8a2a-acbf605753da-jqetFkL (Accessed: 6 January 2020).

Kapur, A. (2019). 'The Rising Threat of Digital Nationalism'. *The Wall Street Journal* (1 November). Available at: www.wsj.com/articles/the-rising-threat-of-digital-national-ism-11572620577?mod=searchresults&page=1&pos=1 (Accessed: 6 January 2020).

Kell, G. (2017). 'When Traditional Culture Meets Modern Corporate Responsibility'. *Huffington Post* (6 December). Available at: www.huffpost.com/entry/when-traditional-culture_b_9658182 (Accessed: 6 January 2020).

Kell, G. (2018). 'The Remarkable Rise of ESG'. *Forbes.com* (11 July). Available at: www.forbes.com/sites/georgkell/2018/07/11/the-remarkable-rise-of-esg/#21e8d1711695 (Accessed: 6 January 2020).

Kell, G. (2019). 'The Energy Transition is not Happening Fast Enough'. *Forbes.com* (11 Sept). Available at: www.forbes.com/sites/georgkell/2019/09/11/the-energy-transformation-is-not-happening-fast-enough/#63b1970923da (Accessed: 6 January 2020).

Knudsen, J.S. and Moon, J.W. (2017). *Visible Hands: Government Regulation and International Business Responsibility.* Cambridge: Cambridge University Press.

Krogh, H. (2019). 'British Columbia als Vorbild bei CO2-Steuer: VW-Chef Diess blickt achtungsvoll nach Kanada'. *Automobilwoche.* Available at: www.automobilwoche.de/article/20191208/BCONLINE/191209917/exklusiv–british-columbia-als-vorbild-bei-co-steuer-vw-chef-diess-blickt-achtungsvoll-nach-kanada (Accessed: 6 January 2020).

Lewis, D. (2015). 'Reagan and Gorbachev Agreed to Pause the Cold War in Case of an Alien Invasion'. Available at: www.smithsonianmag.com/smart-news/reagan-and-gorbachev-agreed-pause-cold-war-case-alien-invasion-180957402/ (Accessed: 6 January 2020).

Lo, A.W. (2017). *Adaptive Markets: Financial Evolution at the Speed of Thought.* Princeton, NJ: Princeton University Press.

MSCI (2017). *Swipe to Invest: Millennials and ESG.* Available at: www.msci.com/documents/10199/07e7a7d3-59c3-4d0b-b0b5-029e8fd3974b (Accessed: 9 January 2019).

Pagoropoulos, A., Pigosso, D.C.A., and McAloone, T.C. (2017). 'The Emergent Role of Digital Technologies in the Circular Economy: A Review'. *Procedia CIRP, 64*, pp. 19–24.

Porter, M.E. and Kramer, M.R. (2011). 'Creating Shared Value'. *Harvard Business Review, 89*(1/2), pp. 62–77.

Portincaso, M., de la Tour, A., and Soussan, P. (2019). *The Dawn of the Deep Tech Ecosystem.* Available at: www.bcg.com/publications/2019/dawn-deep-tech-ecosystem.aspx (Accessed: 6 January 2020).

Rangan, K., Chase, L., and Karim, S. (2015). 'The Truth about CSR'. *Harvard Business Review, 93*(1/2), pp. 40–49.

Reeves, M., Kell, G., and Hassan, F. (2018). *The Case for Corporate Statesmanship.* (BCG Henderson Institute): Available at: https://bcghendersoninstitute.com/the-case-for-corporate-statesman-ship-7444d927cab8 (Accessed: 6 January 2020).

Reeves, M. and Levin, S. (2017). *Building a Resilient Business Inspired by Biology* (BCG Henderson Institute). Available at: www.bcg.com/publications/2017/globalization-strategy-reeves-levin-building-resilient-business-inspired-biology.aspx (Accessed: 6 January 2020).

Reiman, J. (2013). *The Story of Purpose: The Path to Creating a Brighter Brand, a Greater Company, and a Lasting Legacy.* Hoboken, NJ: John Wiley.

Rockström, J., Steffen, W., Noone, K., Persson, A., Chapin, F.S., Lambin, E.F., ... Foley, J.A. (2009). 'A Safe Operating Space for Humanity'. *Nature, 461*(7263), pp. 472–475.

Ruggie, J.G. (2004). 'Reconstituting the Global Public Domain—Issues, Actors, and Practices'. *European Journal of International Relations, 10*(4), pp. 499–531.

Rutqvist, J. (2015). *Waste to Wealth: The Circular Economy Advantage.* London: Palgrave Macmillan.

Schueth, S. (2003). 'Socially Responsible Investing in the United States'. *Journal of Business Ethics, 43*(3), pp. 189–194.

Schwalbach, J. and Klink, D. (2012). 'Der Ehrbare Kaufmann als individuelle Verantwortungskategorie der CSR-Forschung' in A. Schneider and R. Schmidpeter (Eds.) *Corporate Social Responsibility*. Berlin/Heidelberg: Springer, pp. 219–240.

Science-Based Targets (2020). *Companies Taking Action*. Available at: https://sciencebasedtargets. org/companies-taking-action/ (Accessed: 6 January 2020).

Stern, N. (2006). *The Economics of Climate Change: The Stern Review*. Cambridge, UK: Cambridge University Press.

Task Force on Climate-Related Financial Disclosures (TCFD) (2019). *TCFD 2019 Status Report*. Available at: www.fsb-tcfd.org/wp-content/uploads/2019/06/2019-TCFD-Status-Report-FI-NAL-053119.pdf (Accessed: 6 January 2020).

Thomas, T., Schermerhorn, J.R., and Dienhart, J.W. (2004). 'Strategic Leadership of Ethical Behavior in Business'. *Academy of Management Perspectives*, *18*(2), pp. 56–66.

UN Global Compact (2004). *Who Cares Wins—Connecting Financial Markets to a Changing World*. Available at: www.unglobalcompact.org/docs/issues_doc/Financial_markets/who_cares_who_wins.pdf (Accessed: 6 January 2020).

UN Global Compact (2020). *The Ten Principles*. Available at: www.unglobalcompact.org/what-is-gc/mission/principles (Accessed: 6 January 2020).

United Nations (1992). *Rio Declaration on Environment and Development*. Report of the United Nations Conference on Environment and Development (Annex 1, Principle 16, 12 August). Available at: www.un.org/en/development/desa/population/migration/generalassembly/docs/globalcompact/A_CONF.151_26_Vol.I_Declaration.pdf (Accessed: 6 January 2020).

United Nations (1999). *Secretary-General Proposes Global Compact on Human Rights, Labour, Environment, in Address to World Economic Forum in Davos* Press Release, SG/SM/6881: New York: United Nations.

UNPRI(2017).*AlGore:FiduciaryDutyinthe21stCentury&theSustainabilityRevolution*(Video).Availableat: www.unepfi.org/news/industries/investment/al-gore-fiduciary-duty-in-the-21st-century-the-sustainability-revolution/ (Accessed: 6 January 2020).

UN PRI (2020). *Fiduciary in the 21st Century—Final Report*. Available at: www.unpri.org/download?ac=9792 (Accessed: 6 January 2020).

World Intellectual Property Organization (WIPO) (2019). *WIPO Technology Trends 2019—Artificial Intelligence*. Available at: www.wipo.int/publications/en/details.jsp?id=4386 (Accessed: 6 January 2020).

Zuboff, S. (2019). *The Age of Surveillance Capitalism. The Fight for a Human Future at the New Frontier of Power*. New York: Public Affairs.

4

Good governance

Navigating on purpose and complexity-based principles

Theo Kocken and Stefan Lundbergh

INTRODUCTION

Why are so many companies and institutions across the globe incapable of adapting to a changing environment? With hindsight, it is easy to write case studies analysing the Kodaks of the world, identifying the series of strategic mistakes leading towards their demise. These cases demonstrate that management were already aware of, or could have easily identified, that the commercial environment was changing. The pertinent question is: how could management have been so wilfully blind to a changing environment that it refrained from taking sufficient actions? A more nuanced question is: why did the governance framework fail to support management to be adaptive in a fast-changing and complex world?

A financially sustainable company, or institution, needs to be robust to survive in the short term and adaptive to survive in the long run. In addition, the company needs to attract good employees, pay taxes in the local community, and maintain its 'licence to operate'. We argue that good governance requires companies and institutions to have:

1. A clear purpose, acting as a compass helping the organisation to adapt in an ever-changing world;
2. A principle-based corporate culture that fosters a robust decision process, benefitting from an integrated open worldview of the trends and non-linear changes shaping our future; and
3. Tools and processes which help the organisation to deal with uncertainty, mitigate human biases, and effectively tap the 'wisdom of employees'.

This might sound like a utopia, but it is supported by many real-life examples. At the end of this chapter we will also discuss three real-life examples: how purpose drift and a cultural transformation ultimately brought Enron down; how Dutch pension funds used purpose as a beacon when changing the pension contract and introduced tools for dealing with fundamental uncertainty; and finally, how a clear purpose and a principle-based culture helped IKEA to revolutionise the furniture business.

SUSTAINABILITY IN A COMPLEX WORLD REQUIRES BOTH PURPOSE AND PRINCIPLES

Adaptiveness in a fast-changing world is essential for companies to sustain long-term profitability, customer satisfaction and the hiring and retention of engaged employees – in short, being sustainable. To achieve this, we must acknowledge that the world is a complex place and that we often face ambiguous situations which cannot be captured by 'complicated' models alone as we will illustrate below. In our complex world, a clear purpose acts as a compass helping the organisation to navigate an ever changing environment. Through a principle-based culture that defines how the purpose should be achieved, it is possible to decentralise decisions and create an adaptive organisation that does not shy away from ambiguity.

The world is often a complex, not a complicated, place

A modern car is comfortable and provides a safe journey for both its driver and passengers. The car is a complicated piece of machinery that involves scores of components designed to interact with each other in a strictly predefined manner. The mechanical and electronic systems are bounded by the laws of physics. A car mechanic can therefore diagnose and repair a car that has broken down by applying their detailed and expert knowledge about this complicated system. In fact, the car is a top–down system. When the driver hits the accelerator, this causes the engine to react, which generates motion in the wheels and the car picks up speed in a totally predictable manner. The causal relationships – the responses from input to output – of complicated systems do not change over time and are therefore largely predictable, bar any unexpected failures of components.

The traffic flow on a busy motorway is best described as a complex system. Watching the traffic flow from a helicopter, it appears to be organised and orchestrated, but what we observe is the emerging result of self-organisation. It is a bottom–up process. In order to avoid bumping into nearby cars, drivers adapt by keeping their distance, changing lanes, and adjusting the speed relative to the other cars. One car moving significantly slower than the general traffic flow may cause unexpected traffic jams, known as 'ghost jams'. These effects are caused by the interactions between drivers, but this human interaction is not constant over time. The human drivers react to their environment, in turn creating feedback loops. It is not a one-way causal relationship but a two-way dynamic interaction which cannot be fully determined. Small changes in individual behaviour can lead to large changes on a higher aggregated ('macro') level such as the traffic jam as a whole. It is therefore impossible to predict how a traffic flow will evolve, even if we have access to historical GPS coordinates and the speed of all individual cars. It is the behaviour of, and the interaction between, drivers that create uncertainty.

About a century ago, the economist Frank Knight contrasted probabilities with fundamental uncertainty (Knight, 1921). Probabilities can be defined as quantifiable deviations from a 'mean' in a complicated system. When the system itself follows various fundamental laws that do not change over time, we can assess the likelihood that a car engine running without oil will break down within a certain timeframe. Uncertainty is defined as events arising from a complex system which is not possible to quantify – for example, predicting the movements of an individual car on a busy highway. The uncertainty does not exclude us from observing 'patterns' emerging that may give us a better understanding of the dynamics in a complex system, but that does not make it possible to predict it in a precise manner.

By applying the same reasoning to the economy and the financial markets, it becomes apparent that we are faced with complexity. The economy is nothing but the result of an intricate interaction between billions of humans in various frameworks. Our daily decisions are influenced by our emotions and we adapt as the world evolves. Daniel Kahneman, Amos Tversky, Paul Slovic, and many other behavioural economists and psychologists revealed via experiments how we make irrational, inconsistent, and emotion-driven decisions that do not fit a complicated worldview where people are very consistent in their decisions and have static utility functions over time (Kahneman, Slovic, and Tversky, 1982). In practice, investors' behaviour creates self-reinforcing feedback loops which add significantly to uncertainty. Investors react to market movements (i.e. their 'utility function' changes), which is then driving market movements, which impacts the reaction of investors. George Soros called this endless loop 'reflexivity', which can lead to speculative bubbles that eventually burst (Soros, 1986). The economist Hyman Minsky formulated the 'Financial Instability Hypothesis' to describe how these feedback loops always lead to instability (Minsky, 1986). As private debt levels grow, the economy endogenously creates its own booms and busts. This fits with Brian Arthur's view on the economy and financial markets as hardly ever being in an equilibrium, but most often they are in disequilibrium due to human feedback loops (Arthur, 2014). Mark Buchanan argued that based on what we observe in physic, one should view financial risk as following a power distribution instead of a normal distribution (Buchanan, 2002).

Innovations add another layer to the non-static behaviour of our economic system. The smart phone and many other information technology related innovations have fundamentally changed business models in ways that no one could imagine in the late 1990s, when mobile phones first became a mainstream consumer product. The companies that emerged from these new technologies often required much less capital than traditional firms. This has created ripple effects across capital markets, changing the dynamics of interest rates. How the world will develop is uncertain and that makes it impossible to consistently predict the future. In other words, the world is a complex, not complicated, place.

Emotionally, it is reassuring to have a complete mathematical representation; using complicated statistical models to 'predict' the future removes our perceived ambiguity. As humans we dislike ambiguity and want to be in control. It is therefore compelling for us to use models which assume a complicated world and we become wilfully blind when the underpinning assumptions are not valid. We must therefore remain vigilant to the fact that these complicated models must not be mistaken for the complex world itself. A complicated model will sometimes help us gain some understanding of the complex world, but it is only a partial description of the reality based on several strong (refuted) assumptions and generalisations. Still, we have a tendency to pursue making decisions based on complicated models, even if we know we deal with a complex system. Ellsberg showed with experiments that we have a preference to change from a game in which we do not know the probabilities to a game where we do know the probabilities, even if it is not to our benefit (Ellsberg, 1961). This is called ambiguity aversion.

A counterproductive result of ambiguity aversion is to assume that the complicated model is the correct description of how the world works – and pursue 'optimal' strategies based on that model. This is particularly important for financial institutions and investors, who often fall prey to the so-called 'model trap'. In a complex world, 'optimal' is the enemy to short-term robustness and long-term adaptivity. In his book *Adaptive Market*, Andrew Lo argues that investors should not optimise their portfolio based on one model; instead, they should select the portfolio that delivers satisficing outcomes, while being resilient to what we do not know under as many situations as possible (Lo, 2017). The same holds for management of a company when evaluating different projects and business lines.

Purpose is more than profit, but key to sustainability

In a complex world, a clear purpose is the compass helping a company to navigate uncertainty without jeopardising its licence to operate. A purpose, such as reducing old-age poverty or creating wider financial inclusion, is often linked to the UN Sustainability Goals and provides invaluable guidance on how to adapt a business as society evolves. If the purpose is fuzzy, it is not clear why the company exists nor how it should adapt to change.

Profits are necessary to sustain both business and society. Without profits, it is not possible to retain the right people, pay taxes, conduct research, create new products, and pay interest and dividends to investors. Profit is a boundary condition, but it is only one of several critical factors that need to be managed in an integrated way. Ultimately, a company needs to earn the trust of its clients and society.

This includes finding a balance between short-term robustness and long-term adaptivity. Reducing investments in research and innovation will boost profits in the short term but hamper long-term sustainability. Being a good corporate citizen includes paying taxes in the countries where the business operates and being mindful of externalities, such as reducing the environmental footprint. It also involves avoiding the notion that the society has to 'nationalise' its losses. A strong purpose makes employees proud and results in a genuine engagement.

Companies lacking a purpose often replace this by profit alone. When profits become the only purpose, things can go terribly wrong. Profit is a too narrow measure that doesn't provide any guidance for setting the direction for the future. Replacing purpose with profit is tempting, since it creates an easily observable metric against which everything can be monitored and managed. A simple metric reduces the need for management to make judgement calls choosing between different potential solutions. For companies whose largest shareholders, of which most are money managers, only hold a few per cent of the outstanding stock, profits may serve as the least common denominator and therefore replace the purpose.

Without a clear purpose, management assumes the world is a complicated place and often end up optimising short-term profit alone. By failing to include all available information, particularly the information that is not easily quantifiable, management becomes blind to longer-term developments that could either kill the profitability or risk losing the licence to operate. By lacking a purpose, combined with too narrow an optimisation, management have sealed the fate of many 'great' companies over the years. Peter Drucker once wrote that 'what gets measured, gets managed' (Drucker, 1955). If we don't know what to measure, apart from profits, things can drift into the wrong direction.

A clear purpose helps senior management and staff to channel their energies towards innovation by pursuing new initiatives that fit the purpose and 'fail fast', if necessary. It will help to find 'real options' for the longer term that management can turn into strategies to re-invent the company. This is also important for investors allocating money to these companies, ensuring that they invest in a long-term sustainable company, instead of optimised short-term profits.

Principles – the foundation of good governance

To serve 'purpose', an organisation needs clear principles – for example, how to interact with each other inside the company, how to treat clients and learn from failures. Principles are guidelines that embody a sound corporate culture. Good governance is often referred to as having clear delegation of responsibility and accountability, from the board of trustees down to each employee. In most of the large corporate scandals, the formal governance structure, processes, and systems were in place, but the underlying corporate culture was corrupt. Good governance not only has a sound formal structure, but sound principles for working together. In practice, this boils down to creating an environment that encourages diversity in thinking, does not shy away from dealing with ambiguity, and has a sound way of learning from mistakes, plus incrementally improving the company.

The culture is much more powerful than leaders themselves. For example, the mayor of a city is an important person, but less influential than we think. The city is a decentralised system: citizens and companies decide to live there or move somewhere else. A city is prosperous simply because its citizens make it thrive. Thriving cities attract new talented people, creating more opportunities. It is a decentralised process where individuals and companies are mainly self-organizing. The mayor is not in control of this complex environment – far from it. The mayor can only nudge behaviour in certain directions by creating and maintaining an environment that in turn makes the city an attractive place.

The board of a company faces the same challenges as a mayor of a city. A large company is too complex to manage top–down by using one simple metric, such as profit. But still, many companies try to control their entire organisation top–down. Leadership is about nudging emergence in an organisation using principles as the main tool. The role of principles is to guide decentralised decisions by providing guidance on how to deal with each other, to get the most out of everyone working in the company and de-bias the internal decision processes. Adaptiveness requires freedom and autonomy to innovate, but it is central that non-viable ideas are stopped. A principles-based culture can guide this process and therefore the principles should, at least, target the following areas:

- **Improving decisions under fundamental uncertainty**. The principles should address how decisions are formed in the company. Diversity in thinking is an extremely important tool for dealing with the different aspects of a complex environment. How are we getting individuals involved and how do we have constructive dialogues and 'conflicts'? How do we mitigate individual cognitive biases and reduce effects of negative group dynamics? How do we structurally make use of real opposing views to improve the quality of decisions? One of the companies that has written down its principles on decision-making and lives by those is Bridgewater. Their main objective was to create an 'idea meritocracy' to improve investment decisions (Dalio, 2017).

- **Learning from failures**. How do we deal with and learn from failures and errors made by management and employees? How do we create a true learning culture without blame, learning from mistakes? In complex environments, failures are often caused by changes to the environment which impact the dynamics of the complex system. Most of the time, the changing dynamics of the complex system dominate the human error as the main cause of failure. A culture based on an open mindset that embraces failure as an opportunity to improve turns out to be much more successful than a culture where mistakes are seen as human failures. Mathew Syed referred to this as black box thinking, inspired by the civil aviation industry that effectively learns from failures and disseminates this knowledge across the industry (Syed, 2015).

- **Empowering employees**. How do we give employees the courage and empowerment to make them try new things? What tools are available to boost creativity without being reckless or inefficient? How do we balance the need for local autonomy of business units to allow for emergence, but centralise some functions that are best shared across business units? In his book *The Tipping Point*, Malcom Gladwell describes W.L. Gore & Associates, the manufacturer of Gore-Tex, that opted for a decentralised and flat organisation structure (Gladwell, 2000). When a division grows beyond 150 employees, they split it into two smaller divisions since they believe it improves employees' communications and makes the business more efficient. The limit of 150 employees is known as the Dunbar's number, which is the average number of relationships an individual can handle simultaneously without hampering the effectiveness of the group.

No doubt the stakes are high. A company that fails to be adaptive in a complex world will not just disappoint its shareholders and employees, but also negatively affect the wider community in which it operates. It is necessary for a sustainable company to have a purpose as the compass, complemented by principles as bearer of corporate culture. For sustainable goals to be effective over the long term, they must be derived from the purpose and the principles, otherwise it is just window dressing.

Robust long-term decisions can be very painful in the short term, both in terms of profit and for the organisation itself. The history books are full of 'successful' companies that were not able to adapt, not because of a lack of knowledge or insight, but mostly because they were not able to face the pain of adapting, which was necessary to continue to fulfil their purpose. Peter Drucker captured this with 'Management is doing things right; leadership is doing the right things' (Drucker, 2000). In many cases, shareholders pay a significant leadership premium in the CEO's remuneration but end up appointing a manager.

WAYS TO BECOME MORE ADAPTIVE

In our daily life, we regularly make decisions where the information is incomplete. This is the case for minor decisions, such as choosing a restaurant, as well as life-defining decisions, such as choosing a career or getting married. When looking for restaurant for a dinner with friends, we typically choose between a set of known restaurants that satisfice our needs, rather than looking for the optimal restaurant. Herbert Simon, Noble Laureate, explained this using his theory of bounded rationality (Simon, 1984). The idea is that when making decisions, our rationality is limited due to the complexity of the problem, our behavioural biases, and the time available. When making a decision, we act as satisficers trying to find a satisfactory, instead of optimal, solution.

We are ignorant, by definition, to what we do not know. Unfortunately, we are easily framed by social conventions, corporate culture, and most importantly, our existing knowledge. In addition, we have a strong aversion for ambiguity, which is a consequence of fundamental uncertainty. To deal with that, we seek comfort from ideologies around how we want the world to look and our confirmation bias helps strengthen that view. Ironically, much of what we do not know could be better understood if we only tried to see the world for what it is, not for what we want it to be.

When deciding a business model, or strategy, it should satisfice our goal (i.e. fulfil our purpose) while being robust against our own ignorance. To do this successfully, we need diversity in thinking as well as applying de-biasing tools and techniques to mitigate our human biases and prevent negative effects of group dynamics. This applies to all decisions, at all levels in the organisation, so it is essential to cultivate a principles-based culture that does not shy away from dealing with ambiguity.

In the following, we will focus on the challenges facing institutional investors, but this approach is generically applicable to most decision situations.

Becoming robust to our own ignorance

We do not know, by definition, what the future innovations will be. Even if we could know, we cannot predict how individuals will adapt to the innovations.

We are left with making decisions based on incomplete information. In this context, the role of the purpose cannot be underestimated. To become robust to our own ignorance, we should aim for a sufficient outcome that lets us achieve the purpose. Among the set of possible solutions that fulfil this goal, we choose among those that are robust against the worst possible outcomes we can imagine. This forces us to think in terms of consequences of what we do not know (our ignorance).

Mainstream finance relies heavily on complete mathematical models and historical data to describe the world. The narrative is that markets are mean-reverting and that a long-term strategic investor should choose the optimal portfolio at the efficient frontier and adjust the level of risk by allocating between the optimal portfolio and cash (or borrowing money). From these base recommendations, investors can derive 'optimal' solutions premised on the mathematical model and historical correlations. The 'optimal' solution is very attractive to many investors since it eliminates the need for complex discussions and making difficult judgements. But the solution is 'optimal' if, and only if, the complicated model is a correct description of the complex reality. In finance, the 'optimal' solution is, unfortunately, nothing more than beggars' belief.

Abandoning this false sense of control induced by complete mathematical models and historical probabilities means that it is impossible to find optimal solutions. Instead, investors must judge the consequences of a multitude of alternative solutions under different worldviews. This seems discouraging at first, but let us take a step back and reflect on what we are trying to achieve in the first place. For most investors, the goal is probably not to earn a maximum investment return under a wished-for worldview, but to earn a sufficient return without risking losing almost all in the process if our wished-for worldview turns out to be wrong.

Diversity in thinking and models

Specialising in, or optimising for, a certain environment can lead us into disaster due to the inherent uncertainty of the world. The negative consequences of optimisation can be illustrated by the fate of the banana plantations in the 1950s and 1960s. Back then, the most popular banana variety in the West was Gros Michel (also known as Big Mike). It was so popular that vast monocultures of these variety were established throughout the tropical parts of Latin America. A contagious fungal disease, known as the Panama disease, infected the Gros Michel plantations, killing the plants and nearly wiping out this banana variety.

Inspired by the philosopher Ayn Rand, former Federal Reserve Chair Alan Greenspan had a strong belief in the free market hypothesis (Rand, 1966). He heavily relied on the assumption that people are rational and that both banks and consumers will never be exposed to (collective) irrational, overconfident behaviour. This made him a strong proponent for deregulating the financial markets and removing constraints on consumers, since he believed that this would lead to 'optimal' outcomes. In a Senate hearing after the 2007/08 crisis, Greenspan admitted that he relied too much on one simple theory based on very strong assumptions of rationality and equilibrium. The collective reliance on this worldview was one of the root causes of the great financial crisis.

Uncertainty is a real danger for monocultures and nature's cure is biodiversity. In finance, the cure is diversity in thinking. Diversity in thinking results in diversification between different complicated approximations of how the complex world might work. This is a higher-order diversification compared with diversifying between strategies within one specific complicated model. In other words, we should not put all our eggs in the basket of one theoretical model; even if that particular basket has different padded compartments, it only provides us with a second-order diversification.

In a complex world, we have to make decisions based on incomplete information. We don't know what the world looks like; however, the main challenge for us is what our theories and models do not capture. Looking at a problem from multiple angles using theories from different disciplines helps us to get a more complete picture of the world. Examples of theories are: agent-based modelling, stochastic models, network theories, and scenario thinking, which all bring different perspectives.

- **Agent-based modelling**. In a complex world, we must be careful generalising findings on a micro level to a macro level (or the other way around). To better understand the 'ghost jam' problem mentioned previously, an agent-based model is used to bridge micro behaviour of drivers with the observed macro dynamics of the traffic flow. A simple model of how individual drivers behave contains simple rules for matching speed with traffic, avoiding bumping into other cars, and staying on the motorway. Based on this simplified model of the drivers, dynamics, and interactions, it is possible to simulate macro behaviour of traffic flow. The same can be done for interactions between different players (investors, institutions, brokers, etc.) in financial markets. For example, by modelling how the players 'learn' subjectively from changes in the market and analysing how this learning changes the market dynamic and vice versa. This modelling of social feedback loops increases our understanding of financial instability and helps financial institutions to make them more robust. It also helps to improve the effectiveness of regulations and creates a bit more macro stability (although never 'equilibrium') in financial markets.

- **Stochastic models**. Stochastic models can be helpful by providing insight in the dynamics over a long horizon. Acknowledging that probabilities derived from the stochastic models are far from 'exact', stochastic modelling can help us to better understand the consequences of changes to strategies. For example, a pension fund can use stochastic modelling to assess the impact on its long-term sustainability, due to changes of the contribution policy and investment policies. In addition, the consequences of closing a pension fund for new employees or unexpected changes in longevity can be better understood using stochastic models.

- **Network theory**. In the 1960s, Stanley Milgram performed an experiment illustrating that we are more closely linked to each other than we intuitively think (Milgram, 1967). He found that there are six degrees of separation between any two individuals. In social networks some individuals are more connected than others, and we think of these individuals as networkers or influencers. Interconnectivity also applies to countries, institutions, and organisations, and understanding how it works could give us a better understanding of the world. For example, which institutions are system-critical in a financial system (too connected to fail; not so much too big to fail)? How can a monoculture, driven by strict regulation, create system instability? Analysing networks can help us to understand non-linear phenomena by propagating shocks through a network and seeing how a shock goes from one institution to another to another and then affects the initial institution. Banks have complex debt relationships that can create non-linear self-reinforcing feedback effects that cannot be explained by traditional 'equilibrium' tools.

- **Scenario thinking**. When the uncertainty around key input parameters dominates the outcomes, it is better to apply a scenario thinking methodology. For example, the solvency of a defined benefit pension scheme is dominated by unexpected changes to life expectancy, interest rate movements, investment returns, and the credit quality of its sponsor. The goal in scenario thinking is to imagine, not assume, how a broad set of plausible futures could impact the pension scheme. This will help decision-makers to live through possible events and consider consequences of different actions. By familiarising ourselves with the events leading to a certain future scenario, it can also help us find signals that will help us to recognise in a timely manner that a world turns in a certain direction. Herman Kahn's pioneering work during the Cold War provides us with tools that helps us to remember the future.

Box 4.1 The road to hell is paved with good intentions

After the Global Financial Crisis of 2007/08, regulators concluded that the lack of transparency of bilateral trades was an important factor exacerbating the crisis. No one quite understood the extent of inter-connectivity between the many different banks, insurance companies, and pension funds. The regulatory response was to introduce Central Clearing Platforms (CCP) for derivatives. These platforms act as centralised institutions for both trading and clearing derivatives. From a stand-alone perspective, the CCP were safer than the previous approach with bilateral trades. From a network theory perspective, the CCP are centralised nodes and the systemic risks have increased compared with the past decentralised network of bilateral trades. Research shows that small players particularly incur more risk in a CCP network. A recent lesson from the Nasdaq Nordic Commodities Exchange accentuates this systemic risk. A relatively small incident by one individual trader resulted in knock-on effects that eventually wiped out 70% of all the buffers of all the traders involved in that particular Central Clearing Platform. And the management of the platform had to start an investigation but could not explain how so much capital could be wiped away. Sounds like a complex system that is treated as a complicated system. This should trigger alarms at the worldwide financial stability authorities.

In practice, tools and models should be combined. Agent-based models can help us to understand how markets might evolve under new regulations. Scenario thinking can use this as input for more broad scenarios that not only look at economics but also demographics, technological breakthroughs, ecological and social/political changes.

Adaptivity and the innovator's dilemma

Scenario thinking includes imagining different worlds and anticipating how the company would need to adapt in order to fulfil its purpose. This is not a claim on being able to predict how the world may emerge, but it helps us understand what could happen. Identifying the signals that are inherent for the different potential worlds will help management to take action and adapt in a timely manner when observing early warning signals.

By thinking through how to act in each of the scenarios and what the consequences might be, management can take action if one of the scenarios should materialise. This will give a headstart versus competitors who have not been thinking in scenario terms, whose first response will be denial and then gradually trying to cope with the new reality. The outcome of this scenario thinking analysis might challenge how the company is structured today. Maybe management realises that under several scenarios it will need to take action today in order to survive in the future. With a clear purpose as a compass, the company is better positioned to implement adaptive solutions even if it will result in short-term pain.

Many of today's management tools and techniques have been designed for efficiently managing complicated production processes. Unfortunately, these tools and techniques are also often applied routinely when managing complex processes. Trying to optimise the business strategy based on an incomplete complicated model of the complex world could result in failing despite management doing everything 'right'. If the world is changing, it is not sufficient to continue doing what we are doing today a bit more efficiently. To adapt, we must be prepared to ask ourselves three soul-searching questions:

- What are we really good at?
- What could the potential future look like?
- How can we contribute to fulfil our purpose in these potential futures?

In addressing these central questions, a clear purpose acts as the compass for the organisation and principle-based culture broadens the chances of reaching an adaptive strategy, addressing the answers to these questions. A company with purpose has a 'why' and, as Nietzsche once wrote, 'Hat man sein Warum des Lebens, so verträgt man sich fast mit jedem Wie'[1] (Nietzsche, 1889). The consequences may be painful for the organisation and many of its employees, but failing to address these questions will lead to even more pain in the future.

In his book *The Innovator's Dilemma*, Clayton Christensen concludes that it is very difficult, but not impossible, for a company to adapt a new technology (Christensen, 1997). A company has its own lifecycle: it begins as an innovative startup exploring a new technology, challenging the incumbents. As the company matures, it refines its technology and eventually becomes a defensive and monopolistic incumbent that will be challenged by a new startup. Sometimes companies can rejuvenate themselves and adapt to the new technology, but most companies are not able to do so. The natural inclination of many companies is to pursue a defensive strategy that will deliver attractive profits in the short term by not investing in the future. A clear purpose can help a company to rejuvenate itself. As the company begins to drift away from its purpose, it is a clear signal for triggering innovation before it is too late.

Living with uncertainty

Successful application of these theories requires that we have tools and processes in place to help mitigate our behavioural biases, as well as reduce the negative elements of group dynamics such as groupthink. A principle-based culture is central to achieving this and we need to proactively design processes that will de-bias decision-making and effectively tap into the 'wisdom of the employees'.

Looking at the world through a multitude of models will make us more robust, and more adaptive to changes in our environment. The question is how to do this, since we simply don't know how likely, or severe, extreme events could be. Diversity in thinking provides us with more information and that can be contrasted using different perspectives. A diversity of models and theories will not help us predict the future, but they will help us to better understand the market dynamics and help us to calibrate how bad, 'bad' could be and how to react.

THREE EXAMPLES FROM PRACTICE

The considerations above have scientific foundations in cognitive science and complexity theory and are illustrated by practical examples: Enron, Dutch pension funds, and IKEA. This section discusses three diverse cases that show in a more elaborated context the role of purpose and principles.

Losing the purpose – the cautionary tale of Enron

In December 2001, Enron filed for Chapter 11 bankruptcy protection after one of the largest accounting frauds in history was unravelled. Its auditor, Arthur Andersen, one of the world's most renowned accounting firms at the time, was also dragged down in the aftermath of the Enron debacle.

Enron is a clear example of how purpose drift can lead to failure, and there are some important lessons to be learned for managers. The demise of a 'great' company is often the result of several factors acting in concert, of which purpose drift is one. Lacking a purpose is not a sufficient condition for failure, in the same way that a stable purpose is not a sufficient condition for success. We argue that having a clear, well-defined, and stable purpose *helps* in avoiding a destructive drift into new business areas which do not fit the culture of the company.

In the late 1980s, Enron was a boring traditional natural oil and gas company with distribution capabilities in the form of an interstate gas pipeline. After the energy deregulation in the mid-1980s, Enron provided its clients with a fixed gas price while hedging the volatile spot price using financial instruments. This required a solid risk management culture, both to avoid physical accidents and financial blow-ups. Enron's top management had a clear ambition to take advantage of the deregulation and expand the business internationally. Jeffrey Skilling was hired as the head of trading and he set a new strategic direction which implied a quick transition away from distributing gas towards becoming a financial institution, or even a hedge fund, running a largely unregulated trading operation which combined market making, trading, securitisation, and project financing.

The purpose changed from safely delivering gas at a fixed price towards profit-making in general, mainly through proprietary trading. In that process, the balance sheet began to fill up with financial contracts, crowding out heavy assets such as production and pipelines. Only heavy assets that provided 'information' for the trading were kept. To make the profits visually more attractive, Enron begun to apply mark-to-market techniques developed by the financial sector in the early 1990s. A significant difference was that most of Enron's assets were not traded on a public market; for example, Enron could finance a plant and in the valuation they embedded future profits even before the plant had been completed.

Enron's purpose had drifted towards making money on trading, and management keenly ventured into new markets such as trading in electricity contracts and, later on, broadband contracts. Trading in itself can be a sensible purpose, but requires an even more prudent, elaborate financial risk management culture compared with producing and distributing highly flammable gas. In addition, it was a big step moving from trading on the gas market, where Enron had a deep expertise, towards a new market such as broadband. Since management accidentally drifted into these new markets, none of Enron's top people had experience from these new markets, nor had they defined what was needed to build a top-notch safe trading company. Surprisingly, Enron's ill-prepared moves towards other markets were not punished, but rewarded, by investors. On the day, in 2000, when the new broadband 'strategy' was announced, the Enron stock price increased by 26%.

As often happens with companies where the purpose begins to drift, a new organisation culture emerges. Enron's talent management program was an annual 360 review by a committee, where employees in the lowest-performing quintile were at risk of redundancy. This created a toxic culture of not asking questions in combination with complex internal political gaming (Heffernan, 2011). The organisation gradually began to lose its diversity, as more and more people with a heart for the original business left and were replaced by people with a similar lack of interest in risk management as top management. In the end, there were no natural cultural breaks left in the organisation.

During the second half of the 1990s, everybody in the market expected Enron to present stellar profit growth and Enron used more and more innovative accounting tricks to meet the market expectations. The purpose shifted from making profit to increasing the share price. Enron's unprecedented level of 'innovative' financial engineering passed the realm of what was legally allowed by deliberately hiding loss-making activities off-balance sheet by placing them in special purpose vehicles.

As often happens in good times, financial regulators were so impressed by Enron's financial performance that they did not take action until Enron dramatically failed in 2001. In retrospect, the excessive performance in Enron's case was not an indicator of exceptional visionary skills; instead, Enron's management showed an exceptional creativity in systematically fooling people. It is clear that one of the biggest bankruptcies in US history was the result of a decade-long drifting away from the original purpose of the company combined with an unhealthy corporate culture (Dekker, 2018).

The purpose as beacon still requires the right principles to navigate – the Dutch pension funds

Dutch pension funds are organisations with a clear purpose. They are a central pillar of security in society and reduce the risk of old-age poverty among their members. The pension funds facilitate saving while working and mitigate the individual risk of members outliving their pension savings. The member gets a lifelong income at the end of their working life, which reduces financial insecurity. Society benefits since a robust pension makes the financing of the social welfare system more protected against changes in demographics. In addition, the reduction of financial insecurity during old age improves happiness and wellbeing. For pension plan design and long-term strategic investment plans, the standard practice through the 1990s was to use linear 'stochastic' projections based on complicated models of expected investment return and life expectancy. Based on these complicated models, plan members were 'promised' an inflation-linked retirement income, and an 'optimal' long-term asset allocation between different asset classes was chosen. The sponsoring employer agreed to bear the financial consequences of the difference between the projections of the complicated models and the realisation based on the complex reality.

There were massive changes between the late 1980s and late 2010s. Over this 30-year period, long-term interest rates declined from over 10% to almost 0% and the remaining life expectancy, at retirement, increased by over 50%. In addition, the Global Financial Crisis unfolding in 2007/08 came as a surprise to many well-renowned investors and academic professors. Even the best complicated models did not incorporate any of these 'extreme' events and yet they happened in the complex world we live in.

After the dot.com crash in 2000, it became clear that the projections of the complicated models deviated too much from the complex reality. Sponsoring employers could no longer afford to fill the funding gap. Compared with many other countries where pension funds were rapidly closing, the Dutch started from the purpose and accepted that the design was no longer fit for purpose. This resulted in pension design innovation, through an adaptive process lasting for two decades, where the scale of benefits was gradually adjusted and the financial risks were eventually transferred from the employer to the members.

With this change, pension fund trustees took sole responsibility for navigating the investment portfolio in a complex world. Instead of disregarding extreme events as too unlikely in the mid-2000s, many pension funds proceeded asking questions such as: 'how can we best navigate a diverse range of (beneficial and adverse) extreme scenarios?' This resulted in taking effective actions around, for example, interest rate hedging and adjustments to the pension design, because the trustees imagined these potential outcomes and concluded that they would not be able to fulfil their purpose if these adverse scenarios would materialise. Of course, such a shift in thinking did not occur overnight and didn't happen to all pension funds at once. Over time, some pension funds suffered more from still thinking in a 'complicated worldview', relying more on bold projections about how the world worked than others.

Going forward, Dutch pension funds must adaptively manage their investments accepting a complex world. This means that their portfolio needs to be made resilient against future challenges such as climate change, innovations in energy supply, and other potential developments that cannot be captured by a complicated model.

In summary, the strong purpose of the Dutch pension system helped them change the pension contract so that it better reflects a complex world. The challenge ahead is to deal with investing in an uncertain, complex world. Many of the well-intended investment beliefs are still based on a complicated worldview, which, applied to a complex world, could lead to fragile outcomes. Purpose is a great beacon but good principles around sound worldviews are needed to create real sustainability.

The Testament of a Furniture Dealer – the IKEA Bible

Ingvar Kamprad grew up in Sweden on the Elmtaryd farm near the village Agunnaryd. The farm is located in heart of the province Småland, where inhabitants have a reputation of being extremely careful with their money and not letting anything go to waste.

In 1943, at the age of 17, Kamprad registered IKEA as a business and over the following decades it evolved into one of the world's leading furniture manufacturers. At his death in 2018, Kamprad had an estimated net worth of $59 billion, making him the world's eighth richest person. Compared with his ultra-wealthy peers on the Bloomberg Billionaires Index, Kamprad's lifestyle was quite frugal. Honouring the spirit of Småland, Kamprad flew economy, did not stay at luxury hotels, recycled teabags, bought secondhand clothing, drove a 1993 Volvo estate, and did his own grocery shopping.

In 1976, in preparation for the international expansion of IKEA, Kamprad wrote 'The Testament of a Furniture Dealer' in which the purpose of IKEA – 'to create a better everyday life for the many people' – is outlined and explained in plain English (Kamprad, 1976). It also contains the critical elements of the IKEA culture summarised in his nine 'commandments':

1. The product range – our identity
2. The IKEA spirit – a strong and living reality
3. Profit gives us resources
4. Reaching good results with small means
5. Simplicity is a virtue
6. Doing it a different way
7. Concentration – important to our success
8. Taking responsibility – a privilege
9. Most things still remain to be done. A glorious future!

Kamprad wrote the testament at a time when IKEA had grown, and the bureaucracy and the layer of management had increased. IKEA was preparing for an international expansion and he was worried that the organisation would lose its way as it expanded internationally. Kamprad's ambition was to keep the culture similar to a small firm, by reducing layers of management and pushing the responsibility down in the organisation. Quite similar to the Gore-Tex approach, it reduced the amount of communication and management overload an expanding company usually acquires. Although the IKEA culture is not for everyone, those who like the culture tend to stay for many years.

Sara Kristofferson outlines the history and culture of IKEA in her book *Design by IKEA*, and mentions how the 'commandments' influenced the company's way of working (Kristoffersson, 2014). Traditionally, furniture designers were not constrained by the production process, but at IKEA, production efficiency and logistics constraints posed hard restriction on the furniture designers. This was new to the industry, but it made the products affordable to a broad market. One such constraint was that the flat package had to fit on a standard European pallet.

The IKEA culture is driven by narratives, where the legend of Ingvar Kamprad has a clear role as the cultural bearer. He is often portrayed as an underdog who found innovative solutions to the problems he faced by looking at things differently. An example is the narrative around the origin of the short pencil in the IKEA stores. Kamprad met the producer of the standard yellow pencils in Sweden and challenged why they looked the way they did. The producer responded that this is what a pencil looks like in Sweden. Kamprad took a pen, broke it in the middle and said, 'This way you have two pencils for the price of one', and don't paint it yellow. He added, 'this is the IKEA way of doing things.'

IKEA has become a sustainable company because it follows a clear purpose as a beacon, has clear principles of how to work collaboratively and allows for decentralised working – avoiding the pitfalls of larger organisations that want to have top–down control, a structure which, in the end, reduces profitability and innovation as size increases.

IKEA is a privately held family-owned company that has grown organically. This has allowed them to be long term and do things their own way, since they did not have to worry about what stock analysts would say or short-term fluctuations of the share price. At Kamprad's death, the stewardship of the culture had been handed over to the second generation and the question is to what extent the purpose and culture will be able to continue to develop in the spirit of Kamprad's philosophy. The deepest root cause of sustainability is in consistency of purpose and culture. There is a possibility that, over time, IKEA might transform into a more 'traditional' multinational company. Only the future will tell.

CONCLUDING REMARKS

Having a clear company purpose as a beacon for the long-term navigation of a complex world is very helpful. Each time a company needs to adjust to new circumstances, the purpose will help to reflect what the best strategy is. It avoids dilution of activities: business expansions, acquisitions, changes of strategy all benefit from having a clear purpose. For long-term investors, it is therefore relevant to assess a company based on its clearly and consistently expressed purpose as it is probably a better predictor than the snapshot provided by the current balance sheet.

We only provide casuistry evidence using examples and reasoning. People may argue that being able to change the purpose means flexibility in pursuing new profitable strategies. In practice, many companies do not have the experience or organizational strength to make proper strategic judgements after a shift in purpose. The knowledge of the new territory is not in the genes of the company – the Enron case is a lucid example of that. In addition, a shift in purpose may demotivate current staff and prompt the best talent to leave, leading to increased vulnerability, especially in a stage of expansion.

Apart from a distinctive purpose, sustainability benefits from clear principles of how to work together and how to see the world. Being able to accept that part of the external and internal world are complexity-driven systems will make companies better equipped to deal with uncertainty and be more adaptive. The Dutch pension fund case shows how a worldview of complexity is beneficial in navigating unprecedented longevity growth and interest rate declines. Taking into consideration that the largest part of the world is still embracing a 'the financial world is complicated' worldview, the shift in the Netherlands displays a relatively high adaptivity.

The success of IKEA provides some evidence that the narrative of the leader, which provided both purpose and clear successful principles, is beneficial to success. There is a risk that this founder-based narrative and therefore purpose and principles will dilute over time. It is up to the management of this and many other firms to make sure there is stability in purpose and that this is reflected in the principles which will help keep the business fit for purpose. Principles need to incorporate modern insights from behavioural sciences and complexity theory in order to avoid counterproductive decisions based on narrow worldviews.

The analysis around purpose and principles in this chapter applies to every company in the world. But especially in finance, the abstract nature of services and products, the long horizons and extremely high uncertainty of financial markets makes people – professionals included – more prone to behavioural pitfalls and a flight into safe 'complicated but unambiguous' models. Consistency in purpose combined with adequate principles of how to effectively work together in a complex world will be particularly beneficial to sustainability in the financial sector.

NOTE

1   This is often translated as, 'He who has a why to live, can bear almost any how.'

REFERENCES

Arthur, W.B. (2014) *Complexity and the Economy*. Oxford: Oxford University Press.
Buchanan, M. (2002) *Ubiquity: Why Catastrophes Happen*. Portland: Broadway Books.
Christensen, C. (1997) *The Innovator's Dilemma: When New Technologies Cause Great Firms to Fail*. Boston: Harvard Business Review Press.
Dalio, R. (2017) *Principles: Life and Work*. New York: Simon & Schuster.
Dekker, S. (2018) *Drift into Failure: From Hunting Broken Components to Understanding Complex Systems*. London: Routledge.
Drucker, P. (1955) *The Practice of Management*. Oxford: Butterworth-Heinemann.
Drucker, P. (2000) *The Essential Drucker*. London: Routledge.
Ellsberg, D. (1961) 'Risk, Ambiguity, and the Savage Axioms', *Quarterly Journal of Economics*, 75(4), pp. pp. 643–669.
Gladwell, M. (2000) *The Tipping Point. New York*. Boston, MA: Little, Brown and Company.
Heffernan, M. (2011) *Wilful Blindness: Why We Ignore the Obvious at Our Peril*. New York: Walker & Company.
Kahneman, D., Slovic, P., and Tversky, A. (eds.) (1982) *Judgment under Uncertainty: Heuristics and Biases*. Cambridge: Cambridge University Press.

Kamprad, I.F. (1976) *The Testament of a Furniture Dealer*. Available at: www.ikea.com/ms/fr_FR/media/This_is_IKEA/the-testament-of-a-furniture-dealer-small.pdf (Accessed 08.01.2020).

Knight, F. (1921) *Risk, Uncertainty and Profit*. 2006 republication of 1957 edition. Mineola: Dover Publications.

Kristoffersson, S. (2014) *Design by IKEA: A Cultural History*. London: Bloomsbury Publishing.

Lo, A.W. (2017) *Adaptive Markets: Financial Evolution at the Speed of Thought*. Princeton, NJ: Princeton University Press.

Milgram, S. (1967) 'The Small World Problem', *Psychology Today*, 2(1), pp. 60–67.

Minsky, H. (1986) 'Stabilising an Unstable Economy', *Hyman P. Minsky Archive* (Paper 144) [Online]. Available at: http://digitalcommons.bard.edu/hm_archive/144 (Accessed 08. 01.2020).

Nietzsche, F. (1889) *Götzen-Dämmerung Oder Wie Man Mit Dem Hammer Philosophiert*. Leipzig: CG Naumann.

Rand, A. (1966) *Capitalism. The Unknown Ideal*. New York: New American Library.

Simon, H.A. (1984) *Models of Bounded Rationality, Volume 1: Economic Analysis and Public Policy*. Boston: MIT Press Books.

Soros, G. (1986) *The Alchemy of Finance*. Hoboken, NJ: John Wiley & Sons.

Syed, M. (2015) *Black Box Thinking: The Surprising Truth about Success*. Hachette, UK: John Murray.

5

The end of the beginning

Next-generation responsible investment

Fiona Reynolds and Nathan Fabian, with Rory Sullivan

INTRODUCTION

Since its launch in 2006, the Principles for Responsible Investment (PRI) has placed responsible investment at the centre of mainstream investment practice. It has provided a framework for investors' efforts on responsible investment, it has built market capacity on active ownership (engagement) and on the financial analysis of environmental, social, and governance (ESG) issues, and it has helped coordinate and facilitate investor action on issues such as climate change and the Sustainable Development Goals (SDGs).

These efforts have built competence and expertise at scale across the investment industry, with many institutional investors increasing the attention they pay to ESG issues in their investment practices and processes. These changes have, in turn, contributed to significant improvements in the quality and quantity of corporate disclosures on ESG issues, and to improvements in corporate governance and corporate social and environmental performance.

It is, however, clear that much more is needed if investors are to play their full role in responding to the climate emergency, in enabling the transition to a low-carbon economy, in enabling the SDGs to be achieved and in ensuring the stability and resilience of the global financial system. The aim of this chapter is to chart the current and the potential future landscape for responsible investment, with a particular focus on the role and contribution of the PRI.

THE STATE OF PLAY IN RESPONSIBLE INVESTMENT

Investment practice

The PRI was launched in 2006 with 68 founding signatories. By November 2019, it had over 2,500 signatories, including 465 asset owners and over 1,800 asset managers, representing US$86.3 trillion in assets under management.

The PRI's mission is presented in Box 5.1. The PRI's signatories commit to incorporating ESG issues into their investment analysis and decision-making processes and into their ownership policies and practices, and to reporting on their activities and progress towards implementing the Principles (see Box 5.2).

Box 5.1 The PRI's mission

We believe that an economically efficient, sustainable global financial system is a necessity for long-term value creation. Such a system will reward long-term, responsible investment and benefit the environment and society as a whole.

The PRI will work to achieve this sustainable global financial system by encouraging adoption of the Principles and collaboration on their implementation; by fostering good governance, integrity and accountability; and by addressing obstacles to a sustainable financial system that lie within market practices, structures and regulation.

Source: www.unpri.org/pri/about-the-pri

Box 5.2 The Principles for Responsible Investment

As institutional investors, we have a duty to act in the best long-term interests of our beneficiaries. In this fiduciary role, we believe that environmental, social, and corporate governance (ESG) issues can affect the performance of investment portfolios (to varying degrees across companies, sectors, regions, asset classes and through time). We also recognise that applying these Principles may better align investors with broader objectives of society. Therefore, where consistent with our fiduciary responsibilities, we commit to the following:

Principle 1: We will incorporate ESG issues into investment analysis and decision-making processes.

Principle 2: We will be active owners and incorporate ESG issues into our ownership policies and practices.

Principle 3: We will seek appropriate disclosure on ESG issues by the entities in which we invest.

Principle 4: We will promote acceptance and implementation of the Principles within the investment industry.

Principle 5: We will work together to enhance our effectiveness in implementing the Principles.

Principle 6: We will each report on our activities and progress towards implementing the Principles.

Source: www.unpri.org/pri/an-introduction-to-responsible-investment/what-are-the-principles-for-responsible-investment

PRI signatories have taken these commitments seriously. For example, 62% of the PRI's asset owner signatories consider ESG-related factors in all stages of asset manager selection, appointment and monitoring, and 89% and 98% of signatories incorporate ESG issues to at least some extent in fixed income and listed equity investments respectively (PRI, 2019a). In relation to active ownership, many signatories actively engage with the companies and other entities in which they invest. For example, more than 370 investors from across dozens of countries, collectively managing more than US$35 trillion in assets, support Climate Action 100+, a collaborative investor initiative coordinated by five partner organisations including the PRI to ensure the world's largest corporate greenhouse gas emitters take necessary action on climate change.[1] Other examples include the 477 investors representing more than US$34 trillion in assets who signed a letter,[2] coordinated by five partner organisations including the PRI, strongly urging all governments to implement the actions needed to achieve the goals of the Paris Agreement on Climate Change,[3] and the more than 500 investors that support the Carbon Disclosure Project's (CDP) annual climate change, water and forests disclosure requests.[4]

The materiality argument

Investor interest in ESG issues is being driven by the compelling evidence of the positive relationship between ESG and investment performance. A recent analysis of more than 2,000 empirical studies on the relationship between ESG criteria and investment performance concluded that approximately 90% of studies had found a non-negative relationship between ESG performance and corporate financial performance; in fact, a large majority reported positive findings (Friede, Busch, and Bassen, 2015). This general finding is supported

by studies into the relationship between ESG and corporate financial performance (Eccles, Ioannou, and Serafeim, 2014; Khan, Serafeim, and Yoon,
2016), by evidence of the financial benefits that can accrue to companies with
better ESG performance (see, for example, Cheng, Ioannou, and Serafeim,
2014; El Ghoul et al., 2011), and by the billions of dollars in corporate fines
and settlements that were imposed on the banking sector in the wake of the
2008/09 global financial crisis (Clark, Feiner, and Viehs, 2015).

There are also significant investment opportunities associated with ESG
issues. For example, it is estimated that, between now and 2030, US$5–7 tril-
lion a year is needed to achieve the SDGs worldwide (UNCTAD, 2014; recent
OECD estimates indicate that around US$6.3 trillion of infrastructure invest-
ment is needed each year to 2030 to meet development goals, and that this
number would increase to US$6.9 trillion a year if this investment was to be
compatible with the goals of the Paris Agreement (OECD, 2017)).

The changing regulatory landscape

Across the world's 50 largest economies, there are now over 730 hard and
soft law policy revisions, across some 500 policy instruments, that support
investors in their consideration of long-term value drivers, including ESG
factors (PRI, 2019b). Forty-eight of the top 50 economies now have some
form of policy designed to help investors consider sustainability risks,
opportunities, or outcomes. As illustrated in Figure 5.1, the introduction

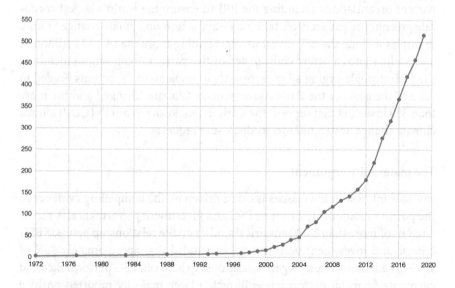

FIGURE 5.1 The growth in responsible investment regulation and policy

Source: PRI

of regulation and policy relating to ESG and responsible investment is very much a twenty-first-century phenomenon, and the rate of adoption of these policy measures has accelerated in recent years.

These policy instruments include pension fund disclosure requirements, regulations requiring pension funds to adopt responsible investment practices, stewardship (or active ownership) codes, and requirements for companies to discuss ESG issues in their annual reports and accounts and to report on specific ESG issues. In jurisdictions where these regulations have been in place for some time, we are starting to see greater emphasis on ensuring that they are effectively implemented (PRI, 2019b). The rate of adoption of responsible investment-related legislation has been such that, in 2019, the PRI concluded that incorporating financially material ESG factors into investment decision-making, active ownership, and supporting the stability and resilience of the financial system are all now part of the duties (or fiduciary duties in common law jurisdictions) that investors owe to their clients and beneficiaries (PRI, UNEP FI and The Generation Foundation, 2019).

Another major change has been the increased emphasis on the role of the finance sector in delivering the SDGs and the goals of the Paris Agreement on Climate Change. Governments recognise that the capital required to deliver their commitments on climate change and development cannot be provided by governments alone, and that they need to adopt policy measures that engage the finance sector in these efforts. An example of what a policy framework might look like is provided by the Chinese guidelines establishing the green financial system, issued in 2016 by the People's Bank of China alongside six other government agencies (see Table 5.1). The European Commission has proposed a similarly ambitious agenda. Building on recommendations made by its High-Level Expert Group (HLEG) on Sustainable Finance in 2018, the Commission has started to develop legislative proposals on a taxonomy of what can be considered environmentally sustainable economic activities, on disclosures relating to sustainable investment and sustainability risks, on benchmarks to help investors better understand the relative carbon impact of their investments, and on the inclusion of ESG considerations into the advice that investment firms and insurance distributors offer to their clients.

The PRI's role and contribution

The PRI has played a central role in the changes that have been seen in investment practice and in the wider investment industry. It has built capacity across the investment industry, through the PRI Academy providing formal training for investment professionals on how ESG issues impact company performance, shareholder value, and investment decision-making,[5] through developing practical guides on ESG integration in asset classes such as listed

TABLE 5.1
Guidelines for establishing the green financial system in China

1. Develop green lending	Establish a policy framework, support financial institutions to establish a credit management system
2. Enhance the role of the securities market	Improve rules and regulations for green bonds, guide international investors to invest in green assets, etc.
3. Launch green development funds and public–private partnerships (PPP)	Improve relevant rules and regulations on green PPPs, etc.
4. Develop green insurance	Establish a compulsory environmental pollution system in areas of high environmental risks, etc.
5. Improve environmental rights trading market	Develop variety of carbon finance products, promote establishment of markets for pollutant emission rights, energy use rights, etc.
6. Support local government initiatives	Explore supportive measures such as bank re-lending, macro-prudential measures, and capital market instruments
7. Promote international cooperation	Promote cooperation through the Belt and Road Imitative (BRI), South–South cooperation, and the AIIB
8. Prevent financial risks	Improve supervision mechanisms, rules, and standards

Adapted from: PRI, UNEP FI and The Generation Foundation (2018), *Investor Duties and ESG Integration in China* (PRI, London; UNEP FI, Geneva).

equities, fixed income, forestry, property, infrastructure, and hedge funds,[6] through providing practical guidance on how asset owners and asset managers can develop and implement their responsible investment policies and strategies,[7] and through enabling signatories to share their experiences and lessons learned through events and through regional networks.[8]

The PRI has recognised the importance of increasing transparency and accountability among its signatory base. All signatories are required to report on how they have implemented their approach to responsible investment, allowing them to be benchmarked against their industry peers.[9] In 2018, the PRI introduced minimum requirements for membership. These require signatories to have a responsible investment policy covering at least half of their assets under management, to have nominated staff with explicit responsibility for implementing the policy and to have clear senior-level commitment and accountability mechanisms for implementing responsible investment.[10] Signatories that fail to meet these requirements following engagement with the PRI may be delisted.[11]

The PRI has also introduced two programmes to incentivise leadership on responsible investment.[12] The first, the Leaders' Group, showcases signatories at the cutting edge of a specific aspect of responsible investment practice; in 2019, for example, the topic was asset owners' selection, appointment, and monitoring of external managers, and in 2020 the topic was climate change. The second, the PRI Awards, recognises individually excellent projects conducted by signatories across four categories: ESG incorporation, active ownership, ESG research, and real-world impact.

The PRI has supported and convened collaborative engagement programmes on a wide variety of ESG issues, both as a formal supporter or convenor (e.g. Climate Action 100+[13] and the Investor Agenda on climate change[14]), and through supporting, facilitating, or enabling the engagement efforts of its members. In addition, the PRI has engaged with national, regional, and global governments and with other global organisations to build a more sustainable financial system and to support effective global action on climate change and on the SDGs. The PRI ensures that the investor voice is heard through its participation in major global meetings (e.g. the Conferences of the Parties to the United Nations Framework Convention on Climate Change, the annual World Economic Forum meetings in Davos, the annual meetings of the World Bank) and through offering suggestions and proposals to governments on the development and implementation of responsible investment.[15]

Two examples illustrate the leadership role that the PRI has played. The first is PRI's Chief Responsible Investment Officer, Nathan Fabian, acting as the Rapporteur for the Taxonomy Group of the EU Technical Expert Group on Sustainable Finance. The EU Taxonomy[16] is a tool to understand whether an economic activity is environmentally sustainable; it sets performance thresholds for economic activities which make a substantive contribution to environmental objectives – starting with climate change mitigation or climate change adaptation – and avoid significant harm to other EU environmental objectives (pollution, waste and the circular economy, water, biodiversity). The Taxonomy is a key tool in the EU's efforts to bridge the gap between international sustainability goals, like the Paris Climate Agreement, and investment practice. Financial products offered in the European Union will be required to make reference to the Taxonomy and large companies will be required to disclose how and to what extent their activities are aligned with the Taxonomy.

The second example is the PRI's CEO, Fiona Reynolds, chairing the Financial Sector Commission on Modern Slavery and Human Trafficking (the Liechtenstein Initiative).[17] The Commission brought together leaders from across the financial sector, global regulators, survivors, and non-governmental organisations to find innovative ways to end modern slavery. Its final report, *A Blueprint for Mobilizing Finance Against Slavery and Trafficking* (Liechtenstein Initiative, 2019), set out five goals, underpinned by a series of detailed proposals on the actions that might support these goals, towards which financial sector actors could work. The goals were: (1) compliance with laws against modern slavery and human trafficking; (2) knowing and showing modern slavery and human trafficking risks; (3) using leverage creatively to mitigate and address modern slavery and human trafficking risks; (4) providing and enabling effective remedy for modern slavery and human trafficking harms; and (5) investment in innovation for prevention.

THE EVOLVING ROLE OF THE PRI

The 2012 Strategic Review and the 2012–2015 Strategic Plan

By 2012, the PRI had achieved significant success in its goal of building the market for responsible investment. It had over 1,000 signatories, an increasing number of asset owners were looking for responsible investment capabilities when appointing investment managers, and large investment managers were increasingly seeing "PRI compliance" as an essential requirement for them to win new business with large asset owners. The PRI had also developed its own capabilities; it had workstreams across most asset classes and investment types, an established reporting process for signatories, a well-functioning collaborative engagement platform, and credibility and legitimacy as a global investor body. Yet, gaps remained; many investors were implementing the Principles to a limited extent only, the PRI had limited penetration in a number of important geographic regions (in particular, the United States, South East Asia, and Spanish-speaking Latin America) and wider market or public knowledge of responsible investment was limited. The PRI saw that, despite the ongoing fallout from the 2008/09 global financial crisis, investors were only playing a limited role in discussions around long-term sustainable capital markets and in discussions around regulatory frameworks and policies that supported responsible investment.

In response, the PRI concluded that it needed to evolve from a focus on individual ESG issues and their effects on companies, to a more holistic, system-wide approach focusing on how ESG issues in the round affect companies and affect the structure and operation of the financial system. Through the period 2012 to 2015, it built its analytical resources and expertise, it strengthened its collaboration platform, and it increased the resources allocated to recruitment and signatory support. One of the key changes was the increased emphasis on public policy. The PRI saw that policy engagement was a new activity for many of its signatories, and that it needed to demonstrate that (a) this was an area where investors had a role to play and could make a difference, (b) public policy engagement was aligned with the PRI's mission and purpose, and (c) the PRI could effectively and credibly engage with policymakers. The PRI established a public policy programme to develop its analytical and advocacy capabilities, it encouraged investors to work together on policy-related and financial system related issues, and it proactively communicated its work on these areas to its signatories (see, PRI and UNEP Inquiry into the Design of a Sustainable Financial System, 2014).

The blueprint for responsible investment

To mark the PRI's ten-year anniversary in 2016, it undertook a series of initiatives to review progress so far and to create an ambitious and achievable vision for how the PRI and the wider responsible investment community should progress over the next ten years. This included global signatory and stakeholder surveys, an independent impact evaluation, and major signatory consultations.[18] The overall conclusion was that the PRI had been remarkably successful – through its engagement with the investment industry, through its sharing of best practices and learning, through its own leadership, and through enabling the efforts of other investors – in creating global awareness about responsible investment, in helping progress responsible investment within the core processes of investors around the world, in supporting investor engagement on ESG issues, in influencing public policy, and in enhancing investor disclosures. Yet, the PRI saw that it had not succeeded in mainstreaming responsible investment, either in terms of investment practice or in terms of the policy environment within which investors operated. It was clear that the challenges faced by society – for example, global warming, modern slavery, biodiversity loss – were of a scale and an urgency that much, much more was demanded and needed of the investment community. The PRI concluded that it needed to much more explicitly focus on outcomes and impact. To take just one example, in 2014/15, global climate flows were approximately US$400 billion per annum, less than half of the amount estimated to be needed to reorient the global energy system to one that is consistent with the goal of keeping global temperature rise below 2°C above pre-industrial levels (Climate Policy Initiative, 2015).

In 2017, the PRI launched its Blueprint for Responsible Investment (PRI, 2017), setting the direction of the PRI's work for the ten years ahead. The Blueprint set the objective of bringing responsible investors together to work towards sustainable markets that contribute to a more prosperous world for all. It stated that the PRI should do this through focusing efforts on the nine priority areas indicated in Box 5.3.

Box 5.3 Priority areas identified in the PRI's Blueprint for Responsible Investment

Responsible Investors: We will strengthen, deepen and expand our core work to lead responsible investors in their pursuit of long-term value and to enhance alignment throughout the investment chain.

1. Empower asset owners
2. Support investors incorporating ESG issues
3. Foster a community of active owners
4. Showcase leadership and increase accountability
5. Convene and educate responsible investors

Sustainable Markets: We will address unsustainable aspects of the markets that investors operate in, to achieve the economically efficient, sustainable global financial system that responsible investors and beneficiaries need.

6. Challenge barriers to a sustainable financial system
7. Drive meaningful data throughout markets

A Prosperous World for All: We will enable signatories to improve the real world – now and in the future – by encouraging investments that contribute to prosperous and inclusive societies for current and future generations.

8. Champion climate action
9. Enable real-world impact aligned with the SDGs

Source: www.unpri.org/pri/a-blueprint-for-responsible-investment

In the introduction to the Blueprint, Fiona Reynolds, the PRI's CEO, commented:

> Responsible investors need a financial system that works with, not against, their pursuit of long-term value: a system that incentivises long-term investment, that takes into account social and environmental impacts beyond the reach of any individual investor and that works in the interests of its ultimate beneficiaries. Ultimately this work will manifest itself in the societies and environment in which beneficiaries live, and that will be passed on to the next generation. [...] Across the globe, governments have come together and for the first time achieved meaningful, widespread agreement on a sustainable direction for the

world – including ending poverty, improving education and protecting natural resources through the SDGs, and a zero-carbon future through the Paris Agreement. The PRI's role over the next decade is to work with investors on playing their part in delivering this future.

(PRI, 2017)

The following case studies illustrate how the PRI has implemented the Blueprint since 2017.

Case study 1   Climate change and the Inevitable Policy Response – developing core scenarios for investors

The PRI's Inevitable Policy Response (IPR) project[19] starts with the recognition that government action to tackle climate change has so far been insufficient to achieve the commitments made under the Paris Agreement. This has led to the market's default assumption being that no further climate-related policies are coming in the near term. Yet as the realities of climate change become increasingly apparent, it is inevitable that governments will be forced to act more decisively than they have so far.

The question for investors is not if governments will act, but when they will do so, what policies they will use, and where the impact will be felt. The IPR project forecasts a response by 2025 that will be forceful, abrupt, and disorderly because of the delay. The most likely policy levers that governments will use to tackle climate change are starting to emerge. These include bans on coal, and on internal combustion engines; an increase in nuclear capacity and bioenergy crops; greater effort on energy efficiency and re/afforestation; wider use of carbon pricing and increasing the supply of low-cost capital to green economy projects.

The project involves the development of a Forecast Policy Scenario which lays out the policies that are likely to be implemented up to 2050 and quantifies the impact of this response on the real economy and financial markets. This scenario is then used to model the impacts on the macro economy, on key sectors, regions, and asset classes, and on the world's most valuable companies.

The IPR is not just another piece of scenario analysis or modelling. The PRI is clear that failing to prepare properly for the inevitable policy response will have a materially negative effect on the value of many investment portfolios and on the pensions of many millions of people.

Furthermore, the greater the delay in responding, the greater the potential cost. The PRI is encouraging its investor signatories to engage in forward-looking analysis and strategic planning to better prepare for transition and mitigate financial losses associated with the IPR; this recommendation applies to investors' strategic asset allocation, portfolio design, governance, and risk management processes. The PRI has extended this recommendation by encouraging investors to ensure that their advisors and consultants, data providers and investment managers have built their knowledge and understanding of the IPR and are building this knowledge into the advice and services that are being provided.

Case study 2 Active Ownership 2.0 – focusing on outcomes

Active ownership is one of the most effective strategies available to investors to minimise risks and maximise returns. Active ownership has also enabled investors to have a positive impact on society and the environment. By raising corporate awareness of environmental and social issues and by encouraging them to take effective action and to report on these issues, investors have encouraged companies to minimise their negative impacts and maximise their positive contribution.

While active ownership has been demonstrably effective in improving corporate practice and performance, it is not clear that these efforts have led to substantial improvements in the aggregate social and environmental performance of companies. Nor is it clear whether active ownership has made a substantial contribution to the goals of an "economically efficient, sustainable global financial system" as set out in the PRI's mission. There are various reasons including: a tendency for investors to focus on processes (governance, management systems, disclosure) rather than on outcomes/impacts, a tendency for investors to focus on short-term drivers of value performance rather than long-term value creation, a tendency for investors to focus on issues with direct financial relevance to the company rather than the wider impacts on the economy.

In 2019, the PRI released its paper, *Active Ownership 2.0* (PRI, 2019c). Active Ownership 2.0 is a proposed aspirational standard for improved stewardship. It builds on existing practice and expertise but explicitly prioritises the seeking of outcomes over process and activity, collaboration rather than individual action, and a focus on outcomes at the economy or society-wide scale rather than the risks and returns of individual holdings. Essentially, it means prioritising the long-term, absolute returns for universal owners, including real-term financial and welfare benefits for beneficiaries more broadly.

Active Ownership 2.0 will demand more of both the PRI and many of its signatories. It will entail a shift in prioritisation and resources, as well as a level of ambition that corresponds to the gravity and urgency of issues facing responsible investors today. As part of this work, the PRI will continue to work with signatories to overcome the structural barriers investors face in working to achieve outcomes. For example, the PRI will: pursue investor rights, including a right to advocate; address information asymmetries that limit investor participation; work to address barriers to collaboration; work further on structural issues in the investment chain where these limit effective outcome-focused stewardship.

Case study 3 A legal framework for impact – changing the rules

There has been significant progress – both in terms of practice and in terms of the law and policy – in making the case that investors, as part of their fiduciary duties, should account for ESG issues in their investment and in their active ownership practices and processes. However, much less progress has been made in defining how and under what circumstances investors are responsible for the real-world outcomes of their investment activities. As currently defined, fiduciary duties do not require a fiduciary to account for the sustainability impact of their investment activity beyond financial performance. In other words, fiduciary duties require consideration of how sustainability issues affect the investment decision, but not how the investment decision affects sustainability.

In January 2019, UNEP FI, the PRI, and the Generation Foundation launched the Legal Framework for Impact project,[20] with the aim of making, assessing, and accounting for the sustainability impact of investment decision-making a core part of investment activity. The project will explore questions such as whether there are legal impediments to investors adopting "impact targets" (e.g. that an investor's investment activity is consistent with no more than 1.5 degrees of warming), whether investors are legally required to integrate the sustainability impacts of their investment activity in their decision-making processes, and on what positive legal grounds could or should investors integrate the realisation of the SDGs into their investment decision-making.

The project will publish analysis of the legal framework for investors to consider sustainability impact in five major economies, propose practical recommendations for investors and policymakers on how policies, regulation, and investment practice may evolve to achieve the systematic integration of sustainability impact in investment decision-making, and support wider implementation of the recommendations through investor and policymaker outreach.

Case study 4   The Just Transition – ensuring that social consequences are considered in environmental decision-making

When the PRI developed the Inevitable Policy Response (see case study 1 above), it was acutely aware of the challenges it would face of convincing policymakers and other stakeholders of the need for change, in particular when advocating for changes that could lead to job losses (e.g. in sectors such as mining), changes in demand for skills (e.g. as energy systems move from being fossil fuel-based to renewable energy-based) and impacts on communities (both those losing existing industries and jobs, and those being asked to accommodate new industries).

The PRI concluded that the transformative changes needed in order for society to successfully and effectively transition to the low-carbon economy meant that the PRI needed to explicitly focus on the human and societal costs of these changes, and to ensure that issues such as fairness and equity were central to its decisions. The PRI recognised that, while the low-carbon transition should generate net new jobs, should produce sustainable, inclusive growth, and should support decent employment and thriving communities, these benefits would not happen automatically. Policies were needed to ensure that jobs and workers in the "new" low-carbon economy had working conditions that were at least as good as, or better than, those in the "old" high-carbon industries, and that workers and communities were not stranded as a consequence of the transition.

In September 2019, the PRI published its paper *Why a Just Transition is Crucial for Effective Climate Action* (PRI, 2019d), setting out the case for investors to support the Just Transition. The paper argued that five key elements are needed for successful transitions, namely: anticipating changes in advance to enable adjustment; empowering those impacted so that human rights are respected, enabling people to participate in the process of change; investing in the human and social capital and capabilities needed to underpin the transition; focusing on the spatial and place-based dimensions; and mobilising the capital required from the public and private sectors, including from institutional investors as holders of corporate as well as public assets (e.g. sovereign bonds). The paper pointed to the critical role that could be played by institutional investors, through their engagement with the companies and other entities in which they are invested, through the allocation of capital to support the Just Transition (and, critically, ensuring that capital allocation explicitly accounts for the human and societal consequences of the decisions being made) and through ensuring that Just Transition is an integral element of policy measures directed at supporting the low-carbon transition.

Without a strong focus on social issues, there is likely to be delay in meaningful climate action and the actions that are taken may well have more serious or disruptive consequences for those workers and communities most affected. The PRI has, therefore, built consideration of the potential consequences into its analysis of the Inevitable Policy Response, positioning worker and community needs at the heart of the recommendations being made to governments, investors, and other stakeholders.

WHERE DO WE GO FROM HERE?

We are proud of the contribution that the PRI has made since it was founded in 2006. The PRI has helped create scale in terms of the number and size of the investment institutions that have committed to responsible investment, and it has helped build a global community of practitioners with real knowledge and expertise on responsible investment. In turn, these institutions and individuals have made important contributions to improving corporate and investor practice and performance on a variety of ESG issues.

Yet, we are also acutely aware that much more is needed if we are to deliver an economically efficient, sustainable global financial system that rewards long-term, responsible investment and that benefits the environment and society as a whole. In that context, we see that we are very much at the end of the beginning of our work on responsible investment.

We see our future work as falling into two distinct strands. The first relates to implementation of the Principles across the investment industry. The second relates to explicitly focusing on outcomes and impacts.

Supporting implementation of the Principles

Despite the progress that we – and our signatories and policymakers – have made since the PRI was established in 2006, we have a long way to go in many markets before we can consider responsible investment to be properly integrated into investment practice or into policy frameworks. Depending on the issue, the actors, and the jurisdiction, we will focus our efforts in six main areas:

1. We will press for legal clarity on the roles and responsibilities of investors. We will support policy measures that require investors to take account of ESG issues in their investment practice and processes, to proactively engage with the companies and the other entities in which they invest, and to play a constructive role in the policy discussions on issues such as climate change, human rights, and wider financial system stability and resilience.

2. We will continue to raise awareness of the evidence base for responsible investment, and of the robustness of the relationship between ESG issues and investment performance. We will work with professional bodies such as the CFA Institute to produce practical guides on the investment case for responsible investment and on how ESG issues might be integrated into investment research and decision-making.

3. We will work with our signatories to improve the quality of responsible investment implementation. We will support them in their efforts to integrate analysis of ESG issues into their decision-making across all asset classes, and to engage with the companies and other entities in which they are invested.

4. We will drive transparency on responsible investment practices, processes, performance, and outcomes across the investment industry, through our signatory reporting requirements, through benchmarking, through highlighting leadership and best practice, and through tightening the disclosure and performance requirements we expect of our signatories.

5. We will continue to support efforts (e.g. through regulation, through listing rules) to improve corporate reporting, as this is a key barrier to investors wishing to assess the investment implications of these issues and to investor engagement. and making it difficult to engage with companies.

6. We will help build capacity and expertise across the investment industry, in particular in smaller funds and in markets where responsible investment is still relatively immature.

We will continue to work on the systemic and structural barriers to responsible investment. This is not just about regulation and policy, but also about the role and influence of key actors within the investment system. These include: the large passive investors (e.g. Blackrock Vanguard), the investment consultants,[21] and credit ratings agencies.[22]

Focusing on outcomes and impacts

The PRI's Blueprint for Responsible Investment envisages that we will move well beyond ensuring that the Principles are implemented across the investment industry. It will potentially require us to take on projects and initiatives that potentially look quite different from those that we have taken on to date. Where might we focus our attention? We have identified the following as key priorities:

1. We need to accelerate our efforts on climate change to ensure that we transition to net zero carbon emissions by 2050. Our work on the Inevitable Policy Response is one part of this effort. Another is our convening, alongside the UN Environment Programme's Finance Initiative, of the Net-Zero Asset Owner Alliance an international group of institutional investors delivering on a bold commitment to transition their investment portfolios to net zero greenhouse gas emissions by 2050.[23]

2. We need to address the SDG and Paris Agreement investment gaps. UNCTAD's 2019 analysis suggests that there is a US$2.6 trillion gap between the estimated annual investment needs in developing countries and the current private sector contribution (UNCTAD, 2019). Similarly, the Climate Policy Initiative estimates that annual climate finance averaged US$579 billion in 2017 and 2018, far short of the estimated annual investment of US$1.6–3.8 trillion required between 2016 and 2050, for supply-side energy system investments alone (Climate Policy Initiative, 2019).

3. We need to ensure that social issues are integral to ESG. Social issues have been a relatively neglected part of the responsible agenda for a variety of reasons, including gaps and inconsistencies in corporate disclosures, a tendency for indicators to be qualitative rather than quantitative, and a lack of clarity on how they affect cash flows or balance sheets. Yet it is clear – as we discussed in the context of the Just Transition above – that we cannot address the world's environmental problems if we do not explicitly address the impacts on workers, on families and on communities. Furthermore, many of the greatest sources of risk to investors – issues such as inequality, human rights, poverty – are clearly social issues. We have a critical role to play, in ensuring that social issues are on the ESG agenda and in ensuring that investors take effective and meaningful action on these issues. We have initiated a series of major programmes on social issues, including modern slavery (through our Chairing of the Liechtenstein Initiative as discussed above), conflict minerals, labour conditions in apparel supply chains, and migration.

What these priorities all have in common is that they see us moving much more quickly and much more assertively to ensure that we transition in time to a low-carbon economy, that we respond effectively to unavoidable climate change, and that we deliver the SDGs. They see us focusing on delivering positive and concrete outcomes and impacts at scale. Ultimately, delivering these goals is the core challenge for the PRI and, over the next decade, our success in delivering these goals is the single measure on which we should be judged.

NOTES

1 www.climateaction100.org/.
2 The letter is available here: https://igcc.org.au/wp-content/uploads/2019/06/GLOBAL-INVES-TOR-STATEMENT-TO-GOVERNMENTS-ON-CLIMATE-CHANGE.pdf
3 http://unfccc.int/paris_agreement/items/9485.php.
4 www.cdp.net/en.
5 https://priacademy.org/
6 www.unpri.org/investor-tools
7 www.unpri.org/asset-owners and www.unpri.org/signatories/getting-started
8 www.unpri.org/signatories/regional-support
9 www.unpri.org/signatories/reporting-for-signatories
10 www.unpri.org/signatories/minimum-requirements
11 Signatories that are delisted at the end of the engagement period would be named, in the same way that signatories who fail to complete their annual reporting to the PRI. See www.unpri.org/annual-report-2019/how-we-work/more/new-and-former-signatories
12 www.unpri.org/signatories/showcasing-leadership/3608.article
13 http://www.climateaction100.org/
14 https://theinvestoragenda.org/
15 The PRI's policy submissions and proposals can be viewed at www.unpri.org/sustainable-markets/briefings-and-consultations.
16 https://eur-lex.europa.eu/legal-content/EN/TXT/PDF/?uri=CELEX:32019R2088&from=EN
17 www.fastinitiative.org/
18 www.unpri.org/pri/a-blueprint-for-responsible-investment
19 www.unpri.org/inevitable-policy-response/what-is-the-inevitable-policy-response/4787.article
20 www.unepfi.org/investment/legal-framework-for-impact/
21 www.unpri.org/sustainable-financial-system/investment-consultants-services-review/571.article
22 www.unpri.org/credit-ratings
23 www.unepfi.org/net-zero-alliance/

REFERENCES

Cheng, B., Ioannou, I., and Serafeim, G. (2014) 'Corporate Social Responsibility and Access to Finance', *Strategic Management Journal*, 35(1), pp. 1–23.
Clark, G.L., Feiner, A., and Viehs, M. (2015) *From the Stockholder to the Stakeholder: How Sustainability Can Drive Financial Outperformance*. Oxford et al.: University of Oxford & Arabesque Partners.
Climate Policy Initiative. (2015) *Global Landscape of Climate Finance 2015*. London: Climate Policy Initiative.
Climate Policy Initiative. (2019) *Global Landscape of Climate Finance 2019*. London: Climate Policy Initiative.
Eccles, R., Ioannou, I., and Serafeim, G. (2014) 'The Impact of Corporate Sustainability on Organizational Processes and Performance', *Management Science*, 60(11), pp. 2835–2857.

El Ghoul, S., Guedhami, O., Kwok, C., and Mishra, D. (2011) 'Does Corporate Social Responsibility Affect the Cost of Capital?', *Journal of Banking and Finance*, 35(9), pp. 2388–2406.

Friede, G., Busch, T., and Bassen, A. (2015) 'ESG and Financial Performance: Aggregated Evidence from more than 2000 Empirical Studies', *Journal of Sustainable Finance & Investment*, 5(4), pp. 210–233.

Khan, M., Serafeim, G., and Yoon, A. (2016) 'Corporate Sustainability: First Evidence on Materiality', *The Accounting Review*, 91(6), pp. 1697–1724.

Liechtenstein Initiative. (2019) *A Blueprint for Mobilizing Finance against Slavery and Trafficking. Final Report of the Liechtenstein Initiative's Financial Sector Commission on Modern Slavery and Human Trafficking*. New York: Liechtenstein Initiative.

Organization for Economic Co-operation and Development (OECD). (2017) *Investing in Climate, Investing in Growth*. Paris: OECD.

Principles for Responsible Investment (PRI). (2017) *A Blueprint for Responsible Investment*. London: PRI.

Principles for Responsible Investment (PRI). (2019a) *Annual Report 2019*. London: PRI.

Principles for Responsible Investment (PRI). (2019b) *Taking Stock: Sustainable Finance Policy Engagement and Policy Influence*. London: PRI.

Principles for Responsible Investment (PRI). (2019c) *Active Ownership 2.0: The Evolution Stewardship Urgently Needs*. London: PRI.

Principles for Responsible Investment (PRI). (2019d) *Why a Just Transition Is Crucial for Effective Climate Action*. London: PRI.

Principles for Responsible Investment (PRI) and United Nations Environmental Programme (UNEP) Inquiry into the Design of a Sustainable Financial System. (2014) *Policy Frameworks for Long-Term Responsible Investment: The Case for Investor Engagement in Public Policy*. London: PRI.

Principles for Responsible Investment (PRI), United Nations Environmental Programme Finance Initiative (UNEP FI) and The Generation Foundation. (2018) *Investor Duties and ESG Integration in China*. London and Geneva: UNEP FI and PRI.

Principles for Responsible Investment (PRI), United Nations Environmental Programme Finance Initiative (UNEP FI) and The Generation Foundation. (2019) *Fiduciary Duty in the 21st Century*. London and Geneva: PRI and UNEP FI.

UN Commission on Trade and Development (UNCTAD). (2014) *World Investment Report 2014 - Investing in SDGs*. Geneva: UNCTAD.

UN Commission on Trade and Development (UNCTAD). (2019) *SDG Investment Trends Monitor*. Geneva: UNCTAD.

6

Planetary boundaries

A compass for investing for the common good

Johan Rockström, Almut Beringer, Beatrice Crona,
Owen Gaffney, and Daniel Klingenfeld

INTRODUCTION

The global financial system is exposed to a new type of systemic risk. Science can now confirm the risk of destabilizing Earth's critical life support systems, upon which societies and economies depend, is extraordinarily high. This chapter will discuss a safe operating space for the global economy. We will introduce a framework for managing risk at a global scale – the Planetary Boundaries Framework. We will explore how economies and businesses can develop within planetary boundaries in order to reduce risks of crossing climate and other tipping points that jeopardize further economic development. Finally, we will discuss how the finance sector can support transformations towards a sustainable planet. But first, we begin at the dawn of civilization and the emergence of the first financial system.

GOODBYE HOLOCENE

The resilience of our complex societies depends on environmental stability. This is as true now as it was when the first civilization – the Sumerians – arose approximately 8,000 years ago.

From isolated farming communities, the first Sumerian cities emerged on the Fertile Crescent of Mesopotamia in modern-day Iraq. Within three millennia, 12 cities existed between the Tigris and Euphrates Rivers. Some had populations of up to 80,000 people. The Sumerians were farmers, carpenters, weavers, accountants, brewers, astronomers, and traders. It was here that the first writing system – cuneiform – was invented. The Sumerians used cuneiform primarily for financial tracking – trades and stocktaking – before branching out into governance, law, history, and storytelling.

The timing of the emergence of human civilization is no coincidence. The last ice age ended 11,700 years ago and Earth entered a new geological epoch geologists call the Holocene. While warmer than the ice age preceding it, the climate of the early Holocene was unpredictable. Planting seeds is a risky investment if there are high chances of drought, freezing, or flooding. But climate and environmental conditions settled down 10,000 years ago, first in the Middle East, then later in China, India, and the Americas (Kavanagh et al., 2018). Since then – for ten millennia – global average temperature has fluctuated no more than 1°C (Marcott et al., 2013). This uncanny stability is arguably the most significant force to enable agriculture and higher population densities. Complex civilizations grew from the seeds laid down by those early farmers.

Earth's average temperature is now at least 1.1°C above temperatures at the start of the industrial revolution, and instabilities are increasingly visible. As a result of industrial activity, farming, and deforestation, we are responsible for the warmest temperature on Earth since leaving the last ice age, and it continues to rise rapidly. Human activity is pushing Earth beyond the *only known safe operating space for civilization*. To add to the drama, the Holocene itself is quite unusual. If we telescope out to view Earth over billions of years, we see that the extraordinarily stable Holocene falls within a longer geological period of *deep instability* (Lenton and Williams, 2013). Earth has been locked in unstable ice age cycles for 2.6 million years, where our planet flicks between two states – ice age and interglacial. Currently the length of the ice-age-interglacial cycle is around every 100,000 years and it is quite predictable because the cycle is driven by slight variations in Earth's orbit and inclination around the sun. Based on the current configuration of Earth's orbit around the sun and estimated changes, recent research shows that without additional influence, Earth would likely remain in a Holocene state for another 50,000 years (Ganopolski, Winkelmann and Schellnhuber, 2016).

For over 2 million years this oscillation between warm interglacials and cold ice ages has a very narrow limit cycle of between −5°C and +2°C (Willeit et al., 2019). Average temperatures on Earth have never exceeded 2°C above the pre-industrial average temperature of approximately 14°C over that timeframe. How has Earth been able to self-regulate within such a narrow limit cycle? It is largely due to the resilience of the biosphere – the capacity of oceans, forests, soils, and species-rich biomes to regulate the stocks and flows of carbon, nitrogen, and other natural cycles along with the ability of Earth's ice sheets to reflect heat back to space and the oceans' ability to store heat. These are the fundaments of Earth resilience that regulate the final state of the planet.

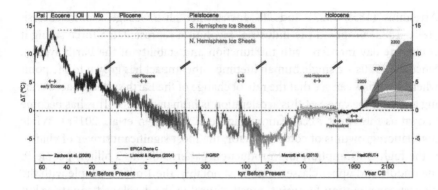

FIGURE 6.1 Temperature trends for the last 65 million years

Source: Adapted from Burke et al. (2018); Design: Félix Pharand-Deschênes (Globaia)

For much of Earth's history the planet has been in a "Hothouse Earth" state with little ice at the poles, sea levels ten meters or more higher than today and temperatures over 3°C warmer than today (Burke et al., 2018) (see Figure 6.1), or, alternatively, and less frequently, Snowball (or Slushball) Earth conditions prevailed where ice reached the equator and life clung on in rare places warm enough to sustain it.

These insights allow us to draw three conclusions: first, the dominant states of the planet are either deep freezes or Hothouse Earth conditions. Second, currently Earth is in neither. Rather, it is in an unusual state of climatic stability but within an unstable "icehouse" period. And third, Earth's stability rests on a hair trigger and humans are pushing and pulling the trigger with some considerable force and wanton abandon given what is at stake – a stable, resilient life-support system.

WELCOME TO THE ANTHROPOCENE

In 1800 the global population reached 1 billion people. Starting first in the UK, the industrial revolution began in earnest, creating self-reinforcing feedback mechanisms. The discovery of the steam engine led to steeply increasing demand for coal mined at ever-larger quantities, due to mechanization and the use of coal-powered pumps. People swarmed to cities. Economic productivity rose dramatically. New inventions made agriculture more productive and new medicines saved millions of lives. While human activity had long had an impact on the environment, now the impact could be detected in the Earth system – the chemistry of the atmosphere, the carbon, water, and nitrogen cycles, the rate of species extinctions, ocean acidification, and the stability of the climate. Academics such as Swedish meteorologist and chemist Svante

Arrenhius (1859–1927) and US environmentalist George Perkins Marsh (1801–1882) proposed the industrial revolution represented a force so big it could one day interfere with the function and stability of the Earth system. Since the 1950s – a single human lifetime – the impact has grown to the point where scientists can see that the rate of change of the Earth system is accelerating and that the cause of this acceleration is human activity. This has become known as the Great Acceleration (Figure 6.2) (Steffen et al., 2015a). While population growth is of course a factor, the most significant driver of change is the high consumption and production patterns of the 3 billion people in the middle and upper classes, and most notably, the 1 billion people with the highest consumption footprint, mostly found in the developed countries but also including elites scattered around the world.

In 2000, Nobel-prize winning chemist Paul Crutzen observed that as a result of the Great Acceleration, Earth's vital signs have clearly moved outside of Holocene boundary conditions. Along with freshwater ecologist Eugene Stoermer, he proposed that Earth has entered a new geological epoch, which they named the Anthropocene (Crutzen and Stoermer, 2000). Since 2000, geologists have been evaluating whether to formally announce an end to the Holocene and the beginning of a new epoch. In May 2019, the Anthropocene Working Group of the International Commission on Stratigraphy agreed that there was now sufficient evidence to conclude decisively that Earth has entered the Anthropocene. This represents a new, unprecedented responsibility for

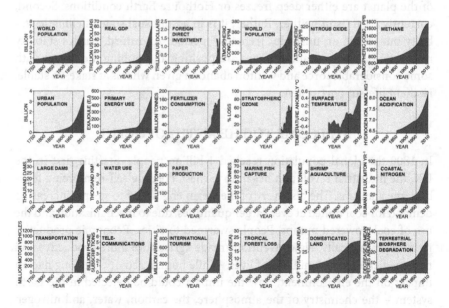

FIGURE 6.2 The Great Acceleration in human activity, 1750–2015

Source: Adapted from Steffen et al. (2015a); Design: Félix Pharand-Deschênes (Globaia)

humanity: In just 50 years *Homo sapiens* has altered a system that has remained stable for 10,000 years. What we do in the next 50 years will determine the trajectory of the planet for the next 10,000 years.

EARTH SYSTEM STABILITY NOW AT SEVERE RISK

Greenhouse gas levels as high as today are unique in the last 3 million years. In 2019, carbon dioxide concentrations in the atmosphere exceeded 412 parts per million (ppm) for the first time in human history. During the Holocene levels were a third lower at around 280ppm, and in ice ages, much lower still at about 180ppm (Lüthi et al., 2008). This is a shock to the Earth system. The warmest 20 years on record occurred in the last 22 years. The five warmest years on record have been the five years 2014–2018. Methane, a greenhouse gas over 20 times the potency of carbon dioxide, is rising again after a period of stabilization (Mikaloff Fletcher and Schaefer, 2019) and, if anything, we are altering the nitrogen cycle more profoundly than the carbon cycle (Gruber and Galloway, 2008). The chemistry of the oceans is changing faster than at any point in perhaps 300 million years (Hönisch et al., 2012). And the planet is losing biodiversity at mass extinction rates (Barnosky et al., 2011).

Like the finance system, global environmental change can be linear and incremental or abrupt and dramatic. Tipping points, captured by the phrase "the straw that broke the camel's back", can be found in complex financial systems, in rapidly unfolding political events and in ecosystems. Research shows that sub-components of the Earth system – for example the Greenland or Antarctic ice sheets, or the boreal and Amazon forests, or ocean circulations – have changed abruptly in the past after small changes have compounded to push the system closer and closer to a critical threshold. Once crossed it can be difficult, or impossible, to return the original state. If a species goes extinct, it cannot come back. If an ice sheet starts melting, it can enter a reinforcing cycle that drives further melting, even if the original forcing is removed. Or if a fishing ground is depleted, like the Grand Banks off the coast of Newfoundland in the 1990s when biomass collapsed to 1%, it may not recover once it passes a critical threshold.

In 2008, a group of researchers identified 15 large-scale Earth system "tipping elements" – systems or ecosystems with lurking tipping points (see Figure 6.3) (Lenton et al., 2008). These include Arctic sea ice, the north Atlantic overturning circulation, the Amazon rainforest, the El Niño system in the Pacific Ocean, warm-water coral reefs, and the great ice sheets of Greenland and Antarctica. If one tipping point is crossed, it may bring other systems closer to phase changes (Steffen et al., 2018). A critical area of research is to identify if Earth is approaching tipping points, the implications of crossing tipping points, and the precise conditions under which the system might tip.

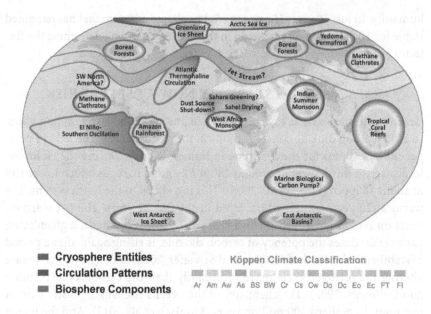

FIGURE 6.3 Tipping elements in the Earth system
Source: PIK, adapted after Lenton et al. (2008)

Since the first assessment, additional potential tipping points have been proposed, for example the jet stream – a band of fast moving air high in the atmosphere in the northern hemisphere (Francis and Skific, 2015; Nakamura and Huang, 2018). Researchers have also reduced some uncertainty regarding the temperature range (or other variables) that is likely to result in crossing a threshold. Worryingly, in most cases, it seems the threshold is closer than earlier estimates suggested. For example, in 2001, the Intergovernmental Panel on Climate Change (IPCC) estimated that high risk of large-scale abrupt events might be expected if temperatures rise 5–6°C above pre-industrial temperatures. In 2018, the IPCC estimated that even between 1°C and 2°C we face high risks (Figure 6.4). Indeed, the 2019 IPCC special report on oceans and the cryosphere suggests that parts of the West Antarctic ice sheet may have already crossed an irreversible tipping point (IPCC, 2019). Recently, Lenton et al. (2019) concluded that nine tipping elements are now active – changing at unprecedented scales and speeds – including the Amazon, the Atlantic overturning circulation, and coral reefs.

In sum, we need greater understanding of the resilience of the Earth system. But in complex, dynamic systems, achieving high levels of precision may be impossible.

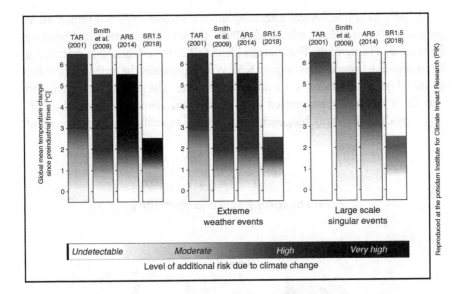

FIGURE 6.4 Changing risk assessments over time in reports from the
Intergovernmental Panel on Climate Change

Source: United In Science, High Level Synthesis Report to the UN Climate Action Summit 2019
(Part: New Insights In Climate Science 2017–2019; Future Earth)

INTRODUCING THE PLANETARY BOUNDARIES FRAMEWORK

Based on the knowledge gained over the last two decades, we can now make
three unequivocal statements about the Earth system: first, the Holocene is the
only state of the Earth system we know that is conducive to complex societies.
Second, human activities have pushed Earth beyond Holocene boundaries.
And third, within the Earth system lurk tipping points it would be wise to
avoid. From this we can conclude that societies are in need of an early warning system to manage the risk of crossing tipping points in the Earth system.

In 2008, a team of international scientists met to discuss the resilience of
the Earth system. They sought answers to the questions:

1. What environmental processes regulate the stability of the Earth system
   in a Holocene-like state?
2. Do these processes have well-defined thresholds at global or regional levels, or do they contribute significantly to the resilience of the Earth system?
3. What boundary positions do they have?

This was a scientific effort to identify the ample evidence that Earth is not only
a coupled system with homeostatic behaviours, but also a system with finite
limits. The researchers sought to characterize the conditions needed for our
planet to continue in a stable, Holocene-like state.

In 2009, an article, "A safe operating space for humanity", was published in the journal *Nature* (Rockström et al., 2009). The article presented the Planetary Boundaries Framework. The analysis identified nine variables that maintain a Holocene-like homeostasis (Figure 6.5). Where possible, the authors provided an initial quantification of each of the boundaries. The assessment concluded that Earth has now transgressed three of the nine boundaries related to climate, biodiversity, and biogeochemical cycles (specifically, human use of

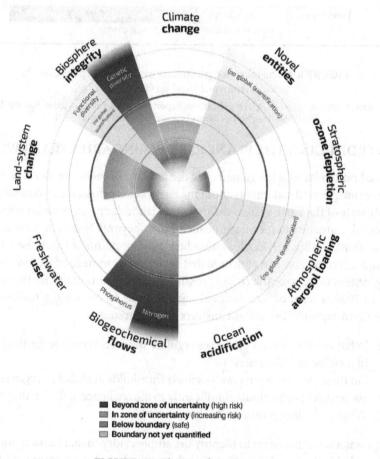

FIGURE 6.5 Planetary boundaries

Source: Adapted from Steffen et al. (2015b) and Rockström et al. (2009); Design: Félix Pharand-Deschênes (Globaia)

nitrogen and phosphorus in fertilizers). In 2015, a re-evaluation of the frame-work confirmed the nine boundaries but assessed Earth had transgressed a fourth boundary related to deforestation (Steffen et al., 2015b). Two of the nine boundaries are considered core boundaries – climate and biosphere integrity. The biosphere regulates material and energy flows in the Earth system and increases its resilience to change.

As mentioned above, Earth is now outside the Holocene boundary for cli-mate and in a danger zone. Paleoclimatic data indicates that a 1°C rise above pre-industrial temperatures carries low risks of crossing a global tipping point. But a global average warming of 1–2°C has caused significant climate changes in the past, not least sea-level rise has been 6 meters or more higher, probably as a result of destabilized ice sheets (Dutton et al., 2015). Below 2°C, the risk of runaway greenhouse-gas feedbacks are limited (Fischer et al., 2018), at least within an Earth system without human forcing. Beyond this limit, the risks rise substantially. Indeed, given the interglacial limit in the last 3 million years has been 2°C, we cannot rule out a domino effect as Earth moves beyond 2°C that leads to an inexorable hike in temperature to beyond 3°C – a Hothouse Earth state – if self-reinforcing feedbacks kick in, for example permafrost, for-est dieback, methane hydrate release, and changing fire regimes (Steffen et al., 2018). Based on current commitments to reduce greenhouse gas emissions, there is a 90% probability of global average temperature increases exceeding 2°C. This rises to 97% when we consider what countries are actually doing (Climate Action Tracker, 2019). In fact, Earth is currently on a Hothouse Earth pathway.

While the global political discourse is dominated by climate, scientific assessments of biosphere integrity show an even greater alarm is warranted when considering anthropogenic causes of species extinction and maintain-ing ecosystem services and functioning (IPBES, 2019). Biosphere integrity relates to Earth's living resources and how they interact within ecosystems to provide resilience. The framework identifies two control variables related to biodiversity and ecosystem stability. Genetic diversity – the number of spe-cies and their extinction rates – provides knowledge of the long-term capacity of the biosphere to persist under and adapt to abrupt and gradual change. The second variable – functional diversity – captures the role of the biosphere in Earth-system functioning through the value, range, distribution, and relative abundance of the functional traits of the organisms present in an ecosystem. The severe reduction in Earth's resilience due to biodiversity loss (along with deforestation and other changes) makes the Hothouse Earth pathway more difficult to avoid.

Within the planetary boundaries framework, two boundaries remain without quantification: atmospheric aerosols and novel entities. Atmospheric aerosols refer to small particles in the atmosphere that affect how much of the sun's energy reaches the surface of the planet. Aerosols can be natural or manmade. Volcanic eruptions can inject billions of tonnes of sulphate particles into the atmosphere. These particles act to cool the planet by reflecting heat back to space. Indeed, in 1991, the Mount Pinatubo eruption in the Philippines caused a small cooling of Earth for almost two years following the eruption. Larger eruptions, such as Tambora in 1816 or Krakatoa in 1883, have had an even more dramatic impact on climate, but the climate, as a resilient system, bounces back within years if the forcing is relatively small and transient. The Tambora eruption led to "the year without summer" in the northern hemisphere and major crop failures but eventually returned to normal. Another natural aerosol is sea spray containing salt particles. Manmade aerosols, such as the Asian brown cloud, are the result of factory and power-generation effluence – usually soot particles – and vehicle emissions.

Novel entities are the second unquantified boundary. There are over 100,000 substances in circulation today. Novel entities that should come under consideration for their potential global geophysical or biological impact include plastics, pesticides and herbicides, nano-particles, genetically modified organisms, and biotechnology more generally. Work is under way to identify and quantify these boundaries.

STABILIZING THE EARTH SYSTEM

Risks are always associated with uncertainty. Humanity now faces a new spectrum of global risks related to Earth's self-reinforcing tipping points. Collective human action is required to steer the Earth system away from a potential threshold and stabilize it in a habitable interglacial-like state – a Stabilized Earth. Such action entails stewardship of the entire Earth system – biosphere, climate, oceans, and ice sheets – and includes biodiversity protection, decarbonization of the global economy, enhancement of biosphere carbon sinks, behavioural changes, technological innovations, new governance arrangements, and transformed social values.

Ultimately, the transformations necessary to achieve the Stabilized Earth pathway require a fundamental reorientation and restructuring of national and international institutions toward more effective governance of the Earth system, as well as a reorientation of capital flows to support this trajectory and away from economic activities that undermine it. There must be a much stronger emphasis on planetary concerns in economic governance, global trade, investments and finance, and technological development.

Pathways limiting global warming to 1.5°C with no or limited overshoot require rapid and far-reaching transitions in energy, land, urban infrastructure (including transport and buildings), and industrial systems. Indeed, it requires reaching net zero emissions of greenhouse gases by 2050 at the latest.

The pathway to achieve this that is consistent with the Paris Agreement is to halve greenhouse gas emissions every decade – a pathway called the Carbon Law. That is, cut emissions 50% by 2030, and cut again by 50% by 2040 and again by 2050, while turning agriculture from a source of greenhouse gases to a sink and building new carbon sinks (Rockström et al., 2017). These systems transitions are unprecedented in terms of scale, but not necessarily in terms of speed, and imply deep emissions reductions in all sectors, a wide portfolio of mitigation options, and a significant upscaling of investments.

ECONOMICS, FINANCE, AND PLANETARY BOUNDARIES

The risks societies are now taking demand a re-evaluation of the global commons. Global commons have traditionally been defined as areas beyond national jurisdiction, for example Antarctica, the high seas, the atmosphere, and outer space. We now need to redefine the global commons as a resilient and stable Earth system (Nakicenovic et al., 2016). Under this definition, then, ocean circulations, ice sheets, rainforest and boreal forests, the water cycle, and Earth's rich biodiversity should be considered global commons.

Our long-term future on Earth depends on our ability to manage the global commons. This amounts to a paradigm shift in thinking about society, the economy, and the Earth. These new perspectives are not yet reflected in academic economic discourse. The world's leading journal on economics, the *Quarterly Journal of Economics*, has never published an article on climate. The top nine journals in economics have published 57 climate-related articles out of about 77,000 articles (Oswald and Stern, 2019). Of the 50 top-ranking journals, only 11 articles have appeared on biodiversity out of 47,000 articles since 2000 (Financial Times, 2019). As a result, the notion of systemic risk from changes in the Earth system has been severely under-developed (Stern, 2016).

Of course, several prominent economists now have climate and the Earth system as the focus of their work. Even so, the value of a stable Amazon rainforest or Antarctic ice sheet (now and in the future) is treated as if they were a typical luxury good where standard discount rates apply. But this is based on two flawed assumptions: first, people will be wealthier in the future, and second, that lives in the future are less important than lives now (Stern, 2016).

While mainstream economic scholarship has been caught napping (or perhaps "catatonic stupor" may be more accurate), the financial system is beginning to wake up, largely as a consequence of the growing sense of risk. Following the global financial crisis of 2008, the G20 set up the Financial Stability Board, led by the chairman of the Bank of England Mark Carney. Carney has said repeatedly that climate change is a bigger systemic risk than the 2008 crash. This statement is an accurate reflection of the risk, though the risks relate to Earth processes that span beyond just climate. We face a planetary emergency: the impact of inaction will be catastrophic and the window to act is closing rapidly (Lenton et al., 2019). The key message is twofold. First, the finance sector now needs to deal with a new and rapidly growing systemic risk. And second, the finance sector must face up to its role in driving this systemic risk, through sustained investments in sectors that are destabilizing the Earth system – and fundamentally change its role and investment logic going forward.

Closing the risk loop

The finance sector faces multiple threats from climate change. Insurance companies are facing greater risks as "natural" disasters such as floods, hurricanes, and droughts, amplified by climate change, wreak more havoc (Coronese et al., 2019; Keucheyan, 2018). Company supply chains can grind to a halt due to these events, and, as climate policies become tighter, the finance sector is exposed to stranded assets – worthless coal mines, pipelines, and other infrastructure – as the growing carbon bubble pops (Caldecott, 2017).

As noted elsewhere in this book, environment, social, and governance (ESG) criteria have emerged as the dominant way to think about sustainability in the financial sector. However, ESG still suffers from a number of challenges also outlined in the introduction, including lack of coherent standards resulting in several competing rating systems. Another critical impediment to the usefulness of ESG integration as a mechanism for driving a rapid transition towards truly sustainable investments is that most ESG frameworks dominating the market are fundamentally built around the notion of risk *to* the financial sector from various social and environmental change processes. The Task Force on Climate Related Risk Disclosures (TCFD) – created by the Financial Stability Board – has been ground-breaking in bringing climate change risks to the top of investors' agenda and is being increasingly adopted. It centres around three types of risk – physical, transition, and liability – likely to materially affect companies in the future. However, with risk conceptualized as an external force afflicting the financial sector, the TCFD (and most other ESG frameworks) does not recognize that investee companies directly contribute to exacerbating the very risk landscape they are trying to quantify (Figure 6.6).

Take companies operating in the Brazilian beef and soy industry. Most ESG ratings tend to focus on, and measure, environmental risk as the reputational or even litigation risk if caught with deforestation-associated products in the supply chains. Another common risk assessed is the future risk to the company of stricter deforestation policies. They might also consider the effect on production of drought or floods, but would not conventionally ponder the

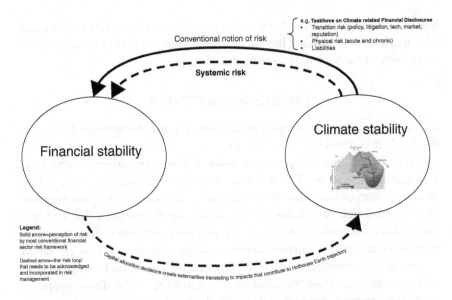

FIGURE 6.6 Climate change is a systemic risk for the financial sector

effect that deforestation associated with company practices might directly be contributing to bringing the Amazon rainforest closer to a tipping point in which it turns to savannah with detrimental repercussions for rain-fed agriculture in the entire region (Galaz et al., 2018). This noted, some investors are however waking up to their role in deforestation and thus their contributing to heightened global systemic risk. In 2019, growing alarm at the scale of destruction of the Amazon rainforest (over 40,000 fires in the region in the year), and perceived political negligence on behalf of the new Brazilian government, led to a statement[1] from 230 investors, coordinated by the Principles for Responsible Investment (PRI), and underpinned by research illuminating the direct links between equity investors and forest-related Earth system tipping points (Galaz et al., 2018). These investors, with US$16 trillion under management, demanded that companies demonstrate clear commitment to eliminating deforestation from their supply chains and improve transparency.

This simple example highlights the cognitive decoupling in current risk frameworks between the fact that risk is both something *affecting* companies and investors, but also something directly *affected by* capital allocation decisions. Recognizing this direct influence of capital allocation decisions on the ultimate risk landscape of the financial sector itself means we cognitively "close the risk loop" (see Figure 6.6).

This is a first critical step towards developing investment practices that help societies and economies stay within the boundaries set by the planet. The next one is to begin the discussion around what measures and metrics can best capture a broader spectrum of the environmental (and social) impacts that are needed to evaluate how investments steer our trajectory towards or away from transgression of these boundaries.

EMERGING SOLUTIONS

So how can sustainable investment be scaled rapidly? In the introduction to this book, it is noted that sustainable investing assets in the five major markets (i.e. Europe, the United States, Japan, Canada, and Australia and New Zealand) accounted for US$30.7 trillion in the beginning of 2018, a 34% increase in the last two years. While impressive, it is worth noting that this way of conceptualizing sustainable investment has significant flaws. The US$30.7 trillion refers to investments that are, in any way, associated with any one of a set of sustainability strategies including positive, negative, and norm-based screening, ESG integration, sustainability themed and impact investment, as well as engagement and shareholder action (GSIA, 2018). These strategies range from investments with potentially clear and direct positive impact on sustainability (notably impact investments), to ones with more unclear sustainability contributions. The former represent only a small fraction of the global total. In quarter one of 2019, green bonds represented less than 0.01% of total debt securities issued (Climate Bonds Initiative, 2019). The sustainability of the latter, such as positive screening or "best-in-class" approaches, applied to fossil-intensive industries or industries with high deforestrisks, remain questionable as they provide merely relative measures. Without a clear benchmark against which to judge the actual negative and positive contribution of a company to a particular variable like CO_2 or total area deforested, this type of screening risks providing a false sense of security in the direction and progress of sustainable investment.

Another growing mechanisms for achieving a greening of capital markets is divestment, particularly from fossil-intensive industries. Between 2017 and 2018/19, the value of divested assets came to US$4 trillion, thus dwarfing any other green investment instruments. This move undoubtedly is an indication of a shift in norms and values in the financial sector, however, it is still not the norm across the large index funds that increasingly dominate the market, even though decarbonized indexes can match or even outperform benchmark indexes (Andersson, Bolton and Samama, 2016). Second, most divestment initiatives, and the broader sustainability and ESG debate, have focused almost entirely on greenhouse gas emissions reduction (with the exception of some recent big divestment initiatives linked to deforestation). Yet as this chapter shows, greenhouse gas emissions reduction alone will not be enough to divert us from a "Hothouse Earth" trajectory.

Climate targets for businesses

In the absence of regulations and standardized reporting mechanisms, some bottom–up initiatives have nonetheless emerged. To date these largely focus on reducing greenhouse gas emissions from industry, but efforts are broadening. Below we outline one such effort, the Science Based Targets Initiative (SBTI). This collaboration between the CDP (Carbon Disclosure Project), the United Nations Global Compact (UNGC), the World Resources Institute (WRI), the World Wide Fund for Nature (WWF), and We Mean Business provides a broad platform along with methodologies for companies to set greenhouse gas reduction targets in line with climate science to meet the goals of the Paris Agreement – to limit global warming to well below 2°C above pre-industrial levels and to pursue efforts to limit warming to 1.5°C. To date, over 900 companies have subscribed to this initiative from across business sectors, public and private, large and small, yet only around 400 actually have approved targets. Financial institutions feature prominently, with around 50 companies headquartered on all continents having set targets. The initiative has developed targets it claims are aligned with 1.5°C; however, these largely ignore equity issues related to distributing the remaining carbon budget and fail to incentivize very rapid emissions reductions.

The Science Based Target (SBT) Initiative argues that the benefits of taking action are internal as well as external. They list four major areas based on surveys of participating companies: (i) increasing innovation, (ii) improving profitability and competitiveness, (iii) strengthening investor confidence and credibility, and (iv) reducing regulatory uncertainty. Each of these factors carries weight and could in itself become a decisive argument for other companies to adapt their strategies accordingly.

When it comes to increasing innovation, setting targets initially requires measuring the current carbon and greenhouse gas performance of the company. This exercise creates transparency and, once a target and pathway is set for the future, accountability. It also sets a compass direction for innovation towards greenhouse gas neutrality. Profitability and competitiveness can be improved if carbon is priced internally as this drives operational and resource efficiency. This also anticipates higher resource prices in the future, ensuring future competitiveness.

From a finance perspective, strengthening investor confidence and credibility is key to bolstering stock valuation and also to attracting new capital. In the coming decade, as the climate becomes increasingly chaotic and stronger policies to tackle the challenge are implemented, setting science-based targets and pursuing them in a verifiable way increases credibility and reputation. In addition, setting a price on carbon internally within a company hedges against future carbon pricing.

In summary, even in the current absence of policies that set strong enough incentives for bending the emissions curve towards a Paris Agreement trajectory in line with the Planetary Boundary for climate, companies around the world have found value in moving forward together and in becoming frontrunners in their sectors of activity. This shows the power of alliances to move at scale to address sustainability and enhance the scope and quality of reporting. Yet so far, SBT focuses only on greenhouse gas reduction.

Financial tools are emerging to help asset managers incorporate ESG and climate metrics into their investment decisions. Arabesque, for example, provides tools to assess a broad set of indicators covering ESG metrics. Another, Carbon Delta, focuses on what is called Climate Value-at-Risk (CVaR). Here, possible physical climate impacts are being assessed on a company level in order to calculate each company's cost of climate change. This information is then used to assess the impact on the company's equity, bonds, and other asset classes in order to compute changing risk exposures of investors' portfolios. Indeed, based on information from these and other channels, some investor perspectives are changing, leading to the reallocation of some funds away from high-carbon, high-vulnerability assets towards so-called "best-in-class" companies that are on a verifiable low-carbon pathway with adequate contributions towards climate stabilization in line with the Paris Agreement.

Targets for the Earth system

Climate change is just one among nine Planetary Boundaries. Following the pioneering work on science-based targets for climate, the concept is now being expanded to explore targets for all relevant Planetary Boundaries. This is being undertaken by the Global Commons Alliance.

In September 2019, ahead of the 74th session of the United Nations General Assembly, the alliance announced the launch of the Earth Commission to identify relevant targets. Hosted by Future Earth and supported scientifically by the Potsdam Institute for Climate Impact Research (PIK) as well as the International Institute for Applied Systems Analysis (IIASA), the Earth Commission will provide the science for defining the environmental boundary conditions for a stable Earth system. Based on the work of its 19 leading scientists in both natural and social sciences from 13 countries, the Earth Commission's findings shall serve to develop practical goals for sustainably managing land, water, oceans, and biodiversity. Beyond that, a new Science Based Targets Network, also part of the Global Commons Alliance and comprising of leading NGOs, will work to translate and operationalize the information into achievable, science-based targets for companies and cities worldwide.

IMPACT OF THE PLANETARY BOUNDARIES FRAMEWORK

A decade after publication, the Planetary Boundaries Framework has emerged as a useful tool to assess the stability of the Earth system. It has generated significant academic, cultural, political, and business interest.

Over 3,000 academic papers reference the framework (Downing et al., 2019). This grows to over 10,000 citations when including the updated boundaries framework (Steffen et al., 2015b) and grey literature, according to Google Scholar, indicating significant academic and policy interest and scrutiny.

In international policy, the framework was included in discussions around the development of the Sustainable Development Goals. It is an intellectual foundation for the UN's High Level Panel Report, *Resilient People, Resilient Planet*, published in advance of the Rio+20 Earth Summit. It has also been central to the development of the Global Commons Alliance, spearheaded by the Global Environment Facility and partners. And it is the key framework for recent WWF Living Planet Reports.

Researchers have used planetary boundaries to explore governance challenges in the Anthropocene. Other research groups have advanced the Planetary Boundaries Framework, iterating and improving on quantification of specific boundaries or groups of boundaries, or critiquing the analysis and proposing alternative solutions to quantification. For example, the biodiversity and land-use boundaries have been updated to reflect these advances (Mace et al., 2014). Yet other researchers have explored how to use the concept, for example, translating it to national or regional scales or exploring links to social dimensions, such as behaviours, impacts, needs, or aspirations. While the framework was not designed to be "downscaled" to regions, nations, and city levels owing to complexities, for example when defining "fair shares" or what is equitable, there is growing momentum to do precisely that.

In addition, the framework has been used to help identify "keystone actors" – the largest international corporations working in sectors that affect the stability of the Earth system, including the seafood industry and the finance sector. Often just a handful of companies dominate these extractive industries. This means they have disproportionate influence on the state of key regions and ecosystems. After identifying the most influential corporations, efforts have been made to develop collaborations bringing together researchers and business leaders to discuss and implement more sustainable business models.

CONCLUSIONS

Despite examples of progress, on aggregate the world is pursuing a profoundly unsustainable trajectory. We are sleepwalking towards dangerous tipping points. Humanity is now taking severe risks with the stability of the

Earth system. Future generations will have to constantly adapt to a scale of change at the planetary level that civilization has *never experienced*. We are already beginning to see early impacts play out today. This cannot fail to have destabilizing impacts on societies.

We are on a knife edge: permafrost is beginning to melt, the Amazon is undergoing unprecedented changes, and fire regimes in the boreal forests are changing rapidly. Decisions made in the next decade will determine the fate of the Earth system for 10,000 years. Science indicates we can still manage the rate of change of ice sheet collapse, for example, if greenhouse gas emissions reduce precipitously, starting with a peak in 2020 and falling approximately 50% by 2030, for example. And Earth's stores of carbon can be enhanced, for example by reducing deforestation and protecting wetlands, to avoid these essential systems from switching to net emitters of greenhouse gases.

This is a planetary emergency. For the financial sector, businesses, and society more broadly, the 2020s will be critical to make decisive progress towards transforming the global economy to operate within planetary boundaries.

NOTE

1   www.unpri.org/Uploads/r/f/l/investorstatementondeforestationandforestfiresintheamazo-n11oct2019_31358.pdf

REFERENCES

Andersson, M., Bolton, P., and Samama, F. (2016). 'Hedging Climate Risk'. *Financial Analysts Journal*, 72(3), pp. 13–32.

Barnosky, A.D., Matzke, N., Tomiya, S., Wogan, G.O.U., Swartz, B., Quental, T.B., Marshall, C. et al. (2011). 'Has the Earth's Sixth Mass Extinction Already Arrived?'. *Nature*, 471(7336), pp. 51–57.

Burke, K.D., Williams, J.W., Chandler, M.A., Haywood, A.M., Lunt, D.J., and Otto-Bliesner, B.L. (2018). 'Pliocene and Eocene Provide Best Analogs for Near-Future Climates'. *Proceedings of the National Academy of Sciences*, 115(52), pp. 13288–13293.

Caldecott, B. (2017). 'Introduction to Special Issue: Stranded Assets and the Environment'. *Journal of Sustainable Finance and Investment*, 7(1), pp. 1–13.

Climate Action Tracker (2019). *The CAT Thermometer*. Available at: https://climateactiontracker.org/global/cat-thermometer/(Accessed: 15 November 2019).

Climate Bonds Initiative (2019). *Green Bonds Market Summary: Q1 2019*. Available at: www.climatebonds.net/files/reports/h1_2019_highlights_final.pdf (Accessed 28 January 2020).

Coronese, M., Lamperti, F., Keller, K., Chiaromonte, F., and Roventini, A. (2019). 'Evidence for Sharp Increase in the Economic Damages of Extreme Natural Disasters'. *Proceedings of the National Academy of Sciences*, 116(43), pp. 21450–21455.

Crutzen, P. and Stoermer, E. (2000). 'The "Anthropocene"'. *Global Change Newsletter*, 41, pp. 17–18.

Downing, A.S., Bhowmik, A., Collste, D., Cornell, S.E., Donges, J., Fetzer, I., … Mooij, W.M. (2019). 'Matching Scope, Purpose and Uses of Planetary Boundaries Science'. *Environmental Research Letters*, 14(7), p. 073005.

Dutton, A., Carlson, A.E., Long, A.J., Milne, G.A., Clark, P.U., DeConto, R., Horton, B.P., Rahmstorf, S., and Raymo, M.E. (2015). 'Sea-Level Rise Due to Polar Ice-Sheet Mass Loss during Past Warm Periods'. *Science*, 349(6244), pp. aaa4019.

Financial Times. (2019). *Researchers Obsessed with FT Journals List are Failing to Tackle Today's Problems*. Available at: www.ft.com/content/b820d6f2-7016-11e9-bf5c-6eeb837566c5 (Accessed: 15 November 2019).

Fischer, H., Meissner, K.J., Mix, A.C., Abram, N.J., Austermann, J., Brovkin, V., Capron, E. et al. (2018). 'Palaeoclimate Constraints on the Impact of 2 °C Anthropogenic Warming and Beyond'. *Nature Geoscience*, 11(7), pp. 474–485.

Francis, J. and Skific, N. (2015). 'Evidence Linking Rapid Arctic Warming to Mid-Latitude Weather Patterns'. *Philosophical Transactions of the Royal Society A: Mathematical, Physical and Engineering Sciences*. Available at: https://royalsocietypublishing.org/doi/abs/10.1098/rsta.2014.0170 (Accessed: 28 January 2020).

Galaz, V., Crona, B., Dauriach, A., Scholtens, B., and Steffen, W. (2018). 'Finance and the Earth System–Exploring the Links between Financial Actors and Non-linear Changes in the Climate System'. *Global Environmental Change*, 53, pp. 296–302.

Ganopolski, A., Winkelmann, R., and Schellnhuber, H.-J. (2016). 'Critical Insolation–CO_2 Relation for Diagnosing Past and Future Glacial Inception'. *Nature*, 529(7585), pp. 200–203.

Global Sustainable Investment Alliance (GSIA) (2018). *2018 Global Sustainable Investment Review*. Available at: www.gsi-alliance.org/wp-content/uploads/2019/03/GSIR_Review2018.3.28.pdf (Accessed: 5 February 2020).

Gruber, N. and Galloway, J.N. (2008). 'An Earth-System Perspective of the Global Nitrogen Cycle'. *Nature*, 455(7176), pp. 293–296.

Hönisch, B., Ridgwell, A., Schmidt, D.N., Thomas, E., Gibbs, S.J., Sluijs, A., Zeebe, R. et al. (2012). 'The Geological Record of Ocean Acidification'. *Science*, 335(6072), pp. 1058–1063.

Intergovernmental Panel on Climate Change (IPCC) (2019). *IPCC Special Report on the Ocean and Cryosphere in a Changing Climate*. Available at: www.ipcc.ch/srocc/ (Accessed: 28 January 2020).

Intergovernmental Science-Policy Platform on Biodiversity and Ecosystem Services (IPBES) (2019). *Global Assessment Report on Biodiversity and Ecosystem Services*. Available at: www.ipbes.net/global-assessment-report-biodiversity-ecosystem-services (Accessed: 28 January 2020).

Kavanagh, P.H., Vilela, B., Haynie, H.J., Tuff, T., Lima-Ribeiro, M., Gray, R.D., Botero, C.A., and Gavin, M.C. (2018). 'Hindcasting Global Population Densities Reveals Forces Enabling the Origin of Agriculture'. *Nature Human Behaviour*, 2(7), pp. 478–484.

Keucheyan, R. (2018). 'Insuring Climate Change: New Risks and the Financialization of Nature'. *Development and Change*, 49(2), pp. 484–501.

Lenton, T.M., Held, H., Kriegler, E., Hall, J.W., Lucht, W., Rahmstorf, S., and Schellnhuber, H.J. (2008). 'Tipping Elements in the Earth's Climate System'. *Proceedings of the National Academy of Sciences*, 105(6), pp. 1786–1793.

Lenton, T.M., Rockström, J., Gaffney, O., Rahmstorf, S., Richardson, K., Steffen, W., and Schellnhuber, H.J. (2019). 'Climate Tipping Points — Too Risky to Bet Against'. *Nature*, 575(7784), pp. 592–595.

Lenton, T.M. and Williams, H.T.P. (2013). 'On the Origin of Planetary-Scale Tipping Points'. *Trends in Ecology & Evolution*, 28(7), pp. 380–382.

Lüthi, D., Le Floch, M., Bereiter, B., Blunier, T., Barnola, J.-M., Siegenthaler, U., Raynaud, D. et al. (2008). 'High-Resolution Carbon Dioxide Concentration Record 650,000–800,000 Years before Present'. *Nature*, 453(7193), pp. 379–382.

Mace, G.M., Reyers, B., Alkemade, R., Biggs, R., Chapin, F.S., Cornell, S.E., Díaz, S. et al. (2014). 'Approaches to Defining a Planetary Boundary for Biodiversity'. *Global Environmental Change*, 28, pp. 289–297.

Marcott, S.A., Shakun, J.D., Clark, P.U., and Mix, A.C. (2013). 'A Reconstruction of Regional and Global Temperature for the Past 11,300 Years'. *Science*, 339(6124), pp. 1198–1201.

Mikaloff Fletcher, S.E. and Schaefer, H. (2019). 'Rising Methane: A New Climate Challenge'. *Science*, 364(6444), pp. 932–933.

Nakamura, N. and Huang, C.S.Y. (2018). 'Atmospheric Blocking as a Traffic Jam in the Jet Stream'. *Science*, 361(6397), pp. 42–47.

Nakicenovic, N., Rockström, J., Gaffney, O., and Zimm, C. (2016). *Global Commons in the Anthropocene: World Development on a Stable and Resilient Planet*. Available at: http://pure. iiasa.ac.at/id/eprint/14003/1/WP-16-019.pdf (Accessed: 28 January 2020).

Oswald, A. and Stern, N. (2019). *Why are Economists Letting down the World on Climate Change? VoxEU.Org* (blog), https://voxeu.org/article/why-are-economists-letting-down-world-climate-change (Accessed: 28 January 2020).

Rockström, J., Gaffney, O., Rogelj, J., Meinshausen, M., Nakicenovic, N., and Schellnhuber, H.J. (2017). 'A Roadmap for Rapid Decarbonization'. *Science*, 355(6331), pp. 1269–1271.

Rockström, J., Steffen, W., Noone, K., Persson, Å., Chapin, F.S., Lambin, E.F., Lenton, T.M. et al. (2009). 'A Safe Operating Space for Humanity'. *Nature*, 461(7263), pp. 472–475.

Steffen, W., Broadgate, W., Deutsch, L., Gaffney, O., and Ludwig., C. (2015a). 'The Trajectory of the Anthropocene: The Great Acceleration'. *The Anthropocene Review*, 2(1), pp. 81–98.

Steffen, W., Richardson, K., Rockström, J., Cornell, S.E., Fetzer, I., Bennett, E.M., Biggs, R. et al. (2015b). 'Planetary Boundaries: Guiding Human Development on a Changing Planet'. *Science*, 347(6223), p. 1259855.

Steffen, W., Rockström, J., Richardson, K., Lenton, T.M., Folke, C., Liverman, D., Summerhayes, C.P. et al. (2018). 'Trajectories of the Earth System in the Anthropocene'. *Proceedings of the National Academy of Sciences*, 115(33), pp. 8252–8259.

Stern, N. (2016). 'Economics: Current Climate Models Are Grossly Misleading'. *Nature*, 530(7591), pp. 407–409.

Willeit, M., Ganopolski, A., Calov, R., and Brovkin, V. (2019). 'Mid-Pleistocene Transition in Glacial Cycles Explained by Declining CO2 and Regolith Removal'. *Science Advances*, 5(4), p. eaav7337.

World Meteorological Organization (WMO), UN Environment Program (UNEP), Intergovernmental Panel on Climate Change (IPCC), Global Carbon Project, Future Earth, Earth League and the Global Framework for Climate Services (GFCS) (2019). United in Science: High-level synthesis report of latest climate science information convened by the Science Advisory Group of the UN Climate Action Summit 2019. Available at: https://public.wmo.int/en/resources/united_in_science (Accessed 9 June 2020).

PART II

Rethinking sustainable finance and leadership

7

Navigating the ESG world[1]

Patrick Bolton, Simon Levin, and Frédéric Samama

INTRODUCTION

The rise of environmental, social, and corporate governance (ESG) is undoubtedly a blessing in the current context of government paralysis in the face of increasingly ominous threats like climate change, rising inequalities, secular stagnation, and the rise of populism. But what is holding back the impact of ESG is a lack of clarity on what this movement stands for and what it seeks to accomplish. We have reached the point where a better conceptualization of ESG, a finer classification of its different constituencies, is needed to understand better how this movement can have greater impact and achieve better social and environmental outcomes.

Together with long-term fundamental investors, ESG analysts are well positioned to identify hidden risks through their 360-degree, holistic, analysis. Due to their long-term perspective and attention to multiple criteria, they are well placed to assess long-term risks and shifts in social norms. They are also able to determine which corporations have the DNA that allows them to transform themselves and adapt to new realities and social environments. In addition, they can assess at what horizon unattended problems will materialize and accordingly what short-term biases are reflected in financial markets.

We argue that the dynamics of the emergence of new environmental and social problems, their gradual identification and their materialization can be better understood by recognizing the specific roles of the various ESG constituencies and their interaction. The first to identify the problem are often the ethical investors and activists. They are the avant-garde, and their stance is generally a good predictor of changing societal norms. However, their ultimate impact depends on how quickly they are able to get the attention from another constituency, the long-term, responsible investors, and from policymakers, who have a more pragmatic attitude, are less categorical, seek optimal tradeoffs and compromises, and generally take a risk-management approach. This constituency will align with the ethical investors and activists when they see that social norms are shifting.

Another key variable is how collective action is organized. The ethical stance of an undoubtedly worthy principled community will not shift lines much unless it can be organized as a collective movement that gradually expands the coalition of actors and transforms itself into a mass movement. It is important to ask how this is achieved and what the organizational and institutional underpinnings of the ESG movement are.

The chapter is organized as follows. First we assess the current ESG context. The next section outlines an analytical framework of the different ESG objectives and constituencies. Then the interactions between ESG and evolving social norms are discussed. The following section proposes the notion of an ESG cycle. And the final section offers a summary and concluding comments.

ESG TODAY: A BOOMING BUT STILL CONFUSING SECTOR

The adoption of ESG criteria by asset owners and managers has accelerated in recent years with currently more than US$30.7 trillion (GSIA, 2018) of assets integrating such criteria. Yet, researchers are often puzzled by the information content of ESG ratings and other ESG corporate disclosures (Yang, 2019). For example, a recent study from CLSA and the Asian Corporate Governance Association (ACGA) (see Financial Times, 2018) delivered very different results when analyzing Tesla. It was either ranked as best by MSCI, worst by FTSEE, or in the middle by Sustainalytics. As a second example, the Government Pension Investment Fund (GPIF), which is leading the Japanese market on the topic of ESG, searched for a correlation between MSCI and FTSEE on ESG ratings among 430 Japanese corporations and found that there was essentially no correlation between the results provided by the two providers.[2]

This lack of correlation (as pointed out in Berg et al., 2019) may be due to multiple sources. First, even when focusing on the same theme, there can be multiple ways of assessing the results of corporations leading to very different results. Consider for example (the lack of) gender parity. How would one assess this? Some providers look at the proportion of women on the board of directors, or the fraction of female executives, while others look at the proportion of women that are hired to a first job. Companies may perform differently along these different metrics, delivering a different

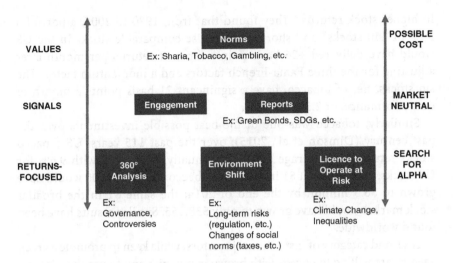

FIGURE 7.1 ESG mapping: a growing split of objectives
Source: Authors

picture depending on the focus of the provider. Second, some data providers are paying more attention to the intent of corporations than to their actions. Third, data providers are often delivering only broad qualitative assessments. But more fundamentally, the objectives of ESG can differ significantly, which may substantially affect the assessment of the ESG performance of a company.

CATEGORIZING ESG OBJECTIVES

What is the purpose of ESG? Clarity on the purpose of the corporation and the objectives of asset managers is important if only to address the legal challenges with respect to managerial fiduciary duties (Schanzenbach and Sitkoff, 2019). Behind the "ESG" label, we identify three main motives, which we refer to respectively as values, signals and risk management, and seeking alpha.

First, for some investors ESG is driven by categorical imperatives. The imperative may be either the investor's personal ethical values (the abhorrence of certain business activities, such as the sale of armaments, tobacco, or alcohol[3]) or the values of the society and culture in which the investor operates (religious beliefs[4] or other ethical norms possibly implemented through organizations like the Council on Ethics in Sweden that establishes the list of exclusion for all the AP Swedish reserve pension funds[5]). As Hong and Kacperczyk (2009) have shown, exclusionary filters based on moral imperatives give rise to under-diversification, which can result in higher stock returns.[6] They found that from 1980 to 2006, a portfolio long in "sin stocks" and short in otherwise comparable stocks in the US would have delivered +26 basis points (bps) of returns per month after adjusting for the three Fama-French factors and a momentum factor. The sin stocks, net of tobacco, have a significant 21 basis points a month of outperformance, or 2.5% per year.

Similarly, tobacco was one of the best possible investments over the past century (Dimson et al., 2015): over the past 115 years, US tobacco stocks returned an average of 14.6% annually, compared with 9.6% for US stocks. It means that $1 invested in tobacco stocks in 1900 would have grown to $6.3 million by the end of 2014; the same $1 in the broader stock market would have grown to only $38,255. Similar results have been found worldwide.

A second category of institutional investors, while keen to promote a green agenda, are willing to engage with brown companies and to use their invest-ments to send green "signals" to both the companies they invest in and to their beneficiaries (like PGGM and APG through an SDG reporting) (APG, 2017). This approach is less likely to have an impact on relative performance unless, in the case of engagement, (i) the investor changes its asset alloca-tion, or (ii) engagement has an impact on the performance of corporations being engaged with. Still, some institutional investors, and especially univer-sal owners like GPIF, consider this is a way, not to obtain an outperformance, but to make the system more resilient, and so ultimately to act for the benefit of their pensioners (Henderson et al., 2019).

The third category, long-term oriented investors, are chasing "alpha" over the long run and seek to exploit short-run deviations from fundamental long-term sustainable values. Partly these investors are betting on societal changes that will put companies under greater scrutiny and expose them to greater reputation risk should their business conduct no longer be compatible with the changed societal norms.

Investors can, of course, have multiple motives: they may divest to man-age their long-term risk exposures, or to send a strong signal that this aligns with their values (see Box 7.1, the AP4 case study). Figure 7.2 illustrates the possible evolution of objectives at three levels. First, institutional investors begin by aligning their investments with the norms of their societies. Second, taking a holistic view, they may seek to avoid reputational risk associated with possible scandals that could hit corporations they invest in. Third, taking into account a possible shift in social norms, any exclusion of some corporations on moral grounds could extend to a call for institutional investors to banish the securities of these companies on risk management grounds (a good exam-ple is coal mines).

From Adaptation to Change of the Environment

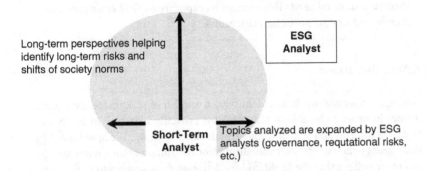

Long-term perspectives helping identify long-term risks and shifts of society norms

ESG Analyst

Short-Term Analyst

Topics analyzed are expanded by ESG analysts (governance, requtational risks, etc.)

FIGURE 7.2 Graph of extended perspectives by ESG analysts
Source: Authors

Box 7.1 AP4 case study

Investors can have multiple objectives as illustrated by AP4, one of the leading European investors with multiple ESG awards.

- First, AP4 has an exclusion list that illustrates their values, with no reference to any returns or profitability. "In the common core values formulated by the AP Funds, it is noted that the principle of legality means that the AP Funds must observe the international conventions ratified by Sweden and the international agreements backed by Sweden. These therefore form the basis for assessing which assets funds should not be invested in. Exclusion means that an AP Fund chooses not to allow an investment for a reason other than a financial one." (AP4, 2019)
- Second, AP4 invests in Green Bonds with an objective that can be analyzed as neutral in terms of performance but that clearly sends a message to issuers: "Help make the green bond asset class attractive and grow: AP4 shall contribute capital in new issues and create a liquid secondary market for green bonds when they meet AP4's criteria for sustainability and profitability."(AP4, 2018a)
- Third, AP4, is trying to improve returns for pensioners in reducing the weightings of assets which could be mispriced by short-term oriented capital markets.

AP4 aims to increase the share of investments that reduce the climate risk in its portfolio. This is done by adhering to low-carbon strategies in the equity portfolio, through which AP4—for each sector—is reducing its

exposure to companies with high CO2 emissions or fossil fuel reserves.
Nor does AP4 have ownership in companies with significant operations in
thermal coal or oil sand. This reduces its exposure to CO2 emissions and
thereby reduces the portfolio's risk profile.

AP4 further states:

During 2018 we also worked at identifying a number of sustainable investment
themes in order to be able to also establish proactive exposure to businesses
that contribute to and benefit from a sustainable transition. We have identified
three areas—the energy shift/mobility, resource efficiency and renewables—
where we believe that the likelihood for a transition is significant at the same
time that there are investment opportunities that are sufficiently mature and
large for AP4 to be able to invest substantial capital and which offers an attractive return.

(AP4, 2018b, p. 29)

ESG metrics can also be applied for different purposes (for example excluding tobacco can be both for risk management reasons and for ethical
reasons). The objectives behind ESG metrics can also switch categories (for
example excluding coal companies is currently justified less on risk mitigation grounds—the stock price of coal companies is already very low—than
on moral grounds).

EVOLUTION OF SOCIAL NORMS AND ESG

A new landscape for corporations

Corporations operate in an ever-evolving social context. Today they are facing more scrutiny as a result of the rise of social media, big data, artificial
intelligence, and machine learning, which have expanded the toolkit and
information sources of financial analysts. In addition, millennials' aspirations
have changed, with a greater emphasis put on mitigating climate change,
gender equality, social justice, and fairer workplace environments. At the
same time, the information technology revolution has greatly increased the
importance of intangible assets (Haskel and Weslake, 2018), including brand
values, increasing corporations' reputational risk.

The most valuable corporations have also grown larger and expanded their
global footprints, directly impacting the day-to-day lives of entire populations. Remarkably, among the top 100 organizations in the world by revenue
and taxes collected, 63 were corporations and only 37 were governments
(Freudenberg, 2015).[7]

Against this growing importance of global corporations, however, there is an increasing disenchantment with capitalism and "globalism" everywhere, including in the US (Harvard University, 2016). All these factors combined put at risk corporations' "license to operate."

Two recent examples illustrate the insights that could be gained by including the possibility of changing social norms into ESG analysis. Even though it did not envisage that a major, respectable, corporation could deliberately engage in a systematic cheating program, MSCI had identified a lack of good governance at Volkswagen months before the scandal was discovered (MSCI, 2018). Similarly, Sustainalytics had put LafargeHolcim for years on a watch list[8] before the discovery of its activities in Syria. By anticipating lower tolerance for bad governance or corporate malfeasance in the future, ESG analysis may be able to identify potential problem companies ahead of any revelations of bad behavior. More generally, as Hong (2019) points out, there is a correlation between ESG ratings and legal penalties.

ESG screens can also reduce exposure to liability from accidents, as Giese et al. (2019) illustrate (see Figure 7.4).

An important recent trend is that corporations are facing a shortening of their life expectancy (Reeves et al., 2016): the 33-year average tenure of companies on the S&P 500 in 1964 narrowed to 24 years by 2016 and is forecasted to shrink to just 12 years by 2027. At the current churn rate, about half of S&P 500 companies will be replaced over the next ten years (Innosight, 2018). This could be due to accelerating technical change and

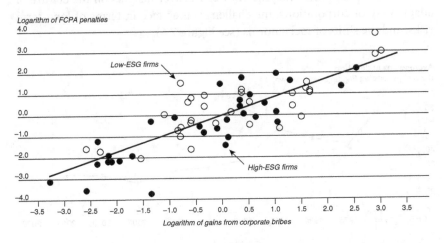

Foreign Corrupt Practives Act Penalties: Low-vs. High-ESG Firms

FIGURE 7.3 Foreign Corrupt Practices Act penalties: low- vs. high-ESG firms

Source: Hong (2019)

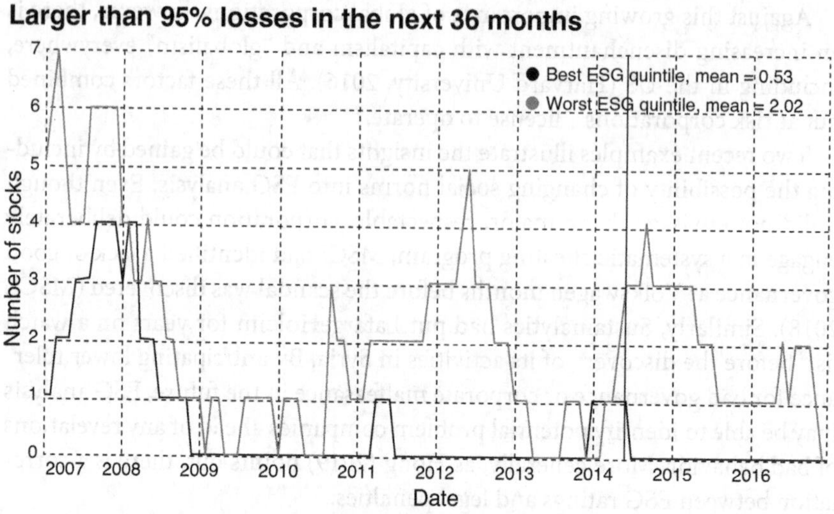

Larger than 95% losses in the next 36 months

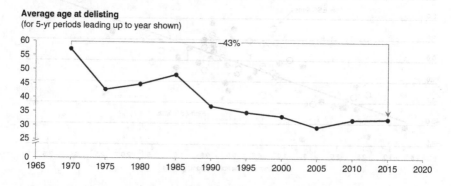

FIGURE 7.4 Idiosyncratic incident frequency of top and bottom ESG quintiles
Source: MSCI ESG Research

more rapid changes in economic, environmental, and social conditions that require major adaptation by corporations. The less nimble corporations, who are slow to adapt, are at greater risk of disappearing in such a dynamic environment.

ESG analysts are well placed to keep track of such rapid transformations of the environment and their implications, as they take a more long-term and holistic view than other analysts. They can deliver insights on the culture of adaptability of corporations, the challenges they face in terms of long-term risks, and the shifts of social norms (see Figure 7.6).

Average age at delisting
(for 5-yr periods leading up to year shown)

FIGURE 7.5 Average firm lifespan almost halved (-43%) since 1970.
Source: S&P Global, BCG Henderson Institute analysis

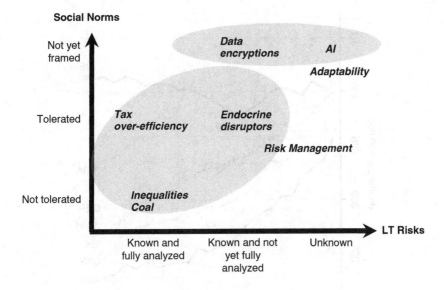

FIGURE 7.6 Mapping of social norms and long-term risk
Source: Authors

It has been noted that it is important for long-term oriented investors to assess the capabilities of corporations to manage their adaptability skills (Deimler and Reeves, 2011; Reeves et al., 2016). One way of making these assessments is to see how much corporations are including scenario analysis into their planning (Gulati et al., 2015), how willing they are to accept failure, how diverse their management and executive teams are, how flexible their financing is, and how long term the outlook of their committed investors is (a lack of long-term investors will not create the conditions for management to pay attention to these factors (Bolton and Samama, 2013), and finally how top management is compensated (do the performance metrics include other criteria than short-term financial performance?).

Investors must continuously assess whether corporations should perfect existing routines or reinforce their adaptability and risk management.

Owners of their environments

Perhaps the two most important challenges corporations are now facing are inequality and climate change. Both are the consequence of their actions and growing importance in society. It is well documented that inequality has reached new highs in Western economies (e.g., Piketty, 2014; Stiglitz, 2013) and that the plight of the poor and disenfranchised is worse than ever (Case and Deaton, 2015; see Figure 7.7).

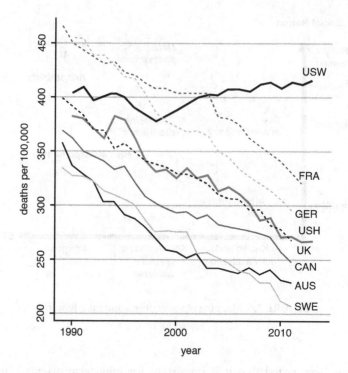

FIGURE 7.7 All-cause mortality, ages 45–54, in the US

Note: All-cause mortality, ages 45–54 for US White non-Hispanics (USW), US Hispanics (USH), and six comparison countries: France (FRA), Germany (GER), the United Kingdom (UK), Canada (CAN), Australia (AUS), and Sweden (SWE). Source: Case and Deaton (2015). "Rising Morbidity and Mortality in Midlife among White Non-Hispanic Americans in the 21st century". *Proceedings of the National Academy of Sciences of the United States of America.* 112(49), pp. 15078–15083. Here: p. 15079.

At the same time the effectiveness of government has diminished (Collier, 2018). Overall, there is a lack of leadership governing modern economies and the rise of inequalities has reached a level threatening capitalism as a whole. This leads us to revisit the objectives of corporations themselves. Chapter 2 stresses the growing recognition that corporations must go beyond the maximization of shareholder value, whether in corporate law (Stout, 2012) or in business practice, as the Business Roundtable (2019)—an association of CEOs of leading US corporations generating around $7tn in annual revenue—has recently advocated. This is an important shift away from its traditional Friedmanite value-maximization perspective towards a more purpose-driven corporation model with multiple objectives such as the support of the welfare of communities in which it operates.

Second, corporations, since the industrial revolution, have benefited from an "almost" free access to energy and interestingly have benefited from a planet that was able to reconstruct its resources at a pace that was matching the use of resources by humans. This situation has changed recently due to a combination of growing populations and reduction in poverty (Klum and Rockström, 2015). However, now the natural environment of corporations is destabilized and threatens financial stability, as illustrated by the mobilization of central banks all around the planet (see the Network for Greening the Financial System),[9] and by the engagement of investors under the Climate Action 100+ coalition (www.climateaction100.org), gathering 360 investors with more than US$40 trillion in assets under management, that aims to challenge the 100 most polluting companies.

In sum, there is certainly now a new situation where corporations must adapt to preserve the environment they operate in—just in order to survive. And they must transform themselves into active players, or possibly even to substitute, governments (see Figure 7.8).

From an energy optimization perspective (that is, a principle that applies to living entities), in a stable environment, corporations must maximize their routines. Alternatively, in a changing environment they must maximize their adaptability skills, and when the environment becomes menacing, they must do their best to protect the environment (or shift entirely their business model; see Figure 7.9).

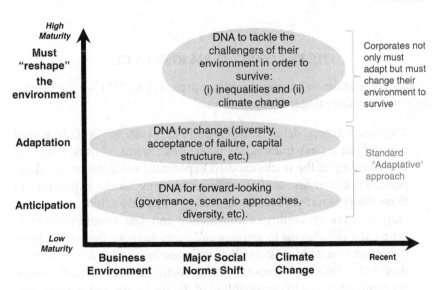

FIGURE 7.8 From adaptation to change of the environment
Source: Authors

TABLE 7.1
Optimal allocation of resources for corporations

	Stable Environment	Moving Environment	Threatening Environment
Optimal Structure of a Corporate	Mimic the external organization	Flexibility	Impact on external environment
Objectives of a Corporate	Polish the internal routines	Anticipate and adapt	Change the environment (or reinvent themselves or manage its programmed vanishing)
Example	Growth in Western economies in the 1960s	Internet and globalization have recently forced corporates to adapt	Inequalities and climate change are forcing corporates to change their environments Ex: fossil fuel companies can (i) ask for a better regulated world on climate, (ii) transform into energy companies helping carbon capture, or (iii) maximize oil production over the short run
Possible Roles of ESG	Assess some potential reputational risks	Indicators of adaptability (through diversity, openness to society, etc.) Identification of shifts of social norms and long-term risks	Indicators on how the corporates are aligned (or not) with the new extreme external conditions

Source: Authors

THE ESG LONG-TERM RISK CYCLE

Interestingly, under an adaptive market approach (Lo, 2017), we can identify four main maturity stages of risk analysis.

- *Stage one:* a general deliberation around a particular subject is developed but without a clear framing for investors in terms of risks. Reducing the weighting of the stocks exposed to potential environmental risks in portfolios can at first lead to *underperformance*, as the importance of these risks has not yet been integrated by financial analysts.
- *Stage two:* the availability of information and data around these environmental risks begins to increase and some financial innovation helps long-term oriented investors align their portfolios with this new situation. As the risks are increasingly being taken into account by the investor community, the underweighting of the stocks exposed to these risks

can lead to *overperformance* (see Andersson et al., 2016b on the outperformance of low-carbon indexes; Eccles and Klimenko, 2019 on their growing adoption).

- *Stage three:* the information is spreading among long-term investors (current situation on climate change as illustrated by various initiatives). The price discovery mechanism then fully prices these risks, offering additional returns, as with similarly to more traditional risk factors like "size" or "momentum." The exclusion or reduction of the weight of these corporations in portfolios could then again lead to a potential *underperformance.*

- *Stage four:* a shift is observed towards "moral imperatives" resulting in above normal returns (Hong and Kacperczyk, 2009), leading to a yet further *underperformance* if there is an exclusion or a reduction of weights in portfolios. This may be the case nowadays for coal companies.

So, the risk (and opportunity) analysis must combine an estimate of (M) the importance of the risk for the corporation (including if they manage or not the risk) and (V) the speed of diffusion of the risk, with (S), the overall risk, being the two factors combined (MxV). And then there is (D) the diffusion of the understanding of the risk (see Figure 7.9) that can reverse expected returns.

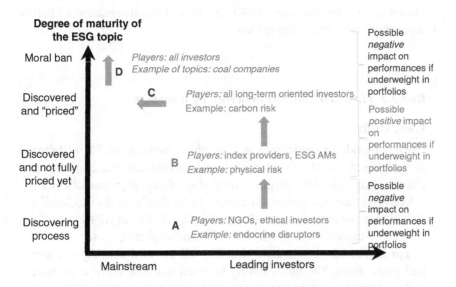

FIGURE 7.9 Different levels of maturities of new ESG long-term risks

Source: Authors

ACCELERATING ESG

In many ways ESG has so far been mostly a "corporate grassroots movement," with minimal organization and structure. Unlike in the realm of politics, ESG has no organizations like political parties that build coalitions, determine policies, and coordinate voting. The closest to a political party organization are the proxy advisers, but they only give voting guidelines and they do not seek to shape policy.

To be truly effective, however, greater coordination among investors in pursuing ESG goals may be needed. How can ESG be accelerated by achieving this greater coordination? As a non-exhaustive list, we can identify, first, at the emergence level, NGOs that can play the role of canaries in the mine, define new skill sets, and help develop "out of the box" topics to frame the debate (as the CDP, formerly known as the "Carbon Disclosure Project," and Carbon Tracker did for climate change more than ten years ago). In parallel, ethical investors can help support the standard-setting process necessary to coordinate investment analysis.

Second, some "leading investors" can request from their asset managers that they disseminate their views on ESG risks that could materialize in the long run. They can even go one step further by encouraging financial innovation to address the ESG risks that have been identified (Andersson et al., 2016a, 2016b), or by scaling new initiatives, particularly in emerging markets (Musca and Samama, 2019; see also Box 7.2) as the recent leadership by GPIF (2018b), the New Zealand Super Annuation Fund (2017), the Fonds de Réserve pour les Retraites (MSCI, 2014), and the International Finance Corporation (IFC, 2018) exemplifies.

Box 7.2 Financial innovation driven by investors

Case study I

Having attended a conference at Columbia University in 2010 (Bolton et al., 2011), the AP4 CEO became convinced of the importance of climate change, although quite skeptical until then. Soon after this, attending a follow-up seminar organized under the umbrella of the Rockefeller Foundation, he took the commitment to align 5–10% of AP4's portfolio with a low-carbon economy in front of the other participants.

For its providers, it became clear that all the then existing solutions had major flaws. The funds having invested into sole green companies had underperformed and there was (although not yet coined) "tragedy of the horizon." Quickly, a solution appeared as very elegant to Amundi: to decarbonize standard market cap weighted indexes. By replacing some constituents exposed to climate change with their peers better positioned, while keeping a low-tracking error, it would generate a "free option" on climate change being analyzed as a mis-priced risk (Andersson et al., 2016a).

And with the adoption of some transparent rules, and a yearly assessment of the corporations' situation on a yearly basis, it creates a form of dynamic and selective pressure on corporations: the ones that have been excluded are informed of it and can be back within the group of selected stocks if they improve their situation.

Although still at the prototype level, FRR (Fonds de réserve pour les retraites) then decided in 2014 to bring this technology to its mainstream level and seeded such approach for EUR1 billion with Amundi (De Swaan, 2020). This is now a technology being adopted around the planet for more than US$50 billion (Eccles and Klimenko, 2019).

Case study 2

In 2017, the IFC decided to tackle the challenge of the lack of green infrastructures in emerging markets. Instead of implementing a traditional business model for a developing bank, it decided to mobilize asset owners.

The IFC then identified two obstacles that investors were facing so far: the risks associated with emerging market debt and the lack of knowledge related to infrastructures financing. To respond to the former, the IFC implemented a risk-sharing mechanism through a junior tranche in order to offer private institutional investors an appropriate risk-return from the senior tranche in line with emerging market debt premiums. To address the latter, the IFC would have a strategic focus on financial institutions issuing green bonds who, in their capacity as intermediaries, would repackage the proceeds into relevant financing for green projects. Financial institutions would play an important role by offering some diversification, doing the due diligence, implementing the necessary currency swaps, and so forth. (Musca and Samama, 2019).

While investing a few hundred million dollars, the IFC selected Amundi to implement and grow the fund that is now deploying more than US$2 billion. Furthermore, this PPP (public–private partnership) capital market approach is now being replicated by the European Investment Bank (EIB), the Asian Infrastructure Investment Bank (AIIB), etc. (Bolton et al., 2020).

Box 7.3 Portfolio Decarbonization Coalition

UN Secretary General Ban Ki-moon initiated a call for one financial sector initiative on climate change mitigation to be showcased at the UN Climate Summit in New York in September 2014. He wanted to prepare the COP21 that was planned one year later in Paris.

Interestingly, different initiatives were set up among investors, usually requesting something before acting (a price on carbon, etc.). The UN team decided to pick up a new one formed by the CDP, the UNEP FI, AP4, and Amundi, and backed by the French and Chinese governments, dedicated to investors already committed to take action to align their portfolios with a low-carbon economy. This coalition then took the commitment to gather investors having such a commitment for US$100 billion by the COP21, although having less than US$20 billion of such will at inception.

As had been anticipated, the platform provided by the UNEP FI and the creation of the Portfolio Decarbonization Coalition (PDC) substantially raised the profile of a number of financial sector initiatives on climate change mitigation and contributed to deepening the ecosystem around portfolio decarbonization. Building on this momentum, the PDC organized three major meetings with asset owners and leading negotiators of the coming Paris COP21 climate accord in the spring and fall of 2015. By fostering a dialogue among institutional investors, academics, and policymakers, each of these meetings furthered the emergence of an ecosystem that was essential to the development of a corporate governance dialogue on climate change and carbon risk. These initiatives also brought the recognition of the socially responsible investor community.

By the time of COP21 in December 2015, it had reached a critical mass by all objective measures. Not only did the number of institutional investors that are signatory members of the CDP grow from 35 to 822 since its creation 15 years ago, but the PDC also recently announced that its membership, which now includes mainstream names such as ABP, Allianz, CDC, ERAFP, Environment Agency Pension Fund, FRR, KLP, and Storebrand, had grown within a year to represent over US$3.2 trillion in assets under management and had already committed US$600 billion of alignment with a low-carbon economy.

Ultimately, the PDC was selected by COP21 organizers to represent the entire finance sector at the Action Day. It was sending a strong message to the negotiators: large asset owners are already counting on your success and taking action on climate change being inevitable.

FIGURE 7.10 Different stages: from ethical to mainstream

Source: Authors

Third, consensus-building efforts could be expanded in at least three possible directions: (1) coalitions such as the Montreal Pledge (https://montrealpledge.org), the Portfolio Decarbonization Coalition (https://unepfi.org/pdc/, see also Box 7.3), and Climate Action 100+ (Andersson et al., 2016b) can increase the effectiveness of investor engagement, (2) similarly, greater coordination among institutional investors in defining ESG reporting standards could substantially enhance investor oversight (Andersson et al., 2016a; Box 7.2 or the JPX 400 index, see Chattopadhyay et al., 2019), and (3) governments can play an important role in codifying emerging investor consensus into new regulations, making the needed data more widely available (e.g., in Japan on gender parity data[10]) and by requiring greater transparency from asset owners (Art. 173 of the French Energy Transition Law that came into force in January 2016 on institutional investor reporting; see Boissinot and Samama, 2017).

CONCLUSION

The future role of ESG is difficult to predict. The past offers few lessons as there has never been a time when ESG rose to such prominence. Undoubtedly, the need for ESG is greater than ever in a world where governments are retrenching, globalization is ebbing, yet the challenge posed by climate change is growing by the day. The promise of ESG, however, can only be fulfilled if corporate leaders can coordinate their actions with governments and civil society. The more corporations take initiatives to address social problems, inequality, and the environment, the more their actions need to be followed up by government intervention and by social policy. The power of finance is an accelerator, bringing forward in time the effects of anticipated future policy interventions. But if governments see the rise of ESG as a convenient excuse to absolve themselves of their responsibility, ESG is doomed to failure. In response to the rise of ESG, governments need to do more than "providing the invitation" for corporations to act.[11] They need to support and assist corporate ESG efforts.

REFERENCES

Andersson, M., Bolton, P., and Samama, F. (2016a). 'Hedging Climate Risk', *Financial Analysts Journal*, 72(3), pp. 13–32.

Andersson, M., Bolton, P., and Samama, F. (2016b). 'Governance and Climate Change: A Success Story in Mobilizing Investor Support for Corporate Responses to Climate Change', *Journal of Applied Corporate Finance*, 28(2), pp. 29–33.

AP4 (2018a). Goals 2018. Available at: www.ap4.se/en/esg/goals-2018/ (Accessed: 26 November 2019).

AP4 (2018b). Annual Report 2018. Available at: www.ap4.se/globalassets/dokument/rapportarkiv/2018/arsredovisning-2018/ap4-annual-report-2018_final.pdf (Accessed: 26 November 2019).

AP4 (2019). The First, Second, Third, and Fourth AP Funds' Common Guidelines on Which Assets Funds Should Not Be Invested In. Available at: www.ap4.se/globalassets/dokument/vardegrund/ap-funds-common-guidelines-assets-should-not-be-invested-in.pdf (Accessed: 26 November 2019).

APG (2017). Sustainable Development Investments (SDIs). Available at: www.apg.nl/en/article/Potential%20sustainable%20development%20investments%20bridging%20the%20gap%20between%20the%20UN-s%20targets/919 (Accessed: 27 November 2019).

Axa (2016). Axa Says No to Tobacco. Available at: www.axa.com/en/newsroom/news/axa-says-no-to-tobacco (Accessed: 26 November 2019).

Berg, F., Koelbel, J., and Rigobon, R. (2019). Aggregate Confusion: The Divergence of ESG Rating. MIT Sloan School Working Paper 5822-19.

Boissinot, J. and Samama, F. (2017). 'Climate Change: A Policy Making Case Study of Capital Markets' Mobilization for Public Good' In R. Arezki, P. Bolton, K. El Aynaoui, and M. Obsetfeld (Eds.). *Coping with the Climate Crisis*. New York: Columbia University Press, pp. 179–200.

Bolton, P., Musca, X. and Samama, F. (2020). 'Global Public-Private Investment-Partnerships (GPPIPs): a Financial Innovation with a Positive Impact on Society', *Journal of Applied Corporate Finance*, 32(2).

Bolton, P., Samama, F. and Stiglitz, J. (2011). *Sovereign Wealth Funds and Long-Term Investing*. Columbia University Press.

Bolton, P. and Samama, F. (2013). 'Loyalty-Shares: Rewarding Long-term Investors', *Journal of Applied Corporate Finance*, 25(3), pp. 86–97.

Business Roundtable (2019). Business Roundtable Redefines the Purpose of a Corporation to Promote 'An Economy That Serves All Americans [Online]. Available at: www.businessroundtable.org/business-roundtable-redefines-the-purpose-of-a-corporation-to-promote-an-economy-that-serves-all-americans (Accessed: 11 November 2019).

Case, A. and Deaton, A. (2015). 'Rising Morbidity and Mortality in Midlife among White Non-Hispanic Americans in the 21st Century', *Proceedings of the National Academy of Sciences of the United States of America*, 112(49), pp. 15078–15083.

Chattopadhyay, A., Shaffer, M., and Wang, C. (2019). 'Governance through Shame and Aspiration: Index Creation and Corporate Behavior', *Journal of Financial Economics*, forthcoming. https://doi.org/10.1016/j.jfineco.2019.07.005

Collier, P. (2018). *The Future of Capitalism: Facing the New Anxieties*. New York: Harper Collins.

Deimler, M. and Reeves, M. (2011). 'Adaptability: The New Competitive Advantage', *Harvard Business Review*, 89(7–8), p. 7.

De Swaan, J.C. (2020). *Seeking Virtue in Finance: Contributing to Society in a Conflicting Industry*. Cambridge University Press.

Dimson, E., Marsh, P., and Staunton, M. (2015). *Credit Suisse Global Investment Returns Yearbook 2015*. Zurich: Credit Suisse Research Institute.

Eccles, R.G. and Klimenko, S. (2019). 'The Investor Revolution: Shareholders Are Getting Serious about Sustainability', *Harvard Business Review*, 97(3), pp. 106–117.

Financial Times (2018). Lies – Damned Lies and ESG Rating Methodologies. Available at: https://ftalphaville.ft.com/2018/12/06/1544076001000/Lies–damned-lies-and-ESG-rating-methodologies/ (Accessed: 26 November 2019).

Freudenberg, N. (2015). The 100 Largest Governments and Corporations by Revenue. Available at: www.corporationsandhealth.org/2015/08/27/the-100-largest-governments-and-corporations-by-revenue/ (Accessed: 27 November 2019).

Giese, G., Lee, L.-E., Melas, D., Nagy, Z., and Nishikawa, L. (2019). 'How ESG Affects Equity Valuation, Risk, and Performance', *The Journal of Portfolio Management*, 45(5), pp. 69–83.

Global Sustainable Investment Alliance (GSIA) (2018). Sustainable Investment Review [Online]. Available at: www.gsi-alliance.org/wp-content/uploads/2019/06/GSIR_Review2018F.pdf (Accessed: 11 November 2019).

GPIF (2017). Results of ESG Index Selection. Available at: www.gpif.go.jp/en/investment/pdf/ESG_indices_selected.pdf (Accessed: 26 November 2019).

GPIF (2018a). ESG Report 2018. Available at: www.gpif.go.jp/en/investment/190905_Esg_Report.pdf (Accessed: 26 November 2019).

GPIF (2018b). Stewardship Activities Report 2018. Available at: www.gpif.go.jp/en/investment/gpif_stewardship_activities_report_2018.pdf (Accessed: 26 November 2019).

Gulati, R., Henderson, R., and Tushman, M. (2015). *Leading Sustainable Change: An Organizational Perspective*. Oxford: Oxford University Press.

Harvard University (2016). Survey of Young Americans' Attitudes Towards Politics and Public Service (29th edition). Available at: https://iop.harvard.edu/sites/default/files/content/160423_Harvard%20IOP_Spring%202016_TOPLINE_u.pdf (Accessed: 26 November 2019).

Haskel, J. and Weslake, S. (2018). *Capitalism without Capital: The Rise of the Intangible*. Princeton, NJ: Princeton University Press.

Henderson, R., Jinjo, N., Lerner, J., and Serafeim, G. (2019). *Should a Pension Fund Try to Change the World? inside GPIF's Embrace of ESG*. Harvard Business School Case Series (HBR 9-319-067).

Hong, H. (2019). The Sustainable Investing Proposition. Available at: https://data.nber.org/reporter/2019number2/hong.html (Accessed: 26 November 2019).

Hong, H. and Kacperczyk, M. (2009). 'The Price of Sin: The Effects of Social Norms on Markets', *Journal of Financial Economics*, 93(1), pp. 15–36.

IFC (2018). IFC, Amundi Successfully Close World's Largest Green Bond Fund. Available at: *https://ifcextapps.ifc.org/ifcext/pressroom/IFCPressRoom.nsf/0/F4D6285A3177879A85258252005DE769* (Accessed: 26 November 2019).

Innosight (2018). 2018 Corporate Longevity Forecast: Creative Destruction is Accelerating. Available at: www.innosight.com/wp-content/uploads/2017/11/Innosight-Corporate-Longevity-2018.pdf (Accessed: 26 November 2019).

Klum, M. and Rockström, J. (2015). *Big World, Small Planet: Abundance Within Planetary Boundaries*. New Haven, NJ: Yale University Press.

Lo, A. (2017). *Adaptive Markets: Financial Evolution at the Speed of Thought*. Princeton, NJ: Princeton University Press.

Marantz, A. (2016). Greener Pastures: Secretary of State John Kerry Bounces around the U.N. and Signs the Paris Climate Agreement. Available at: www.newyorker.com/magazine/2016/05/09/john-kerrys-earth-day (Accessed: 26 November 2019).

MSCI (2014). MSCI Launches Innovative Family of Low Carbon Indexes. Available at: www.msci.com/documents/10199/447d3ba7-e215-45c9-8b14-74031a80f4bc (Accessed: 26 November 2019).

MSCI (2018). MSCI ESG Ratings May Help Identify Warning Signs. Available at: www.msci.com/documents/1296102/6174917/MSCI-ESG-Ratings-Equifax.pdf/b95045f2-5470-bd51-8844-717dab9808b9 (Accessed: 26 November 2019).

Musca, X. and Samama, F. 2019. *IFC and Amundi's Innovative Partnership to Finance Green Projects in Emerging Markets*. LSE Global Policy Lab. Available at: https://digital.thecatcompanyinc.com/

g20magazine/japan-2019/ifc-and-amundis-innovative-partnership-to-finance-green-projects-in-emerging-markets/ (Accessed: 26 November 2019).

New Zealand Super Annuation Fund (2017). NZ Super Fund Shifts Passive Equities to Low-Carbon. Available at: https://nzsuperfund.nz/news-media/nz-super-fund-shifts-passive-equities-low-carbon (Accessed: 26 November 2019).

Piketty, T. (2014). *Capital in the Twenty-First Century*. Cambridge, MA: Harvard University Press.

Reeves, M., Levin, S., and Ueda, D. (2016). 'The Biology of Corporate Survival', *Harvard Business Review*, 94(1), pp. 46–55.

Schanzenbach, M. and Sitkoff, R. (2019). Reconciling Fiduciary Duty and Social Conscience: The Law and Economics of ESG Investing by a Trustee. Available at: https://papers.ssrn.com/sol3/papers.cfm?abstract_id=3244665 (Accessed: 26 November 2019).

Stiglitz, J. (2013). *The Price of Inequality: How Today's Divided Society Endangers Our Future*. New York/London: W.W. Norton & Company.

Stout, L. (2012). *The Shareholder Value Myth: How Putting Shareholders First Harms Investors, Corporations and the Public*. San Francisco: Berrett-Koehler.

Yang, R. (2019). What Do We Learn from Ratings about Corporate Social Responsibility (CSR)?, Columbia Business School Research Paper No. 18–37. Available at: https://papers.ssrn.com/sol3/papers.cfm?abstract_id=3165783 (Accessed: 26 November 2019).

NOTES

1   We thank Jean Boissinot, Tegwen Le Berthe, Kasper Elmgreen, Niklas Ekvall, Arnaud Faller, Timothée Jaulin, Augustin Landier, Olivier Rousseau, Matthias Seewald, Ikho Suh, Rachel Teo, for helpful comments. The views expressed in this chapter are those of the authors and do not necessarily reflect the position of the Crédit Agricole Group.

2   See the discussion in the GPIF (2018a) ESG Report 2018 (pp. 37–38).The report can be accessed here: www.gpif.go.jp/en/investment/190905_Esg_Report.pdf. See also GPIF (2017).

3   As illustrated by Axa (2016): "Tobacco kills six million people a year and costs society more than war and terrorism combined. Yet it is also considered to be an attractive investment offering strong returns. This contradiction means that while doctors, healthcare organizations and governments call for tighter tobacco controls and new rules on point of sale advertising, the people who manage pension funds and investments for you, I and millions of people across the world invest money into the tobacco industry. (…) As an investor, divesting from tobacco may cost us money in the short term but we know this is the right thing to do in the long run"

4   The standard examples are related to religious rules. See S&P 500 Catholic Values Index at https://us.spindices.com/indices/equity/sp-500-catholic-values-index or Shariah compliant https://us.spindices.com/indices/equity/sp-500-shariah-index

5   See http://etikradet.se/?lang=en

6   The explanations behind this outperformance can be attributed to: (1) lower institutional ownership (institutional ownership ratio of sin stocks is 23% lower than that of their comparable), (2) sin stocks are less held by pension funds, university endowments and other socially responsible institutional investors and, (3) less analyst coverage: sin stocks on average are followed by 1.3 analysts, while their comparable received 1.7 analysts on average.

7   The list can be accessed here: www.corporationsandhealth.org/2015/08/27/the-100-largest-governments-and-corporations-by-revenue/

8   See the Sustainalytics ESG blog: www.sustainalytics.com/esg-blog/lafargeholcim-human-rights-high-risk-countries/

9   This coalition gathers more than 46 central banks and supervisors. See: www.banque-france.fr/en/financial-stability/international-role/network-greening-financial-system

10 See "The Act on Promotion of Women's Participation and Advancement in the Workplace":www.gender.go.jp/english_contents/about_danjo/lbp/pdf/promotion_of_woman.pdf

11 Secretary of State John Kerry's remark on climate change mitigation at the UN in 2016: "The governments aren't going to do it—we're providing the invitation, and the structure, but it's the private sector that's going to lead the way" (Marantz, 2016).

8

A new age for responsible banking[1]

Eric Usher

INTRODUCTION: A NEW AGE FOR RESPONSIBLE BANKING

The newly launched Principles for Responsible Banking (PRB) will herald a new age for the industry in setting out a clear framework for what it is to be a responsible bank. The Principles can be traced back to the 1990s, when banks began to understand their increasing responsibility to limit financing for environmentally, and later socially, unsound economic activities and from a transactional perspective began to implement systems aimed at doing no harm. During the same period, however, financial sector deregulation helped drive bank interest towards some questionable market practice, ultimately contributing to the mortgage-backed securities debacle and global financial crisis of 2007/08.

Ten years later, the banking industry remains in a state of uncertainty. The post-crisis reform known as Basel III shored up bank balance sheets and closed some regulatory loopholes but at the cost of decreasing long-term lending to the economy. And although many banks are considered too big to fail, they are criticized for being slow to innovate and are increasingly challenged by a new generation of financial technology (fintechs) companies ready to challenge their primacy in the financial system.

The focus of some regulators has shifted from short-term concerns over financial stability to the role of banks in the economy, with the overall purpose of banking increasingly questioned and challenged. In the UK an All Party Parliamentary Review on Fair Business Banking has been examining problems between private businesses and their finance providers, while in

Australia the Royal Banking Commission has come down heavily on purported misconduct and conflicted remuneration schemes (APPG Banking, 2019; Hayne, 2019).

Banks have made progress in managing environmental and social risks at the transactional level, but their bigger role in society and the economy remains in a state of flux. Corporate leaders have begun questioning the shareholder primacy established by Milton Friedman in the 1970s, the view that seeking profits for shareholders would alone allow a company to prosper, keep people employed, and fuel the economy. In August 2019 America's most influential group of corporate leaders, the Business Roundtable, mooted a form of "conscious capitalism" whereby a company has a broader responsibility to society, which it can better serve if it considers all stakeholders in its business decisions. Meanwhile a new law in France may rewrite the 200-year-old definition of corporate purpose such that companies must now be managed "in furtherance of its corporate interest [...] while taking into consideration the social and environmental issues arising from its activity" (Robé, Delaunay and Fleury, 2019). Along these lines, Bob Eccles has further proposed that company boards should publish an annual "Statement of Purpose" that clearly articulates the company's purpose to profitably achieve value for society (Eccles, 2019).

A new age of responsible banking

Clear purpose and strategic alignment with society's goals is becoming a crucial determinant of a bank's competitiveness. Whether in its search for the most talented employees, its competition for customers, or in its engagement with shareholders, sustainability is becoming increasingly material to corporate valuations and ever more decisive to a bank's comparative advantage.

This context sets the stage for a growing constituency in the banking community recognizing that re-instilling legitimacy and trust in banks increasingly depends on the industry clearly showing its purpose and value to society.

These considerations helped inspire leaders in the banking community to come together in 2018 to draft, under the auspices of the UN, a set of global PRB. UN Secretary-General Antonio Guterres and 132 founding signatory banks formally launched the Principles at UN Headquarters on 22 September 2019. Forty-three of the bank CEOs attended the launch in person. These Principles provide a framework for defining the notion of a responsible bank for the 21st century, a bank that not only manages the risks involved with the shift towards sustainable economies, but also plays an active role in channeling financing towards new economic activities which need to be developed. Put simply, this is both greening finance and financing the green.

With the PRB, these founding banks have set out a vision for the banking industry, a clear purpose and responsibility to serve and contribute to society. The signatories committed to making society's goals an integral part of their own strategic objectives and decision-making and to aligning their strategy, portfolio, and business practices with the UN Sustainable Development Goals (SDGs) and the Paris Climate Agreement.

They aim to set a global benchmark for what it means to be a responsible bank and to provide a single framework that guides banks in clearly defining their purpose, their strategy to create value for society and shareholders while enabling them to remain competitive, to seize the opportunities of, and thrive in, a changing economy and society.

This chapter reviews the context in which a leading group of banks stepped up and drafted the PRB, and examines the individual Principles and what they will require in practice for implementation. Finally, the chapter considers whether their adoption can herald a new age of responsible banking.

HISTORY OF BANKING INDUSTRY ENVIRONMENTAL RISK MANAGEMENT

Establishment of UNEP FI and its Statement of Commitment

The UNEP Finance Initiative was created in 1991 when a small group of banks, including Deutsche Bank, HSBC Holdings, NatWest, Royal Bank of Canada, and Westpac, joined forces with the UN Environment Programme (UNEP) to catalyze banking industry awareness of the environmental agenda. In May 1992, in the run-up to the Rio Earth Summit, the *UNEP Statement by Banks on the Environment and Sustainable Development* was launched in New York and the Banking Initiative formed. Three years later, UNEP worked with a group of insurance and reinsurance companies, including General Accident, Gerling Global Re, National Provident, Storebrand, Sumitomo Marine & Fire, and Swiss Re to launch the *UNEP Statement of Environmental Commitment* by the insurance industry, and in 1997, the Insurance Industry Initiative was formed. In 2003, the banking and insurance initiatives merged into one UNEP Finance Initiative, which eventually drafted a single *UNEP Statement of Commitment by Financial Institutions on Sustainable Development* (UNEP FI, 2011).

By signing the Statement of Commitment, financial institutions recognized the role of the financial services sector in making the economy and lifestyles sustainable and committed to the integration of environmental and social considerations into *all* aspects of their operations. Financial institutions wishing to join UNEP FI were required to adhere to the Statement, although how to put it into practice remained somewhat unclear.

On UNEP FI's 25th anniversary in 2017, UNEP FI's banking members commissioned an independent review of the Statement of Commitment and its use by banking members (UNEP FI, 2017). The review considered whether the Statement should be updated or whether a set of principles specifically designed to promote responsible banking should be created. The results from this review led to the development of the PRB.

Before going into detail on the PRB's development, it is important to review other developments in the banking industry which influenced how and why environmental risk management systems where being established across the sector.

History of modern banking

Although money lending can be traced back to the ancient world, modern banking began in 16th-century Italy as an alternative to private lenders and loan sharks. The Catholic Church set clear rules from which ethical guidelines were developed to prevent usury, money lending at unreasonable rates of interest. For instance, one of the largest banks at the time, Monte di Pieta, had guidelines akin to a 21st-century corporate social responsibility statement with an emphasis on lending to women, to the local community, public institutions, and helping finance local social activities (Weber and Remer, 2011).

Credit unions and cooperative banks arose in the second half of the 18th century. Urban-centered credit unions' main clientele were the lower-income classes and the new middle class arising from the industrial revolution, from whom they collected and channeled savings into entrepreneurial initiatives to support local economic development (Weber, 2012). The cooperative banks were more rural and aimed at fighting usury and to enable savings and loans. A specific example was the establishment in 1900 in Quebec of a project by Alphonse Desjardins to allow the working class to become their own bankers. The goals of what would become Desjardins Group, now one of the largest cooperative banks in the world and a founding signatory of the PRB, included constituting a system of popular credit accessible to workers and farmers.

US super fund law and lender liability

In the 1990s, US federal and state environmental laws increased the scope of liability faced by lenders, leading banks to establish proper environmental risk management systems. The most important environmental laws were the Comprehensive Environmental Response, Compensation and Liability Act (CERCLA), known as the Superfund Law, and the Resource Conservation and Recovery Act. These federal laws imposed strict and joint liability on responsible parties for the cleanup and reimbursement of costs associated with releases of hazardous substances (Schnapf, 2005). Lender liability continued to evolve through the decade with the CERCLA Lender Liability Rule in 1992 and the 1996 Lender Liability Amendments.

Financial institutions also began to face increased environmental risk from loans or properties acquired during bank mergers or acquisitions. Banks which did not perform thorough environmental due diligence during these consolidations found themselves facing a new form of environmental liability (Ibid).

Equator Principles

In parallel to developments in the US, during the 1980s and 1990s the structural adjustment programs implemented by the World Bank and International Monetary Fund in many developing nations resulted in increasing privatization of public and state-owned services such as energy, water, resource extraction, and basic industries. This set the stage for private banks to play a larger role in infrastructure investment globally than they had previously. This trend was, however, viewed with dismay by a number of global environmental NGOs and led to the development of the Equator Principles (EP) first promulgated in 2003 then revised in 2006, 2013, and most recently in 2019 (Williams, 2013).

The EPs are a voluntary agreement among banks to set standards for assessing and managing environmental and social risk in infrastructure investment that was taken directly from International Finance Corporation (IFC) Performance Standards on Environmental and Social Sustainability. The EPs are primarily intended to provide a minimum standard for due diligence and monitoring to support responsible risk decision-making in project and related finance and advisory services, including project-related corporate loans and bridging loans above specific thresholds. As of 2019, 101 financial institutions were implementing the EP across 38 countries, representing a majority of international project finance debt within developed and emerging markets (Equator Principles, 2014).

The rise of ethical banking and the Global Alliance for Banking on Values

Although enjoying a long history, ethical banks really began to grow in the 1990s as sustainable alternatives specifically concerned with the social and environmental impacts of their investments and loans. While there are differences between ethical banks, they generally share a desire to uphold principles in the projects they finance, the most frequent including transparency and social and/or environmental values. The Global Alliance for Banking on Values (GABV) was established in 2009 as a network of ethical banks, banking cooperatives, credit unions, microfinance institutions and community development banks committed to transparency and supporting economic, social, and environmental sustainability (GABV, 2009). As of 2019, GABV comprises 55 financial institutions operating globally and collectively serving 50 million customers, with nearly US$200 billion of assets under management.

CONTRASTING THE MORE STRATEGIC APPROACH OF INVESTORS AND INSURERS

Principles for Responsible Investment

In 2005, UNEP FI's Asset Management Working Group together with the legal firm Freshfields Bruckhaus Deringer published a pivotal report on investor fiduciary duties titled *A Legal Framework for the Integration of Environmental, Social and Governance Issues into Institutional Investment* (UNEP FI, 2005). The report, widely referred to as the Freshfields report, argued that "integrating ESG considerations into an investment analysis so as to more reliably predict financial performance is clearly permissible and is arguably required in all jurisdictions" (Ibid, p.13). This led UNEP FI and the UN Global Compact to work with a group of investors to draft the Principles for Responsible Investment (PRI), which were launched in 2007 by UN Secretary-General Kofi Annan and 20 institutional investors on the balcony of the New York Stock Exchange.

The PRI aimed to incorporate ESG issues into mainstream investment decision-making and ownership practices. At that time, there were relatively few globally applicable codes of conduct or frameworks that specifically linked responsible or sustainable practice and long-term asset management and investment by either the public or private sector.

Many of the PRI signatories have since established processes to research and analyze ESG issues and to take account of these in their investment processes, and there are now multiple examples of these issues materially affecting investment decisions. Today, the PRI has grown to over 2,700 signatories collectively managing US$89 trillion in assets.

Leaving the early progress of the UNEP FI Statement of Commitment aside, the establishment of the PRI was the first time that a global normative effort began to shift the focus of financial institutions from transactional environmental/social risks management to more institution-wide strategic ESG considerations. For example, the first of the six PRI principles states "Principle 1: We will incorporate ESG issues into investment analysis and decision-making processes" (PRI, 2020). The other five PRI principles are similarly brief, strategic, and high level in nature.

In comparison, the EPs are much more detailed and meant for environmental and social risk management specialists. For example, Principle 1 states as follows:

> When a Project is proposed for financing, the EPFI (Equator Principle Finance Institution) will, as part of its internal environmental and social review and due diligence, categorise the Project based on the magnitude of potential environmental and social risks and impacts, including those related to Human rights, climate change, and biodiversity. Such categorisation is based on the International Finance Corporation's (IFC) environmental and social categorisation process.
>
> (Equator Principles, 2014)

This is only half of the EP Principle 1 wording, after which a project categorization is provided and then the following closing statement: "The EPFI's environmental and social due diligence is commensurate with the nature, scale and stage of the Project, and with the categorised level of environmental and social risks and impacts" (Equator Principles, 2014).

Whereas the PRI principles take up half a page of text, the EPs are 17 pages long, indicating that they are meant for a more technical audience and not intended to be familiar to leadership and senior management within the financial institutions that have adopted them.

Based on the approach employed by the PRI, this shift towards higher-level, institutional-wide approaches was then picked up by the insurers for their insurance underwriting lines of business.

Principles for Sustainable Insurance (PSI)

The Principles for Sustainable Insurance (PSI) were launched with the support of UN Secretary-General Ban Ki-moon in 2012 as the product of a multi-year negotiation by industry players and UNEP FI. This framework established the norm for the global insurance industry to address environmental, social, and governance risks and opportunities.

When the process to develop the PSI was initiated, there were very few, if any, global initiatives that created both a framework to drive change and awareness in the insurance industry or directly linked sustainability to the industry's risk or operational considerations. There were, however, examples from around the world of insurers proactively identifying and managing climate change risk and risk to biodiversity and ecosystems as well as insurers tackling the needs of the poor communities and those underserviced by insurance products.

National and regional codes and principles

Focusing in geographically, a number of countries, regions, and banking associations around the world have adopted specific codes of conduct and principles that apply on either a voluntary or mandatory basis to banking industry actors within those jurisdictions. In 2012 the Nigerian Central Bank adopted Nigerian Principles for Sustainable Banking. Also in 2012, China's Banking and Regulatory Commission published Green Credit Guidelines aimed at encouraging banks to adjust their credit structures, to manage environmental and social risks, better serve the real economy, and promote transformation and new models of economic growth.

Meanwhile, banking associations in Ghana, Kenya, South Africa, India, Brazil, and China also began addressing environmental and social issues through a variety of policy and voluntary instruments. Common elements included building awareness of and incorporating ESG risk assessment into transactions to be financed, the engagement of stakeholders, developing green credit lines, programs, and products, and adopting commitments.

The central banks of many countries also began working collaboratively with the International Finance Corporation to create or enhance green credit guidelines or banking principles in a number of different countries where such instruments currently do not exist.

2015 AS A LANDMARK YEAR FOR SUSTAINABILITY UPTAKE

The inflection point for the banking community came in 2015. Fifteen years earlier, at the turn of the millennium, 191 governments had come together to establish the Millennium Development Goals, or MDGs, a set of eight global goals to be achieved by 2015. The MDGs framed global development priorities such as eradicating extreme poverty and hunger, reducing child mortality, and improving maternal health, helping build a common language focusing limited aid flows and other public resources on human development needs. Although they helped generate some major advancements and improvements, MDG progress was uneven and by 2012 UN Secretary-General Ban Ki-moon was starting to plan for a Post-2015 UN Development Agenda. This ultimately led to the drafting by 195 governments of the UN 2030 Agenda for Sustainable Development with its 17 SDGs, launched in New York in September 2015.

Meanwhile on the climate front, after the failure of climate negotiations in Copenhagen at the 2009 Conference of Parties to the UN Framework Convention on Climate Change (COP15), countries began to regroup and eventually agreed in Paris in December 2015 on a landmark agreement for stabilizing global climate change.

These two UN agreements marked the first time that the private sector was significantly engaged in successful outcomes. This was in part due to a strategy initiated by the UN Secretary-General to foster mutual signaling between governments and the private sector on the need to deliver ambitious agreements.

The financial sector was particularly engaged. In the lead-up to Paris, over 400 investors, representing more than US$24 trillion in assets, signed a Global Investor Statement on Climate Change calling for a robust agreement and clear market signal on climate policy (IIGCC, 2015). The PRI launched that year the Montreal Pledge, which had investors committing to measure and publicly disclose the carbon footprint of their investment portfolios, while UNEP FI and CDP launched the Portfolio Decarbonization Coalition aiming to mobilize institutional investors committed to decarbonizing their portfolios.

Investors and insurers were more visibly acting in 2015, but in the following years banks started to engage, in large part due to pressures coming from new areas. Banking regulators, starting with Mark Carney, Governor of the Bank of England and Chair of the Financial Stability Board, began to speak about climate change and the need for actors in the financial sector to take heed of climate risk exposure within company strategy and portfolios. The French and Dutch central bank governors started to send similar signals and by 2018 a new Network for Greening the Financial System was established of central banks and financial supervisors.

Although banker participation on the Taskforce for Climate Related Financial Disclosures was limited, the reporting guidance was picked up quickly by the industry and significant effort employed, including through UNEP FI, to develop appropriate methodologies for forward-looking scenario analysis of future physical and transitional climate risks.

A growing body of investors, particularly coming from the Nordic markets, also began to influence bank greening via the capital markets. In the green bonds market, commercial banks became the largest class of issuer, ahead of corporates and the development banks, who had been the main players early on.

A few years on from the 2015 launch of the SDGs and the Paris Climate Agreement, the banking sector was doing a lot to help build out the green finance market, using increasing financial innovation to build out portfolios in areas such as renewable energies and other low-carbon infrastructure. But the overall impact on loan books and bank strategy remained limited, indicating that something more was needed.

THE PRINCIPLES FOR RESPONSIBLE BANKING

Ever since the launch of the PRI in 2007, the banking community had been considering whether to draft their own set of principles. Banks were initially reluctant given their use of other frameworks, including the EPs and later the Green Bond Principles. However, by 2017, when UNEP FI conducted a survey of its banking members, the majority view had shifted, leading UNEP FI's Banking Committee to commission a review of its Statement of Commitment. The results from this review pointed towards the need for banks to go the Principles route as the Statement was viewed to be outdated and the existing frameworks all transactional in nature, lacking the higher-level strategic orientation needed for banks to navigate the new sustainability-oriented challenges and opportunities.

UNEP FI's Banking Committee subsequently invited interested members to join a Core Group of banks to draft a set of PRB. This Core Group numbered 30 banks from around the world, including some of the largest, but also some small and many varied in their local contexts and lines of business. The Core Group, advised by a group of 12 civil society institutions to take account of wider societal considerations, released in November 2018 a draft set of Principles for a six-month consultation process during which 250 banks and more than 500 stakeholders provided inputs.

With the PRB, the Core Group of banks aimed to set a global benchmark for what it means to be a responsible bank and to provide a single framework that guides banks in clearly defining their purpose and their strategy to create value for society and shareholders while remaining competitive in a changing economy.

The PRB, as drafted and later adjusted and finalized, include a preamble and six specific principles on: alignment, impact and target-setting, clients and customers, stakeholders, governance and culture, and transparency and accountability (see Figure 8.1).

Several aspects of the PRB framework are unique, from the focus on aligning all lines of business to contribute to individual needs and societal goals to the forward-looking orientation around impact assessment and target-setting, and finally to having a firm accountability framework with assurance of signatory reporting.

PRINCIPLE 1: ALIGNMENT	**PRINCIPLE 2: IMPACT & TARGET SETTING**	**PRINCIPLE 3: CLIENT & CUSTOMERS**
We will align our business strategy to be consistent with and contribute to individuals' needs and society's goals, as expressed in the Sustainable Development Goals, the Paris Climate Agreement and relevant national and regional frameworks.	We will continuously increase our positive impacts while reducing the negative impacts on, and managing the risks to, people and environment resulting from our activities, products and services. To this end, we will set and publish targets where we can have the most significant impacts.	We will work responsibly with our clients and our customers to encourage sustainable practices and enable economic activities that create shared prosperity for current and future generation.
PRINCIPLE 4: STAKEHOLDERS	**PRINCIPLE 5: GOVERNANCE & CULTURE**	**PRINCIPLE 6: TRANSPARENCY & ACCOUNTABILITY**
We will proactively and responsibly consult, engage and partner with relevant stakeholders to achieve society's goals.	We will implement our commitment to these Principles through effective governance and a culture of responsible banking.	We will periodically review our individual and collective implementation of these Principles and be transparent about and accountable for our positive and negative impacts and our contribution to society's goals.

FIGURE 8.1 The Principles for Responsible Banking
Source: UNEP FI

In their October ESG Research Report published soon after the Principles were launched, Moody's Investor Services noted that they expect the Principles "to have more far reaching implications for the banking industry than previous sustainability initiatives. [...] Target setting, transparency and accountability are key features of the principles, which will facilitate market scrutiny of bank progress and compliance" (Moody's Investor Service, 2019).

The following sections present the preamble and six PRB principles individually and explain some of the implications for their application by signatories. Reference is made to the framework documents and particularly to the Reporting Framework, which includes accountability requirements for each Principle. There is a specific timeline for implementation that banks must meet, or risk being delisted. This is explained under Principle 6.

> PREAMBLE: Banks play a key role in society. As financial intermediaries, it is our purpose to help develop sustainable economies and to empower people to build better futures. Banking is based on the trust our customers and wider society put in us to serve their best interests and to act responsibly. Our success and ability to remain profitable and relevant is intrinsically dependent on the long-term prosperity of the societies we serve. We believe that only in an inclusive society founded on human dignity, equality and the sustainable use of natural resources, can our clients and customers and, in turn, our businesses thrive. We therefore want to take a leadership role and use our products, services and relationships to support and accelerate the fundamental changes in our economies and lifestyles necessary to achieve shared prosperity for both current and future generations.

The preamble provides a framing to establish the purpose of the PRB as a new framework for redefining the role of banking in society. It is closely linked to the first principle on alignment.

> Principle 1 – ALIGNMENT: We will align our business strategy to be consistent with and contribute to individuals' needs and society's goals, as expressed in the Sustainable Development Goals, the Paris Climate Agreement and relevant national and regional frameworks.

Along with the Preamble, Principle 1 sets out the objective and vision of the Principles: aligning a bank's strategy with society's goals. This means elevating sustainability considerations, a bank's contribution to society – from the transactional level to the strategic level – making society's goals an integral part of a bank's own strategic objectives.

The UN agreements cited in Principle 1, the SDGs and the Climate Agreement, articulate globally agreed challenges to meeting an individual's needs and building a more sustainable future. By aligning bank strategy with society's goals, it shows that its business, and the products and services it provides, can support a sustainable future while achieving long-term business benefits. It signals that the bank accepts its shared responsibility for shaping and securing our common future.

While the SDGs and the Paris Climate Agreement are directed at governments, they are underpinned by a series of specific targets and program areas where banks can make substantial contributions and, by doing so, align themselves clearly with the needs of society, their countries, clients, and customers. In Boxes 8.1 and 8.2, Standard Bank and CIMB provide two examples of banks aligning their business strategy with society's goals in a national or regional context.

Box 8.1 Standard Bank – How an African bank targets impact

This African banking group's strategy is underpinned by the understanding that the profitability of the banking group in the long term depends on the stability and wellbeing of the African continent (where it has operations in 20 countries), and that its pursuit of profit should produce outcomes that are beneficial to the societies, economies, and environments in which it does business. Its purpose and strategy are to drive sustainable and inclusive growth across Africa by meeting the needs of Africa's people, its entrepreneurs, and businesses; these needs overlap with the SDGs. As such, positively impacting on the achievement of the SDGs is integrated into the bank's strategy. Positive impact is both a driver of sustainable financial value, and an outcome of doing the right business, the right way. The bank has identified seven areas in which it will drive impact: health; education; infrastructure; financial inclusion; climate change; jobs and enterprises; and African trade and investment.

Box 8.2 CIMB – How a Malaysian bank integrates the SDGs with Islamic banking

Activities supported by Islamic banks are in line with Islamic law, which emphasizes the maximization of benefits to individuals and society and the minimization of harm. The main areas of consideration tend to be the protection of morality and life, family, intellect, and wealth. These elements form the primary basis of the business screens used by Islamic banks. As the SDGs address the most necessary elements of these considerations, they can be used to augment existing screens and form a useful yardstick for Islamic banks in managing both the positive and negative impacts of their activities.

In terms of the requirements set out in the PRB framework documents, banks are required to describe how they are aligning their business strategies with these societal needs. The bank's business strategy may be articulated in one or across several of its strategy documents.

To achieve this alignment with society's goals requires first and foremost that the banks understand and implement the notion of impact assessment and target-setting across their different lines of business.

> Principle 2 – IMPACT & TARGET SETTING: We will continuously increase our positive impacts while reducing the negative impacts on, and managing the risks to, people and environment resulting from our activities, products and services. To this end, we will set and publish targets where we can have the most significant impacts.

In the Preamble to the Principles, the banks define their purpose as helping to develop sustainable economies and to empower people to build better futures. To put this purpose into practice, banks need to identify, assess, and improve the impact on people and planet resulting from their activities, products, and services. For the banks to continuously increase positive impact while reducing negative impact, they need to incorporate assessment of risks and impacts on all three dimensions of sustainability (environmental, social, and economic) into business decision-making at strategic, portfolio, and transaction levels. This constitutes a significant change in viewpoint: this is no longer just about what impacts do developments in the world have on a bank's portfolio, but what impact does the bank's portfolio have on the world? Banks commit to assess and be transparent about their impact – positive and negative.

The impact analysis is informed by the bank's core business areas, its products and services across the main geographies that the bank operates in, its major client areas in terms of industries and technologies, the most relevant challenges and priorities related to sustainable development in the countries/regions it operates in, and the scale and intensity/salience of the actual and potential social, economic, and environmental impacts. The bank should engage with relevant stakeholders, including civil society, to inform aspects of the analysis.

Although conducting impact analysis across all lines of business is a significant undertaking, what really distinguishes these Principles from other frameworks is a clear mechanism for driving ambition and continuous improvement: target-setting. Principle 2 requires banks to identify their most significant impacts and to set a minimum of two targets that address at least two of the identified impact areas. Chosen targets need to be in the areas where the bank has the most significant impact, so banks are required to focus where it matters most.

Example approaches to impact assessment and target-setting are described in text boxes for the Dutch bank ING and the largest bank in the world, Industrial and Commercial Bank of China (see Box 8.3 and Box 8.4).

Box 8.3 ING – A European bank setting climate targets

Based in the Netherlands, ING has a loan book of approximately €600 billion, which it intends to use to contribute to the Paris goal of keeping global warming well below two degrees Celsius. To do this, the bank intends to focus on the sectors in its loan book that are responsible for most GHG emissions, including energy, automotive, shipping and aviation, steel, cement, residential mortgages, and commercial real estate.

The bank is among a few in the industry that have been developing methodologies to align their portfolios with a well-below two-degree pathway. Specifically, the bank aims to double by 2022 its funding to sectors and companies that contribute to a low-carbon economy, including in areas such as renewable energy and the circular economy. ING has also committed to reduce its coal exposure to nearly zero by 2025. The Principles require that the bank now sets a specific timeline with milestones for achieving its climate-related targets.

The bank also intends to set a second target in a non-climate area for which they first plan to undertake a much more detailed assessment of their social, economic, and environmental impacts before deciding where the most progress can be made and the sort of target and implementation plan needed to get there.

Box 8.4 ICBC – World's largest bank responding to policy objectives

With over US$7 trillion in assets, Industrial and Commercial Bank of China is the largest bank in the world. As a state-owned bank, it has a responsibility to respond to policy objectives, which include poverty alleviation, green finance, inclusive finance, and social welfare.

As part of its poverty relief policy, the bank has provided loans to farmers, allowing them to use technology in getting connected to the market and selling their produce. As part of its policy to drive green finance, ICBC has issued two climate bonds with the purpose of financing solar power, wind power, low-carbon transport, and marine renewable energy.

The bank has indicated that it is planning to set a target to strengthen its contribution to the Paris Climate Agreement and, in line with China's priorities, to set a second target that furthers the work the bank is doing in the areas of financial inclusion or air pollution

The targets of PRB signatories, and their level of ambition, should be linked to the SDGs, Paris Climate Agreement, and other relevant national, regional, or international frameworks. Targets may be qualitative or quantitative but are expected to be specific, measurable, achievable, relevant, and time-bound (SMART). Banks are required to establish milestones for monitoring progress against their targets. When setting and monitoring progress against targets, banks should be conscious of any negative impacts that may result from this process and should address these as they arise. By setting public targets, banks commit themselves to a clear ambition and course of action towards external stakeholders and – more importantly – internal teams.

Banks are expected to revise their targets and establish additional targets at their own pace. However, banks are required to have set a minimum of two targets within the first four years of implementing the Principles. They are also expected to put in place a governance and oversight structure responsible for monitoring target implementation and, if required, remedial action.

Banks achieve this improvement in impact and deliver on their targets by following Principle 3.

Principle 3 – CLIENTS & CUSTOMERS: We will work responsibly with our clients and our customers to encourage sustainable practices and enable economic activities that create shared prosperity for current and future generations.

A bank's most significant impacts on society, the economy, and the environment are indirect. Thus, banks can achieve some of their most significant contributions to society's goals by working with their customers and clients and by accompanying and proactively supporting their customers and clients in their transition towards more sustainable technologies, business models, and lifestyles.

Banks are vital economic intermediaries and as such can make their most significant contributions to society's goals by creating synergies with customers and clients, encouraging sustainable practices and accompanying their customers and clients in their transition towards more sustainable business models and practice. In addition to contributing towards shared prosperity for current and future generations, enabling sustainable economic activities in this way presents a clear business case for banks: clients that are shifting to sustainable business models and technologies are better prepared for emerging regulations and changes in market sentiment. Accompanying their clients in their own journeys to contribute to society's goals enables stronger relationships with customers and clients and positions the bank as the partner of choice. Further, getting to know the bank's customers and client's better drives business growth and supports improved risk management. A strong relationship between the banks and its clients and customers – built on trust – is crucial for any bank's success. Responsible conduct is the foundation of trust.

In line with the PRB Framework Documents, signatories are required to report – at a high level – on how their policies and practices promote responsible conduct on the part of their clients and customers, encouraging sustainable practices and enabling sustainable economic activities.

Banks on their own can only make so much progress in achieving society's goals. Stakeholders have important roles to play and are the subject of Principle 4.

Principle 4 – STAKEHOLDERS: We will proactively and responsibly consult, engage and partner with relevant stakeholders to achieve society's goals.

To help create an enabling environment for the economic and social changes required to achieve society's goals, banks need to work and transparently engage with policymakers and regulators, employees, academia and civil society, trade unions, and communities. To understand their impact, understand how they affect people and the environment, and how they can align better with societies goals requires banks to consult, listen to, and engage with this broad range of stakeholders. Proactively consulting stakeholders ensures that a bank benefits from their knowledge and drives legitimacy and capacity to identify positive and negative impacts.

In line with the PRB Framework Documents, signatories are required to consult, engage, collaborate, and/or partner with relevant stakeholders for the purpose of implementing the Principles, which includes engaging on its impacts. Banks are required to give a high-level account of the stakeholders they identified and engaged with, as well as the key issues raised by stakeholders and how they were addressed by the bank.

Successfully implementing these first four Principles and aligning a bank with society's goals will require anchoring them in day-to-day business practice.

Principle 5 – GOVERNANCE & CULTURE: We will implement our commitment to these Principles through effective governance and a culture of responsible banking.

For banks' strategic objectives regarding their contribution to society's goals to be implemented effectively, they need to become part of day-to-day decision-making and the bank's culture. To be able to respond with the speed and scale necessary to address global challenges requires leadership, buy-in, and active support of the board of directors, the CEO, and senior and middle management. It requires establishing a daily business culture and practice in which all employees understand their role in delivering the bank's purpose and to integrate sustainability in their work and their decision-making. Clarity of purpose not only drives change; it also enables transparency and accountability.

In line with the PRB Framework Documents, banks are required to develop governance structures that enable and support effective implementation of the Principles. This includes having appropriate structures, policies, and processes in place to manage significant impacts and risks, and to achieve set targets. Signatories are also required to disclose measures being implemented to foster a culture of responsible banking among its employees. Box 8.5 provides some examples of how European banks are integrating sustainability-related considerations into the performance assessment and remuneration of staff.

From alignment, through impact assessment and target-setting, new approaches to client, customer, and stakeholder engagement, and finally the governance needed to drive this new agenda through the organization, the final principle is outward-looking, creating the transparency and accountability for commitments and progress made.

Box 8.5 European approaches to establishing governance and culture

Banks are beginning to incorporate sustainability-related considerations into the performance assessment and remuneration of staff throughout the organization, including for their executive committees and board members. Aligning remuneration programs with the sustainability agenda creates awareness, delivers action, and demonstrates credibility.

For example, a major European bank measures the share of its lending portfolio that strictly contributes to at least one of the 17 SDGs. This indicator is embedded in a set of sustainability-linked KPIs (e.g., exposure to renewable power sector, operational carbon footprint, number of individuals that have benefited from a financial education session provided by the group, etc.). Part of the long-term compensation for the bank's 5,000 top managers across the group is linked to these criteria.

Another European bank has a Corporate Responsibility Committee (CRC), chaired by its CEO, which has the overall oversight of the implementation of the PRB. The CRC reports directly to the Board Ethics Committee and Executive Committee. High-level "Ambassadors for Responsible Banking" have been appointed by the CEO, which include top executive managers and a working group coordinated by the CRC, to develop an implementation action plan. The bank is in the process of incorporating the Principles into its sustainability policy and in other policies (e.g., credit, risk, human resources).

And a third European bank has set up a "responsible banking, sustainability, and culture committee" to assist the board of directors in fulfilling its oversight responsibilities with respect to the responsible business strategy and sustainability issues of the company.

Principle 6 – TRANSPARENCY & ACCOUNTABILITY: We will periodically review our individual and collective implementation of these Principles and be transparent about and accountable for our positive and negative impacts and our contribution to society's goals.

Banks are accountable to shareholders, employees, and society for their positive and negative impact and with that their contribution to society's goals. They thus commit to integrate information on PRB implementation in their annual public reporting. Public disclosure is critical because it enables internal and external stakeholders to assess a bank's contribution to society, and the progress it is making. This, in turn, helps build confidence in the bank's sustainability-related commitments and helps to distinguish it from its competitors. Making targets public and reporting progress increases the potential for success in achieving them. Progress reports are key to ensuring the effectiveness of approaches, to motivating employees, competing with peers, driving innovation, and strengthening reputation and trust.

In line with the PRB Framework Documents, banks are required to provide information on their implementation of the Principles in their existing public reporting within the first 18 months of becoming a signatory, and every year thereafter. Reporting should include information about their positive and negative impacts, risks, and targets.

Using the PRB Reporting and Self-Assessment Template, banks are expected to provide references/links to where in their public reporting the relevant information on their implementation of the Principles can be found (UNEP FI, 2019). In the same template, banks assess their progress against six criteria: (1) impact analysis, (2) target-setting, (3) plans for target implementation and monitoring, (4) progress on implementing targets, (5) governance structure for implementation of the Principles, and (6) progress on implementing the Principles.

Limited assurance is required of bank self-assessments and must be included in the bank's reporting. Where third-party assurance is not feasible, an independent review may be conducted.

Based on the signatory banks' aggregated individual reporting, UNEP FI will take stock of collective signatory progress and publish an assessment every two years. This periodic review of collective progress will support continuous improvement, enable banks to share lessons learned, and establish the credibility of the Principles, signatory banks, and of the sector as a whole.

PRB AS A TOOL FOR POLICY ENGAGEMENT

As previously described, what makes the PRB framework unique for the financial sector is the impact assessment and target-setting process, asking signatories to provide forward guidance on the bank's strategy and projected contributions to society's most significant challenges. The signaling this provides is both internal, as business targets to be allocated and tracked across the organization, and external, communicating to investors, customers, civil society, regulators, and policymakers.

Governments also provide their own forward guidance on many of the issues that the banks will be focusing on. For instance, the parties to the UN Framework Convention on Climate Change have agreed a "Paris Rulebook," the set of the rules that makes the Paris Agreement operative. This Rulebook spells out how countries plan their national climate actions and how they review individual and collective progress to strengthen climate commitments over time.

Clearly, there are similarities between what the Paris Rulebook means for governments and what the PRB means for bank signatories. The PRB can be described as a Paris Rulebook for the banking sector.

A government which sets national climate mitigation and adaptation targets will need to propose appropriate policy actions and investment requirements, including how much capital they expect to be mobilized through the private sector, where public financing may be required, and how it can be deployed most effectively. Countries undergoing such policy developments – most today – can benefit from a dialogue with PRB signatories, and particularly those focusing efforts on climate action. Bringing together the public and private sectors in this way can help to make the capital mobilization challenge more feasible and based on current and expected future realities.

This policy engagement potential goes far beyond climate change to the rest of the SDGs and other major societal challenges. A current example would be the Green New Deal proposed by European Commission President von der Leyen in December 2019 (European Commission, 2019). This Green Deal legislative package for driving green economic development across the continent is projected to require €260 billion of additional annual investment, about 1.5% of 2018 GDP, to achieve 2030 climate and energy targets. Some of this will come from the public treasury but much of it will rely on the private sector to deliver. These capital mobilization targets are useful for European PRB signatories to consider in their planning, and the aggregate of their relevant announced targets will also help Brussels in assessing the feasibility of public projections.

CONCLUSION: WILL THE PRB HERALD A
NEW AGE OF RESPONSIBLE BANKING?

This chapter has reviewed recent developments in the banking industry on sustainability integration and specifically how the newly launched PRB heralds a new age for the industry in setting out a clear framework for what it is to be a responsible bank.

The notion of responsible banking conduct dates back to 16th-century Italy and has constantly been evolving up through the Superfund-related environmental liabilities of the 1980s, the EPs for project finance in the 1990s, up to the present-day increasingly sophisticated environmental and social risks management systems most banks have in place.

However, a wider and somewhat more strategic ESG focus of investors has, along with financial regulators and civil society, been increasing the pressure on banks to step up more strategically and holistically in response to the Paris Climate Agreement and the SDGs. In response, the PRB are the product of a group of leading banks seeking to ratchet up ambition and more clearly define the notion of responsible banking.

Drafting the PRB in the post-2015 world made it different from previous frameworks, going beyond responsibility being simply a risk management approach to integrating the purpose of a bank and the impact that it has with and through its clients. This "outcomes" focused orientation and the requirement to set targets and show continuous improvement orients responsible banking more towards business strategy and implementation. This places the emphasis on results and accountability rather than enumerating policies and procedures.

It is still very early days for the PRB. 132 banks signed up in September 2019 as founding signatories, together representing US$47 trillion, a little over one-third of global banking assets. But signing is only the first step. Now, these banks need to establish the systems and capacities to deliver. Many will be watching their actions carefully. Only when targets are set, and clear progress made towards meeting them, will the PRB become a framework fit for defining the notion of the responsible bank, one that is oriented towards financing the greatest needs of society.

NOTE

1   The author wishes to acknowledge the significant efforts on the part of the Core Group of Banks who took the leadership in drafting the Principles for Responsible Banking, the UNEP FI Banking Team, led by Simone Dettling, who so ably facilitated the process, Puleng Ndjwili-Potele, who drafted the Guidance Documents and provided much material to this chapter, and Bruce Usher and Jonathan Clayton, who provided thoughtful feedback on the chapter draft.

REFERENCES

APPG Banking (2019) *Levelling the playing field between businesses and their lenders* [Online]. Available at: www.appgbanking.org.uk/ (Accessed: 20 January 2020).

Eccles, B. (2019) 'The Statement of Purpose and What You Need to Do', *Forbes* (23 August) [Online]. Available at: www.forbes.com/sites/bobeccles/2019/08/23/the-statement-of-purpose-and-what-you-need-to-do/#4bddb7df2393 (Accessed: 20 January 2020).

Equator Principles (2014) *The Equator Principles* [Online]. Available at: https://equator-principles.com/about/ (Accessed: 20 January 2020).

European Commission (2019) *The European Green Deal*. Brussels, 11.12.2019, COM(2019) 640 final. Available at: https://ec.europa.eu/info/sites/info/files/european-green-deal-communication_en.pdf(Accessed: 20 January 2020).

GABV (2009) *About the Global Alliance for Banking on Values* [Online]. Available at: www.gabv.org/about-us (Accessed: 20 January 2020).

Hayne, K.M. (2019) 'Royal Commission into Misconduct in the Banking, Superannuation and Financial Services Industry', *Interim report, Commonwealth of Australia*. Available online: https://financialservices.royalcommission.gov.au/Pages/default.aspx (Accessed: 20 January 2020).

IIGCC (2015) *Global Investor Statement On Climate Change* [Online]. Available at: www.iigcc.org/download/20142015-global-investor-statement-on-climate-change/?wpdmdl=1599&refresh=-5dac4481ebec41571570817 (Accessed: 20 January 2020).

Moody's Investor Service (2019) 'ESG Research Report', October Edition. London: Moody's Investor Service.

Principles for Responsible Investment (PRI) (2020). 'What Are the Principles for Responsible Investment?', Available at: www.unpri.org/pri/an-introduction-to-responsible-investment/what-are-the-principles-for-responsible-investment (Accessed: 20 January 2020).

Robé, J.P., Delaunay, B., and Fleury, B. (2019) *French Legislation on Corporate Purpose* [Online]. Available at: https://corpgov.law.harvard.edu/2019/06/08/french-legislation-on-corporate-pur-pose/ (Accessed: 20 January 2020).

Schnapf, L. (2005) *Making the World Safe for Banks and Commercial Real Estate Developers: Overview of Lender Liability under Environmental Laws* [Online]. Available at: www.environmental-law.net/wp-content/uploads/2011/07/OverviewofLenderLiabilityUnderEnvironmentalLaws.doc+&cd=1&hl=en&ct=clnk&gl=dk (Accessed: 20 January 2020).

UNEP FI (2005) *A Legal Framework for the Integration of Environmental, Social and Governance Issues into Institutional Investment* [Online]. Available at: www.unepfi.org/fileadmin/docu-ments/freshfields_legal_resp_20051123.pdf (Accessed: 20 January 2020).

UNEP FI (2011) *History of the Statement* [Online]. Available at: www.unepfi.org/about/unep-fi-state-ment/history-of-the-statement/ (Accessed: 20 January 2020).

UNEP FI (2017) *North America Regional Roundtable, Banking Session* (20.09.2017). Available online: www.unepfi.org/wordpress/wp-content/uploads/2017/09/EXTRANET-9-35-Simone-BankingSession_20.09.pdf (Accessed: 20 January 2020).

UNEP FI (2019) *PRB Reporting and Self-Assessment Template* [Online]. Available at: www.unepfi.org/prb-reporting-and-self-assessment-template/ (Accessed: 20 January 2020).

Weber, O. (2012) 'Sustainable Banking–History and Current Developments', [Online]. Available at: https://papers.ssrn.com/sol3/papers.cfm?abstract_id=2159947 (Accessed: 20. 01.2020).

Weber, O. and Remer, S. (2011). *Social Banks and the Future of Sustainable Finance*. New York: Routledge, pp. 15–47.

Williams, C.A. (2013) 'Regulating the Impacts of International Project Financing: The Equator Principles', *Proceedings of the ASIL Annual Meeting* (Vol. 107, pp. 303–308). Cambridge University Press.

9

Corporate purpose in play

The role of ESG investing[1]

John G. Ruggie

INTRODUCTION

On August 19, 2019, the U.S. Business Roundtable (BR), comprising the CEOs of more than 200 of America's largest corporations, issued a new mission statement on "the purpose of a corporation" (BR, 2019a). The press release noted that each periodic update on principles of corporate governance since 1997 had endorsed the principle of maximizing shareholder value. In contrast, the new statement commits signatory CEOs "to lead their companies for the benefit of all stakeholders – customers, employees, suppliers, communities and shareholders" (BR, 2019b). "[Milton] Friedman must be turning in his grave," a *Fortune* magazine article declared (Murray, 2019).

Such shifts are not unprecedented. Indeed, Friedman bore significant intellectual responsibility for the last one. William Allen, a highly regarded former Chancellor of the Delaware Court of Chancery, authored an essay some years ago entitled "Our Schizophrenic Conception of the Business Corporation" (Allen, 1992). Allen's thesis was that over the course of the twentieth century there were "two quite different and inconsistent ways to conceptualize the public corporation and legitimate its power. I will call them the property conception and the social entity conception" (Ibid, p. 264). By the property conception he meant that the corporation is literally seen – in the literature and in the courts – as the property of the individuals who constitute the firm. That made perfect sense, Allen affirmed, when the main players actually were a limited number of natural persons who had come together for the purpose of capital formation.[2] It began to make less sense, he states, as the scale and

scope of the modern corporation grew massively, requiring distinctive management skills and risk-sharing through widely dispersed stock holdings.

What Allen called the social entity conception of the corporation became the
predominant form around the time of the New Deal, a time of socioeconomic
crisis. Contributors of capital certainly needed to be assured a decent rate
of return to induce them to invest in a company. "But the corporation has
other purposes of perhaps equal dignity: the satisfaction of consumer wants,
the provision of meaningful employment opportunities, and the making
of a contribution to the public life of its communities" (Ibid, p. 271). This
conception prevailed well into the post-World War II era. By the 1980s,
however, Allen saw the United States reverting to the property conception.
Friedman, already in his famous 1970 *New York Times Magazine* article,
had equated shareholders with business "owners," and considered directors as well as executives as the owners' employees (Friedman, 1970). This
binary differentiation subsequently became the basis for part ideology and
part academic paradigm in the form of principal–agent theory (Jensen and
Meckling, 1976). Allen attributed its broader uptake in the 1980s to innovations in the technology of stock trading, the pressure of growing competition
from globalization, and the upsurge of leveraged corporate takeovers. In
1986, a Delaware court held (in *Revlon v. MacAndrews & Forbes*[3]) that once
a firm was already on the auction block, its directors had the fiduciary duty
to secure the highest share price available. The generalized shareholder primacy doctrine emerged from this mix. By 2001 it was heralded to be nothing
less than "The End of History for Corporate Law" (Hansman and Kraakman,
2001). It became a staple in shaping business school training, corporate law
teaching, and securities regulation.

So, should we consider the BR's mission statement as schizophrenia redux?
As an attempt to preempt left-of-center politicians? A significant normative
departure in the direction of a "stakeholder theory" of the firm (Freeman,
1984)? Unnecessary, because most of those companies already take stakeholder concerns into consideration, and even under Delaware law they have
the discretionary power to do so given the "business judgment rule"? Or, as
IBM CEO Ginni Rometty put it, is it a means for business to regain its "social
license to operate" in the post financial crisis world? (quoted in Murray, 2019).

Of course, at this point no one can know how or even if the idea of "repurposing" the corporation will shape actual day-to-day business conduct. But
it seems safe to conjecture that, whatever the immediate motivations for the
BR statement may have been, the move toward a more social entity conception of the public corporation that it implies will be reinforced by the
remarkable rise of ESG investing – taking into account a company's environmental, social, and governance policies in making investment decisions.
That is my focus in this chapter.

The chapter is organized in three parts. The first briefly summarizes why the narrowly construed shareholder primacy doctrine simply hasn't been an adequate conceptual foundation for the public corporation for some time. The second sketches out the rise of ESG investing, its performance, and its potential role in reinforcing corporate "repurposing." The third addresses potential impediments to the further rapid growth in ESG investing as well as moves to manage them – obstacles posed by traditional practices in the investment industry as well as by weaknesses in ESG itself. A brief conclusion wraps up the chapter.

LETTING GO OF MILTON FRIEDMAN[4]

It is a disservice to the legacy of a brilliant Nobel laureate in economics to keep invoking him in support for the shareholder primacy doctrine. Yes, a half-century ago Friedman wrote "The Social Responsibility of Business is to Increase its Profits," so long as it stays within the rules of the game (Friedman, 1970). He first articulated the core principles even earlier in *Capitalism and Freedom*, a book that has sold more than a half-million copies over the years (Friedman, 1962). But the world in which Friedman lived, thought, and wrote about in his popular works was fundamentally different from ours, which his intellectual progenies today seem to ignore. I make just two points.

The first concerns foundational confusion regarding the concept of property as it applies to the public corporation: "In a free-enterprise, private-property system," Friedman wrote, "a corporate executive is an employee of the owners of the business" (1970, p. 33). But in today's world, owning shares in a large public company with dispersed shareholding does not make one an owner of the company. Friedman's Chicago colleague and fellow Nobel laureate Eugene Fama challenged the equation of the two long ago (Fama, 1980, p. 290):

> Ownership of capital should not be confused with ownership of the firm. Each factor in a firm is owned by somebody ... Dispelling the tenacious notion that a firm is owned by its security holders is important because it is a first step toward understanding that control over a firm's decisions is not necessarily the province of security holders.

And yet, almost a half-century after Friedman's writings, the *Wall Street Journal* (2019) pilloried the BR statement for not "serving the interests of the shareholders who own the company." This is not merely a theoretical issue. It matters for very practical reasons: it reinforces the deep divide in the American variant of capitalism between "private" and "social," which the Business Roundtable statement presumably sought to address and help bridge.

Fama had argued the case on analytical grounds; he viewed the corporation as a nexus of contracts between different parties that contribute to the firm. Empirically, the point he made has greater validity today than ever. Indeed, far from being owners, many investors are not even *investors* as such. They move into and out of individual stocks several times a day or hold them for very short periods of time – sometimes mere seconds – using a variety of trading algorithms and automated means. High-frequency traders are involved in half of the daily trading volumes on America's stock market (The Economist, 2019). In turn, indexers buy the whole market at today's price without "valuing" the price of any one stock as a potential owner would do.

Moreover, as Robé observes:

After the process of incorporation, shareholders have *no right of access* to the assets of the corporation; they *do not enter into any contract* in its name. *No liability* can arise for them from the corporate activity. They *do not run* the corporation and *do not own it.*

(Robé, 2012, p. 6, italics in original)

Yes, shareholders are entitled to a dividend at the discretion of the board, and at the annual general meeting they can vote on a pre-set slate of directors and on non-binding resolutions. If a shareholder owns a lot of shares in a single company, they might bhe able to demand a seat on the board or otherwise exert influence. And in case of bankruptcy or liquidation, shareholders are entitled to any residual assets left over after all secured obligations have been paid. But in no sense does any of this make them "owners" of the firm.[5] The challenge raised by the BR statement is how best to accommodate this fact without "undermining the morality of free markets and the moral and fiduciary duty" of the corporation, as a *Wall Street Journal* (2019) editorial hyperbolically characterized the BR statement.

My second point concerns the assumed role of government in Friedman's scheme: "We have established elaborate constitutional, parliamentary and judicial provisions to control these functions [dealing with externalities, providing social goods], to assure that taxes are imposed so far as possible in accordance with the preferences and desires of the public" (Friedman, 1970, p. 122). Executives who invade this space by undertaking corporate social responsibility commitments, he argued, not only violate their fiduciary responsibility; they also usurp governmental functions and democratic principles. By "we" Friedman presumably meant countries like the US and those in Western Europe at the time he was writing. Leaving aside the question of business influence on those governments, then and since, his model of state and market became highly problematic once corporate globalization broadened and deepened in the 1990s. There is no global regulator to match the functional and juridical space in which the multinational firm operates. International law generally does not apply to corporations. With some exceptions, the reach of national law typically does not go beyond the individual entities comprising a multinational group that are domiciled within a country's jurisdiction.

Moreover, in numerous domestic jurisdictions Friedman's characterization of government simply does not hold. Sir Mark Moody-Stuart worked for Shell in the 1990s, at the time the Movement for the Survival of the Ogoni People engaged in massive protests against the company's environmental and other practices in the oil-rich region of Nigeria. Nigeria's military government executed nine Ogoni leaders after a sham trial, while Shell became the target of a global campaign for not speaking out to oppose the execution. Shell meekly stated: "A commercial enterprise like Shell cannot and must never interfere with the legal process of any sovereign state" (quoted in Manby, 1999, p. 157). Friedman might well have agreed. But Moody-Stuart (2015, p. 237), who had advocated for a more robust position by Shell at the time and ultimately became its chairman, later observed that "these economists live in cloud cuckoo land when they say that."

In short, the combination of these two factors – the absence of a global regulator and national governance failures – led firms, Shell being an early mover, to adopt enterprise-wide social responsibility policies and practices with the aim of managing stakeholder-related risk and gaining social legitimacy (Kell and Ruggie, 2001. Among major firms such practices have moved steadily away from philanthropic approaches to involve the conduct of core business functions (Crane, Matten and Spence, 2014; Crane et al., 2014).

Chancellor Allen described the emergence of shareholder primacy. But what accounts for its ultimate dominance, particularly in the US? Lynn Stout, a longtime critic, suggests several factors (2012, pp. 19–21): it gave the public and the media easy-to-understand sound bites to account for numerous corporate scandals in the 1980s (portrayed as out-of-control C-suites); it provided companies and reformers with a simple metric of corporate performance; it prescribed a solution that fit well with the broader influence of the "Chicago School" economists and the conservative Law and Economics movement; and self-interest. The last because one of the main means the doctrine's proponents advocated for how "principals" should exercise control over "agents" in the corporate context was to link CEO compensation to stock performance – which in practice often came to mean short-term performance. Earnings reports can be easily manipulated. And cost-cutting can be produced through a variety of means including, for example, outsourcing and offshoring jobs into opaque global supply chains, or cutting R&D expenditures and capital investments, all of which could affect not only the targeted factor of production but also the long-term health of the company.[6]

Moreover, through outsourcing and offshoring, manufacturing companies in particular decoupled themselves from large parts of their workforce at both ends of global supply chains, thereby reducing the bargaining power of labor in their home countries (Rodrik, 1997). Similarly, through offshoring profits companies could significantly reduce their home country taxes (Palan, Murphy and Chavagneux, 2010), thereby creating, in the words of former US Treasury Secretary Lawrence Summers, "a significant problem for the revenue capacity of states and an immense problem for their capacity to maintain progressive taxation" (quoted in Porter, 2014). Without getting into the tall grass of methodology of precisely what is measured and how, it seems safe to conclude that the combination of these factors contributed to rising income inequality in the US that began in the 1980s and spiked in the 1990s and into the 2000s.

In short, it is time to let go of Milton Friedman when it comes to constructing a sustainable conceptual foundation for the role of the public corporation. Today, the broad and deep loss of social legitimacy in major institutions, private and public, and the governance failures preventing correction of market failures, has driven large and leading parts of the business community to engage in this paradigmatic challenge (Fink, 2019; Lipton, 2019; Mayer, 2018). The Business Roundtable statement is but one instance. ESG investing already has been and is likely to become even more of a factor in reinforcing the construction of a broader social conception of the public corporation. I turn to it next.

THE RISE IN ESG INVESTING

An institutionalized socially responsible investing industry (SRI) has existed at least since the 1970s, when the first socially screened mutual funds were established (Lydenberg, 2005; Townsend, 2017). SRI initially focused on the exclusion of certain stocks from portfolios (for example, weapons, tobacco, gambling, or alcohol), and also engaging with companies. In the 1980s major pension funds and university endowments took part in the divestment campaign against South Africa's apartheid regime. In the 1990s, the first research firm (Kinder, Lydenberg, Domini & Co.) was established to market social and environmental data on publicly traded companies to the investment community. Rating agencies using such data soon followed. Multi-stakeholder initiatives establishing principles for environmental and social reporting by companies, such as the Global Reporting Initiative, also emerged at this same time. In the US, SRI reached US$2.32 trillion in 2001 (Lydenberg, 2005, p. xii).

ESG investing evolved out of this context. The term ESG was first used in a 2004 United Nations report, "Who Cares Wins" (Kell, 2018), prepared for the launch of the Principles for Responsible Investment (www.unpri.org).

In essence, these Principles were a mission statement for asset owners and managers not unlike the recent BR statement. Today PRI is an independent non-profit entity and the Principles have nearly 2,800 institutional and individual signatories with some US$80 trillion in assets under management. In 2010, Bloomberg terminals began to include ESG data, and by 2016 more than 100 rating agencies were providing ESG information and rankings of companies (Amel-Zadeh and Serafeim, 2017). All major asset managers now offer some form of ESG products.[7]

Depending on definitions, there are a half-dozen or more types and strategies of ESG investing (GSIA, 2018). The most prominent are values-based screening (mostly negative, some positive), and integrating ESG metrics into financial analytics. Engaging with companies can accompany all. Table 9.1 shows ESG categories that the authors of a broad survey found to be representative of the types of issues that can have a material impact on a company (Clark, Feiner and Viehs, 2015, p. 12). Sub-scategories and specific metrics operationalize these.

According to the Global Sustainable Investment Alliance (GSIA, 2018), nearly US$31 trillion of all assets under management (AUM) globally, or more than 25%, apply some form of ESG criteria. This space is still largely dominated by institutional investors, but the share of retail investing is increasing. In Australia and New Zealand, ESG investing accounts for 60% of AUM; in Canada and Europe it hovers around 50%. In the US it is 26% but growing quickly: it rose substantially after the 2008 financial sector meltdown, and then spiked by nearly 38% between 2016 and 2018. An article in *Barron's*,

TABLE 9.1
Typical ESG factors

Environmental ("E")	Social ("S")	Governance ("G")
Biodiversity/land use	Community relations	Accountability
Carbon emissions	Controversial business	Anti-takeover measures
Climate change risks	Customer relations/product	Board structure/size
Energy use	Diversity issues	Bribery and corruption
Raw material sourcing	Employee relations	CEO duality
Regulatory/legal risks	Health and safety	Executive compensation schemes
Supply chain management	Human capital management	Ownership structure
Waste and recycling	Human rights	Shareholder rights
Water management	Responsible marketing and R&D	Transparency
Weather events	Union relationships	Voting procedures

Source: Clark, Feiner and Viehs (2015)

the business magazine, called the latter the "Trump Bump" (Fonda, 2018), presumably reflecting the view that the new administration was unlikely to advance an ESG-friendly agenda. Indeed, the US Department of Labor, the Securities and Exchange Commission, and the White House have all issued Friedmanesque warnings that ESG investing by pension funds possibly violates their fiduciary responsibilities (BakerMcKenzie, 2019). Even so, ESG investing continues to grow rapidly (Nauman, 2019; Thompson, 2019).

An upward trend in ESG investing has also been reported in private equity markets. In addition, ESG is expected to get a boost from millennial investors (born 1981–1996), who are reported likely to inherit some US$30 trillion from their baby boomer parents (1946–1964) over the next decade or two. Surveys conducted by consultancies suggest that millennials have stronger commitments to sustainability investing (another way of labeling ESG) than their parents, and that the commitment is even higher among millennial women than men (Ruggie and Middleton, 2019). Millennial employees are reported to exhibit similar preferences for workplaces (Henderson, 2019; Mooney, 2019; Tett and Nauman, 2019).

The most persuasive drivers for investors and companies is the fact that ESG investing has begun to perform as well as, and often better than, its mainstream counterparts. Although causal inference remains complex, a meta-analysis of 200 academic papers and other research reports found either a positive or neutral correlation between ESG equity funds and conventional indexes (Clark, Feiner and Viehs, 2015; also see Kotula, 2019; Thompson, 2019). A similar although somewhat weaker correlation has been reported for bond indexes (Haefele, 2017). A survey of more than 400 mainstream senior investment professionals found that performance is the most frequent reason they cite for using ESG data, followed by client demand and product strategy (Amel-Zadeh and Serafeim, 2017; on client demand, also see GSIA, 2018). In 2017, the *Wall Street Journal* reported that "Do-Good Funds Finally Are Paying Off in Performance" (Weil, 2018). Because ESG investing considers a broader array of issues it also may be more alert to risks that mainstream counterparts do not yet consider. For example, of 1,200 ESG funds Bloomberg tracks, only 34 were reported to have held stock in Pacific Gas & Electric, the California utility that triggered the wildfires destroying the town of Paradise and creating the first climate-related corporate bankruptcy (Rise Financial, 2017). In a similar vein, ESG funds have tended to avoid Facebook (Hale, 2018). And S-Ray, the big-data affiliate of Arabesque Asset Management, on numerous occasions has lowered the ESG scores of major global brands well before the companies and their share price were hit by scandals, detecting significant shortcomings in one or more categories.[8]

In sum, ESG investing has grown rapidly. Bank of England Governor Mark Carney views it as "a new horizon" for the investment universe (Carney,

2019). Performance is critical. But clearly these trends also reflect a desire by many in the investment community to move beyond the narrow strictures of shareholder primacy – to become more deeply embedded in the increasingly fragile social fabric and natural ecosystems in which they operate and live.[9] Virtually by definition these preferences will advance the move toward more of a social entity conception of the public corporation.

MANAGING MATURATION

The fact that roughly 25% of global assets under management employ some form of ESG criteria is impressive, as is how rapidly this has occurred. But continued expansion into the mainstream also faces obstacles. Some are due to traditional perspectives and practices of investment-related professionals, others to current weaknesses in ESG itself. This section addresses some of the challenges as well as moves to begin managing them.

Tradition

Perhaps the most deep-seated impediment to ESG investing resides in the binary thinking of many mainstream investment-related professionals, including influential media. As already discussed, in recent decades the dominant paradigm has been shareholder primacy. The hard-core response to efforts that advance a broader concept of corporate responsibility, including the BR statement and ESG investing, goes something like this: it amounts to *stakeholder* primacy; it violates fiduciary duties as well as corporate charters and corporate law; besides, stakeholder primacy is impossible to execute and therefore will destroy the public corporation as we know it; and if directors and officers want to start a charity or give money to one, they are free to do so using their own. This was Friedman's argument, close to verbatim; it remains the editorial position of the *Wall Street Journal*; and it pervades large parts of the mainstream investment profession, including academics and think-tank experts.[10]

But the dichotomy of shareholder vs. stakeholder primacy is a false one. There is vast space between the two. Shareholders have an important say over company performance via their role in the election of directors, through shareholder activism, and by means of exit. Shareholder rights are protected by corporate law and securities regulation. Directors have fiduciary duties of care, loyalty and good faith, and shareholders can bring suit if those duties have not been met. But none of this logically implies that any move beyond shareholder primacy ipso facto is a move toward stakeholder primacy. At bottom, it represents a desire to move beyond the narrow confines of the principal–agent construct, beyond the "owners" and "employees" conception of the body corporate that may operate in more countries than there are UN member states.

It acknowledges that there are forms of "capital" other than financial that affect the success of a company and the society in which it operates: human, social, and natural capital (Mayer, 2018). Not all shareholders may care about these matters. But directors and officers should, in the best interest of the corporation itself. No specific institutional formula necessarily follows.

A closely related corollary has been the pressure on CEOs to produce short-term results. Among many other ways, this has played out in the quarterly reports controversy. I noted earlier that Paul Polman discontinued the practice of issuing such reports when he became CEO of Unilever, a consumer products company with some 300 factories, 400 brands serving 2.5 billion customers around the world. He found quarterly reports to be both distracting and unproductive – distracting from his commitment to achieving longer-term sustainable growth, and unproductive because he was never asked questions about the environmental and social dimensions of his business model at investor and analyst meetings or calls (Boynton, 2015; Buckley, 2017; Ignatius and Polman, 2012). Since 2015 or so, the number of major companies issuing quarterly guidance has declined and ESG issues are discussed more frequently, although starting from a low base (Langley, 2019; Samuelson, 2018; Walker, 2018).

Finally, there is the issue of "materiality." According to the International Federation of Accountants:

> [w]hether information is material is a matter of judgment. The concept of materiality works as a filter through which management sifts information. Its purpose is to make sure that the financial information that could influence investors' decisions is included in the financial statements.
>
> (IFAC, 2017)

Here again the issue is how narrowly a particular category, in this case materiality, is interpreted. In some domains, including climate change and human rights, potentially high-impact risks that are emergent but not yet imminent may not receive the attention they require and thus fail to register in board or management "judgment" before serious and possibly irreversible harm has been done.

Current ESG shortcomings

ESG investing is also faced with intrinsic maturation challenges. The most widely reported is significant inconsistencies in ESG data generated by data providers. Common taxonomies and templates are still in their infancy and evolving haphazardly even as demand for ESG products is increasing. This poses potential problems for investors who seek ESG opportunities and may be paying a high price for deficient data, as well as companies striving to improve their practices that go unrecognized. According to Hans

Hoogervorst, Head of the International Accounting Standards Board, it also means that so-called greenwashing – putting an ESG label on old funds – "is rampant" (quoted in Rajan, 2019). The lack of transparency regarding metrics and algorithms that data providers and raters use compound these problems.

An MIT Sloan study did have access to the data of five rating agencies. Using novel statistical tools it found that the major source of divergence among ratings is due to how raters measure different elements within each of the ESG categories, more so than the categories used or the relative weights assigned to them (Berg, Koelbel and Rigobon, 2019). They also detected a "rater effect," meaning that an agency's (human) assessment of one category seems to be influenced by its view of the company as a whole. Another statistical study focused on corporate social responsibility ratings more broadly. It found that in only 3 of 12 pairs of raters was the correlation between them higher than 0.5 (barely); the lowest was –0.12, and the mean 0.3 (Chatterji et al., 2016).

The "S" scores in ESG appear to be the least reliable (O'Connor and Labowitz, 2017; Ruggie, 2018). In addition to the factors already noted, the way in which human rights elements are conceptualized in the S domain contributes to this poor performance. Look back for a moment at Table 9.1. The S column includes ten elements (community relations, diversity issues, union relationships, health and safety, and so on), each of which will have numerous indicators that get measured and that algorithms will ultimately aggregate into the S score. The conceptual oddity is that virtually all of these elements are well-established human rights issues – while, at the same time, the list *also* includes a separate human rights category. By well-established I mean that they reflect human rights that states have formally recognized in UN treaties, International Labour Organization Conventions as well as the UN Guiding Principles on Business and Human Rights, unanimously endorsed by the UN Human Rights Council (UN, 2011).[11]

This is a widespread practice. In a survey of 14 different raters and rating frameworks, 74 out of 85 S elements were standard business and human rights issues; yet 8 of the 14 raters also included a separate human rights category (Ruggie and Middleton, 2019). Indeed, even under the E domain in Table 9.1 we find categories that have critical human rights impacts, including raw materials sourcing (community relations), supply chain management (workers' rights), and water usage (the right to water). This oddity likely reflects a lack of familiarity on the part of ESG raters – and perhaps the investment community as a whole – with human rights, the core of the S.

Ongoing developments

According to Lady Lynn Forester de Rothschild, founder of the Coalition for Inclusive Capitalism, more than "150 ratings systems exist, covering over 10,000 sustainability performance metrics, that are trying to fill the gap that is left by the lack of a generally accepted standard" (quoted in Edgeclifff-Johnson, 2019). For ESG investing, no such standard is imminent. But greater depth of understanding and overlap around core issues is occurring, typically led by nonprofit entities and coalitions. One example is the Sustainability Accounting Standards Board (SASB). It identifies ESG issues that are deemed likely to affect a company's financial performance, across different industries and sectors. SASB has partnered with the Climate Disclosure Standards Board to translate the principles developed by the Task Force on Climate-Related Financial Disclosures into more specific implementation guidance (sasb. org). As its name suggests, the International Integrated Reporting Initiative seeks to promote integrated financial and non-financial reporting by companies, and to make the practice a norm. According to the Global Reporting Initiative, its sustainability standards are used by nearly all of the world's 250 largest corporations in their sustainability reporting (globalreporting.org). The various such efforts may be described as resources for the willing.

There is some reinforcement of these trends on the governmental front, mainly by or within the European Union. The European Commission has issued a directive requiring large companies to report on their social and environmental impacts (Directive 2014/95/EU). The Commission is also developing a Sustainable Finance Action Plan, which will include more detailed guidance and voluntary standards in several environmental domains. And in 2021 an EU regulation will come into force aiming to stem the trade in conflict minerals (tin, tantalum, tungsten, and gold) by requiring supply chain due diligence and reporting. France has a "due vigilance" law that requires large French companies or foreign companies with a significant business presence in France to have and report on "effective" due diligence systems for human rights and environmental matters (Law 2017–399). Anti-slavery legislation in the United Kingdom (UK Public General Acts 2015 c.30) and Australia (Modern Slavery Act 2018) also require human rights due diligence systems and reporting. Some form of mandatory human rights due diligence is currently under consideration by the EU, Germany, and Finland, while the UK is expected to roll out a requirement for all large asset owners to start disclosing their climate risks by 2020 (Hale, 2019). A move in the US House of Representatives Financial Services Committee to require the Securities and Exchange Commission to write ESG disclosure rules failed to advance (Temple-West, 2019). This brief listing is not inclusive, but it does suggest that governments have begun to respond to the increased need for better and more standardized nonfinancial data, and where such issues are addressed the environment, particularly climate, and human rights in global supply chains have attracted the most attention.

Front-line market players are responding to the data challenge in two ways. One, investment research firms, ESG rating agencies, and asset managers are both diversifying their sources of data and reducing their dependence on external data providers by building or acquiring in-house capacity. For example, UBS has built a proprietary base; Morningstar, an investment research firm, has acquired a 40% stake in Sustainalytics, an ESG research and ratings firm; Moody's, the rating agency, has bought Vigeo Eiris, a data provider (Mair, 2019). Second, in terms of stock picking, there is shift toward a combination of big data and artificial intelligence (Thomas, 2017). BlackRock, the world's largest asset manager, has moved partially in this direction, while the algorithms of relative newcomer Arabesque are entirely machine based.

In short, there appears to be a high-level convergence among private and public actors regarding issues that are of interest to ESG investors and companies seeking to improve their ESG scores. But if the MIT study has it right, this may produce overlap and similarities in what is measured, but not convergence of actual metrics. At the same time, the development of proprietary systems by individual asset management firms raises transparency issues that may be more troubling than when those asset managers drew data from several different sources that were also being used by other asset managers. These issues are unlikely to be fully resolved anytime soon without governments setting clearer parameters, as they did in the evolution of financial accounting.

CONCLUSION

The rise in ESG investing and the debate on repurposing the public corporation are not unrelated. Both express a view that the large public corporation should be more than a piece of private property that has been excavated and is insulated from its social and natural ecosystems. Both express a concern that the public corporation is not managing its adverse impacts on people and planet well enough. And both reflect a growing belief among investors and business leaders that there is unlocked value in creating shared value (Porter and Kramer, 2011).

At the same time, neither is without challenges. But getting ESG right is not fundamentally different from past instances of standard-setting, whether by market actors, public authorities, or a combination of both. In contrast, the repurposing debate is deeply philosophical while also involving innumerable interests. Borrowing the wise observation Chancellor Allen made some time ago, the repurposing of the public corporation "will be worked out, not deduced" (1992, p. 281). Continuing to make practical progress on ESG investing is a key driver in working it out.

NOTES

1   I am grateful to Florian Berg for his comments on an earlier draft and sharing his insights on ESG investing. Many thanks also to the team at Arabesque Asset Management, especially Omar Selim and Andreas Feiner, for their inspiring leadership, and to Max Kelton and Emily Matthews for research assistance.

2   This would have been so in the 1919 case of *Dodge v. Ford*, when the Dodge brothers, in business with Henry Ford, wanted to collect dividends but Ford wanted to invest the funds to expand the business. The Dodge brothers won in the Michigan Supreme Court (204 Mich. 459, 170 N.W. 668 (Mich. 1919)). The case is still cited today in support of the idea that shareholders are owners of the firm and, therefore, that shareholder primacy must be preserved (Skapinker, 2019).

3   *Revlon, Inc. v. MacAndrews & Forbes Holdings, Inc.*, 506 A.2d 173 (Del. 1986).

4   This heading was inspired by J.P. Robé (2012).

5   The corporation has legal personality in its own right and a "parent" company can own subsidiaries, just as natural persons can own their business. But to the question of who does "own" the large public corporation with dispersed shareholders there are only two plausible answers: no one; or that the corporation owns itself (Ruggie, 2018).

6   When Paul Polman became CEO of Unilever in January 2009, he announced that investors should no longer expect quarterly earnings reports. He went further and urged shareholders to put their money elsewhere if they did not want to "buy into [my] long-term value creation, which is equitable, which is shared, which is sustainable" (quoted in Boynton, 2015). In 2017, Unilever rejected an unsolicited US$143 billion takeover bid by KraftHeinz, with Polman saying that their corporate cultures would never merge (Gelles, 2019).

7   The proportion of funds allocated to ESG strategies by the top ten asset managers varies but typically remains relatively small.

8   Based on discussions with the firm. Full disclosure: I sit on the board of Arabesque Asset Management Holding Company.

9   For a formal analysis of why business would want to make such a move, see Bénabou and Tirole (2010); in 2014 Tirole received the Nobel Prize in economics for his work on market power and regulation.

10 On the latter, see Fried (2019) and Epstein (2019) respectively.

11 I developed the Guiding Principles over the course of a six-year mandate as the UN Secretary-General's Special Representative for Business and Human Rights (Ruggie, 2013).

REFERENCES

Allen, W.T. (1992). 'Our Schizophrenic Conception of the Business Corporation'. *Cardozo Law Review*, 14(2), pp. 261–282.

Amel-Zadeh, A. and Serafeim, G. (2017). Why and How Investors Use ESG Information: Evidence from a Global Survey. Available at: https://papers.ssrn.com/sol3/papers.cfm?abstract_id=2925310 (Accessed: 11 November 2019).

BakerMcKenzie. (2019). Trump Executive Order Brings Renewed Scrutiny of ESG Investing and Proxy Engagement by Pension Funds [Online]. Available at: www.bakermckenzie.com/en/insight/publications/2019/05/trump-executive-order (Accessed: 11 November 2019).

Bénabou, R. and Tirole, J. (2010). 'Individual and Corporate Social Responsibility'. *Economica*, 77(305), pp. 1–19.

Berg, F., Koelbel, J.F., and Rigobon, R. (2019). *Aggregate Confusion: The Divergence of ESG Ratings*. MIT Sloan School of Management, Working Paper 5822-19.

Boynton, A.C. (2015). Unilever's Paul Polman: CEOs Can't Be 'Slaves' To Shareholders. *Forbes* (20 July). Available at: www.forbes.com/sites/andyboynton/2015/07/20/unilevers-paul-polman-ce-os-cant-be-slaves-to-shareholders/ (Accessed: 11 November 2019).

Buckley, T. (2017). Unilever CEO Loses Cool with Goldman Analyst at Investor Day [Online]. Available at: www.bloomberg.com/news/articles/2017-12-01/unilever-ceo-loses-his-cool-with-analyst-at-investor-event (Accessed: 11 November 2019).

Business Roundtable. (2019a). Business Roundtable Redefines the Purpose of a Corporation to Promote 'An Economy That Serves All Americans [Online]. Available at: www.businessround-table.org/business-roundtable-redefines-the-purpose-of-a-corporation-to-promote-an-econo-my-that-serves-all-americans (Accessed: 11 November 2019).

Business Roundtable. (2019b). The Purpose of a Corporation [Online]. Available at: https://opportunity.businessroundtable.org/wp-content/uploads/2019/09/BRT-Statement-on-the-Purpose-of-a-Corporation-with-Signatures-1.pdf (Accessed: 11 November 2019).

Carney, M. (2019). A New Horizon (Speech to European Commission Conference: A Global Approach to Sustainable Finance, March 21) [Online]. Available at: www.bankofengland.co.uk/speech/2019/mark-carney-speech-at-european-commission-high-level-conference-brussels (Accessed: 11 November 2019).

Chatterji, A.K., Rodolphe, D., Levine, D.I., and Touboul, S. (2016). 'Do Ratings of Firms Converge? Implications for Managers, Investors and Strategy Researchers'. *Strategic Management Journal*, 37(8), pp. 1597–1614.

Clark, G.L., Feiner, A., and Viehs, M. (2015). From the Shareholder to the Stakeholder [Online]. Available at: https://arabesque.com/research/From_the_stockholder_to_the_stakeholder_web.pdf (Accessed: 11 November 2019).

Crane, A., Matten, D., and Spence, L.J. (eds). (2014). *Corporate Social Responsibility: Readings and Cases in a Global Context*. 2nd ed. London: Routledge.

Crane, A., McWilliams, A., Moon, J., and Siegel, D.S. (eds). (2014). *The Oxford Handbook of Corporate Social Responsibility*. Oxford: Oxford University Press.

Edgecliff-Johnson, A. (2019). ESG Groups Try to Thin a Thicket of Sustainability Metrics, *Financial Times* (11 June).Available at: www.ft.com/content/1244dc6e-8bec-11e9-a1c1-51bf8f989972 (Accessed: 11 November 2019).

Epstein, R.A. (2019).What Is The Purpose of a Corporation? [Online], Available at: www.hoover.org/research/what-purpose-corporation (Accessed: 11 November 2019).

Fama, E.F. (1980). 'Agency Problems and the Theory of the Firm'. *Journal of Political Economy*, 88(2), pp. 288–307.

Fink, L. (2019). Larry Fink's 2019 Letter to CEOS: Purpose & Profit [Online]. Available at: www.blackrock.com/corporate/investor-relations/larry-fink-ceo-letter (Accessed: 11 November 2019).

Fonda, D. (2018). The Trump Bump and Sustainable Investing. *Barron's* (June 23). Available at: www.barrons.com/articles/the-trump-bump-and-sustainable-investing-1529712001 (Accessed: 11 November 2019).

Freeman, R.E. (1984). *Strategic Management: A Stakeholder Approach*. Marshfield, MA: Pittman.

Fried, J. (2019). Shareholders Always Come First and that's a Good Thing. *Financial Times* (7 October). Available at: www.ft.com/content/fff170a0-e5e0-11e9-b8e0-026e07cbe5b4 (Accessed: 11 November 2019).

Friedman, M. (1962). *Capitalism and Freedom*. Chicago: University of Chicago Press.

Friedman, M. (1970). The Social Responsibility of Business is to Increase its Profits. *New York Times Magazine* (13 September). Available: http://umich.edu/~thecore/doc/Friedman.pdf (Accessed: 11 November 2019).

Gelles, D. (2019). He Ran an Empire of Soap and Mayonnaise. Now He wants to Reinvent Capitalism. *New York Times* (29 August). Available at: www.nytimes.com/2019/08/29/business/paul-polman-unilever-corner-office.html (Accessed: 11 November 2019).

Global Sustainable Investment Alliance. (2018). Sustainable Investment Review [Online]. Available at: www.gsi-alliance.org/wp-content/uploads/2019/06/GSIR_Review2018F.pdf (Accessed: 11 November 2019).

Haefele, M. (2017). Sustainable Performance, UBS House View, Monthly Letter (14 December).

Hale, T. (2018). ESG is Being Discussed More Often on Earnings Calls/Sustainable Funds Exposure to Facebook [Online]. Available at: https://medium.com/the-esg-advisor/esg-is-being-discussed-more-often-on-earnings-calls-sustainable-funds-exposure-to-facebook-1a27da0c4456 (Accessed: 11 November 2019).

Hale, T. (2019). Tougher Rules Will Help Green Finance Take Off. *Financial Times* (17 October). Available at: http://ftalphaville.ft.com/2019/10/17/1571301192000/Tougher-rules-will-help-green-finance-take-off/ (Accessed: 11 November 2019).

Hansman, H. and Kraakman, R. (2001). 'The End of History for Corporate Law'. *Georgetown Law Journal*, 89(2), pp. 439–468.

Henderson, R. (2019). Fund Managers Turn their Focus to Millennials. *Financial Times* (24 July). Available at: www.ft.com/content/bbd9574c-aced-11e9-8030-530adfa879c2 (Accessed: 11 November 2019).

Ignatius, A. and Polman, P. (2012). Unilever's CEO on Making Responsible Business Work [Online] Available at: https://hbr.org/2012/05/unilevers-ceo-on-making-respon (Accessed: 11 November 2019).

International Federation of Accountants (IFAC). (2017). Making Sense of Materiality [Online]. Available at: www.ifac.org/knowledge-gateway/business-reporting/discussion/making-sense-materiality (Accessed: 11 November 2019).

Jensen, M.C. and Meckling, W.H. (1976). 'Theory of the Firm: Managerial Behavior, Agency Costs and Ownership Structure'. *Journal of Financial Economics*, 3(4), pp. 305–360.

Kell, G. (2018). The Remarkable Rise of ESG. *Forbes* (11 July). Available at: www.forbes.com/sites/georgkell/2018/07/11/the-remarkable-rise-of-esg/#74b136816951 (Accessed: 11 November 2019).

Kell, G. and Ruggie, J.G. (2001). 'Global Markets and Social Legitimacy: The Case of the Global Compact'. In Drache, D. (ed) *The Market or the Public Domain: Global Governance & the Asymmetry of Power* (pp. 321–334). London: Routledge.

Kotula, T. (2019). ESG and Financial Returns: The Academic Perspective [Online]. Available at: www.axa-im-usa.com/content/-/asset_publisher/xnQOfhEPDlxp/content/esg-and-financial-returns-the-academic-perspective/23818 (Accessed: 11 November 2019).

Langley, K. (2019). More Companies are Making Noise about ESG. *Wall Street Journal* (23 September). Available at: www.wsj.com/articles/more-companies-are-making-noise-about-esg-11569263634 (Accessed 11 November 2019).

Lipton, M. (2019). *Financial Times* (17 September). Available at: www.ft.com/content/6e806580-d560-11e9-8d46-8def889b4137 (Accessed 11 November 2019).

Lydenberg, S. (2005). *Corporations and the Public Interest: Guiding the Invisible Hand*. San Francisco: Berrett-Koehler.

Mair, V. (2019). State Street Global Advisors Finds the R-Factor as Asset Managers Develop Inhouse ESG Data. *Responsible Investor* (20 May).

Manby, B. (1999). *The Price of Oil: Corporate Responsibility and Human Rights Violations in Nigeria's Oil Producing Communities*. New York: Human Rights Watch.

Mayer, C. (2018). *Prosperity: Better Business Makes the Greater Good*. Oxford: Oxford University Press.

Moody-Stuart, M. (2015). 'Business as a Vocation' in M. McIntosh (ed). *Business, Capitalism and Corporate Citizenship*. London: Routledge, pp. 228–241.

Mooney, A. (2019). ESG Investing Sparks Race in Tech and Hiring at Asset Managers. *Financial Times* (10 August). Available at: www.ft.com/content/247f4034-4280-318a-9900-87608a575ede (Accessed: 11 November 2019).

Murray, A. (2019). America's CEOs See A New Purpose for the Corporation. *Fortune* (19 August). Available at: https://fortune.com/longform/business-roundtable-ceos-corporations-purpose/ (Accessed: 11 November 2019).

Nauman, B. (2019). ESG Money Market Funds Grow 15% in First Half of 2019. *Financial Times* (14 July). Available at: www.ft.com/content/2c7b8438-a5a6-11e9-984c-fac8325aaa04 (Accessed: 11 November 2019).

O'Connor, C. and Labowitz, S. (2017). *Putting the "S" in ESG: Measuring Human Rights Performance for Investors*. New York: New York University Stern Center for Business and Human Rights.

Palan, R., Murphy, R., and Chavagneux, C. (eds). (2010). *Tax Havens: How Globalization Really Works*. Ithaca, NY: Cornell University Press.

Porter, E. (2014). Tax Tactics Threaten Public Funds. *New York Times* (1 October). Available at: www.nytimes.com/2014/10/02/business/economy/multinational-tax-strategies-put-public-coffers-at-risk.html (Accessed: 11 November 2019).

Porter, M.E. and Kramer, M.E. (2011). 'Creating Shared Value'. *Harvard Business Review*, 89(1–2), pp. 62–77.

Rajan, A. (2019). Pragmatism is the Name of the Game in Greenwashing Fight. *Financial Times* (9 September). Available at: www.ft.com/content/4b7165ee-729d-381d-9a8f-ecd1c21d2db1 (Accessed: 11 November 2019).

Rise Financial. (2017). Bloomberg Good Business Review [Online]. Available at: www.responsiblein-vestment.co.nz/news/bloomberg-good-business-review (Accessed: 11 November 2019).

Robé, J.-P. (2012). 'Being Done with Milton Friedman'. *Accounting, Economics, and Law*, 2(2), pp. 1–31.

Rodrik, D. (1997). *Has Globalization Gone Too Far?* Washington, DC: Institute for International Economics.

Ruggie, J.G. (2013). *Just Business: Multinational Corporations and Human Rights*. New York: Norton.

Ruggie, J.G. (2018). 'Multinationals as Global Institutions: Power, Authority, and Relative Autonomy'. *Regulation & Governance*, 12(3), pp. 317–333.

Ruggie, J.G. and Middleton, E.K. (2019). "Money, Millennials, and Human Rights: Sustaining 'Sustainable Investing'". *Global Policy*, 10(1), pp. 144–150.

Samuelson, J.F. (2018). The Case Against Investor Conference Calls [Online]. Available at: www.aspen-institute.org/blog-posts/the-case-against-investor-conference-calls/ (Accessed: 11 November 2019).

Skapinker, M. (2019). Boosting Corporate Social Good Will Not Protect Workers. *Financial Times* (8 October). Available at: www.ft.com/content/d106dc54-e698-11e9-9743-db5a370481bc (Accessed: 11 November 2019).

Stout, L. (2012). *The Shareholder Value Myth: How Putting Shareholders First Harms Investors, Corporations, and the Public*. San Francisco: Berrett-Koehler.

Temple-West, P. (2019). US Congress Rejects European-style ESG Reporting Standards. *Financial Times* (12 July) Available at: www.ft.com/content/0dd92570-a47b-11e9-974c-ad1c6ab5efd1 (Accessed: 11 November 2019).

Tett, G. and Nauman, B. (2019). Climate Crisis Carries Unknown Costs; SEC Backlash; World Leaders Sound Alarm. *Financial Times* (3 July). Available at: www.ft.com/content/fad4b910-9cd9-11e9-b8ce-8b459ed04726

The Economist. (2019). The Stockmarket is Now Run by Computers, Algorithms and Passive Managers: Briefing. Available at: www.economist.com/briefing/2019/10/05/the-stockmarket-is-now-run-by-computers-algorithms-and-passive-managers (Accessed: 11 November 2019).

Thomas, L. (2017). At BlackRock Machines are Rising over Managers to Pick Stocks. *New York Times* (28 March). Available at: www.nytimes.com/2017/03/28/business/dealbook/blackrock-active-ly-managed-funds-computer-models.html (Accessed: 11 November 2019).

Thompson, J. (2019). Sustainable Funds More Likely to be Top Performers, Study Shows. *Financial Times* (11 August). Available at: www.ft.com/content/9e71cf86-ba2d-345c-bb3b-0d5887abbc6a (Accessed: 11 November 2019).

Townsend, B. (2017). From SRI to ESG: Responsible and Sustainable Investing [Online]. Available at: www.bailard.com/wp-content/uploads/2017/06/Socially-Responsible-Investing-History-Bailard-White-Paper-FNL.pdf?pdf=SRI-Investing-History-White-Paper (Accessed: 11 November 2019).

United Nations. (2011). Guiding Principles on Business and Human Rights [Online]. Available at: www.business-humanrights.org/en/un-guiding-principles (Accessed: 11 November 2019).

Walker, O. (2018). The Long and Short of the Quarterly Reports Controversy. *Financial Times* (1 July). Available at: www.ft.com/content/e61046bc-7a2e-11e8-8e67-1e1a0846c475

Wall Street Journal (editorial). (2019). King Warren of the Roundtable (6 October). Available at: www.wsj.com/articles/king-warren-of-the-roundtable-11570395953 (Accessed: 11 November 2019).

Weil, D. (2018). Do-Good Funds Finally Are Paying Off in Performance. Will it Last?. *Wall Street Journal* (6 May). Available at: www.wsj.com/articles/do-good-funds-finally-are-paying-off-in-performance-will-it-last-1525659420 (Accessed: 11 November 2019).

10

What corporates can do to move the financial markets to a longer-term and more responsible mindset

Paul Polman and Halla Tómasdóttir

A SHORTENING INVESTMENT HORIZON...

It's often claimed that the financial and investment markets have moved in recent years to an increasingly short-term focus, and that this shift is affecting how companies are managed and how business leaders make decisions. We believe this view is demonstrably true – and supported by a growing body of anecdotal evidence and research across companies and the investor base.

It's also increasingly clear that if the world is to tackle some of the most pressing challenges of our time – from runaway climate change to widening inequality to declining levels of public trust – corporations need to play their part, by moving to new business models that deliver long-term sustainable and equitable growth. And to do this successfully, corporations must also convince asset managers and investors that this is the type of growth they should be seeking out and investing in.

The need to tackle short-termism in the investment markets is becoming all the more pressing, with the prevailing economic conditions of recent years having had the effect of intensifying their short-term perspective. In an article published in the *Harvard Business Review* in February 2017, entitled "Finally, Evidence That Managing for the Long Term Pays Off," authors Dominic Barton, James Manyika, and Sarah Keohane Williamson cite academic studies linking "the possible effects of short-termism to lower investment rates among publicly traded firms and decreased returns over a multi-year time horizon" (Barton, Manyika and Koehane Williamson, 2017).

The implication is that in a world where interest rates are effectively zero or even negative, and there is a lot of capital out there seeking a home, the people managing the investment of that money go shorter term in an attempt to chase a return. At the same time, the current high – and arguably increasing – levels of geopolitical and economic uncertainty make people discount future cash flows, increasing the pressure on the market to adopt a shorter-term view. This thesis is supported by a welter of market statistics. For example, the average holding for shares in a public company is now estimated to be four months, down from eight years in the 1960s. And, according to JP Morgan research in 2017, traditional "stock-picking" accounts for only about 10% of trading volume in stocks, while passive and quantitative investing represents about 60%, a proportion that's more than doubled in a decade (Cheng, 2017).

Not surprisingly, the markets' focus on the short term influences the decisions made by corporates. In an interesting analysis produced in 2016 by FCLTGlobal, entitled *Rising to the Challenge of Short-termism*, Dominic Barton, Jonathan Bailey, and Joshua Zoffer attribute corporate short-termism to multiple factors ranging from activist investor pressure to how management teams are incentivized (Barton, Bailey and Zoffer, 2015). And drawing on interviews with corporate executives, they point out that short-termism manifests itself through a negative feedback loop: "While executives may feel that investor pressure forces their hand, the short-term objectives and metrics they set also push investors to shorten their horizons to match the data available to them" (Ibid). The authors depict this vicious cycle in the diagram shown in Figure 10.1 – with the causes of corporate short-termism being continually reinforced by their effects.

More recent research by FCLTGlobal suggests that the problem of corporate short-termism is continuing to increase, resulting in a massive loss of value. In a report published in September 2019, entitled *Predicting Long-term Success for Corporations and Investors Worldwide*, authors Bhakti Mirchandani, Steve Boxer, Allen He, Evan Horowitz, and Victoria Tellez note that, on overall measures of long-term behavior, global companies are scoring lower than they did in 2014 and well below the level reached before the financial crisis (Mirchandani et al., 2019). They add: "If companies were more long-term, our research suggests they could earn an additional US$1.5 trillion per year in returns on invested capital" (Ibid).

Finding a way to break out of the cycle of ever more intense short-termism is the challenge facing corporates and the financial markets, and by extension our societies, governments, and the world as a whole. Despite claims to the contrary and some encouraging signs, the fact remains that any move to a longer-term perspective by the financial markets is – at best – slow, patchy, and halting. Ten years on from the financial crisis, Christine Lagarde, head of the IMF, recently despaired in a blog published in September 2018 – entitled "Ten Years after Lehman – Lessons Learned and Challenges Ahead" – about

Cases

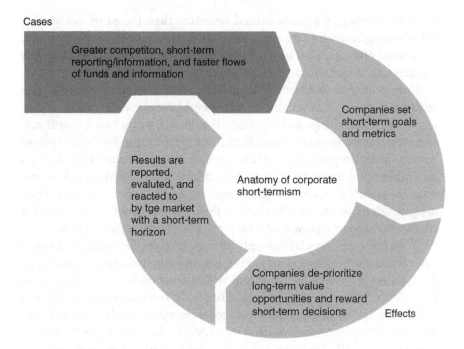

FIGURE 10.1 Causes and effects of corporate short-termism

Source: Barton, Bailey and Zoffer (2015)

an "important area that has not changed much – the area of culture, values, and ethics. As I have noted before, the financial sector still puts profit now over long-range prudence, short-termism over sustainability" (Lagarde, 2018).

...AND A SET OF URGENT GLOBAL CRISES...

It's against this shortening investment horizon that businesses are striving to help the world overcome the massive global challenges it now faces. It's now widely accepted that four of our nine critical planetary boundaries have already been crossed: climate change; loss of biosphere integrity; land-system change; and altered nitrogen/phosphorous cycles (often causing eutrophication). Put simply, we are currently exploiting our natural resources at unsustainable levels and undermining nature's ability to provide for our societies and economies.

The resulting problems are becoming more acute each year as the world's population continues to grow, with a projected rise from around 7.7 billion people today to over 9 billion by 2050. The point at which consumption of natural resources overshoots what the planet can regenerate annually is getting earlier every year, and in 2019 it was reached on July 29 – meaning we're consuming 70% more natural resources than the earth can sustain. What's more, intensive farming means our food system alone is responsible for around 60% of global biodiversity loss, and only a quarter of land now remains free of human activities, projected to fall to 10% by 2050.

It's an ecological cataclysm in the making. And in human terms, two crises related to our use – or rather misuse – of the world's resources are rapidly coming to a head: climate change and inequality. Fortunately, we do have a "north star" to guide our responses to these and other crises, in the form of the United Nations Sustainable Development Goals (SDGs), which provide an ambitious blueprint for a better world. Spanning key areas from climate action to sustaining life below water, from ending poverty to gender equality, and from zero hunger to fairer institutions and peace, the SDGs have as their ultimate objective the mission of rebalancing economic growth with the protection of our people and planet.

While these aims are clearly worth pursuing on planetary grounds, the good news is that the SDG agenda also promises an attractive return. Research by the Business & Sustainable Development Commission has found that in just four areas of the economy – energy, cities, food and agriculture, and health and wellbeing – sustainable business models based on the SDGs could open up economic opportunities worth at least US$12 trillion and up to 380 million jobs a year by 2030 (Unilever, 2017). This uplift would occur in 60 sustainable and inclusive market "hotspots," and would be worth more than 10% of today's global aggregate GDP. As such figures underline, profits and purpose can be highly compatible – as demonstrated by Unilever, which achieved a near-300% shareholder return during the ten-year tenure as CEO of Paul Polman, the co-author of this chapter (more on this topic later). However, regrettably, the world at large is not yet moving fast enough to deliver the SDGs by 2030. We now have barely a decade to alter our trajectory and ensure we live in an equitable way and within our planetary boundaries.

On climate change, we believe we are now witnessing the fallout from the greatest intergenerational crime ever committed in human history. The United Nations Intergovernmental Panel on Climate Change (IPCC) has warned that if we do not hold the rise in global temperatures to below 1.5 degrees Celsius, we will do irreversible damage. And Mother Nature does not negotiate: in fact, she's sending us invoices every month as extreme weather events escalate and proliferate. As Sir David Attenborough told UN-sponsored climate talks in Katowice, Poland in December 2018:

> Right now, we are facing a man-made disaster of global scale, our greatest threat in thousands of years: climate change. If we don't take action, the collapse of our civilisations and the extinction of much of the natural world is on the horizon.
>
> (McGrath, 2018)

On inequality, the facts are equally stark. In 2018 – as Oxfam highlighted in *Five Shocking Facts about Extreme Global Inequality and How to Even It Up* – the poorest half of the world became 11% poorer, while billionaires' fortunes rose by 12% (US$900 billion) – or US$2.5 billion every day (Oxfam, 2018). Partly as a result, the world's 26 richest people owned the same as the 3.8 billion people who make up the poorest half of humanity. And if the richest 1% of the global population paid just 0.5% extra tax, we would raise more than enough money to educate all the 262 million children who are currently denied schooling, and to provide healthcare that would save the lives of 3.3 million people.

The SDGs provide a valuable framework to help businesses, governments, and other participants – including the financial markets – move towards addressing the twin crises of inequality and climate. But the world is looking to tackle these challenges while hamstrung by a further crisis: a loss of trust. The Edelman Trust Barometer for 2019 continues to paint a picture of a world of seemingly stagnant distrust and rising pessimism about the future (Edelman, 2019). Only one in three of the mass-population respondents in the developed world believe their family will be better off in the next five years, just one in five believe the system as a whole is working for them, and 70% want change. Trust levels for various types of institution stand at just 57% for NGOs, 56% for business, 48% for government, and 47% for the media.

Restoring trust in institutions globally is an absolute prerequisite to tackling the most pressing global issues. Without rebuilding trust in those organizations with the capacity and capability to effect real and lasting change, it will be impossible to take the coordinated and united action that's needed on planetary boundaries, or to create the shared purpose and cohesion needed to close the inequality gap by valuing each person's contribution to society. To achieve all this, what's required is a new social contract that clarifies rights and responsibilities on all sides.

Business's side of this new contract will need to include greater transparency, better and more open governance, and deeper and more active engagement with society and governments – all spearheaded by leaders who hold themselves accountable to all stakeholders. We'll say more about leadership later in this chapter. But suffice to say for now that without purpose-driven and principled business leadership that builds trust, it will be very hard to tackle the key global crises – because few people will even trust the motives of those trying to do it.

…DEMAND A LONGER-TERM PERSPECTIVE

For the UN's SDGs to be achieved, and to create a world that is more inclusive and that can mobilize the resources and will needed to tackle issues like climate change, food security, and gender and income inequality, something else is also imperative: the longer-term perspective that we highlighted earlier. If business can have space to make longer-term plans, it will also be better placed to address global issues. A world where systemic environmental and social challenges persist is not a world in which business can thrive and prosper over the long term. That's why a growing number of companies are embedding a long-term focus on the UN global goals in their strategies – whether they be larger corporates, entrepreneurs, or even startups, where we see some of the boldest action being taken. These companies are taking up the mantle and executing the vital move from business-as-usual to business *un*usual, which is something all organizations will need to do if we're to rise to the challenges we face.

However, many pressures are pushing the other way, reinforcing the short-term perspective of business-as-usual – not least the rat-race of quarterly reporting that can act as a straitjacket on businesses' ability to think long term. Several jurisdictions across the world, including the US, have proposed ending quarterly earnings reporting by listed companies, and the US Securities and Exchange Commission has been investigating whether quarterly reporting or forecasting encourages shorter-term thinking and should be dropped. Some research suggests that it should: a McKinsey study has shown that more than 50% of a company's value is created by activities that take place three years from now, but also that 78% of executives would take actions to improve quarterly earnings at the expense of long-term value creation.

Given such findings, and the wider need to tackle critical global issues, our view is that it's vital to move the way value and performance are perceived and measured to a longer-term perspective – a shift that must encompass both businesses themselves and the financial markets that fund them. We'll now go on to look at the benefits of doing this, and how it might be achieved.

BUSINESSES THAT TAKE A LONGER-TERM VIEW CREATE MORE VALUE

Turning to the benefits of a longer-term view, there's growing evidence that companies that invest for the longer term outperform those that focus on the short term. Many examples of this competitive edge can be seen in the private company sector. Free from constraints such as quarterly reporting, and often guided by a strong commitment to their wider stakeholders, privately owned companies can take a longer-term perspective than their listed counterparts. It's no coincidence that a comparison of privately owned and publicly traded companies shows the former tend to invest six times more capital than the latter. Also, companies that are run for the longer term with a focus on multiple stakeholders, and measure performance holistically – including environmental, social, and governance (ESG) measures – attract better people with higher motivation and engagement, and have lower costs and better innovation.

A key step for realizing these benefits – and towards a longer-term view attuned to helping address global crises – is the adoption of more open and transparent reporting, and the building in of externalities like climate change supported by credible, strongly assured evidential data. As Michael Bloomberg, Chair of the Task Force on Climate-related Financial Disclosures, has observed:

> Climate change poses both economic risks and opportunities. But right now, companies don't have the data they need to accurately measure the risks and evaluate the opportunities. That prevents them from taking protective measures and identifying sustainable investments that could have strong returns.
>
> (TCFD, 2017)

As well as being better placed to make more sustainable decisions, research suggests that firms that manage for the long term and with the interests of multiple stakeholders in mind also generate higher value. A 2017 *Harvard Business Review* article that we cited earlier – "Finally, Evidence That Managing for the Long Term Pays Off," whose authors include McKinsey & Co managing partner Dominic Barton – quotes joint research by McKinsey Global Institute and FCLTGlobal showing that "companies that operate with a true long-term mindset have consistently outperformed their industry peers since 2001 across almost every financial measure that matters" (Barton, Manyika and Koehane Williamson, 2017).

Drilling down further into the findings, they show that – from 2001 to 2014 – the long-term companies categorized under the researchers' "Corporate Horizons Index" methodology increased their revenue by an average of 47% more than their counterparts in the same industry group, and their earnings by 36% more. The firms taking a longer-term view also seemed more willing and able to maintain a consistent strategy through times of economic stress: during the global financial crisis of 2008/09, they not only suffered smaller falls in revenue and earnings, but also continued to increase their investments in research and development at a time when others were cutting back. Over the period from 2007 to 2014, the long-term companies' R&D spending rose at an annualized rate of 8.5%, over twice as fast as the 3.7% increase recorded by other companies.

The message is clear: a longer-term focus – one that, by its nature, takes into account multiple stakeholders and non-financial (ESG) impacts and metrics – translates into better, more sustainable, and more consistent business performance over time. A similar conclusion was reached by a Boston

Consulting Group (BCG) study entitled *Total Societal Impact: A new lens for strategy*, published in October 2017 (Beal et al., 2017). Based on an analysis of over 300 businesses in five industries, the research found that companies that outperform in ESG areas relevant to their industry tend to have higher valuation multiples and margins than those with weaker performance in those areas. Top performers in specific ESG topics enjoyed valuation multiples 3–19% higher – all else being equal – than median performers in those topics. BCG CEO Rich Lesser, a co-author of the report, commented: "Our analysis provides compelling evidence that companies can develop a robust strategy to make positive contributions to society with confidence that such an approach will increase enterprise value – not diminish it" (Ibid).

ESG-FOCUSED INVESTMENT YIELDS HIGHER RETURNS – AND IS INCREASING APACE

If companies that take a longer-term and more holistic view outperform their peers, it follows that investment portfolios and strategies that focus on these companies should yield higher returns. Once again, there is a growing body of research that shows this to be the case. As reported in the *Financial Times* on August 12, 2018, research by the risk and portfolio analytics provider Axioma found that investment portfolios that were weighted towards companies with higher ESG scores outperformed their peer benchmarks by a margin of between 81 and 243 basis points in the four-year period up to March 2018 (Thompson, 2018). And in January 2019, Amundi Asset Management published a study called *The Alpha and Beta of ESG Investing*, which found that responsible investing was generally a source of outperformance in the Eurozone and North America from 2014 to 2017 (Mortier and Roncalli, 2019).

As evidence mounts that ESG investing actually gets higher returns, the investment markets are responding to realize the opportunity, driving total global investment in sustainable assets and companies steadily upwards. According to the Global Sustainable Investment Alliance's (GSIA's) *Global Sustainable Investment Review 2018*, sustainable investing assets in five major markets – Europe, the US, Canada, Japan, and Australia/New Zealand – stood at US$30.7 trillion at the start of 2018, a 34% increase in two years, with Japan the fastest-growing region followed by Australia/New Zealand and Canada (GSI Alliance, 2018). The GSIA's figures also show that this rise has helped responsible investment to account for an increasingly significant share of professionally managed assets in each region, ranging from 18% in Japan to 63% in Australia and New Zealand. As the GSIA concludes: "Clearly, sustainable investing constitutes a major force across global financial markets" (Ibid).

There are many signs of progress in this area. One is the rapid growth in the number of signatories to the Principles for Responsible Investment (PRI) – an organization that works to help its members incorporate ESG factors into their investment decisions. As of July 2018, the PRI's global signatory base stood at 2,000, representing over US$82 trillion of assets (PRI, 2018). A year later, in August 2019, it announced it had added more than 500 new signatories in the intervening 12 months (Rust, 2019). Meanwhile, in June 2019 some 477 members of the Institutional Investors Group on Climate Change (IIGCC) – with an aggregate US$34 trillion in assets – issued an urgent call-to-action for world government leaders to limit average global temperature rises to no more than 1.5 degrees Celsius, through measures including putting a meaningful price on carbon (IIGCC, 2019). And in September 2019, a new United Nations-convened Net-Zero Asset Owner Alliance was announced at the UN Secretary-General's Climate Action Summit in New York. This alliance – led by Oliver Bäte, CEO of Allianz and a B Team Leader – includes many of the world's largest pension funds and insurers, who have committed to make their investment portfolios carbon-neutral by 2050.

As such initiatives underline, investors have a pivotal role to play in supporting and facilitating the trillions of dollars of capital investment required to enable the transition to a lower-carbon and more climate-resilient future. A further way they're doing this is through "impact investing," which involves making investments with the aim of generating social or environmental benefits alongside a financial return. In April 2019, a report issued by the Global Impact Investing Network (GIIN) – *Sizing the Impact Investing Market* – estimated the current size of the global impact investing market at US$502 billion (Pioneers Post, 2019). An important part of the impact investing landscape is the "green bond" market, which consists of loans issued to finance projects that will have a demonstrably positive impact on the climate or the environment more generally. According to a report published on the Euractiv website on June 26, 2019, *France Returns to Top of Global Green Bond Ranking*, the global green bonds market grew by 5% in 2018 to US$163 billion, with forecasts for 2019 ranging from US$200 billion to US$250 billion (Cuny, 2019).

However, despite this growth, green bonds still account for a tiny fraction – roughly 2% – of total global bond issuance. More generally, the sad fact remains that short-termism still too often prevails in the financial markets, and that progress towards a longer-term view remains too slow and too gradual. All of this raises some pressing questions. What's missing to move the investment markets to a longer-term and more holistic view at scale? What should corporates be doing to support this move? And what barriers need to be overcome? We'll now look to answer these questions – starting with the hurdles to surmount.

THE BARRIERS: EMBEDDED SHORT-TERMISM AND OPACITY OF VALUE

Turning to the barriers to moving the financial markets to a longer-term view, the first point to make is that the broad, airy statements that many organizations have made in the past are no longer enough – and indeed never were. Over the years, we've seen a lot of statements and plenty of good intentions, with many leaders in business and the financial markets stressing the importance of looking beyond financial profit to the generation of wider societal and environmental value. But the world is long on words and short on actions – and it needs more than lip-service.

However, beneath the surface, the environment is shifting. A key change is that, increasingly, the inherent role of the financial markets is actually to fulfill longer-term obligations. Today, most funds in the financial markets are pension funds, which by their nature want longer-term returns and a focus on generating sustainable value over many years and even decades. Yet while – as we've highlighted above – investors are coming around to a longer-term view, real change in investment priorities and criteria is not yet happening at the speed and scale that is needed.

Alongside the shifts in the financial markets, there has also been a sea-change in where the value of businesses resides. If you look back 40 or 50 years, 80% of a company's market capitalization could usually be explained by its fixed physical assets, mainly operations and buildings. Over the decades since then the polarities have been reversed, with the proportion attributable to fixed assets dropping to around 20%, and a corresponding rise in intangibles. This is partly because industry has moved to a different type of economy – namely the service economy, gig economy, and digital business – and partly because a lot of intangibles are virtually impossible to value accurately or with a high degree of certainty.

The result? Compared with the era when companies' value was dominated by their physical assets, it's now a lot more difficult for the financial market to assess where an organization's main value lies and what it's worth in both financial and societal terms. The solution to this opacity comes back to the greater transparency, clearer sense of purpose, and accountability in leadership that are so vital to rebuilding trust in business. Only when businesses themselves are demonstrably applying a long-term view and focusing on holistic value can they hope to convince the financial markets to do the same.

STEPS TO TAKE: A PROGRAM TO EFFECT REAL CHANGE

So, against this background, what do corporates need to do in order to help move the markets to a longer-term view? First and foremost, companies themselves need to *embrace longer-term and multi-stakeholder governance models*, and become better able to communicate the resulting benefits to the financial markets. Here are six concrete suggestions.

- First, *focus on the interests of a wider group of stakeholders* beyond investors. As well as emphasizing short-termism over long-term value creation, our economic system currently favors the shareholder over all other stakeholders, and fails to measure the real and undeniable costs business inflicts on nature and society. The B Team – whose CEO, Halla Tómasdóttir, is the co-author of this chapter – is at the forefront of tackling these shortcomings. To do this, the B Team engages leaders from business, civil society and government to catalyze a better way of doing business that prioritizes the wellbeing of people and the planet. In mid-2019, the leaders of the B Team committed to becoming "five times bolder" about changing their own practices, shifting societal norms and advocating for governmental policies to create an inclusive economy by 2030. There was a further vindication of the multi-stakeholder model in August 2019, when the US Business Roundtable released a new statement on the purpose of a corporation. Moving away from shareholder primacy, the new statement saw the CEOs of 181 Business Roundtable members commit to lead their companies for the benefit of all stakeholders – including customers, employees, suppliers, and communities, as well as shareholders.

  For an organization seeking to broaden its focus on stakeholders, the first step is to make the case for its overarching societal purpose as a way to create financial value. It can then define for itself where – and with which stakeholders – it can make the biggest contributions to that purpose. In essence, the company has to ask itself, "What is our reason for being?" By answering this question, it can begin to progress from shareholder primacy to multi-stakeholder governance.

  Danone – a leading foods company that is the world's largest yoghurt maker – provides a shining example of this process. Under the leadership of Emmanuel Faber, Danone CEO and a member of the B Team, the company has reinvented its way of doing business as well as its entire supply chain. Mr. Faber's strong commitment to accountability has seen him turn Danone's North American operations into the world's largest "B Corp," a business that holds itself responsible not only for profit but for its impact on people and planet. B Team Leader Guilherme Leal, co-founder of Natura, is another leader who exemplifies the holistic, courageous leadership needed to enhance sustainability and trust with all stakeholders. Natura – one of the world's largest "B Corps" – is widely considered to be Brazil's most sustainable company, and is fast becoming a global leader in the cosmetic sector through its own innovative and sustainable practices as well as acquisitions of like-minded companies such as Body Shop and Avon.

- Second, alongside the adoption of a broader multi-stakeholder focus, take steps to *escape from the straitjacket of short-term quarterly reporting*. This is a step Unilever took in 2009 under the leadership of co-author Paul Polman, and the decade since has proved the wisdom of that move. The company wanted to be anchored firmly in the UN SDGs, a goal that did not fit with a short-sighted focus on quarterly reporting. So, both to send a signal to the markets and create space for people to think long term, Unilever abolished quarterly reporting and analyst guidance while also embracing a multi-stakeholder model.

Initially this move attracted a degree of skepticism, with the stock price falling by 8% because investors thought it might negatively impact profitability. But, bit by bit, the new approach gained credibility. Ultimately, far from damaging Unilever's share price performance over time – as some suspected might happen – the changes saw the company deliver consistent top- and bottom-line growth over a ten-year period, generating a total shareholder return of 282% between 2009 and late 2018, with dividends reinvested. This was way ahead of the average of 131% delivered by the UK's FTSE share index as a whole over the same period.

Experience shows that the most difficult challenges when putting longer-term measures like these in place are getting everybody in the business on board and aligned, and ensuring the capabilities are in place to deal with any tensions and tradeoffs that may arise. A good example of how to manage these tensions for the long term is once again provided by Unilever, which – over the ten-year timeframe mentioned above – succeeded in evolving its corporate culture to be more sustainable, including buying and integrating five "B Corps" (see definition below). Compensation systems also need to be adjusted to a longer-term and multi-stakeholder basis to avoid decisions being driven by short-term priorities and pressures.

- Third, enhance and broaden companies' reporting by *integrating not only financial, but also environmental and social measures*. These measures should be material, significant, and comparable, so the markets can interpret and compare different organizations' performance in the areas they cover. A key to unlocking this opportunity is moving to more open and transparent reporting and the building in of externalities like climate change impacts. If companies "measure what they treasure," this automatically drives greater understanding and accountability for the system changes needed to make the shift – for example – to a low-carbon economy.

A good example of the leadership needed to drive the move to more holistic and relevant reporting measures is the work of the World Business Council for Sustainable Development (WBCSD), a CEO-led membership organization of over 200 international companies. The WBCSD's "Redefining Value" initiative aims to help companies measure and manage risk, gain competitive advantage and seize new opportunities through a better understanding of ESG information (WBCSD, 2019). The ultimate goal is to improve decision-making and external disclosures, eventually transforming the financial system to reward the most sustainable companies.

Major contributions are also being made by the Task Force on Climate-related Financial Disclosures (TFCD) and the World Benchmarking Alliance. These bodies are helping companies reach a more accurate view of the risks and opportunities of climate change, and thereby making it easier for investors to direct capital to more sustainable businesses. The faster and further we can progress towards these goals the better, as they will help overcome the "voodoo economics" that have twisted how we treat the natural world: for example, the clean-up operation following the BP oil spill in the Gulf of Mexico actually boosted US GDP growth.

Progress is also being made in other aspects of ESG. For example, Just Capital surveys the US public about its values, and then rates the companies in the Russell 1000 Index on how well they perform against societal expectations (JUST Capital, 2019). And in the area of equality, the B Team is working with various partners to refine and embed a set of Principles for Equality in the Workplace, with the goal of "ensuring equitable, safe and dignified workplaces that respect human rights and allow people to thrive" (B Team, 2018).

- Fourth, *become part of the B movement that is driving more responsible business models.* We've already mentioned the work of the B Team and the "B Corp" certification. A "B Corp" is an organization that commits to meeting the highest standards of verified social and environmental performance, public transparency, and legal accountability to balance profit and purpose.[1] Through this commitment, B Corps are accelerating the global culture shift to redefine success in business and build a more inclusive and sustainable economy. At the time of writing, 3,023 companies from 150 industries and 64 countries have become B Corps, including household names like Patagonia, Innocent Drinks, and – as mentioned above – B Team companies Danone North America and Natura in Brazil. Unilever's certified B Corps include Ben & Jerry's, Pukka, and Seventh Generation.

Box 10.1 The B Corp Declaration of Interdependence

We envision a global economy that uses business as a force for good. This economy is comprised of a new type of corporation – the B Corporation – which is purpose-driven and creates benefit for all stakeholders, not just shareholders.

As B Corporations and leaders of this emerging economy, we believe:

- That we must be the change we seek in the world.
- That all business ought to be conducted as if people and place mattered.
- That, through their products, practices, and profits, businesses should aspire to do no harm and benefit all.
- To do so requires that we act with the understanding that we are each dependent upon another and thus responsible for each other and future generations.

Source: https://bcorporation.net/about-b-corps

- Alongside such global initiatives, there are now a growing number of countries adopting longer-term corporate governance models, especially those where dropping quarterly reporting and providing greater stakeholder protection have been advocated. Examples of advances in this area include the introduction of "for-benefit corporation" legislation in several jurisdictions, including Italy and 35 US states – Maryland was the first in 2010 – plus the District of Columbia. For-benefit businesses are "fourth sector" for-profit companies that can pursue a broad array of environmental and/or societal goals as their main purpose, ahead of generating shareholder returns.
- Whether operating as one of these new types of business or working as part a movement such as the B Team, and whether working individually or collectively to drive change, companies should also become more proactive and vocal advocates of longer-term models. A great example of this type of advocacy is the Embankment Project for Inclusive Capitalism that Unilever helped to develop with EY. In a press statement released on November 16, 2018, EY revealed that the report – created by the Coalition for Inclusive Capitalism and EY, and based on a multi-stakeholder effort including more than 30 global business leaders – had found that a holistic view of a company's value, including intangible assets and impacts on society and the environment, required a focus on measuring

four components beyond financial returns: talent, innovation, society and environment, and governance (Díaz, 2018).

- Fifth, *collaborate with other companies and with governments to create an "ambition loop"* – a new type of positive feedback loop in which bold government policies and far-sighted private sector leadership reinforce each other. As the world looks to tackle the issues of climate change and inequality, there is huge potential for public–private partnerships to unleash greater corporate action that supports ambitious government policies. In our view, all companies should – at a minimum – be setting science-based emission reduction targets in line with the 1.5 degrees Celsius target. For their part, governments also need to promote policies that give business the clarity and confidence to invest further in a zero-carbon future. Similarly, collaboration between the private sector and government – often supported by regulation – is vital in pursuing social equality goals ranging from better financial inclusion to rural broadband availability.

- Finally, *use the systems and capabilities within companies to help move the financial markets to the longer term.* Organizations have several different tools or levers on hand to do this. These include:

  - Pension fund investments – Businesses should ask several questions, such as: how are the company's own pension funds invested? Are they invested for the long term or the short term? Have they signed up to the principles of responsible investing? And on what basis are the asset managers rewarded – quarterly performance or over the longer term?

  - Procurement – Companies cannot outsource their value chain and think this also means they've outsourced their responsibilities. As the B Team stresses, an important aspect of fostering a longer-term, multi-stakeholder view is for companies to take responsibility for their total value chain, and work with partners in it to embed longer-term responsibility to multiple stakeholders and non-financial measures. To help do this, companies might also apply an SDG (or ESG) lens across all their procurement activities.

  - Shareholder base – Businesses can actively seek out long-term shareholders who share their own view of their intrinsic purpose and role in society. Dropping quarterly reporting and adopting longer-term and more holistic remuneration policies can help to achieve this.

  - Talent and diversity – Experience and research show that workplace diversity makes for better and more holistic decision-making, thanks to input from a wider range of perspectives. So to develop a vibrant, inclusive, and high-performing workplace, companies should identify and close gaps in their workforces in terms of gender, generation, race, sexual orientation, and other personal characteristics. In this context, an article published in the *Harvard Business Review* in September 2019 – "Research: When Women are on Boards, Male CEOs are Less Overconfident" – provides further evidence that gender diversity on boards is a non-financial measure that drives financial returns through improved decisions and reduced risk (Chen et al., 2019). Age diversity is another increasingly important attribute as generational change continues, and is reflected in the different set of social values embraced by the younger generation, including an expectation of greater transparency from businesses and government. These distinct values manifest themselves in many ways, ranging from the strong commitment of younger people to fighting climate change, to their demand for more visibility into companies' social impacts along their global supply chains. All of this points to the younger generation's desire to create a better, more equal, and more sustainable world. After all, it's their future – and today's businesses have a responsibility to help create it by embedding ESG values into the decisions they make today.

CONCLUSION AND LESSONS LEARNED: PROVING THE BENEFITS...

Whatever steps companies may take to encourage the financial markets to take a long-term view, the most powerful tool at their disposal is demonstrating that the longer-term, multi-stakeholder model gives a better return than shorter-term approaches. Two proof-points serve to underline the need for change – and the scale of the potential impacts.

First, as long ago as 2012, Professor Richard Foster of Yale University estimated that the average lifespan of a company listed on the US S&P 500 index had fallen by more than 50 years in less than a century, from 67 years in the 1920s to just 15 years (Gittleson, 2012). Today it may well be even shorter. And this trend has also impacted CEOs. Research from PwC's Strategy& shows that in 2000, the CEO of a large company could expect to remain in office for eight or more years on average (Karlsson, Turner and Gassmann, 2019). Over the past decade, however, the average CEO tenure has fallen to only five years. This shorter period in control means today's business leaders simply don't have the time and space needed to develop models that address long-term challenges and opportunities. Second, public listings are in global retreat. In April 2018, in a paper entitled "What is the Point of the Equity Market?", Duncan Lamont, Head of Research and Analytics at Schroders, noted that "the number of companies listed on the UK main market has fallen by over 70% since the mid-1960s, and both the UK and US markets have witnessed a rough halving in numbers since the mid-1990s" (Lamont, 2018).

Such statistics confirm that if businesses are run without a longer-term view, a deeper sense of purpose, and a multi-stakeholder perspective – as they have been during the period when these declines occurred – we are actually running these companies into the ground: effectively killing the golden goose and throwing away the eggs. But more worryingly, we're failing to fulfill our function of serving society. We are not creating income equality because people cannot participate in wealth creation. And we are in turn fuelling the populism and the discontent we see today in many societies.

If we reverse all this, we can trigger the "fifth industrial revolution" (5IR) – the next step beyond the "fourth industrial revolution" (4IR) that's currently being ushered in by digital technologies. The 5IR will be an era when companies make positive contributions to society, are in sync with the planet, and work to drive inclusive growth – helping people the world over to enjoy healthy and thriving lives. These are all things that initiatives such as the B Team and the United Nations Global Compact are striving to bring about.

...AND EXHIBITING COURAGEOUS, INSPIRING, AND PRINCIPLED LEADERSHIP

To sum up: business cannot succeed in a system that is broken. And business cannot afford to remain a bystander as a system that gives it life in the first place breaks down. We're now seeing that breakdown take place. So, recognizing that we are all operating in a challenging and complex political environment, now is the time for business to step up, accept its responsibilities, help to de-risk the political process, and commit to assisting in the creation of a better future for all.

However, to do all this we must first address a key impediment to progress – today's unprecedented lack of trust in institutions of all kinds. It's because of this trust deficit that meeting today's challenges will require business leaders who are courageous and principled: individuals with a mindset that is bold, brave, and far-sighted, and who can look beyond their own relatively short tenure as a CEO to focus on the long term. Who will not just espouse a compelling purpose, but will act positively to turn it into reality. And who are committed to engaging openly and honestly with stakeholders, society, and governments to build the trust needed to craft a new social contract.

The necessary qualities boil down to strong leadership and willpower, underpinned by an unshakeable belief that real and positive change is both vital and achievable. Ultimately, those are the forces that will move the dial in the financial markets, by serving to shift the perspective in three important ways: first, from short-termism to the creation and stewardship of long-term value; second, from focusing on measuring only financial profit to measuring what really matters; and third, from shareholder primacy to multi-stakeholder inclusion and governance. As mankind faces up to the greatest challenges in its history, these are the overarching leadership imperatives for the 21st century.

NOTE

1   See the accompanying information panel, drawn from the B Corp website: https://bcorporation. uk/about-b-corps

REFERENCES

B Team (2018) *Workplace Equality* [Online]. Available at: https://bteam.org/our-work/causes/workplace-equality (Accessed: 2 January 2020).

Barton, D., Bailey, J., and Zoffer, J. (2015) *Rising to the Challenge of Short-termism* [Online]. Available at: www.fcltglobal.org/docs/default-source/default-document-library/fclt-global-rising-to-the-challenge.pdf?sfvrsn=0 (Accessed: 2 January 2020).

Barton, D., Manyika, J., and Koehane Williamson, S. (2017) 'Finally, evidence that managing for the long term pays off', *Harvard Business Review* (9 February) [Online]. Available at: https://hbr. org/2017/02/finally-proof-that-managing-for-the-long-term-pays-off (Accessed: 23 December 2019).

Beal, D., Eccles, R., Hansell, G., Lesser, R., Unnikrishnan, S., Woods, W., and Young, D. (2017) *Total Societal Impact: A New Lens for Strategy* [Online]. Available at: www.bcg.com/publications/2017/ total-societal-impact-new-lens-strategy.aspx (Accessed: 2 January 2020).

Chen, J., Leung, W.S., Song, W., and Goergen, M. (2019) 'When women are on boards, male CEOs are less overconfident', *Harvard Business Review* (12 September) [Online]. Available at: https:// hbr.org/2019/09/research-when-women-are-on-boards-male-ceos-are-less-overconfident (Accessed: 2 January 2020).

Cheng, E. (2017) 'Just 10% of trading is regular stock picking, JPMorgan estimates', *CNBC* (13 June) [Online]. Available at: www.cnbc.com/2017/06/13/death-of-the-human-investor-just-10-per-cent-of-trading-is-regular-stock-picking-jpmorgan-estimates.html (Accessed: 2 January 2020).

Cuny, D. (2019) *France Returns to Top of Global Green Bond Ranking* [Online]. Available at: www. euractiv.com/section/energy-environment/news/france-returns-to-top-of-global-green-bond-ranking/ (Accessed: 2 January 2020).

Díaz, Y. (2018) *Embankment Project for Inclusive Capitalism Releases Report to Drive Sustainable and Inclusive Growth* [Online]. Available at: www.ey.com/uk/en/newsroom/news-releases/18-11-16-embankment-project-for-inclusive-capitalism-releases-report-to-drive-sustainable-and-inclusive-growth (Accessed: 2 January 2020).

Edelman (2019) *2019 Edelman Trust Barometer* [Online]. Available at: www.edelman.com/trust-barometer (Accessed: 2 January 2020).

Gittleson, K. (2012) 'Can a company live forever?', *BBC News* (19 January) [Online]. Available at: www.bbc.co.uk/news/business-16611040 (Accessed: 2 January 2020).

GSI Alliance (2018) *2018 Global Sustainable Investment Review* [Online]. Available at: www.gsi-alliance. org/wp-content/uploads/2019/03/GSIR_Review2018.3.28.pdf?utm_source=The+IIG+Community&utm_campaign=60a39c9e1c-EMAIL_CAMPAIGN_11_30_2018_11_56_ COPY_01&utm_medium=email&utm_term=0_4b03177e81-60a39c9e1c-71997937 (Accessed: 2 January 2020).

IIGCC (2019) *477 Investors with USD $34 Trillion in Assets Urge G20 Leaders to Keep Global Temperature Rise to 1.5 Degrees Celsius Source* [Online]. Available at: www.iigcc.org/news/477-investors-with-usd-34-trillion-in-assets-urge-g20-leaders-to-keep-global-temperature-rise-to-1-5-degrees-celsius/ (Accessed: 2 January 2020).

JUST Capital (2019) *Survey Reports* [Online]. Available at: https://justcapital.com/survey-report/ (Accessed: 2 January 2020).

Karlsson, P., Turner, M., and Gassmann, P. (2019) 'Succeeding the long-serving legend in the corner office', *strategy+business* (15 May) [Online]. Available at: www.strategy-business.com/article/Succeeding-the-long-serving-legend-in-the-corner-office?gko=90171 (Accessed: 2 January 2020).

Lagarde, C. (2018) *Ten Years after Lehman – Lessons Learned and Challenges Ahead* [Online]. Available at: https://blogs.imf.org/2018/09/05/ten-years-after-lehman-lessons-learned-and-challenges-ahead/ (Accessed: 2 January 2020).

Lamont, D. (2018) *What Is the Point of the Equity Market?* [Online]. Available at: www.schroders.com/en/sysglobalassets/digital/insights/2018/thought-leadership/what-is-the-point-of-the-equity-market_april-2018.pdf (Accessed: 2 January 2020).

McGrath, M. (2018) 'Sir David Attenborough: Climate change "our greatest threat"', *BBC News* (3 December) [Online]. Available at: www.bbc.co.uk/news/science-environment-46398057 (Accessed: 2 January 2020).

Mirchandani, B., Boxer, S., He, A., Horowitz, E., and Tellez, V. (2019) *Predicting Long-term Success for Corporations and Investors Worldwide* [Online]. Available at: www.fcltglobal.org/docs/default-source/publications/predicting-long-term-success-for-corporations-and-investors-worldwide.pdf?sfvrsn=8f00228c_2 (Accessed: 2 January 2020).

Mortier, V. and Roncalli, T. (2019) *The Alpha and Beta of ESG Investing* [Online]. Available at: http://research-center.amundi.com/page/Article/2019/01/The-Alpha-and-Beta-of-ESG-investing (Accessed: 2 January 2020).

Oxfam (2018) *5 Shocking Facts about Extreme Global Inequality and How to Even It Up* [Online]. Available at: www.oxfam.org/en/even-it/5-shocking-facts-about-extreme-global-inequality-and-how-even-it-davos (Accessed: 2 January 2020).

Pioneers Post (2019) 'Global impact investing market soars above $500bn', *Pioneers Post* (1 April) [Online]. Available at: www.pioneerspost.com/news-views/20190401/global-impact-investing-market-soars-above-500bn (Accessed: 2 January 2020).

PRI (2018) *Quarterly Update: Climate Action Gathering Momentum* [Online]. Available at: www.unpri.org/news-and-press/quarterly-update-climate-action-gathering-momentum/3442.article (Accessed: 2 January 2020).

Rust, S. (2019) 'PRI gains 500 new signatories in 12 months', *IPE* (16 August) [Online]. Available at: www.ipe.com/news/esg/pri-gains-500-new-signatories-in-12-months/10032854.article *(Accessed: 2 January 2020).*

Task Force on Climate-Related Financial Disclosures (TCFD) (2017). *Mike Bloomberg and FSB Chair Mark Carney Announce Growing Support for the TCFD on the Two-Year Anniversary of the Paris Agreement* [Online]. Available at: www.fsb-tcfd.org/wp-content/uploads/2017/12/TCFD-Press-Release-One-Planet-Summit-12-Dec-2017_FINAL.pdf (Accessed: 2 January 2020).

Thompson, J. (2018) 'Companies with strong ESG score outperform, study finds', *Financial Times* (12 August) [Online]. Available at: www.ft.com/content/f99b0399-ee67-3497-98ff-eed4b04cf-de5#comments-anchor (Accessed: 2 January 2020).

Unilever (2017) *Sustainable Business Could Unlock US$12 Trillion, Creating 380 Million Jobs* [Online]. Available at: www.unilever.com/news/news-and-features/Feature-article/2017/Sustainable-business-could-unlock-12-trillion-dollars-and-380-million-jobs.html (Accessed: 2 January 2020).

WBCSD (2019) *Redefining Value* [Online]. Available at: www.wbcsd.org/Programs/Redefining-Value (Accessed: 2 January 2020).

11

Embedding values and principles[1]

Mark Moody-Stuart

INTRODUCTION

In order to make a more sustainable investment choice, an investor needs to compare sustainability indicators and governance between companies. To make a longer-term difference an investor also needs to engage with companies, using the power of investment to encourage positive change and improve ESG performance. Investors measure outputs. Outputs are driven by internal factors which are essential to corporate performance but often difficult for an investor to assess. This chapter considers some of the important internal factors and suggests some ways in which an engaged investor can gauge the quality and effectiveness of these factors.

To operate effectively as a cohesive unit a company needs a purpose shared throughout the organisation. It also needs an agreed set of values governing behaviour while working towards that common purpose. Purpose and values are often clearly stated for all to see, but this is a far cry from the leadership of a company, let alone a shareholder, being able to know that these often lofty statements are actually commonly agreed and lived throughout the organisation at all levels and in all parts of the world.

COMMONLY ACCEPTED VALUES ARE MORE IMPORTANT THAN RULES

A major global company cannot be run simply by referring to a rule book. Situations vary enormously from country to country and furthermore can change very rapidly. No rule book could cover this and if it attempted to it would be voluminous and, in any case, almost certainly would not be read. It is therefore essential to try and embed values and principles in such a way that they are absorbed by people in the organisation wherever they are and whatever their background, race, or religion. In this way an individual can respond rapidly and confidently to situations on the ground. However, that does not mean that individuals are on their own. They should be able to refer to other people in the organisation to discuss difficult issues and thus draw on the experience of the whole group. This will only be possible if conditions have been created where real-life past problems have been discussed freely and people know that it is not a confession of weakness or failure to discuss a dilemma.

There is an analogy with the values to which a family subscribe. At best these encompass all members of a family: parents, grandparents, brothers, sisters, and children. There are established patterns of behaviour which are known and accepted by all as part of membership of the family group. The values are not codified but established by example and behaviour. They are also subject to adaptation. The situations encountered by children and grandchildren are different from those experienced by their parents and grandparents and inevitably changes in behaviour and response will be needed, although hopefully the underlying values remain the same.

If this is difficult to achieve in a family, it is even more difficult in a global corporation. The essential first step is a willingness to discuss and debate. One of the reasons that I continued to work for Shell for so many years is that I found it always acceptable to say, "that does not seem quite right to me." You would not simply be told to get on with the job. People at any level were prepared to engage in a discussion as to why it did not seem quite right or fair and what could be done about it.

UNADDRESSED MISBEHAVIOUR NEGATES
ANY CODE OF CONDUCT

Almost every corporate statement of principles will include a commitment to respect for people. To truly embed such a value in a global company requires much thought and discussion between people at all levels and all areas in an organisation. The same value can have many expressions. Even in simple forms of address there can be variations. For example, someone who would be called Yamamoto-san in Japan would probably be comfortable being called "Bob" Yamamoto in the US or Herr Doktor Yamamoto in Germany. The more formal styles of address need not detract from a corporate culture of openness and free exchange of views. The same is true of forms of dress, particularly for women.

At the same time, if breaches of company values or regulations are left unaddressed, the entire structure of values is destroyed. I recall a charismatic and high-performing individual leading a significant business who at the same time could reduce grown men and women to tears by his treatment of them. The individual left the company; had this not been the case, the entire concept of values would have been destroyed. In the same vein, I was told of a star trader at a bank who, before the financial crisis, regularly smoked in the foyer of the bank where other employees had to stand outside in the rain. Small wonder that irregularities went unreported in such an organisation. What was the point? Financial performance clearly trumped values.

Many corporations lay great emphasis on training to instil values. Conventional training has limited effect. What is needed is training which involves a lot of free-flowing discussion and relating of personal experiences – what are sometimes referred to as "war stories". I recall listening to the chief executive of a major financial institution which had suffered from scandals relating to trading in Europe and to other events in Japan. He had put in place a very impressive structured training programme delivered around the world through thousands of hours, with care to ensure maximum coverage (and documentation of that coverage). I was impressed by the effort and systematic approach, but then, in my eyes, he blew it all by remarking somewhat wistfully of his errant traders that if they had done it to Goldman's or Lehman's it would have been alright. He plainly did not get it. Distorting the market, which is what the traders had done, is an abuse whether the victims are Goldman's or Lehman's or a lot of little old ladies. The value is not dependent on the victim, although the severity of the crime may be. Given this attitude of the chief executive, I suspect that the entire structured and rather legalistic training was wasted.

In Shell in the 1990s our safety performance in exploration and production had plateaued after a period of improvement. An analysis of accidents showed that fatal accidents were more likely to occur when operations were started up before all was completely ready. It was also apparent that in the case of many accidents, someone had had some degree of prior concern or uneasiness about the situation but had not felt empowered to act. So we sent out a strong message to all operations over my signature saying that anyone at any level had a right to stop an operation if they felt that it was unsafe and that it was more important to ensure that all was ready – training and testing complete – than to meet a promised deadline.

For two or more years after that when I attended town hall type meetings with people in operations around the world, I found that at some point there would be a question along the lines of: "Mark, are we not sending out mixed messages on the importance of production versus safety?" Initially I was a bit irritated by the question, pointing to the letter which I had signed and which

I thought was absolutely clear. Could people not read? Very soberingly, I soon realised that it was not that people had not read my letter, but that they still had some doubts as to what it really meant. Not to put too fine a point on it, they did not really believe the words or that I really meant what I said. The answer was not to make the message more strident, but to find operations which had been shut down for safety reasons, or where start-up had been delayed and draw attention to them, publicly commending those concerned. If people see an action that, although clearly costing the company money, attracts commendation, they believe the message.

At a different level, the action of Cynthia Caroll when chief executive of Anglo American in shutting down Anglo Platinum mining operations in the wake of an unacceptable series of fatal accidents was not just brave, but transformative. Operations only recommenced when all miners had been trained in safe behaviour and rules. The significant cost was publicised. Interestingly, there was no complaint from shareholders. The message to all was that values trump profit.

I have been much encouraged recently to read of several examples where chief executives of major companies who by all accounts had been very successful in delivering good financial results were nonetheless dismissed as a result of reports of inappropriate behaviour towards others in the organisation. Some of this has undoubtedly been triggered by the #MeToo movement, but it is perhaps an indication of a wider acceptability of a willingness for people in an organisation to speak up and call out unacceptable behaviour, with consequent action. It is encouraging that financial performance or charismatic leadership is not seen to forgive unacceptable behaviour in the corporations.

Less encouraging is an apparent reverse trend in political leadership. In several cases political leaders who are clearly guilty of repeated wilful mis-statements and lies are nonetheless forgiven by their followers. I believe that in corporate life such behaviour would lead to dismissal. Indeed, in the case of one elected leader it had resulted in him being fired from a past employment. A trend of forgiving unacceptable behaviour in public life, as long as the actions of the leader deliver financial benefit to supporters or reflect their own views, is deeply corrosive to our societies. It is indeed ironic if some business leaders, and indeed investors, condone behaviour in political leaders which hopefully they would never accept in their own businesses or in the companies in which they invest.

THE PROCESS OF AGREEING PURPOSE AND VALUES IS IMPORTANT

How values are established can have a significant impact on how they are owned or internalised by people throughout the organisation. Widespread discussion across the organisation can ensure that the purpose and values of the organisation are indeed soundly based and understood by all. A crisis brought on by challenges from stakeholders to a corporation's behaviour can paradoxically be very helpful. The self-esteem of all who work in or for the corporation is challenged and this enables a deeper reconsideration of purpose as well as values and norms of behaviour. Past examples are Nike in relation to abuses in the supply chain, Shell in the case of the execution of Ken Saro Wiwa and challenges to deep-sea disposal of the marine facility Brent Spar, and the mining industry in relation to environmental and human rights issues. In the mining industry, Rio Tinto under their executive chairman Sir Robert Wilson, was deeply involved in the multi-stakeholder consultation in the Mining Metals and Sustainable Development. That process led to the formation of the International Council for Mining and Metals, a CEO-led organisation of leading mining companies with clear principles mandatory for members. In the case of Shell, the wide multi-stakeholder consultation led to modification of existing principles and a commitment to report openly on progress in implementing them. Banks and the banking industry are facing similar challenges, as are the major social media companies. Both industries are still working on developing solutions, although their approaches are not necessarily based on independently chaired multi-stakeholder input. In all cases, the process has to be an ongoing one.

PUBLIC REPORTING OF PROGRESS AGAINST COMMITMENTS IS VITAL

A company's purpose is, by definition, very much related to its own specific activities or perhaps that of the industry in which it operates. The work of the International Integrated Reporting Council has done much to make sure that a company's purpose embedded in its corporate reporting is clear and that reporting makes clear the reason for the existence of the company. It is encouraging that the number of companies that produce integrated reports is increasing.

In relation to principles, the ten principles of the United Nations Global Compact (UNGC) provide a basis or starting point for the development of corporate principles. The principles were developed in 2000 from the late Kofi Annan's challenge to business to join with the United Nations "to initiate a global compact of shared values and principles, which will give a human face to the global market". They are universal principles in that they were developed from the major UN Conventions agreed by all member states and cover human rights, labour, the environment, and anti-corruption.

The UNGC is thus different from most other organisations in that not only do signatories have to subscribe to universal principles, but they must also commit to report annually on progress in embedding these principles into their day-to-day operations. Failure to do so results in sanctions. Other differentiating characteristics of the UNGC are that it is multi-stakeholder in its governance. While business-led and largely business-funded, it involves civil society and labour organisations working on all the areas of the principles. Both civil society organisations and unions are represented on the UNGC board.

A further distinguishing factor is that the UNGC is inclusive of all businesses regardless of size. It embraces, along with major corporations, the small and medium-sized enterprises which employ the bulk of the world's workforce as well as forming the critical supply chains of global companies. This has allowed the UNGC to grow to embrace some 10,000 corporations in over 160 countries, with a further 3,000 civil society organisations. The Local Networks of the UNGC bring together national and international companies, large and small companies as well as local and international civil society organisations in a country context. Apart from sharing experiences and increasing compliance with the principles, the Local Networks of the UNGC can also focus on national progress towards achievement of the Sustainable Development Goals.

Whatever principles and values a company develops, the example of the UNGC demonstrates the importance for credibility of reporting publicly on performance in relation to its principles. Internally, such reporting can highlight which parts of the organisation are making the most progress. This can then provide examples and encouragement to units of the company which are progressing more slowly. Externally, such reporting demonstrates to investors the practical application and impact of the corporate principles.

SPEAK-UP PROGRAMMES AND HOTLINES

Whatever principles a company commits to, developing a feeling that every member of the company is responsible for playing their part in maintaining the values and ensuring that all their colleagues do likewise is critical. There is an analogy with family values and a feeling that all members of the family are responsible for maintaining those values and not letting the family down. The ideal is where all members of the team, at whatever level in the organisation, support each other in maintaining values and there is open discussion of what is, or is not, in line with those values. However, there will be cases where an individual does not feel sufficiently empowered to discuss questionable or improper behaviour or challenge it openly. To address this, independent secure speak-up programmes or hotlines are important. Such lines are also valuable fraud detection and prevention measures: current statistics indicate that about half of all frauds detected in corporations come from such facilities.

When such facilities are first introduced, most reports are anonymous, but as confidence in the security of the system and in non-retaliation grows, more reporters are prepared to give their names. While not essential, it is more helpful if the independent body receiving the report knows the name of the reporter. This makes follow-up easier and it also allows the reporting individual to be told directly of the result of the investigation. Statistics on the source and nature of the reports and the trends can be an important indicator for audit committees and boards of directors. Information on the existence and workings of such systems is also an important indicator for investors.

It is important that such systems or parallel systems be open to companies in the supply chain. In Saudi Arabia and other countries in the Middle East, it is often incorrectly assumed by international companies that local agents or important connections are necessary in order to obtain business. Saudi Aramco encourages all its suppliers and contractors to do business directly with the company and also requires them to sign a "Supplier Code of Conduct" specifying the behaviour expected of suppliers and contractors. This code gives details of confidential reporting lines that can be used by a supplier, any of its staff, or subcontractors to report improper behaviour, including that of any Aramco staff. It is an effective and important mechanism on all sides.

THE USE OF CORPORATE-WIDE SURVEYS

Properly designed and independently run surveys of people at all levels in a company can be an important measure of the state of a company and of directions of progress. Such surveys are often denigrated on the assumption that people only put down what they think that the company wants to hear, but I have not found this to be the case. However, several conditions need to be met if the surveys are to be valid and effective.

First, they should be properly and professionally designed, with multiple questions designed to check on consistency of approach and allowing nuances of feeling. Second, they should be externally run, with anonymity guaranteed. Third, there needs to be feedback to all those surveyed of the results at different levels of aggregation, from the company as a whole to the smallest unit that can be achieved without the possibility of anonymity being compromised. Fourth, there needs to be a detailed response from management on steps which are being taken at all levels to address areas where improvement is needed, with consultation and discussion of the results and these proposed steps.

This fourth step is perhaps the most important. Filling in surveys thoughtfully is time-consuming and people will only continue to do so in successive surveys if they feel that they have been listened to and action taken. The percentage of people taking the trouble to reply to participate in the survey, the so-called "engagement score", is an important indicator of progress or otherwise. Increasing engagement is also normally correlated with more encouraging results. The trends, if not the detailed results, of such surveys can be a valuable indicator for an engaged investor to discuss with a company.

Graded responses to such statements as "I believe the company puts pro-duction performance above safety" will seldom result in a 100% positive score, but the trend is very important. One of the scores which gave me most pleasure in a Shell survey was the very high positive score to the statement, "In this company I can say what I really think", or something similar. If there is free communication and expression, common progress in other areas is made easier. The other side of the coin is that in Shell we sometimes suffered from an excessively deliberative process!

INSIGHTS FROM VISITS TO OPERATIONS AND BOARD PROCESSES

Whether for management, boards of directors, or investors, visits to oper-ations provide a vital reality check. It is not only possible to see physical evidence of principles and values playing out in action, but by talking to oper-atives and asking questions a sense can be gained as to whether those on the front line have really internalised the corporate values. For boards this is a time-consuming process, as it is seldom possible to visit operations in distant parts of the world in less than several days. Nonetheless, the time and effort are repaid in greater understanding of the operations and hopefully greater confidence in their integrity. Such visits are also possible to arrange for repre-sentatives of engaged investors.

A not dissimilar insight can be obtained by non-executive directors at every board meeting. By observing the relationship between the executive team and the chief executive as well as with the chairman and seeing whether there is open discussion or whether everything has been carefully choreo-graphed beforehand gives insight into the company culture. Does the board have access to those outside the executive team? Is an open discussion with differences of opinion between executives on specific points permitted, toler-ated, or even encouraged? Is the company open to separate briefing sessions for board members interested in a specific subject? Are the chairs of board committees expected to have a free hand in determining agendas? All of these and many other points are important indicators of internal workings of the company. An engaged investor can gain insights into this through discus-sions with independent chairs of board committees.

INVOLVEMENT OF COMPANIES IN DIFFICULT COUNTRIES – "BUSINESS FOR PEACE"

One of the challenges for sustainable investing as well as for corporations is the involvement of potentially investible companies in countries with poor human rights records or very high levels of corruption. These are the countries where a company's activities are most likely to appear in critical reporting and thus be flagged up by "controversy monitoring". These are also the countries where strong internal values are required in working towards solutions of complex problems.

A controversy does not necessarily imply wrongdoing. In a country with high levels of corruption and where human rights abuses may undoubtedly have occurred, a company with high standards which is able to run its own operations without becoming entangled in abuses may not only provide decent employment for many in its own operations and in its supply chain, but may also be an example of how high standards are a benefit and not simply a cost. It is incumbent on a responsible investor to be discriminatory in such cases. The concept of responsible business maintaining through investment connections across political divides is the basis of the UNGC's "Business for Peace" initiative.

In 2002 the Canadian company Talisman was forced by the pressure of public opinion and from the Canadian government to sell its oil production operations in Sudan, a country in which not only was there effectively a civil war, but where undoubted human rights abuses were taking place. It is quite possible that Talisman may have at some point made mistakes in its relations with government forces. In discussions that I have had with human rights activists, they admitted that it was not possible to say that the human rights situation had improved as a result of Talisman's withdrawal. In fact, they were concerned that while Talisman had been open to discussion on the nature of their operations, the dilemmas involved, and on actions which could be taken to improve the situation, it was not clear that the successor companies were similarly open to open dialogue with critics.

Shortly after the transfer of Talisman operations to the China National Petroleum Corporation (CNPC), the UN Global Compact was engaged in establishing a local network in Sudan and also promoting the UNGC "Business for Peace" initiative. It was therefore very encouraging that, through the intermediation of the UNGC, representatives of six major long-term investors who were all signatories to the UN Principles for Responsible Investment (PRI) were able to visit CNPC operations in Sudan. The PRI signatories were concerned that their investments in PetroChina, the internationally quoted arm of CNPC, could be criticised as a result of CNPC operations in Sudan.

The visit, hosted by CNPC, established that the operations were indeed of high quality. Security was unarmed and clearly separated from any involvement with the armed state security and was indeed in line with the UN Principles on Security and Human Rights. The treatment of produced water was of high quality through innovative reed bed techniques. There were also creative practices on the employment of Sudanese, including flexible working for nomadic herders for some parts of the year. A very impressive and modern hospital, set up originally by Talisman, was staffed by Sudanese doctors and served not just the local population but accessed by women with difficult pregnancies from a wide area.

An excellent example of the concept of "Business for Peace", although started many years before that initiative was launched by the UNGC, is the Gaesong Industrial Zone. This is well described in a paper by Williams and Park (2019). The Gaesong Industrial Zone (GIZ) is an enclave in North Korea where companies from South Korea have made investments in manufacturing facilities of a high standard, where decent work was provided to some 55,000 citizens of North Korea who enter the zone for work every day. This meant that citizens of the two countries interact in a cooperative way delivering commercial and livelihood benefits and breaking down barriers. Due to enhanced political sanctions the Zone is now closed, but thanks to the Korean Network, my wife and I had the opportunity to visit the GIZ in 2015 and we were very impressed by what we saw, although the operation faces challenges and is controversial in some areas like that of the handling of North Korean workers' wages by North Korean unions. A few months before, at the first Business for Peace annual meeting held in Istanbul, I had been given a gift of some of the ceramic and textile products from the Zone. My wife and I were very moved when we returned home to see that the label on one gift item of clothing did not say Made in the Republic of Korea or North Korea, but simply "Made in Peace". That sums up the spirit and drive behind this imaginative initiative.

A DILEMMA FOR RESPONSIBLE AND SUSTAINABLE INVESTORS

I would argue that the above examples show that a responsible company operating to high standards in a country with high levels of corruption and with even some human rights abuses by governments in areas not related to the company's operations can exemplify the benefits of high standards. Those high standards can spread to local companies in the supply chain and are often seen as supportive by other local businesses, frequently family owned, who also aspire to ethical standards. Responsible and engaged investors should be supportive of companies operating in such countries, provided that they are prepared to be transparent about their approach to the challenges. Such companies also need to be open in their engagement with critical civil society groups. In Myanmar, civil society groups had been very critical of Total's continued operations in the country. Yet when cyclone Nargis struck, some of the same groups found that Total's operations were the most capable and organised in the affected areas. An investment supportive of such companies must take into account the probability that, given the environment, media controversies and criticism are likely to be greater.

The default reaction of some Western governments to regimes of whose actions they disapprove is to impose unilateral economic sanctions. Equally, some investors will avoid investments in companies which operate in countries in which human rights violations are common. Clearly on some occasions financial sanctions, particularly targeted at key individuals, may be justified. But the sanction weapon needs to be applied sparingly and to be coupled with a clarity as to what action is needed for sanctions to be lifted. Sanctions approved by the United Nations, other than arms embargoes, are relatively rare precisely because there is generally only support from a small group of countries with similar political views.

Consider the case of Iran, a country which has been under some form of economic sanctions or restrictions from one or other country for some 40 years. There is no doubt that the present government in Iran has been fomenting problems or threatening destruction on a number of countries in the region, directly or through proxies. It would be highly beneficial if this ceased. There are also clearly human rights violations by the government. A consequence of years of sanctions has been that the economy has been restricted and the very restricted economic activity has been concentrated in the hands of the government who can use it for political purposes and to reward its supporters. This encourages corruption. Furthermore, the government can blame hardships and its own shortcomings on the enemy. The private sector has been squeezed almost out of existence and the wider population has suffered great hardship.

Had an alternative policy been adopted in which responsible foreign investment had been encouraged, contributing also to the growth of the domestic private sector, it is arguable that the outcome would have been very different. The private business sector is one important element of society which, if it is permitted to flourish, is not only independent of government but also helps to grow the economy to the benefit of all. While this increases the government's fiscal revenue, which could be misapplied by the government, there will be pressure from a successful and independent private sector to apply the revenue more constructively and ensure that the benefits of growth accrue to all.

To endure and flourish, trade and investment requires mutually beneficial agreements. Very often business people can reach such agreements across fractious political boundaries. They can maintain communication and understanding even when governments are at loggerheads. This is at the heart of the concept of business for peace.

It is clear that this approach will only work if business indeed behaves responsibly. What is "responsible business" in this context? It requires transparency and openness about its engagement in difficult countries with civil society groups representing various interests from human rights to working conditions, the environment, and anti-corruption (the four areas of the UNGC Principles). It also requires transparency and responsiveness to engaged investors. Being open to consumer pressure directly or indirectly also encourages corporate responsibility. If those conditions are in place, it could be argued that positive change is more likely to come from maintaining open business connections with what might be called difficult countries than in trying to isolate them by sanctions. The investor community together with international financial institutions have an important role to play in evaluating such situations and considering supporting rather than shunning responsible companies engaged in such activities.

TESTING THE PENETRATION OF VALUES

The penetration and ownership at all levels in a company of its principles and values is very important to its ability to respond rapidly and effectively to unexpected situations and challenges and not just in "business as usual" situations. Getting a sense of this is not as easy for engaged investors and indeed for non-executive directors as is examining sustainability indicators largely based on output. To compare performance on sustainability requires a sense of a company's capacity for anticipatory response or how anyone in the company might respond to a situation not necessarily encountered before.

Here is a checklist of a few possible additional lines of enquiry for engaged investors. The list is certainly not exhaustive:

- *What was the "process of discussion" across the company of its purpose and principles or values?* Was there a widespread process of engagement at all levels and around the world in different countries, if appropriate?
- *What was the involvement of external stakeholders in that process?* How were they involved? Was it just reviewing and commenting upon the result or were they engaging in discussions at an earlier formative stage?
- *Does the company openly report against a framework of its principles or principles such as those of the United Nations Global Compact?* Are targets set and is there reporting, internal or external, of progress by area or business division? Internally, such reporting can lead to healthy competition, as no unit or region wants to be the laggard holding back progress. Reporting against the UNGC ten principles in the format of a UNGC communication on progress is a requirement for ongoing membership of the UNGC, but company-specific reporting against its own principles may be equally useful. It should be comprehensive and open to public scrutiny.
- *How does the board function?* This is easier for a non-executive director to answer with direct experience of how free the engagement is, not just with the CEO, but with other members of the executive team and

with other executives outside the executive team. Shareholders can get an indication of how the board works by engaging with the chairs of committees. Whether the company is happy to arrange this is also an indication of an open culture and a lack of a controlling mentality.

- *Does the company use worldwide surveys of its people to determine their view of the company and its performance in relation to its published principles?* The nature of the questions can be revealing and the trend of responses to particular questions can be revealing. Trends in answers to individual questions are important if the company is happy to disclose them. The overall "engagement score" and the trend should certainly be available.
- *Does the company have an effective speak-up process or hotline?* The trend of users can also be a useful indicator, for example a reduction in anonymous reports may indicate growing confidence in the effectiveness and security of the process.
- *Does the company have a supplier code of conduct and is there a confidential complaints mechanism open to both suppliers and their staff?* Access to a secure process is important to detect potential abuse by staff as well as suppliers. Access to the process by supplier employees can reveal problems not necessarily detected in a supplier audit. Clearly, however, it can be the subject of abuse.
- *Does the company arrange regular site visits for its board and for investors?* Site visits allow confirmation that operatives at different levels in the company are aligned with the stated values. It is also an opportunity not just to sense the quality of local operation but to observe the degree of openness between people at different levels in the company.

NOTE

1 Some of the ideas expressed in this chapter are based on prior publications by the author, including: Moody-Stuart, M. (2017). *Responsible Leadership: Lessons from the Frontline of Sustainability and Ethics.* London: Routledge; Moody-Stuart, M. (2013). "UN Global Compact Local Networks and their importance in the implementation of the Guiding Principles." *Business and Human Rights Review.* 1(2), pp. 9–10; Moody-Stuart, M. (2019). "Leadership and the Challenge of Embedding Values in a Global Corporation". *Hawkamah Journal.* 14, pp. 8–11; and Moody-Stuart, M. (2017). "The Governance of Transnational Issues" in Rasche, A, Morsing, M. & Moon, J. (eds). *Corporate Social Responsibility: Strategy, Governance, Communication,* pp. 473–477. Cambridge: Cambridge University Press.

REFERENCE

Williams, O. and Park, S. Y.-S. (2019). '"Business for Peace" (B4P): can this new global governance paradigm of the United Nations Global Compact bring some peace and stability to the Korean peninsula?', *Asian Journal of Business Ethics,* 8(2), pp. pp. 173–193.

PART III

Sustainable investing, technology, and data

12

ESG and AI

The beauty and the beast of sustainable investing

Omar Selim[1]

AN X-RAY FOR FINANCE

It was a cold evening on 8 November 1895 in Würzburg, a small town in the south of Germany. A young physicist, well known for his meticulous experiments and dislike of coincidences, came across what perhaps became the biggest coincidence of the nineteenth century. For years, he had been studying the effects of electrical charges in a vacuum tube and, to his utter surprise, the device he was working on produced a fluorescent ray on a coated screen, somewhere at the back of his laboratory. He locked himself up to understand the full potential of that new phenomenon and discovered that it enabled him to see under the skin of a human body. Professor Röntgen's ground-breaking discovery, which later earned him the first Nobel Prize ever to be awarded in the field of physics, transformed medicine for good.

Finance is now experiencing its own x-ray moment. At the heart of every investment decision is the desire to achieve the best possible outcome for an asset, by selecting the right information, applying the most suitable models and portfolio concepts, under a chosen set of restrictions. In the past, investors would rely primarily on financial information in making such decisions. Only recently, driven by major technological developments in big data and artificial intelligence (AI), non-financial data is being used to supplement financial data. In fact, the authenticity, scalability, and quality of this new non-financial data dimension enables us to look inside the walls, or "under the skin", of companies. The proliferation of and the ability to analyse non-financial information is increasingly becoming important in allowing us to understand not only the sustainability of a company, but also its economic performance and competitiveness.

The reporting of a growing number of non-financial performance metrics by companies, such as water use, energy, CO_2 emissions, diversity, and endless more, enables the integration of sustainability targets into the investment process. Aided by machine learning, we can filter out the background noise of unstructured information, including qualitative-based sources of information, such as news, websites, and social media, in order to integrate such data into the investment process.

However, innovation doesn't come easy in the investment industry, compared with consumer goods or electronic products, for example. It is an industry that prides itself on having long track records of good performance for doing the same thing in the same manner for as long as possible. To understand how investment technology might be shaped by those two disruptive forces, sustainability and AI, it is tempting to compare this with another industry – namely, the transportation sector. There, as in finance, the industry is challenged by two major streams of innovation: electric or alternative engines, and self-driving technology. The first one is taking off predominantly for environmental reasons, and the second one for convenience and safety. Not so long ago, electric cars were considered too slow, limited in range, and perhaps something of an acquired taste. Today, not only do they compete favourably with conventional vehicles on many accounts, but they have become a lifestyle choice. Despite the inevitable problems that come along with the transition of an industry, there is no doubt that these two trends have changed the automotive industry and maybe even the Zeitgeist of tomorrow.

What electric cars are to their fossil-fuel counterparts, sustainable investing is to conventional finance. Still kept behind a wall of opaque acronyms, lacking an established regulatory framework, and sometimes being abused for political gain, an inevitable sea change is under way. This is poised to change the future of the financial industry. Historically, the integration of non-financial factors has been associated with underperformance. That was due to a simplistic approach of industry exclusion that would reduce the available investment universe and, hence, expected financial performance, temporarily aided by a favourable sector overweight. ESG (environmental, social, and governance) integration also felt like incorporating externally imposed conditions, rather than the inclusion of an intrinsic set of values. The limited quality and quantity of non-financial data would not allow for much more, and a discretionary portfolio context would make sustainability appear like a personal preference, rather than a transparent selection process that could be integrated into performance attribution analyses.

There is a lot to be said about the quality issues of non-financial data today, which has a striking similarity to the quality of financial data prior to the

Great Depression. Investment decisions were based on subjective assessments of financial information, mostly unstructured, unregulated, delayed in time, and often unaudited, available only to a narrow circle of stakeholders.

Many would argue that this bears a very close resemblance to the status quo of non-financial data today. The current ESG data landscape embodies a confusing range of subjective interpretations of corporate sustainability. Indeed, ESG data is still infrequently collected, subjectively judged, and largely based on data that is estimated or modelled, instead of representing concrete and verifiable facts and figures. And for what it's worth, the data is often back-fitted in many cases to reflect the benefit of hindsight, rather than adopting a transparent and systematic approach. The search for materiality is as subjective as the choice of the framework, without any meaningful access to the underlying raw data, which is the foundation of a company's sustainability performance. The companies that are being assessed are the usual suspects: the 13,000 mainly large cap listed corporations in developed markets. Within ESG data, there is a growing need for developing the same consistency and quality we require of financial information. Even the glossiest corporate and social responsibility (CSR) reports cannot change the fact that all stakeholders, including the investment community, need to develop a scalable, dynamic, and unbiased picture of large and small companies across the globe that shows the status quo and reveals trends in the performance on non-financial metrics. In other words, what we need is an x-ray for corporates – a diagnostic tool that allows us to look underneath the surface of companies.

THE STATUS QUO OF SUSTAINABILITY DATA: STILL A LONG WAY TO GO

With the rise in company sustainability reporting and disclosure, we have seen a proliferation of non-financial information. According to the Governance and Accountability Institute (GAI), more than 82% of S&P 500 companies issued a sustainability report in 2016, compared with less than 20% in 2011 (D'Aquila, 2018). Indeed, research shows that by 2016, over 13,000 companies had produced more than 80,000 sustainability reports worldwide.[2] The quality and scope of ESG data is growing, enabling better-informed investment decisions. These trends reveal that sustainability reporting is now established practice for large companies. This is compounded by the fact that more than 72% of corporations use ESG ratings to inform their decision-making (SustainAbility, 2019, p. 26). Yet, the majority of sustainability ratings are underpinned by unreliable third-party data, whose sources are not transparent and carry significant errors, costs, and restrictions unrelated to the issuing company. This affects a corporation's cost of capital and long-term profitability in ways that the company is prevented from impacting directly.

Despite the explosive growth of non-financial information, there are numerous challenges that stand in the way of truly mainstreaming corporate sustainability data. These include:

1. lack of data standardisation and comparability;
2. competing reporting and measurement frameworks;
3. diverging materiality assessments;
4. inconsistent reporting methods;
5. opaque ESG ratings methodologies (black box approach);
6. high cost of accessing structured sustainability data insights.

Poor coverage, the unknown scope of data errors, and limited transparency over the data origination process create an inherent lack of trust in sustainability data. In a noteworthy paper by MIT Sloan School of Management, the authors note a perturbing divergence of ESG ratings and rankings (Berg, Koelbel, and Rigobon, 2019). The authors cite three main sources of divergence, namely: scope divergence, measurement divergence, and weight divergence, with measurement divergence contributing the most (over 50%) to the level of overall divergence. The study also detected a "rater effect", whereby subjective elements of assessment influenced the analysis. This in turn brings further challenges for investors who aim to effectively incorporate non-financial information in their decisions.

Particularly troublesome is the process of raw ESG data collection, as well as the quality and coverage of sustainability data itself. In addition to using conventional data sourcing techniques to collect data that is disclosed directly by the reporting company, or is otherwise made publicly available, sustainability data providers deploy a host of statistical models to generate estimates for undisclosed data. Such data estimation techniques are often based on averages and estimations, stemming from what the data provider views as peer group companies and industry benchmarks (State Street Global Advisors, 2019). This is but one example of how investors incorporate potentially biased information into their investment processes.

The uncertainty surrounding the assessment of financial materiality, data acquisition, and estimation, as well as divergent approaches to data aggregation and weighting, need to be overcome in order to allow for a level playing field for decision-makers and broader stakeholders who rely on such information in their processes. These inefficiencies within the current system prevent broader ESG data integration, which in turn would help further mainstream corporate sustainability.

Technological solutions, based on the latest advancements in scalable cloud-based infrastructure, machine learning, and AI, are poised to bring much-needed efficiencies in the space (Deutsche Bank Research, 2018).

This will subsequently enhance the data origination and collection process, enabling a host of underlying analytics and insights from newly structured datasets. This convergence of big data and AI is what the *MIT Sloan Management Review* called "the single most important development that is shaping the future of how firms drive business value from their data and analytics capabilities" (Bean, 2017). This unstoppable wave of technological transformation enables the analysis of unstructured data into actionable insights and forms the subject of the next section.

AI IN FINANCE

Financial decision-makers require quick and robust access to information. Firms in the financial industry always had the capacity to welcome new technologies to gain a competitive advantage over their peers. However, according to a CFA report from 2019, when it comes to AI, relatively few professional investors (<10%) have adopted the technology (Cao, 2019). That is despite their prediction that the winners of the future are the firms that strategically invest in AI now.

The advantages of AI stem from its intrinsic ability to process vast and disparate datasets, its delivery via state-of-the-art computational methods, and its rigorous scientific and research-led underpinning. Such AI applications require high-performance computing and data storage capacities that have only recently become available. From 2016–2018, the number of AI-powered funds rose by 77% and have outperformed traditional funds by 3% on average over the past three years (Friedman, 2019). Yet, as the CFA report showed, only a handful of pioneers have directly incorporated AI into their investment processes, while most have incorporated only limited AI technologies in investment decisions and strategies (Cao, 2019). The main hurdles to successful adoption of AI and big data in investment decision-making require cost, talent, technology, leadership vision, and time.

There has been an exponential growth in data generation over the last few years, with the global internet population reaching 4.39 billion people – an almost 50% increase over the last five years and more than 2.5 billion gigabytes of data being created daily (DOMO, 2019; see Figure 12.1 for a 2025 projection).

Technologies like AI and machine learning have the increased ability to assess vast, complex data sets to identify patterns to bring about greater data transparency and support better investment decision-making. These technologies are helping to capture reported data, as well as news-based data with higher frequency, to solve issues around infrequency and sparseness of sustainability data. A study found that 90% of negative ESG incidents were not reported in company reports (Doyle, 2018). AI and big data can help in

Data Age
The Global Datasphere 2025

175   # 49%   # 30%

Zettabytes

The global datasphere will grow from 33 zettabytes by 2025. IoT devices are expected to create over 90 zettabytes of data in 2025.

By 2025, 49% of all data worldwide will reside in public cloud environments as cloud becomes the new core.

In 2025 nearly 30% of the world's data will need real-time processing as the role of the edge continues to grow.

FIGURE 12.1 The global datasphere 2025

Source: Arabesque & Seagate

these cases and provide a competitive advantage. The Task Force on Climate-related Financial Disclosures (TCFD) laments that the breadth of ESG reports does not yet have the quality and dimensions that the market needs to invest in sustainable solutions, opportunities, and business models (TCDF, 2019).

Two types of AI are currently the most promising: natural language processing (NLP) and computer vision, as well as deep learning and big data analytics. NLP is a method that allows text and language data to be recorded, analysed, and evaluated. The underlying raw data can come in the form of reports, messages, articles, or transcripts. This enables companies to verify the published data, or to identify missing metrics. The best aspect: NLP operates in a fraction of the time it would take an analyst to carry out the same analysis. The latest language models are constantly being improved and refined (e.g. Google's language model BERT beats human performance in text comprehension tests; Pavlus, 2019). Other AI algorithms can process huge amounts of structured data, be it in the form of financial data, share prices, or 10-K reports, and find intricate relationships within the data. Non-linear models, such as neural networks, are becoming increasingly important and are already being used in facial recognition technologies, medicine, and image recognition. These networks can learn relationships from millions of data points, which often go beyond human perception in an objective manner, avoiding underlying human biases.

High-quality, labelled training datasets are usually difficult to obtain or produce because of the large amount of time and effort required to label such datasets. Unfortunately, in the financial sector, there are several recurring issues with data and datasets, such as availability and bias which hinder progress for

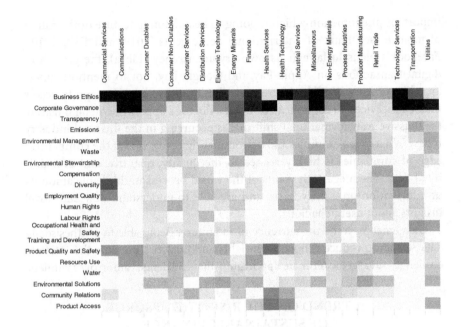

FIGURE 12.2 Data-driven materiality of Arabesque S-Ray score through machine learning

machine learning in this area. In such cases, perhaps one can consider alternative, accessible, and unconventional data sources. For instance, in one study, the authors extracted titles from financial news to predict the S&P 500 stock index and its individual stocks and reported to achieve nearly a 6% improvement as compared with state-of-the-art baseline methods (see Ding et al., 2015).

The opportunity of technology creating more insights for investors is endless. Transcription, voice and image files, satellite data, social media, and digital news content are all indicators of corporate performance that can be measured – going beyond just self-reported corporate data. This digitalisation in turn creates enhanced risk profiling and helps towards improved capital allocation.

As Angelo Calvello (2020) from Rosetta Analytics puts it:

> AI not only fundamentally changes a manager's investment process and investment worldview, but it also radically transforms the entire business – it requires new talent, new data, a different R&D process, a new management structure, a new brand and, perhaps most importantly, new funds to pay for this multimillion-dollar endeavour.

Moreover, the rise of BigTech (e.g. companies like GAFA – Google, Amazon, Facebook, Apple) and their foray into financial services and payments is an important phenomenon which is going to be a defining feature of the future of finance (see Bank of International Settlements, 2019, and FSB, 2019). Facebook's plans to launch its own cryptocurrency (Libra), the growth of digital transactions on Apple Pay and Google Pay, not to mention super-apps like China's WeChat where users don't need to leave the app to access financial services, order a meal, or book a doctor's appointment, all illustrate the massive transformational shift that is occurring in the financial industry today. What these examples most prominently reveal is that the competitive edge of companies is highly related to the quality, quantity, and availability of data. The mega-tech giants of the world process unthinkable amounts of information on a daily basis, and are able to understand new and novel insights about user behaviour.

Data emerges to be the currency of the future. Being able to synthesise big data sets and produce actionable insights and analytics presents the ultimate challenge, but also the ultimate opportunity that will define tomorrow's winners.

A TREND ON THE RISE: THE UPSURGE OF SUSTAINABLE FINANCE

One may legitimately be driven to ask: why do we need access to high-quality, relevant, and actionable sustainability information in the first place? A major reason behind the growing relevance of sustainability data stems from its propagation in mainstream investment decisions. Indeed, the global sustainable investing landscape has experienced a transformation over the past few years. Sustainable investment assets globally rose 34% in just two years, to US$30.7 trillion in 2018 (GSIA, 2018; see also Chasan, 2019). It is noteworthy that nearly half of socially responsible investment (SRI) assets are concentrated in the European market, at around US$14 trillion. Moreover, Japan experienced the biggest growth in responsible investment strategies, which now make up 18% of professionally managed assets (up from only 3% in 2017). Additionally, according to the Global Impact Investing Network, the impact investing market is currently estimated to be at US$502 billion managed by over 1,340 active impact investing organisations worldwide (Mudaliar and Dithrich, 2019).

This trend towards sustainable investing is to a large extent driven by mounting regulatory requirements, rising awareness of the need to integrate sustainability into decision-making, the solidifying link between ESG metrics and financial outperformance (Clark, Feiner, and Viehs, 2015; Friede, Busch, and Bassen, 2015), as well as the massive generational wealth shift whereby US$68 trillion is due to be inherited by millennials (aged 18 to 37) over the next 30 years (Sigalos, 2018). Recent research found 59% of millennials consider sustainability factors when selecting an investment product. According to a Schroders survey, 78% of respondents stated that sustainable investing was more important to them now than it was five years ago (Schroders, 2017).

Sustainable investment can propel long-term financial outperformance and improve risk management. Over 2,200 academic studies undertaken in the last 40 years have examined the relationship between ESG factors and corporate financial performance. More than 90% of them have found that ESG factors have a positive or neutral impact on financial returns (Friede, Busch, and Bassen, 2015). When comparing the performance of the S&P 500 Index to its sustainable counterpart, the S&P 500 ESG Index, there is consistent evidence that integrating ESG into financial products does not compromise financial performance, leads to lower rates of tracking error, and lower volatility.[3] This demonstrates that it is indeed possible to do well by doing good and achieve long-term financial success by being a responsible investor.

ESG regulatory landscape

Growing scrutiny of corporate behaviour by regulators and stock exchanges is shedding new light on companies' business practices regarding their non-financial performance, with an increased focus on environmental, social, and governance performance metrics. ESG regulation globally has skyrocketed, from nearly non-existent in the 1950s to approximately 400 ESG-related policy instruments worldwide in 2016 (PRI and MSCI, 2016). As of 2016, 14 members of the G20 and 32 of the 50 largest country economies had at least one regulation covering an aspect of environmental, social, and governance disclosure (Sustainable Stock Exchange Initiative, 2016).

These developments demonstrate that there has been significant regulatory advancement both globally and across regions over the past three to five years. The European Commission's "Action Plan on Financing Sustainable Growth" closely follows historical political progress in the field.[4] The ambitious agenda builds upon the climate-related goals of the Paris Agreement and the larger commitments made by international political leaders to achieve the SDGs by 2030. The progress and initiatives being developed by the EU, EC, the High-Level Expert Group (HLEG), and the Technical Expert Group (TEG) all support the Action Plan on Sustainable Finance. That Action Plan sets out a comprehensive strategy to further connect finance with sustainability. Its key actions include:

- establishing a clear and detailed EU classification system – or taxonomy – for sustainable activities;
- establishing EU labels for green financial products – this will help investors to easily identify products that comply with green or low-carbon criteria;

- introducing measures to clarify asset managers' and institutional investors' duties regarding sustainability;
- strengthening the transparency of companies on their environmental, social, and governance (ESG) policies;
- introducing a "green supporting factor" in the EU prudential rules for banks and insurance companies.

Furthermore, there have been a number of reports published by the working groups and scientific committees on the actual implementation of the EU's Action Plan. Those reports include:

- *Sustainable Finance Taxonomy*: A proposal for a regulation on the establishment of a framework to facilitate sustainable investment. This regulation establishes the conditions and the framework to gradually create a unified classification system ("taxonomy") on what can be considered an environmentally sustainable economic activity. This is a first and essential step in the efforts to channel investments into sustainable activities.
- *European Non-Financial Reporting Directive*: A proposal for a regulation on disclosures relating to sustainable investments and sustainability risks and amending Directive (EU)2016/2341. This regulation will introduce disclosure obligations on how institutional investors and asset managers integrate ESG factors into their risk management processes. Delegated acts will further specify requirements on integrating ESG factors into investment decisions, which is part of institutional investors' and asset managers' duties towards investors and beneficiaries.
- *Low-carbon benchmarks*: In 2019 the EU introduced two low-carbon benchmarks, a climate-transition benchmark and a specialised Paris-aligned benchmark which brings investment portfolios in line with the Paris Agreement goal to limit the global temperature increase to 1.5 degrees Celsius above pre-industrial levels (European Commission, 2019). This stems from a proposal for a regulation amending the benchmark regulation. The proposed amendment will create a new category of benchmarks, comprising low-carbon and positive carbon impact benchmarks, which will provide investors with better information on the carbon footprint of their investments. This new category of benchmarks will help investors compare the carbon footprint of their investments in a drive to promote sustainable finance.

Additionally, proposed legislation on promoting sustainability in EU capital markets would require firms to identify their clients' ESG preferences so that their advice and investment decision-making reflects the clients' financial objectives and ESG preferences (European Securities and Markets Authority, 2018). Europe's Sustainable Finance Action Plan, as well as the European Non-Financial

Reporting Directive, mandating corporate sustainability disclosure and transparency regarding sustainable finance objectives, are paving the way towards a more consistent and rules-based accountability and measurement framework.

Governments are also becoming more attuned to climate risk. For instance, in the United Kingdom, the Financial Conduct Authority (FCA) issued a discussion paper on Climate Change and Green Finance in October 2018, noting that the "FCA must consider all major risks that have an impact on the markets and institutions we regulate including those posed by climate change" (Financial Conduct Authority, 2018). It is particularly notable that regulations at the regional and global levels related to climate change disclosure have increased by 90% in the last ten years (Volkman, 2019). ESG regulations in Asia are taking off as well, demonstrating that this is not an isolated or region-specific phenomenon, confined to developed markets only. From 2019, listed companies in Hong Kong have to make mandatory public disclosures about company policies and how they intend to deal with the operational risks that have implications for the environment and the wider society (Ng, 2016). Non-financial accounting standards are also on the rise, as illustrated by Figure 12.3.

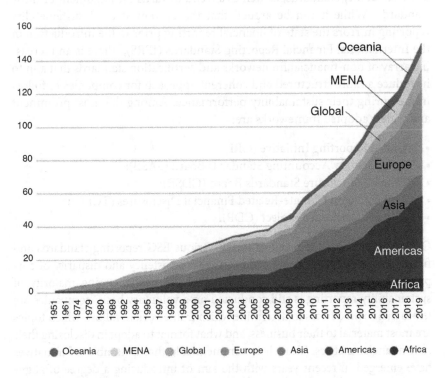

FIGURE 12.3 Growth of climate change and GHG regulations

Source: Datamaran & Arabesque

Additionally, the Sustainable Stock Exchanges Initiative (SSE) was launched in 2009 by the UN Conference on Trade and Development (UNCTAD), the UN Global Compact, the UN Environment Programme Finance Initiative (UNEP FI), and the Principles for Responsible Investment (PRI).[5] As of April 2019, there were 86 SSE Partner Exchanges, representing more than 50,000 globally listed companies, with nearly US$86 trillion market cap. Asian Stock exchanges, including those in India, Sri Lanka, Malaysia, South Korea, Vietnam, and Thailand, are now members of the UN-backed Sustainable Stock Exchanges Initiative (International Organization of Securities Commissions, 2019). Seventeen stock exchanges globally require ESG reporting as a listing rule, covering over 15,000 listed companies with a domestic market capitalisation of US$16,627,067 million. Additionally, 42 exchanges offer written guidance on sustainability reporting, while 35 stock exchanges have sustainability-related indices.[6]

The evolution and alignment of ESG reporting standards

In addition to an evolving global ESG regulatory environment, over the past few years we have also witnessed the growing formalisation and evolution of sustainability standards, as well as a trend towards the alignment of those standards. While it can be argued that the current state of sustainability reporting mirrors the state of financial reporting prior to the introduction of the International Financial Reporting Standards (IFRS),[7] there is an increasing array of non-financial frameworks and certification standards that aim to introduce a more structured and coherent approach for companies to follow in measuring their sustainability performance. Among the most prominent and widely adopted frameworks are:

- Global Reporting Initiative (GRI);
- Sustainability Accounting Standards Board (SASB);
- Climate Disclosure Standards Board (CDSB);
- Task Force on Climate-Related Financial Disclosures (TCFD);
- Climate Disclosure Project (CDP).

On the other hand, the proliferation of various ESG reporting standards and frameworks arguably serves to add to the inconsistency and disparity of corporate sustainability data today. Given that the overwhelming majority of sustainability reporting is still conducted on a voluntary basis, companies are left to their own devices to determine which framework to follow, which topics are most material to their business, and what format to adopt in disclosing their non-financial metrics. Thus, it is commendable that a number of initiatives have emerged in recent years with the aim of introducing a degree of alignment and harmonisation between the acronym-ridden and jargon-heavy field of sustainability standards that are currently in place. Among these initiatives are the International Integrated Reporting Council (IRRC), as well as the Better Alignment Project.

In view of the high levels of overlap between frameworks, and the growing reporting burden for corporates to comply with a mushrooming number of sustainability disclosure requests, it is a welcome development that such organisations are working on introducing efficiencies into the data reporting process. Developing a systematic methodology that maps the overlapping indicators and enables companies to report in a more streamlined manner is essential in truly mainstreaming the current state of sustainability data and empowering stakeholders to derive actionable insights from ESG information.

From negative screening to positive impact: the sustainable finance pyramid

While negative ESG screening (meaning the screening out of investments in controversial business activities such as fossil fuel, weapons, tobacco, etc.) remains the most widely adopted strategy, we are witnessing the growth of more positive impact-driven approaches to integrating sustainability into investment decisions. Figure 12.4 aptly illustrates the pyramid of sustainable

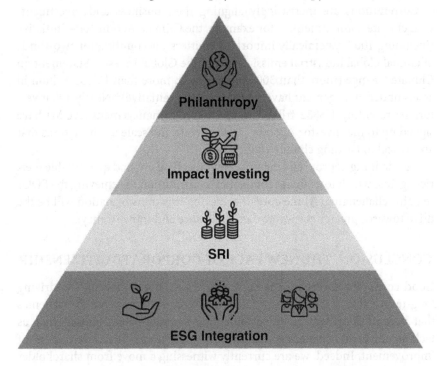

FIGURE 12.4 The sustainable investing pyramid
Source: Arabesque

investing strategies, evolving from an approach based on ESG factor integration in traditional investment strategies, to one based on screening holdings in or out according to investor preferences, and third – an impact-focused method that identifies investment strategies poised to lead to positive sustainable outcomes (impact investing).

Indeed, the global sustainable development agenda embodied by the United Nations SDGs requires the deployment of a vast amount of capital in order to achieve its objectives of poverty alleviation, universal access to education and health care, tackling climate change and decent employment opportunities, among others. The UN Commission on Trade and Development (UNCTAD) estimates that meeting the SDGs will require US$5 trillion to US$7 trillion in investment each year from 2015 to 2030 (PRI, 2017). This investment gap will have to be filled by public and private sources of capital alike, as well as the conclusion of public–private partnerships between government bodies and the private sector. Indeed, multi-stakeholder collaboration is a crucial element in unlocking the amount of development capital needed to realise the UN Global Goals. The case for sustainable business is clear: an estimated €966 billion opportunity exists for brands that make their sustainability credentials more transparent (Unilever, 2017).

Corporations are increasingly aligning their business and investments with climate commitments – for example, the Climate Action 100+ initiative (including 100 "systemically important emitters", accounting for two-thirds of annual global industrial emissions)[8] and the Global Investor Statement on Climate Change (more than 300 investors with more than US$33 trillion in assets under management have signed on to the initiative).[9] Nearly 400 investors representing US$32 trillion in assets under management (AUM) have signed up to the Investor Agenda[10] to accelerate and scale up the actions that are critical to tackling climate change.

Yet, defining appropriate measurement mechanisms and quantifiable metrics against which to evaluate companies' contribution to achieving the SDGs remains challenging. At the core of achieving this transformation will be the drive towards greater corporate data disclosure and transparency.

CONCLUSION: THE NEW FACE OF CORPORATE CITIZENSHIP

Good corporate governance is becoming ever more important for driving long-term value. Transparency, adequate executive compensation schemes that reward long-term and sustainability-focused objectives, as well as tackling diversity challenges within corporations are significant areas of improvement. Indeed, we are currently witnessing a move from shareholder to stakeholder capitalism, as companies' behaviour is being evaluated based on a broader stakeholder agenda. This drive towards "conscious capitalism" pushes companies to become better corporate citizens and implement a triple-bottom-line approach that considers the impact not only on short-term profitability, but also on stakeholder groups such as employees, customers, suppliers, local communities, and the environment.

The World Economic Forum unveiled in November 2019 the "Davos Manifesto 2020", proclaiming that "the purpose of a company is to engage all its stakeholders in shared and sustained value creation" (WEF, 2020), coinciding with the Forum's 50th anniversary. Indeed, we have seen issues such as climate change move from the sidelines of high-profile corporate gatherings to centre stage in the space of just a few years. A true sign of mainstreaming business sustainability stems from the recognition that ESG concerns have progressed from being the purview of marketing or CSR departments into the C-suite and the chief financial officer. In fact, there was a doubling of S&P 500 companies citing "ESG" on their earnings calls in Q2 of 2019 compared with Q1 (Factset, 2019).

Truly embedding sustainability into companies' DNA will be accomplished when ESG data becomes just "data", widely accessible and comparable across sectors and jurisdictions. This creates the need for a next-generation technology tool and an underlying scalable infrastructure that empowers companies and allows them to become better corporate citizens by sharing their sustainability practices and demonstrating transparency. With the improving quality, coverage, and consistency of sustainability information, stakeholders become more empowered to shed light on unsustainable business practices, demand actionable change on the ground, and implement better-informed investment and purchasing decisions, in turn influencing companies' behaviour. Sustainability dies in darkness,[11] so let's make sure we shine a light on these most salient issues that will define the shape of the twenty-first century and beyond.

NOTES

1   Founder and CEO, Arabesque Partners.
2   See: Corporate Register, an online directory of corporate responsibility reports, available at: www.corporateregister.com.
3   Source: S&P Dow Jones Indices LLC. Performance data from May 31, 2014, to May 31, 2019. See also Leale-Green (2019) and Rotonti and Lomax (2019).
4   See, European Commission (COM (2018) 97): https://ec.europa.eu/info/publications/180308-action-plan-sustainable-growth_en.
5   See the website: www.sseinitiative.org/.
6   See: https://sseinitiative.org/.
7   See: www.ifrs.org/.
8   See: www.climateaction100.org/.
9   See: http://globalinvestorcoalition.org/wp-content/uploads/2016/09/2014_GlobalInvestState_ClimChange_092316.pdf
10 See: www.theinvestoragenda.org.
11 An allusion to the *Washington Post*'s motto: "Democracy dies in darkness." See: www.washingtonpost.com/lifestyle/style/the-washington-posts-new-slogan-turns-out-to-be-an-old-saying/2017/02/23/cb199cda-fa02-11e6-be05-1a3817ac21a5_story.html.

REFERENCES

Bank of International Settlements (BIS). (2019). *Big Tech in Finance: Opportunities and Risks.* Available at: www.bis.org/publ/arpdf/ar2019e3.pdf (Accessed: 4 February 2020).

Bean, R. (2017). *How Big Data is Empowering AI and Machine Learning at Scale* (MIT Sloan Management Review Online). Available at: https://sloanreview.mit.edu/article/how-big-data-is-empowering-ai-and-machine-learning-at-scale/ (Accessed: 4 February 2020).

Berg, F., Koelbel, J. F., and Rigobon, R. (2019). *Aggregate Confusion: The Divergence of ESG Ratings (MIT Sloan School Working Paper 5822-19).* Cambridge, MA: MIT.

Calvello, A. (2020). *Fund managers must embrace AI disruption (Financial Times).* Available at: www.ft.com/content/e58a767a-fbe8-4461-8cdf-cfc0f8a80de9 (Accessed: 4 February 2020).

Cao, L. (2019). *AI Pioneers in Investment Management* (CFA Institute, Research Reports). Available at: www.cfainstitute.org/-/media/documents/survey/AI-Pioneers-in-Investment-Management.ashx (Accessed: 4 February 2020).

Chasan, E. (2019). Global sustainable investments rise 34% to 30.7 trillion (Bloomberg). Available at: www.bloomberg.com/news/articles/2019-04-01/global-sustainable-investments-rise-34-percent-to-30-7-trillion (Accessed: 4 February 2020).

Clark, G. L., Feiner, A., and Viehs, M. (2015). *From the Stockholder to the Stakeholder: How Sustainability Can Drive Financial Outperformance.* Oxford: University of Oxford and Arabesque Partners.

D'Aquila, J. M. (2018). *The Current State of Sustainability Reporting: A Work in Progress.* The CPA Journal. Available at: www.cpajournal.com/2018/07/30/the-current-state-of-sustainability-reporting/ (Accessed: 4 February 2020).

Deutsche Bank Research. (2018). *Big Data Shakes Up ESG Investing* (konzept). Available at: www.dbresearch.com/PROD/RPS_EN-PROD/PROD0000000000478852/Big_data_shakes_up_ESG_investing.PDF (Accessed: 4 February 2020).

Ding, X., Zhang, Y., Liu, T., and Duan, J. (2015). Deep learning for event-driven stock prediction Xiao. *Proceedings of the Twenty-Fourth International Joint Conference on Artificial Intelligence (IJCAI),* pp. 2327–2333.

DOMO. (2019). *Data Never Sleeps: How Much Data is Generated Every Minute?* Available at: https://web-assets.domo.com/blog/wp-content/uploads/2019/07/data-never-sleeps-7-896kb.jpg (Accessed: 4 February 2020).

Doyle, T. M. (2018). *Ratings that Don't Rate: The Subjective World of ESG Rating Agencies.* Available at: https://accfcorpgov.org/wp-content/uploads/2018/07/ACCF_RatingsESGReport.pdf (Accessed: 4 February 2020).

European Commission. (2019). Sustainable finance: Commission welcomes agreement on a new generation of low-carbon benchmarks. Available at: https://ec.europa.eu/commission/presscorner/detail/en/IP_19_1418 (Accessed: 4 February 2020).

European Securities and Markets Authority. (2018). ESMA consults on measures to promote sustainability in EU capital markets. Available at: www.esma.europa.eu/press-news/esma-news/esma-consults-measures-promote-sustainability-in-eu-capital-markets (Accessed: 4 February 2020).

Factset. (2019). 100% increase in S&P 500 companies citing "ESG" on earnings calls in Q2 vs. Q1. Available at: https://insight.factset.com/100-increase-in-sp-500-companies-citing-esg-on-earnings-calls-in-q2-vs.-q1 (Accessed: 4 February 2020).

Financial Conduct Authority. (2018). Climate change and green finance (Discussion Paper DP18/8). Available at: www.fca.org.uk/publication/discussion/dp18-08.pdf (Accessed: 4 February 2020).

Financial Stability Board (FSB). (2019). BigTech in finance: market developments and potential financial stability implications. Available at: www.fsb.org/wp-content/uploads/P091219-1.pdf (Accessed: 4 February 2020).

Friede, G., Busch, T., and Bassen, A. (2015). ESG and financial performance: aggregated evidence from more than 2000 empirical studies. *Journal of Sustainable Finance and Investment,* 5(4), pp. 210–233.

Friedman, B. (2019). *The Rise of the Machines: AI Funds are Outperforming the Hedge Fund Benchmark.* Available at:www.preqin.com/insights/blogs/the-rise-of-the-machines-ai-funds-are-outperforming-the-hedge-fund-benchmark/26411 (Accessed: 4 February 2020).

Global Sustainable Investment Alliance (GSIA). (2018). *2018 Global Sustainable Investment Review*. Available at: www.gsi-alliance.org/wp-content/uploads/2019/03/GSIR_Review2018.3.28.pdf (Accessed: 5 February 2020).

International Organization of Securities Commissions. (2019). Sustainable finance in emerging markets and the role of securities regulators. Available at: www.iosco.org/library/pubdocs/pdf/IOSCOPD621.pdf (Accessed: 5 February 2020).

Leale-Green, B. (2019). Which performs better, the S&P500 or the S&P500 ESG index? Available at: www.evidenceinvestor.com/which-performs-better-the-sp-500-or-the-sp-500-esg-index/ (Accessed: 5 February 2020).

Mudaliar, A. and Dithrich, H. (2019). *Sizing the Impact Investing Market (Global Impact Investing Network)*. Available at: https://thegiin.org/research/publication/impinv-market-size (Accessed: 5 February 2020).

Ng, E. (2016). ESG is the new buzzword for listed firms, investors in HK, Asia as regulations tighten. Available at: www.scmp.com/business/companies/article/1971837/esg-new-buzzword-listed-firms-investors-hk-asia-regulations (Accessed: 4 February 2020).

Pavlus, J. (2019). Machines beat humans on a reading test: but do they understand? Available at: www.quantamagazine.org/machines-beat-humans-on-a-reading-test-but-do-they-understand-20191017/ (Accessed: 4 February 2020).

Principles for Responsible Investment (PIR). (2017). The SDG investment case. Available at: www.unpri.org/download?ac=5909 (Accessed: 4 February 2020).

Principles for Responsible Investment (PRI) and Morgan Stanley Capital International (MSCI). (2016). Global guide to responsible investment regulation. Available at: www.msci.com/documents/1296102/0/PRI_MSCI_Global-Guide-to-Responsible-Investment-Regulation.pdf/ac76bbbd-1e0a-416e-9e83-9416910a4a4b (Accessed: 4 February 2020).

Rotonti, J. and Lomax, A. (2019). Does ESG investing produce better stock returns? Available at: www.fool.com/investing/2019/05/22/does-esg-investing-produce-better-stock-returns.aspx (Accessed: 4 February 2020).

Schroders. (2017). Schroders global investor study 2017: sustainable investing on the rise. Available at: www.schroders.com/en/media-relations/newsroom/all_news_releases/schroders-global-investor-study-2017-sustainable-investing-on-the-rise/ (Accessed: 4 February 2020).

Sigalos, M. (2018). *$68 trillion is About to Change Hands in the US (CNBC)*. Available at: www.cnbc.com/2018/11/20/great-wealth-transfer-is-passing-from-baby-boomers-to-gen-x-millennials.html (Accessed: 4 February 2020).

State Street Global Advisors. (2019). *The ESG Data Challenge* (March 2019). Available at: www.ssga.com/investment-topics/environmental-social-governance/2019/03/esg-data-challenge.pdf (Accessed: 4 February 2020).

SustainAbility. (2019). *Rate the Raters 2019: Expert Views on ESG*. Available at: https://sustainability.com/wp-content/uploads/2019/02/SA-RateTheRaters-2019-1.pdf#page=26 (Accessed: 4 February 2020).

Sustainable Stock Exchange Initiative. (2016). *2016 Progress Report*. Available at: https://unctad.org/en/PublicationsLibrary/unctad_sse_2016d1.pdf (Accessed: 4 February 2020).

Task Force on Climate-Related Financial Disclosures (TCFD). (2019). *TCFD 2019 Status Report*. Available at: www.fsb-tcfd.org/wp-content/uploads/2019/06/2019-TCFD-Status-Report-FINAL-053119.pdf (Accessed: 6 January 2020).

Unilever. (2017). Reports shows a third of consumers prefer sustainable brands. Available at: www.unilever.com/news/press-releases/2017/report-shows-a-third-of-consumers-prefer-sustainable-brands.html (Accessed: 4 February 2020).

Volkman, S. (2019). Six trends that will shape sustainability transparency in 2020 and beyond. Available at: https://sustainability.com/our-work/insights/trends-sustainability-transparency-2020/ (Accessed: 4 February 2020).

World Economic Forum (WEF). (2020). The Davos manifesto. Available at: www.weforum.org/the-davos-manifesto (Accessed: 4 February 2020).

13

FutureMakers and climate change modelling

Method to the madness

Helga Birgden

INTRODUCTION

The potential impact of climate change as a systemic issue – arguably *the* investment theme of our time – represents a challenge for large global investors with long time horizons and portfolio exposure across the global economy. Environmental, scientific, political, and technological developments continue to evolve and disrupt incumbent industries and regional economies. As such, the Paris Agreement presents challenges to many investors.

Investors often use scenario analysis and stress testing as a part of strategic asset allocation and portfolio construction decisions leading to portfolio construction addressing decarbonisation and transition risk. Model and data selection is important to investors to build resilient portfolios that perform well throughout volatile market conditions and deliver investment returns to shareholders and beneficiaries. When it comes to climate change, many questions arise regarding the data and methods used. Is it madness to attempt to understand the impact and likelihood of climate change (World Economic Forum, 2019) on assets for a 2°C or less[2] aligned world in an institutional investment portfolio? How is climate-related data relevant to investors? This chapter will explore some of the challenges and results when investing in a time of climate change, using a case study about the FutureMakers,[3] a group of about 30 institutional investors that apply common climate scenario modelling and stress testing to their investments.

WHY IS IT IMPORTANT TO QUANTIFY
CLIMATE CHANGE RISK?

Investors use quantitative data and statistics to assess and measure investments against benchmarks and other economic indicators. Given the deep uncertainty and complexity of climate change, investors increasingly are seeking scientific data sources and data science analytics to better understand what the implications of climate change are for investment portfolios. There is a trend towards data-intensive analytics in climate-change-related studies, taken from research applications (Hassani, Huang and Silva, 2019) for climate mitigation and adaption investing. For example, investors use reported carbon emissions data against the Greenhouse Gas (GHG) Protocol to calculate the future "glide path" or "scenario pathway" of how much emissions need to reduce in a portfolio to meet a 2°C or lower science-based target. This is part of a wider trend of multi-disciplinary use of climate data by policymakers, resource planners, and investors alike (Overpeck et al., 2011).

A TOP–DOWN APPROACH TO SCENARIO ANALYSIS

Institutional investors are undertaking climate scenario analysis and portfolio stress testing, typically framed around the risks and investment opportunities associated with a transition to a low-carbon economy and the impact of physical damages on assets. Transition risk consists of the technology and policy changes necessary (and to some extent, already under way) to transform the economy away from fossil fuels as the primary energy source and to mitigate additional temperature increases. Top–down assessment might include views on trends, such as drivers of technology take-up, the interactions between energy policy and technology development and integrated fossil fuel supply curves, to model stranded fossil fuel reserves (Mercer, 2019, p. 30). The top–down approach works by taking views on the investment and economic environment and applying them portfolio-wide at asset class and sector level.

Modelling climate change physical damages is a significant challenge for investors because of the lack of data coverage and deep uncertainty about the future. Physical risk damages capture the impacts that come with temperature increases that we have failed to avoid. The frequency of storms, wildfires, floods, and droughts is unpredictable, as is the outlook on the availability of natural resources with, for example, the impact of biodiversity loss on agriculture.

Top–down, economy-wide damage functions, which are most often used to estimate the long-term physical impacts of climate change, greatly underestimate the speed/magnitude of physical damages given the way models tend to treat uncertainty, narrowing down wide dispersions and "tail risks" oriented to equilibrium (Mercer, 2019, p. 30). The Intergovernmental Panel on Climate Change (IPCC) reports that physical damage estimates typically exclude high-uncertainty "feedback loops" that can create climate tipping points, such as permafrost melting and releasing methane (see also Stoerk, Wagner and Ward, 2018).

Top–down models are important to long-term investors because they allow for governance of the entire investment process and to make strategic portfolio decisions to manage complex risks and invest in sustainable assets.

WHERE DO BOTTOM–UP MODELS FIT?

The meaning of the term "bottom–up" is dependent on perspective. For instance, in the model used by Mercer (2019) in *Investing in a Time of Climate Change: The sequel*, a bottom–up approach was taken to develop physical impact estimates. This entailed sourcing peril – specific damage estimates and combining them to develop a uniform multi-peril physical damage function. Although such an approach carries benefits (for example, transparency into the peril/region-specific drivers of damage), it also carries drawbacks. For example, very few peril-specific damage functions exist with global consistency, meaning any bottom–up approach is likely to have gaps; also, more research would be needed into the interactions between perils to avoid double counting.

Alternatively, some investors work from bottom–up company-level assessment to better understand the exposures in the portfolio, before developing views about sectors, asset classes, and the portfolio as a whole. For example, carbon footprinting is a bottom–up way of assessing historical carbon emissions intensity, relative to benchmarks and targets, and is now commonly undertaken. Bottom–up mapping of potential physical damages perils on a location-specific basis, particularly in relation to directly held real assets, is also an exercise undertaken by investors. While the majority of bottom–up approaches being employed now provide beneficial granularity on near-term risks, often they focus on short-term transition risk (as with carbon footprinting) and only cover certain sectors or asset classes, such as equities and fixed income (Mercer, 2019, p. 30).

Such bottom–up approaches are also typically most useful for tactical decisions – e.g. which specific security to buy, sell, or engage with – and may not be applicable to broad asset allocation decisions or portfolio construction aimed at science based alignment for a 1.5 degree scenario.

HOW ECONOMIC THEORY INFLUENCES THINKING ABOUT CLIMATE CHANGE

Investment practice today among large institutional investors such as pension funds, sovereign wealth funds, insurers, and asset managers is heavily influenced by "neoclassical economic theory" and the many Nobel-prize-winning investment theories based on neoclassical premises, including Markowitz's Modern Portfolio Theory (MPT), which dates back to the late 1950s. Along with widely used capital asset pricing model (CAPM) and mean variance optimisation (MVO) techniques, mainstream portfolio analysis in many investment houses presupposes the efficient market hypothesis (EMH).[4] This hypothesis states that stock prices fully reflect available information and represent unbiased estimates of underlying values.

Externalities such as climate change are not readily factored into such analytical frameworks. This is in part because neoclassical theory is grounded in our ability as investors to act rationally – ignoring the fact that we likely have over 200 cognitive biases (McKenzie, 2019), including salience and loss-aversion biases.

A new way of thinking is needed and there are in fact many alternative economic theories that try to better recognise the role of transition and disruption associated with environmental, social, and governance factors and climate change – described as ecological, adaptable, low-growth, degrowth, sustainable, feminist, doughnut, neurological/brain, and complexity economics. Some efforts have been made to tie these alternative theories with more rigour to investment practice.

For example, Andrew Lo (2004) and Richard Bookstaber[5] articulate potential alternatives to the EMH as a means of incorporating greater consideration of complexity in their work as investors. Other examples include women economists like Phyllis Deane working in 1941, and New Zealand-born Marilyn Waring (1999), who highlighted the failure of economists to count the economic contribution of women measured by gross domestic product (GDP).[6] Such economists will not be discussed at length here; they are, in their own right, worthy of a separate and full discussion.

There is a wide body of literature indicating that our understanding of economic indicators is poor – GDP only considers market activities and GDP estimation techniques involve judgement at many levels and have known gaps (Pilling, 2018). We are also still actively debating the relationship between interest rates, debt, and inflation (Kelton, 2019). Such economic indicators are at best blunt instruments and at worst underestimate or fail to capture real-world impact of the systemic nature of climate change.

INTEGRATED ASSESSMENT MODELS

This new way of economic thinking is needed when it comes to climate change, scenario modelling and stress testing.

Integrated assessment models (IAMs) are a solid starting point for investors. IAMs include a diverse array of modelling tools, each with varying degrees of reliance on theory, dynamism, scope, and regional/sectoral granularity. Computable general equilibrium (CGE) models are a form of IAM and are tools used for climate policy analysis and forecasts of economic growth by many policymakers (Cambridge Econometrics, 2019). Some IAMs focus on estimating the impacts of transition risk, others on the impact of physical risk. Some are economy-wide, others focus on specific sectors (e.g. energy or agriculture) and others on specific regions. All try to draw a link between GHG emissions from human activities and the long-term physical and economic impacts these may have.

Markets may not be fully pricing in climate change for a variety of reasons, such as different investor (or even country-level) expectations, and therefore, the data gathered does not reflect adequately drivers of risk in the economy, which is due to:

- Time horizon mismatches: Across the capital markets value chain present long-term asset owners.
- Complexity and uncertainty: Uncertainty regarding the global pathway toward a given temperature outcome also causes confusion about which risks are likely to manifest and when.
- Pricing failures: Carbon pricing is still too low to reflect the full social cost of net emissions and send a meaningful signal to the market; therefore, they remain as "externalities" not captured in valuations.
- Behavioural economics: Research in behavioural economics points to the inability of humans to properly account for the effects of future risks, especially those that are large and infrequent. This relates to prospect theory, hyperbolic discounting, and other behavioural economics concepts that are well studied.
- Peer practices: To date, a low proportion of institutional investors have adopted climate change risk management strategies. As peer practices are a key input for many investors' decisions, this can have a depressive effect on market behaviour until norms shift over time (see "The FutureMakers" case later in this chapter, which highlights an exception to this phenomena; Mercer, 2019, p.50).

IAMs as a class (and some particular models) have been held out as being useful for climate policy on abatement by, for example, Metcalf and Stock (2017) and Weyant (2017). However, IAMs are also considered by some as inadequate to the task because they are oversold as being "scientific" when equations and parameter values are widely different from model to model.

IAMs can be used to calculate a social cost of carbon (SCC) or an estimate of the long-term future damage caused by ton of carbon dioxide equivalent (CO_2e) emissions. Robert Pindyck argues compellingly that relying on IAMs to get insight from data, generated by computation, should be avoided and that rather investors should focus on the extreme tail (i.e. catastrophic outcomes), and the emission reductions needed to eliminate that tail. He suggests: "a simple sensitivity analysis on key parameters [...] would be more informative and transparent than a Monte Carlo simulation using ad hoc probability distributions" (Pindyck, 2017, p. 112).

While IAMs are ambitious tools, they are some of the more coherent tools available for the quantitative assessment of climate impact.

IS BIGGER DATA BETTER?

Data analytic methods of regression, classification, and statistical significance used for climate scenario modelling is highly subject to uncertainty introduced at many levels, including (a) the overall construct of the modelling approach, (b) the specific assumptions made, and (c) the time horizon over which the analysis is performed (Mercer, 2019). Data sources needed for climate modelling – in situ, remote sensed, model output, and paleoclimatic – are extremely diverse to start with (Faghmous and Kumar, 2014). The sheer quantity of data available today is reflected in the next generation Climate Model Intercomparison Project, CMIP-6, which will need 30 petabytes available for modelling and analytics.

In the past, computational constraints severely limited the way in which CGE models operated with small data sets, focusing only on a particular group of countries or a few regions using historic price-level expectations conditional only on past or current prices. Instead, many academics agree that intertemporal modelling is needed to account for the various effects of global warming (e.g. species loss, soil erosion, water impacts, sea-level rise, human health effects) on GDP growth and other economic variables in order for investors to account for future climate effects (Kompas, Pham and Tuong, 2018).

Current software packages are incapable of solving large intertemporal CGE models. Dixon et al. (2005) shows that these models, using over 100 industries or commodity groups, can only solve the system simultaneously for a relatively small number of time periods. Nordhaus (1991) sought to model effects from climate change impacts on GDP and rated them as low as 1%, or up to 2%, on the global economy in first iterations.

There are many different ways of trying to assess climate scenarios as investors, including the use of earth science models to improve understanding of forecasting meteorological events, for example, and implications for climate change-driven (Ford et al., 2016) physical damages (Knüsel et al., 2019). Different complex climate models used for scenario modelling produce widely dispersed results that also can grossly underestimate (or ignore) possible catastrophic outcomes (Stern, 2016). There are arguments against large data analytics when it comes to practice, which include a disregard for common domain knowledge [...] some of the most popular data analysis techniques are ill-suited to analyze noisy, heterogeneous, and auto-correlated data that are found in climate and other sciences. Thus, while these methods will certainly produce output, they may rarely yield insight.

(Faghmous and Kumar, 2014)

In *Investing in a Time of Climate Change: The Sequel* (Mercer, 2019), there is discussion of the wide dispersion of results when modelling a carbon pathway and its impacts on global GDP. It's a case for acknowledging widely different possible outcomes, given deep uncertainty, recognising data gaps. Different approaches have tried to address dispersion; for example, Kriegler et al. (2009) tried to overcome some of these issues by estimating tipping points in the climate system for potential catastrophic outcomes as a way to overcome it.

There are a number of studies (see, e.g., Knüsel et al., 2019) that promote the application of big data analytics in climate change modelling and scenario analysis (Faghmous and Kumar, 2014), combining process-based and machine learning together, as one is not adequate without the other. There is also a call for the development of "contextual cues" as part of deep learning (an approach that is able to extract spatio-temporal features automatically) to gain further process understanding of Earth system science problems. All this is to enable the predictive ability of seasonal forecasting and modelling of long-range spatial connections across multiple timescales, which is critical to investors with long-term investments. Hybrid modelling approaches, coupling physical process models with the versatility of data-driven machine learning, are considered to be the best pathways forward (Reichstein et al., 2019).

Case-study The FutureMakers use climate scenario modelling

Since 2009 Mercer has prepared papers and researched into the implications of climate change for institutional investors and began developing a methodology, modelling, and portfolio tools to assess climate change. The *Mercer Sustainable Growth Framework* is the foundation for this work and starts with establishing climate governance through the introduction of climate change in investment beliefs as a strategic view adopted by the board. The next stage is to build contemporary governance through crafting investment policy that fully applies these views to drive how the investment institution embeds climate considerations in investment processes and, finally, how to construct climate-resilient portfolios. The framework is top–down and this methodology influenced

> the development of the top–down portfolio modelling approach adopted by Mercer when developing its climate scenario modelling and stress testing and transition implementation. In line with other top–down models, the Mercer climate scenario method starts with strategic asset allocation as an input to then calculate the additional climate impact on investment return at the whole of portfolio, asset class, and sector level.

The FutureMakers

A group of about 30 global institutional investors agreed to form the FutureMakers Working Group because they all use or have used Mercer's climate scenario modelling tools to guide their investment decision-making. Mercer named these investors the FutureMakers,[7] defined as:

> advocating for and creating the investment conditions that support a well-below 2°C scenario outcome through investment decisions and engagement activities most likely to provide the economic and investment environment necessary to pay pensions, endowment grants and insurance claims over the timeframes required by beneficiaries.

These investors, representing well over $3 trillion in assets under management, are a cross-section of the institutional investment industry and include pension and superannuation investors as well as insurers and endowments and foundations and have worked with Mercer's top–down modelling for more than five years. This investor group collaborates in discussions on the climate scenario and stress-testing process and research needed with Mercer. The FutureMakers are bound together by the fact they have all worked with the same scenarios and models, though these too have evolved over time.

Examples of FutureMakers who share overview cases of their approaches to climate change as a result of using the Mercer scenario modelling in both *Investing in a Time of Climate Change* (Mercer, 2015, p. 3 and p. 80) and *Investing in a Time of Climate Change: The Sequel* (Mercer, 2019) include funds such as the Guardians of the NZ Super Fund, which at the time of writing invests approximately NZ$14 billion of its global passive equity portfolio, 40% of the overall fund, into low-carbon strategies, with the total fund's carbon emissions intensity 19.6% lower, and its exposure to carbon reserves 21.5% lower, than if the changes hadn't been made, along with a comprehensive climate change valuation framework. GPIF the Sovereign Wealth Fund of Japan invests US$8.9 billion in ESG indices and is actively assessing its climate approach to investing of its portfolio of approximately US$1.4 trillion. QIC, a US$63 billion manager that began assessing its climate exposures through modelling, focuses on real assets and physical damages (Mercer, 2019, p. 70). The input from FutureMakers is significant and shaped the method that Mercer took over the decade of its work and is reflected in the activities and results outlined below The FutureMakers continue to provide input to Mercer's next generation climate modelling on decarbonisation and transition in portfolio construction.

Which models are useful and why?

Mercer consciously chose to use an econometric[8] rather than a CGE model and methodology, to capture relationships on an empirical basis and to not assume optimal, "rational" behaviour as per neoclassical economic theory, discussed earlier in this chapter. CGE models might optimise for all resources being fully utilised, so that if it were to increase output and employment by adding regulation, it would not register the change. The econometric model in comparison allows for the possibility of unused capital and labour resources that may be utilised under the right legislation; it is therefore possible (although not guaranteed) that additional regulation could lead to increases in investment, output, and employment (Cambridge Econometrics, 2019).

The econometric model seeks to better equip investors as they assess portfolio impacts, such as uncompensated-for risks they are currently exposed to (as climate risk is a financial risk) and also newly assumed risk they may take on when decarbonising portfolios. Econometric modelling used by Mercer helped investors understand the inter-linkages between the economy, energy systems, and the environment using economic data points – GDP, gross value added (GVA), interest rates, along with other factors.

Climate scenarios

The Mercer climate scenario model isolates transition and physical risk factors and maps the relative impact of those risk factors under three climate scenarios. In a trajectory known as the global carbon law, emissions peak in 2020 and halve every decade thereafter. The "carbon law" concept is based on Moore's Law in the computer industry, applied to cities, nations, and industrial sectors to show that to reduce emissions sooner rather than later reduces the risk of exceeding the remaining global carbon budget (650 GtCO2) in order to stay well below 2°C (Mercer, 2019, p. 20).

Many investors accept that a 2°C or less scenario (with a carbon budget of 1,100 GtCO2 between 2018 and 2100) in a low-carbon economy transformation is most closely aligned with both successful implementation of the Paris Agreement's ambitions and represent the greatest chance of lessening physical damages. In a 3°C scenario, the carbon budget is estimated at 3,500

GtCO2 between 2018 and 2100, where some climate action would see limited abatement, but also a failure both to meet the Paris Agreement and be impacted heavily by physical damages. In a 4°C+ scenario (carbon budget of 5,100 GtCO2 between 2018 and 2100), a fragmented policy pathway sees current commitments not implemented and a serious failure to alleviate the physical damages. These three scenarios and carbon budgets were selected in collaboration with the FutureMakers, who decided in 2015 that they were the most relevant to global institutional investors using these tools. Since then the IPCC Special Report on 1.5 degrees was published and it is acknowledged that a lower warming scenario is important for future modelling.

In support of the scenarios and its outputs, Mercer developed resources for investors to supplement the model results such as scenario signposts as a guide to help monitor the latest scenario policy signals about the progress of the low-carbon transition and developments in physical damage impacts. These resources alert investors to issues around technology and policy developments, such as the importance of reducing air and plastics pollution and other risks such as climate-related litigation, not captured in the economic modelling report outputs (Mercer, 2019).

Scenario pathways and risk factors

The 2019 Mercer report determined scenario pathways that show the direction of climate impact over time on risk factors which are proxy for different

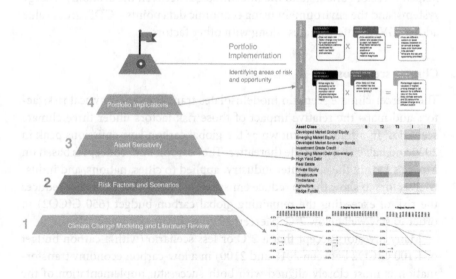

FIGURE 13.1 Mercer Climate Scenario Modelling Overview

Source: Mercer (2019)

climate change impacts. The method chosen was to develop global scenario scripts which describe the relative impact of four risk factors (defined below) in three different temperature scenarios spanning the time period between 2018 and 2100 at annual time steps. We refer to these global time series values as "scripts". When it came to coverage of regions and sectors for the 82-year period, the climate impact was modelled over 16 regions and 20 sectors. The scripts and risk factors are measured by the relative overall cumulative impact on global GDP and other economic indicators and factors.

Each risk factor is a summary of a significant aspect of the effect of climate change and are called the STIR factors, where:

S = spending
T = transition (2°C and 3°C versions – T2 and T3)
I = impact of natural catastrophes
R = resource availability (Mercer, 2019, p. 22)

The climate impact for a given region or sector, under a given scenario using the STIR risk factors described above, is calculated as Return = Σ Sensitivities × Script. The return impacts as defined by the econometric model and the STIR risk factors are compared for consistency over the time period.

The Spending (S) and Transition (T) risk factors both capture transition risk, while physical risks are represented by the impact of natural catastrophes (I) and resource availability (R).

The (S) factor seeks to account for the increase needed in public and private spending in the first few years of the transition, but is not in this instance considered beyond 2025. It is primarily relevant under the 2°C scenario for the most climate-sensitive sectors and asset classes, e.g. coal, oil and gas, utilities, renewables, and sustainable infrastructure.

The (T) factor captures policy and technology interactions as a single transition risk factor, with different asset sensitivities in a 2°C and a 3°C scenario.

The (I) Impact and (R) climate risk factors assess the physical damage of climate change. "Impact of natural catastrophes" is the risk to investors of physical damages due to acute weather incidence/severity, for example, extreme or catastrophic events. The "Resource availability" factor captures the effect of long-term weather pattern changes, for example, in temperature or precipitation on natural resources like agricultural commodities. Physical damages are not considered in the original model that Mercer sourced from Cambridge Econometrics. Instead, to estimate physical impacts, Mercer conducted a survey of available literature on specific climate-affected catastrophe perils/natural resources and selected best-in-class research to inform the development of peril-specific physical damage functions which could be embedded in the econometric model. The catastrophe perils and natural resources ultimately addressed by this "bottom–up" approach and embedded in the econometric modelling are:

- agriculture damage function (wheat, maize, soy, rice) (Moore et al., 2017);
- coastal flood damage function (Hinkel et al., 2014);
- wildfire damage function (Howard, 2014).

Stress testing for climate impacts now

Mercer developed a stress-testing tool in 2019 to consider longer-term return impacts as shorter-term climate-related market re-pricing events reflecting short-term changes in how and to what extent the market prices climate change risks and opportunities, including changing views on the probabilities of different climate scenarios. As a result, the stress-testing tool was designed to capitalise expected future impacts in present-value terms, using a dividend discount modelling (DDM) approach (Mercer, 2019, p. 50). The scenario probabilities allow investors to decide to what extent they consider changes in either transition risk or physical damages risks and why they might become more likely. Market pricing changes are considered in the stress test, to think about how much the market is under- or overpricing assets. The stress test allows investors to consider the percentage impact on valuation if market pricing changed to (a) account for a different view on the more likely climate scenario and (b) account for climate change to a different extent. These stress tests are run at a whole of portfolio level, asset class level, and sector level, and allow for consideration of the additional climate-related impact on investment return within a 12-month period.

Results

The outputs from the econometric modelling produce scenario analysis that provide asset class and sector-level detail which investors can workshop and apply to asset allocation decisions. The relative magnitude of investment return impact produced by the scenario analysis is considered by Mercer to be significantly underestimated – especially in relation to physical damages – and invariably small in absolute terms due to the effect of averaging over many years in some cases.

In two typical well-diversified, multi-asset sample portfolios, the modelling results show there is a return opportunity to 2030 of between 0.10% per annum and 0.30% per annum in a 2°C scenario compared with –0.07% per annum in a 4°C scenario. To 2100, a 4°C scenario leaves each portfolio down more than 0.10% per annum compared with a 2°C scenario. Compounding these gains or losses over a period of years gives some insight as to the additional climate impact on investment return.

THE LOW-CARBON TRANSITION PREMIUM

Transition opportunities emerge from a 2°C scenario according to the model outputs, with transition expected to be a benefit from a macroeconomic perspective (Mercer, 2019, p. 50; OECD, 2017), including the potential to capture a "low-carbon transition premium". Although a 2°C scenario presents transition risk (especially for portfolios aligned to a 3°C or 4°C+ world), the data suggests investors can target investment in the many mitigation and adaptation solutions required for a transformative transition. In the two sample portfolios, the sustainability-themed version is nearly 0.20% per annum better off to 2030.

Expected annual return impacts remain most visible at an industry sector level, with significant variations by scenario, particularly for energy, utilities, consumer staples, and telecoms. Asset class returns can also vary significantly by scenario, with infrastructure, property, and equities being the most notable. Variations in results between asset classes and across regions, cumulative impacts, and the emphasis on sustainable opportunities provide multiple portfolio construction possibilities for investors.

The low-carbon transition premium in lower warming scenarios is not equivalent to other investment-risk factors (for example, inflation, liquidity) that would apply across scenarios. It also cannot be calculated historically, as

TABLE 13.1
Example of additional climate impact on return on sectors and asset classes

Example Industry sectors and asset classes	% p.a. to 2030 in 2°C scenario	% p.a. to 2060 in 2°C scenario	% cumulative impact to 2030 in 2°C scenario	% cumulative impact to 2060 in 2°C scenario
Coal	−7.1	−8.9	−58.9	−100.0*
Oil and gas	−4.5	−8.9	−42.1	−95.1
Renewables	+6.2	+3.3	+105.9	+177.9
Electric utilities	−4.1	−3.3	−39.2	−65.7
Developed market equities	0.0	−0.2	−0.5	−5.6
Emerging market equities	+0.2	−0.1	+1.8	−4.0
All-world equities – sustainability themed	+1.6	+0.9	+21.2	+32.0
Infrastructure	+2.0	+1.0	+26.4	+39A
Infrastructure – sustainability themed	+3.0	+1.6	+42.3	+67.1
All-world real estate	0.0	−0.2	−0.1	−4.7

* Effective absolute loss of value is expected to occur in 2041 under a scenario in which global warming is limited to 2°C by 2100.

Source: Mercer (2019).

it is based on forward-looking assumptions. It can be assumed that an asymmetric assessment of carbon-risk pricing is appropriate – as neither priced in nor mispriced – and that fossil-fuel-exposed stocks will underperform over time. It is more likely that carbon risk is under-priced today than either fairly priced or overpriced (Mercer, 2017).

In *The Sequel* report (Mercer, 2019), two sample asset allocations were used to illustrate the key findings: (1) the same diversified growth asset allocation introduced in the 2015 report, and (2) a 2019 portfolio that is equivalent to the 2015 portfolio but with explicit allocations to sustainability-themed investments in multiple asset classes.

A key emphasis in the climate modelling is the testing of how tilting existing portfolios to a greater exposure to sustainable assets, including low-carbon equity, active and passive, fossil-fuel-free equity, sustainable public equity, sustainable private equity, sustainable infrastructure, and green bonds, for example, might render a portfolio more climate-resilient. The sustainability-themed equivalents in *The Sequel* differ only in terms of their climate change sensitivities, as the source of the quantum of the low-carbon transition premium Mercer finds exists in the context of a 2°C or less scenario or a scenario getting meaningfully closer to 2°C or less than our current trajectory (Mercer, 2019, p. 57).

WHAT'S THE NEXT FUTUREMAKER STEP FOR INVESTORS?

It can be argued that it is "madness" to attempt to model the impact and likelihood of climate change on assets for a 2°C or less scenario, given the influence of neoclassical economic theory on our thinking about climate change, modelling methods, and data gaps. Econometric models and big data approaches that combine forecasting and modelling of long-range spatial connections across multiple timescales, with links to physical process models, provide long-term investors with a way forward to manage transition risk and physical damages risk. Big data models, however, do not necessarily lead to accelerated institutional investor action. However, investors can and should focus on the catastrophic outcomes ahead and the emission reductions needed. As the FutureMakers case illustrates, it is possible for a peer group of major global investors to use common climate scenario and stress-testing tools and integrated assessment models (combining top–down and bottom–up methods) to take investment action. Models and data translated by practitioners and subject-matter experts can help institutional investors identify key risks and work to eliminate them and are decision-useful. The models and data we have access to today indicate that current methods can support the transition to a 2°C or less scenario and that all investors can become Future Makers (Mercer, 2019, p. 35).

NOTES

1 I would like to thank my colleagues Alex Bernhardt, Steven Sowden, and Dr Harry Liem for their review.

2 See the United Nations Framework Convention on Climate Change (2015) Paris Agreement. In October 2018, the Intergovernmental Panel on Climate Change (IPCC) released a report on 1.5°C and the difference between that and 2°C to illustrate the additional impact that 0.5°C is expected to have, why the Paris Agreement ambition is for "well below" 2°C, which I acknowledge here.

3 The FutureMakers are a group of global institutional investors facilitated by Mercer representing over US$3 trillion in assets that all use or have used Mercer's climate scenario analysis and show leadership in climate investment practices.

4 An "efficient" market is defined as a market where there are large numbers of rational, profit "maximisers" actively competing, with each trying to predict future market values of individual securities, and where important current information is almost freely available to all participants. In an efficient market, competition among the many intelligent participants leads to a situation where, at any point in time, actual prices of individual securities already reflect the effects of information based both on events that have already occurred and on events which, as of now, the market expects to take place in the future. In other words, in an efficient market, at any point in time the actual price of a security will be a good estimate of its intrinsic value. See Fama (1970).

5 See the discussion by Brenda Jubin (2017).

6 See also the discussion by Messac (2018).

7 The FutureMakers group was formally established after the Mercer *Investing in a Time of Climate Change* 2015 report, with membership evolving as new clients conduct the analysis and elect to participate.

8 The climate modelling is explained by Holden et al. (2018).

REFERENCES

Cambridge Econometrics (2019). *E3ME Technical Manual V6.1*. Available at: www.e3me.com/wp-content/uploads/2019/09/E3ME-Technical-Manual-v6.1-onlineSML.pdf (Accessed: 17 January 2020).

Dixon, P. B., Pearson, K., Picton, M. R., and Rimmer, M. T. (2005). 'Rational Expectations for Large CGE Models: A Practical Algorithm and a Policy Application'. *Economic Modelling*, 22(6), pp. 1001–1019.

Faghmous, J. H. and Kumar, V. (2014). 'A Big Data Guide to Understanding Climate Change: The Case for Theory-Guided Data Science'. *Big Data*, 2(3), pp. 155–163.

Fama, E. (1970). 'Efficient Capital Markets: A Review of Theory and Empirical Work'. *Journal of Finance*, 25, pp. 383–417.

Ford, J. D., Tilleard, S. E., Berrang-Ford, L., Araos, M., Biesbroek, R., Lesnikowski, A. C., ... Bizikova, L. (2016). 'Big Data Has Big Potential for Applications to Climate Change Adaptation'. *Proceedings of the National Academy of Sciences of the United States of America*, 113(39), pp. 10729–10732.

Hassani, H., Huang, X., and Silva, E. (2019). 'Big Data and Climate Change'. *Big Data and Cognitive Computing*, 3(1), pp. 1–17.

Hinkel, J., Lincke, D., Vafeidis, A. T., Perrette, M., Nicholls, R. J., Tol, R. S. J., ... Levermann, A. (2014). 'Coastal Flood Damage and Adaptation Costs under 21st Century Sea-level Rise'. *Proceedings of the National Academy of Sciences of the United States of America*, 111(9), pp. 3292–3297.

Holden, P. B., Edwards, N. R., Ridgwell, A., Wilkinson, R. D., Fraedrich, K., Lunkeit, F., ... Viñuales, J. E. (2018). 'Climate–Carbon Cycle Uncertainties and the Paris Agreement'. *Nature Climate Change*, 8(7), pp. 609–613.

Howard, P. (2014). *Flammable Planet: Wildfires and the Social Cost of Carbon*. Available at:https://costofcarbon.org/files/Flammable_Planet__Wildfires_and_Social_Cost_of_Carbon.pdf (Accessed: 17 January 2020).

Jubin, B. (2017). *Bookstaber, the End of Theory*. Available at: https://seekingalpha.com/article/4068311-bookstaber-end-of-theory (Accessed: 17 January 2020).

Kelton, S. (2019). *Paul Krugman Asked Me about Modern Monetary Theory: Here are 4 Answers*. Available at: www.bloomberg.com/opinion/articles/2019-03-01/paul-krugman-s-four-questions-about-mmt (Accessed: 17 January 2020).

Knüsel, B., Zumwald, M., Baumberger, C., Hirsch Hadorn, G., Fischer, E. M., Bresch, D. N., and Knutti, R. (2019). 'Applying Big Data Beyond Small Problems in Climate Research'. *Nature Climate Change*, 9(3), pp. 196–202.

Kompas, T., Pham, V. H., and Tuong, N. C. (2018). 'The Effects of Climate Change on GDP by Country and the Global Economic Gains from Complying with the Paris Climate Accord'. *Earth's Future*, 6(8), pp. 1045–1173. [Online Journal].

Kriegler, E., Hall, J. W., Held, H., Dawson, R., and Schellnhuber, H. J. (2009). 'Imprecise Probability Assessment of Tipping Points in the Climate System'. *Proceedings of the National Academy of Sciences of the United States of America*, 106(13), pp. 5041–5046.

Lo, A. W. (2004). 'The Adaptive Markets Hypothesis'. *Journal of Portfolio Management*, 30, pp. 15–29.

McKenzie, R. B. (2019). *Market Competitiveness and Rationality: A Brain-Focused Perspective*. Available at: www.econlib.org/library/Columns/y2019/McKenziemarketcompetitiveness.html (Accessed: 17 January 2020).

Mercer (2015). *Investing in a Time of Climate Change*. Available at: www.mercer.com/content/dam/mercer/attachments/global/investments/mercer-climate-change-report-2015.pdf (Accessed: 17 January 2020).

Mercer (2017). *Preparing Portfolios for Transformation: Assessing the Prospective Investment Impacts of a Low Carbon Economic Transition*. Available at: https://www.mercer.com/our-thinking/assessing-the-prospective-investment-impacts-of-a-low-carbon-economic-transition.html (Accessed: 17 January 2020).

Mercer (2019). *Investing in a Time of Climate Change: The Sequel*. Available at: www.mmc.com/content/dam/mmc-web/insights/publications/2019/apr/FINAL_Investing-in-a-Time-of-Climate-Change-2019-Full-Report.pdf (Accessed: 17 January 2020).

Messac, L. (2018). *Woman's Unpaid Work Must Be Included in GDP Calculations: Lessons from History*. Available at: http://theconversation.com/womens-unpaid-work-must-be-included-in-gdp-calculations-lessons-from-history-98110 (Accessed: 17 January 2020).

Metcalf, G. E. and Stock, J. H. (2017). 'Integrated Assessment Models and the Social Cost of Carbon: A Review and Assessment of U.S. Experience'. *Review of Environmental Economics and Policy*, 11(1), pp. 80–99.

Moore, F. C., Baldos, U., Hertel, T., and Diaz, D. (2017). 'New Science of Climate Change Impacts on Agriculture Implies Higher Social Cost of Carbon'. *Nature Communications*, 8(1), pp. 1–8.

Nordhaus, W. D. (1991). 'To Slow or Not to Slow: The Economics of the Greenhouse Effect'. *The Economic Journal*, 101, pp. 920–937.

Organization for Economic Co-operation and Development (OECD) (2017). *Investing in Climate, Investing in Growth*. Available at: www.oecd.org/environment/investing-in-climate-investing-in-growth-9789264273528-en.htm (Accessed: 17 January 2020).

Overpeck, J. T., Meehl, G. A., Bony, S., and Easterling, D. R. (2011). 'Climate Data Challenges in the 21st Century'. *Science*, 331(6018), pp. 700–702.

Pilling, D. (2018). *5 Ways GDP Gets It Totally Wrong as a Measure of Our Success*. Available at: www.weforum.org/agenda/2018/01/gdp-frog-matchbox-david-pilling-growth-delusion/(Accessed: 17 January 2020).

Pindyck, R. S. (2017). 'The Use and Misuse of Models for Climate Policy'. *Review of Environmental Economics and Policy*, 11(1), pp. 100–114.

Reichstein, M., Camps-Valls, G., Stevens, B., Jung, M., Denzler, J., and Carvalhais, N. Prabhat. (2019). 'Deep Learning and Process Understanding for Data-driven Earth System Science'. *Nature*, 566(7743), pp. 195–204.

Stern, N. (2016). 'Current Climate Models are Grossly Misleading'. *Nature*, 530(7591), pp. 407–409.

Stoerk, T., Wagner, G., and Ward, R. E. T. (2018). 'Policy Brief—Recommendations for Improving the Treatment of Risk and Uncertainty in Economic Estimates of Climate Impacts in the Sixth

Intergovernmental Panel on Climate Change Assessment Report'. *Review of Environmental Economics and Policy*, 12(2), pp. 371–376.

United Nations Environmental Program Finance Initiative (UNEP FI) (2011). *Universal Ownership: Why Environmental Externalities Matter to Institutional Investors*. Available at: www.unepfi.org/fileadmin/documents/universal_ownership_full.pdf (Accessed: 17 January 2020).

United Nations Framework Convention on Climate Change (UNFCC) (2015). *The Paris Agreement*. Available at: http://unfccc.int/files/essential_background/convention/application/pdf/english_paris_agreement.pdf (Accessed: 17 January 2020).

Waring, M. (1999). *Counting for Nothing: What Men Value and What Women are Worth*, 2nd edition. Toronto: University of Toronto Press.

Weyant (2017). 'Some Contributions of Integrated Assessment Models of Global Climate Change'. *Review of Environmental Economics and Policy*, 11(1), pp. 115–137.

World Economic Forum (2019). *The Global Risks Report 2019*. Available at: www.weforum.org/reports/the-global-risks-report-2019 (Accessed: 17 January 2020).

14

Data defense in sustainable investing

Ashby Monk, Marcel Prins, and Dane Rook

INTRODUCTION

Investors are increasingly drawing upon unconventional datasets to support their decision-making processes.[1] Use of *alternative data* ("alt-data") – such as geolocation data, social media data, and remote-sensing data – is helping investors to more comprehensively understand all sources of risk, and thus better value all types of assets (Monk, Prins, and Rook, 2019). In particular, alt-data is fast becoming a crucial ingredient in many investors' approaches to sustainable investing. It is enabling them to more thoroughly integrate environmental, social, and governance (ESG) factors into investment decisions, and thereby gain a deeper comprehension of assets' sustainability impacts (whether positive or negative). In short, alt-data is now a powerful tool for unlocking sustainable investing's full potential, which is itself vital for beneficially transforming society and preserving the natural world.

But, as with any tool, increased power translates into an increased need to ensure that power is used responsibly. In using alt-data for sustainable investing, investors must be mindful of what vulnerabilities can be created if it is used irresponsibly – and what constitutes irresponsible use in the first place. To be clear, in our view, the benefits from using alt-data to improve sustainable-investing capabilities vastly outweigh the costs. Nevertheless, there are several emerging threats to which investors may become exposed if they improperly manage and govern how they use alt-data (not just in sustainable investing, but in general). Some of these threats are external, i.e., they come from entities outside investors' organizations (as opposed to, e.g., poor decisions caused by internal analysts making errors in data processing). In this chapter, we characterize these external threats. We then uncover how investors can successfully combat them by playing *data defense*.

The need for data defense is perhaps strongest when alt-data is used for purposes other than long-term asset ownership: namely, when investors use alt-data to incorporate ESG factors into their decisions, but still prioritize capturing quick gains from short-term trading – rather than the more reliable advantages that come through focusing on long holding periods, alignment with intermediaries, and other practices of truly long-term asset ownership (see Monk, Sharma, and Sinclair, 2017).[2] Operating as a long-term owner should alleviate many of the dangers of alt-data, as the vulnerability is often associated with the time pressure that market participants with short horizons face in using this form of data. By taking a long-term view, however, asset owners have more opportunity to study, vet, and responsibly govern data on which they base decisions, which in turn makes them more likely to identify any problems with the data that could become abused by bad actors. A key takeaway from this chapter is thus that operating as a long-term owner is the overall best way for an investor to play data defense.

Our research further finds that, when playing data defense, it is important for investors to:

- closely scrutinize how alt-data enters, and is used, in their organizations;
- be aware of how alt-data, and its role in investment decision-making, might become visible to and misused by third parties for purposes such as greenwashing, frontrunning trades, or other adversarial activities; and
- take appropriate measures to conceal from outsiders what alt-data they use for investment decision-making.

These aspects of data defense are linked by the (perhaps counterintuitive) need to limit transparency to third parties regarding the specific alt-data that is used for decision-making – be it for sustainable investing or otherwise.

Emphasis on limiting transparency may at first seem strange in the context of sustainability, which is usually more closely associated with openness and visibility.[3] This sense of strangeness is typical, and stems from a pervasive belief that alt-data must somehow be treated differently from "normal" data, for example, by following a separate track outside the organization's main systems for data management and governance. Certainly, alt-data enables sustainable investing capabilities that more conventional forms of data cannot. But there is, *a priori*, no valid reason that alt-data should exist in a management and governance sphere that segregates it from other data.[4] For instance, few investors would deem it responsible to exactly disclose what data and factors they use for making "ordinary" investment decisions that neither account for sustainability nor use alt-data. Indeed, to do so would often be deemed reckless, as it can expose investors to being exploited. Things are no different if alt-data is used for sustainable investing: excessive visibility can result in exploitation.

This threat of exploitation is growing – not just where alt-data or sustainable investing are concerned, but in general. This trend is being propelled by significant advances in technology and its accessibility: in specific, sophisticated algorithms for forging data, and potent machine-learning tools for analyzing data. We dissect these trends and detail some strategies to guard against them. Our aim is to encourage an appropriate degree of organizational prudence so that investors can increase the use of alt-data to drive more thoughtful investment decisions and better outcomes over the long term.

The rest of this chapter proceeds as follows. In the next section, we dive into detail on why the responsible use of alt-data in sustainable investing should be a top priority for investors. Then we reveal some of the motives bad actors may have for using alt-data as a weapon against investors, and why the possibility of their doing so is on the rise. We then address specific ways in which various entities may use alt-data to harm investors, and then turn in to discuss the main considerations to weigh in assessing how vulnerable an investor is to having alt-data (as well as conventional data) used against it. Then we introduce strategies for data defense that investors can use to protect themselves from such threats. The final section summarizes.

Most of the findings in this chapter come from a four-year (and counting) research program that aims to understand how institutional investors (e.g., public pensions, endowments, sovereign wealth funds) are using alt-data and technology now, and how they can realistically embrace advanced technology in the (immediate) future. The project has involved interviews, surveys, and embedded observation of hundreds of practitioners situated in dozens of institutional investment organizations across the globe. While many of our findings were derived within the institutional investment community, our conversations with industry professionals and other experts prove that they are also applicable to other investment organizations. Throughout the chapter we make explicit note of any findings or insights that may apply distinctly to institutional investors, but not necessarily to other organizations.

CHARACTERIZING THE THREAT

Exploitation imposes negative externalities on an investor; an investor being exploited means it bears the costs for some third party's gain. The costs borne by an exploited investor can take many forms, including buying or selling assets when they otherwise would not have done, trading at worse prices than they otherwise would have, or assuming unwanted or unanticipated risks.

The severity of these costs to a given investor depends on its strategy and portfolio.[5] Similarly, the nature of the gains to the exploiter depends on its identity and intentions.

What types of entities would try to exploit investors – especially, institutional investors – by using alt-data, and how would they stand to benefit? Why would they find sustainability-related data appealing for doing so?[6] And how exactly are such exploitations executed? This section is devoted to answering those questions.

Who exploits investors and why?

Greenwashing and *adversarial trading* are the core motivations for exploiting an investor by (mis)using sustainability data.[7] These motivations separately explain the types of organization that are likely to try exploiting investors by using sustainability data: corporations are more disposed to being driven by a desire to greenwash, whereas short-term-oriented market participants (e.g., arbitrage-focused hedge funds or criminal actors) are more likely to engage in adversarial trading.

For the most part, these two motivations are mutually exclusive. Corporations are unlikely to have a goal of trading against investors after having misrepresented themselves as being more sustainable than they actually are. Meanwhile, adversarial traders may use greenwashing or reverse greenwashing as a means to an end (e.g., inducing an investor to sell a company's stock by causing the investor to mistakenly believe the company is "dirty"), but their only real goal is to generate trading profits at investors' expense.[8]

The gains associated with these two motives are relatively clear. Greenwashing can lead to a higher corporate valuation, whereas adversarial trading can boost the profitability of a market participant's trades. But why would exploiters try to specifically target *institutional investors*? Or, rather, why may institutional investors be more vulnerable to exploitation by such methods than other types of investor are?

For one, institutional investors are vulnerable due to their size. Institutional investors often are responsible for portfolios of tens or hundreds of billions of dollars in assets. At those scales, dealing in small positions and trade executions becomes challenging, in terms of coordination as well as cost. Institutional investors therefore tend to own larger stakes in corporations and place trades in larger batches than other organizations do, which means it is often relatively more efficient to attempt to exploit them specifically than other market participants broadly. What is more, most institutional investors also own heavily diversified portfolios comprising hundreds or thousands of different securities and other assets. Intensively monitoring all data on each of these holdings is highly resource-intensive, yet most institutional investors are very resource-constrained. As such, institutional investors are – all else equal – less likely to (quickly) detect exploitation than other entities would. This disadvantage is compounded by the fact that institutional investors tend to suffer from weak data management and governance systems (Monk and Rook, 2018, 2019). Hence, institutional investors are, by and large, more susceptible to data-based exploitation than are other market participants.

Institutional investors are also presently facing considerable external pressure to invest in sustainable assets. This pressure comes from pensioners, governments, universities, and other groups to which institutional investors are responsible. In some cases, this pressure is "hard": institutional investors are forced to consider specific sustainability factors in their investment decisions, and are outright prevented from owning assets with features that are deemed to make them unsustainable.[9] Such hard constraints can increase investors' vulnerability to exploitation. For example, they can force an investor to hurriedly sell an asset that is perceived to violate those constraints, or compel them to reallocate capital to an asset that meets pre-stipulated sustainability criteria.

Regardless of whether pressure to invest sustainably is hard or soft, many institutional investors' systems for handling sustainability considerations are not fully integrated with their organizations' general decision-making processes (often because such systems have only recently been adopted). That is, sustainability considerations are often treated as add-ons to institutional investors' core processes and portfolios.[10] It is not uncommon for institutional investors to claim they invest sustainably by reserving a (small) fraction of their portfolios for sustainability-focused assets, or by first selecting candidate assets based on features unrelated to sustainability and then selectively filtering these using a (generic or weak) sustainability criterion. These addendum approaches often cause institutional investors' systems and processes for handling sustainability considerations to be under-resourced, and so are more exposed to exploitation. Thus, it is often easier to manipulate, deceive, or otherwise exploit an institutional investor with sustainability-related data than with other forms of data.

Why target sustainability data?

Beyond the fact that many institutional investors are weaker in managing, and making decisions from, sustainability data, there are other reasons why sustainability data may be easier to use in exploiting them than other data types. For one, there remains a lack of widespread consensus in the financial community about what sustainability factors matter most for various kinds of investments, and how to properly measure them (In, Monk, and Rook, 2019). This absence of consensus militates against the emergence of prescriptive and enforced standards for producing sustainability data. Consequently, organizations that generate sustainability data may calculate it in different – even idiosyncratic – ways, which can make detecting attempts at manipulation (for example, through misstating numbers) more challenging. Relatedly, much of the sustainability data that does exist is not governed by strict regulation in the way that standard accounting figures are. There are often no requirements to release such data publicly, nor large penalties for errors in published data.

Moreover, sustainability data can be a more enticing tool for exploitation than other types of data because it is often harder to verify, e.g., it may require sophisticated physical measurement, or (expert) subjective judgment. Finally, the emotive nature of some sustainability data can endow it with a viral property that other types of business data lack. Plainly, a claim that a company is responsible for human sufferings or the deaths of charismatic megafauna (sea turtles, polar bears, whales, etc.) is more likely to attract media attention than news of skipped dividend payments. Such virality can be a boon for those looking to exploit investors (especially via adversarial trading or reverse-greenwashing): even if the data on which it is based is clearly questionable, the scale of negative attention can force investors into rushed action – e.g., to avoid unwelcome publicity.

Why now?

Why are these threats intensifying now? The rising popularity of sustainable investing is only part of the answer. There are two other critical components: First, *alternative data* (alt-data) has become more prevalently used among investors in recent years (see Monk, Prins, and Rook, 2019). That is, investors are more extensively using unconventional forms of data – such as satellite imagery, web-scraped data, geolocation data, social media streams, and other novel data from millions of diverse sources – than ever before. Proliferation of sustainability data has been, to some degree, a byproduct of broader and deeper demand for alt-data in general. Market participants are increasingly seeking unconventional data, irrespective of whether they are motivated by sustainability objectives. The fact that most sustainability data is unconventional – and is thereby alt-data – just serves to fuel an expansion in both the demand for and supply of it.

The corresponding increase in availability of sustainability data is, on balance, beneficial to investors. But it creates a problem of selectivity. The growing volume of data that could be used to judge sustainability makes vetting all sources of it impossible. Nevertheless, ignoring all but a few sources runs the risk of excluding informative, material signals on sustainability. Hence, for many alt-datasets, investors are thrust into a precarious position of having to pick between active ignorance and blind trust. Opting for the latter exposes them to exploitation, while the former can introduce significant reputational risks – among others.[11]

Another key reason that the threat of exploitation (not just by means of sustainability data) is currently accelerating is technological. Emergence of vastly improved algorithms for generating fake data – especially forged images and text – has hit a feverish pace over the past few years. The most convincing of such algorithmically produced forgeries are becoming nearly indistinguishable from reality and are, in many instances, widely and freely available (we discuss their specific use in more detail below). At the same time, sharply improved analytical technologies (e.g., machine-learning algorithms) are becoming broadly accessible – for instance, via user-friendly interfaces that require little mathematical background and low digital fluency. Although this has benefitted investors by reducing barriers to their own use of advanced analytics, these tools can also be turned against them. For example (and as discussed next), these tools can be readily fooled by various types of the digital forgeries we mentioned above. Similarly, such tools can be used to more accurately predict when an investor is likely to place trades and then exploit them accordingly.

HOW CAN SUSTAINABILITY DATA BE USED FOR EXPLOITATION?

Overall, there are two primary ways by which data (in general) can be used to exploit investors: detection and manipulation. Detection permits exploitation because it allows other parties to infer what data an investor uses to drive its decisions, or else to forecast when (and possibly how) it is likely to trade based on that data. An organization's *data exhaust* is what enables detection – i.e., the data that it produces over the course of its operations that becomes visible to entities outside the organization (data exhaust is not just internal data that leaks out from the organization; it also includes "footprints" from the organization's digital activities, such as online behavior).[12] Loosely, detection can be considered a passive form of exploitation, in the sense that it (on its own) does not involve attempts to control the actions of the organization it victimizes.

Manipulation, on the other hand, directly aims to influence a victim's behavior by altering the data and information it receives. The chief mechanism by which manipulation functions is *data ingestion*: manipulation works by targeting the data that enters a victim organization (i.e., data that organization ingests) and changing that data in ways that induce the victim organization to take exploitable actions.[13] Detection and manipulation are not mutually exclusive, but they do tend to correspond to different motives. Namely, manipulation is more strongly linked with greenwashing, whereas detection is more associated with adversarial trading.[14]

Exploitation via detection

Conventionally, detection has been the main way that data is used to exploit investors. Perhaps the simplest (and until recently, the only widespread) form of data exhaust that enables detection is investors' trading patterns. For the most part, these are observable, even though they might not explicitly identify the investor itself. But anonymity is not necessarily a safeguard. Adversarial traders do not need to know investors' identities outright to exploit them. They only need to know how an investor's trading activity correlates with some observable variable.[15] Clearly, pinpointing the data on which an investor actually makes trading decisions will yield the tightest correlations, which is precisely why investors should be cautious in disclosing what sustainability data they use for investment decision-making.

But official disclosure is not the sole way exploiters can detect data use. All organizations produce data exhaust: "the assortment of log files, cookies, and other digital footprints created by people's online browsing (including geolocation data from searches on mobile devices)" (Monk, Prins, and Rook, 2019, p. 14). Collectively, these footprints can be used to assemble a telling picture of what data sources an investor uses to drive its decision-making, and thus make it vulnerable to exploitation.

Problematically, digital footprints are a challenge to manage for individuals, and are even more so for organizations. Any entity's digital footprint has both an active and passive component. An active footprint is composed of data that the entity knowingly and voluntarily provides online. It can include submission of users' email addresses, posted comments or other content, submitted contact/mailing details, or the contribution of any other data the entity willingly chooses to yield to web services with which it interacts. Worryingly, however, even though an active footprint is made up of voluntarily surrendered data, access to it can – and often does – slip outside the control of the party that initially receives it (e.g., the website from which it was collected). Active-footprint data can become used for purposes other than those agreed to or envisioned by its original owner.

The passive part of an entity's digital footprint, meanwhile, is made up from data on which it never knowingly gives consent for another party to use or distribute. In many cases, such consent may be implicit – e.g., granted by agreeing to vague or open-ended terms-of-use agreements for web services. Still, in all cases, data in an entity's passive footprint is data that it never intentionally approves for use or distribution by third parties. Common examples of passive-footprint data are geolocation data (whether tied to coordinates from an IP address or GPS), activity logs on pages in a website (or across sites), or even information on a user's specific device configuration (maker, browser, peripherals, battery life, etc.). Broadly, an entity's active footprint tends to more plainly reveal *who it is*, whereas its passive footprint usually gives a more comprehensive view into *what it does* in the digital realm – including where it sources data.[16]

Our research on institutional investors indicates that they have increasing awareness of the vulnerabilities created by large and visible digital foot-prints. Yet our studies also show that many institutional investors are taking few focused measures to either reduce or control their footprints, despite awareness of the risks. We find that a significant cause of this disconnect is organizational; many institutional investors treat their digital footprint as a concern for cybersecurity teams, rather than an issue of data management or governance. This problem can be viewed from another angle: too few insti-tutional investors' systems for data management and governance pay enough attention to what happens to data after it leaves the organization, relative to how data is handled inside of it.

Our interviews and other interactions with institutional investors suggest this imbalance is worse for sustainability data – partly because sustainability data is so often treated differently from other forms of data (and thus may not be subject to the same quality controls required for other data types). But there also appears to be another reason. The need to manage digital footprints is frequently associated only with short-term trading activities, while sustainability data is often seen as relevant mainly for long-term asset ownership. As such, sustain-ability data is treated exclusively as an asset, without recognizing the fact that it creates organizational liabilities (as do the processes involved in obtaining it).

Yet the liabilities that digital footprints create are rapidly becoming more severe with the rise of more sophisticated inference algorithms – in specific, those related to improved machine-learning techniques. These tools are increasing the resolution at which exploiters can detect what data sources investors are using to inform their decision-making, and thus enabling more targeted attacks. Later, we will cover some remedies that investors might take to shield themselves against this trend. But the first step to doing so is acknowledging the reality that all data has the potential to be both an asset and liability, and that one of the chief liabilities for investors is the creation of footprints from obtaining and handling data, irrespective of whether it is sustainability data or not.

Exploitation via manipulation

Detection is an indirect exploitation strategy: an exploiter responds to learn-ing a data source used by its victim. Exploitation by manipulation, however, is more direct, as the exploiter aims to induce a specific response from its victim by altering or fabricating part of a dataset that its victim uses for deci-sion-making. This latter type of exploitation targets an investor's process for data ingestion – i.e., how it converts external data into investment decisions. Knowing what data an organization ingests is obviously crucial to this form of exploitation. As such, there is some overlap between exploitation by detection and exploitation by manipulation. For example, an exploiter may examine investors' data exhaust to discover what data resources they consume. But manipulation goes a step further by actually trying to influence the data an investor consumes: by tampering with data it already ingests, or forcing it to ingest data from new sources.

The threat of exploitation by manipulation is not new to investors. Recall that there is a long history in finance of corporate accounting fraud and attempts to sow rumors. The chief recent change has come through increased scale. Thanks to a raft of improving technologies, exploiters can generate counterfeit data at speed, volume, and quality not previously achievable. Advances in these technologies are most dramatic in the domain of *generative* algorithms – specifically, machine-learning models that are rapidly able to create output (e.g., text, photos, time-series) with very (and increasingly) high fidelity to reality.

Before describing these tools and their implications for exploitation, it is instructive to note that their success depends on continued decentralizing of data provision in the financial services industry. That is, the extent to which these tools can be used to manipulate investors heavily relies on data continuing to come from unconventional sources in unconventional forms. Appreciably, exploitation by manipulation is challenging when issuance of data is controlled by a small number of credible authorities (like the Securities and Exchange Commission) that issue official data in a limited number of forms (e.g., official filings or recorded corporate earnings calls).

Yet, using only official data creates a bottleneck on how comprehensively investors can understand investable assets. Rising popularity of alt-data is helping to alleviate this bottleneck in data sources and forms, and also helping investors to gain fuller understanding of assets they own (or could own). But the cost of this expanded access is a heightened susceptibility to unknowingly using data that has been corrupted – whether maliciously or unintentionally. The rise of alt-data in finance is therefore a mixed blessing for investors, but is wind in the sails for would-be exploiters. This is especially true for sustainability data.

For investors, *deep-fakes* present one of the more harmful results of alt-data's ascendance. We will be somewhat loose in our application of the term, and take it to encompass all forms of data that are synthesized by artificial neural networks for purposes of deception – whether to fool humans or other algorithms.[17] The pace at which deep-fakes are improving (in the sense that they are becoming harder to distinguish from reality) is staggering and is being driven by the ferocious progress in the sophistication of artificial neural networks (which nowadays fall mostly under the banner of *deep learning*).[18] This progress is being fueled by intense funding from technology giants like Google, Facebook, and Microsoft. But it is also an outgrowth of the zeitgeist of transparency which dominates that research space: researchers are expected to publicly release the code behind any breakthroughs they make, so that others may test and further experiment with it.

Troublingly, this openness also means the latest algorithmic advances (e.g., generative adversarial networks [Goodfellow et al., 2014] or transformers [Vaswani et al., 2017]) are easily available to exploiters who would abuse them. Worry over this potential for abuse is what drove a leading artificial intelligence research organization, OpenAI, to choose not to publicly release code for one of its major innovations: a text-generation model dubbed "GPT-2".[19] GPT-2 is notable for its ability to generate article-length passages of text that are cogent, non-repetitive, and replete with plausible (even if false) arguments – without human intervention. Capacity to produce text of such length and quality was a first, and OpenAI researchers observed that, in experimental testing, human subjects often had a tough time identifying whether text was written by GPT-2 or a person. The following is a passage generated by GPT-2 in response to the prompt "recycling is not good":

> Recycling is NOT good for the world. It is bad for the environment, it is bad for our health, and it is bad for our economy. I'm not kidding. Recycling is not good for the environment. It is destructive to the earth and it's a major contributor to global warming. Recycling is not good for our health. It contributes to obesity and diseases like heart disease and cancer. Recycling is bad for our economy. It increases the cost of a product, and in turn, the price of everything that is made with that product. Recycling is not good for our nation. We pay a tremendous price for the privilege of having the world's most advanced and efficient recycling system. Recycling is a huge, colossal waste of time, energy, money, and resources.
>
> (OpenAI, 2019)

Within the community of artificial intelligence research, OpenAI has drawn criticism for not open-sourcing GPT-2. Still, their stated desire to prevent abuse of the model is understandable, and stems from recognition of a well-established principle in social psychology: the *popularity* of information can often substitute for credibility. While it is true that many people could easily write a deceptive passage that meets or surpasses the quality of what GPT-2 can write, no one (nor any large group of individuals) could write diverse versions of such a passage – that are both consistent with one another and individually convincing – as GPT-2 can. This ability to be hyper-prolific matters: robust empirical studies show repeated exposure to similar messages from diverse sources can cause a subject's confidence in the message to meet or exceed their confidence in the opposite message from a trusted source. By this token, models like GPT-2 could conceivably be used to manipulate people – as well as investment organizations – by generating floods of misinformation.

Developments such as those connected to GPT-2 are especially relevant for how investors manage and govern sustainability data, as most sustainability data is – and likely will remain – textual. That said, a sizable proportion of sustainability data is in visual or audio form, and includes satellite imagery, voice recordings, and video footage. Deep-fakes, however, exist in each of these forms and their quality regularly exceeds that of their textual counterparts.[20] Despite intense efforts by many organizations to pinpoint reliable ways for humans to spot deep-fakes, no universal methods for distinguishing deep-fakes have been discovered (nor should they soon be expected).[21]

It is not only humans that lack foolproof methods for detecting deep-fakes, but also other algorithms – i.e., many decision algorithms are vulnerable to being exploited by deep-fakes that specifically target them. This machine-versus-machine manipulation is problematic due to the data inundation that investors now face. Decision algorithms can combat data inundation by automating some of the processing that ordinarily would be done by humans. But algorithmic automation can make investors vulnerable when those algorithms can be deceived by other algorithms.

One example of such deception involves the injection of distorted pixels into images that cause computer-vision algorithms to misidentify the contents of images. These distortions can take place both after the original image is captured, or when the image itself is recorded. A high-profile example of the latter was demonstrated when a team of researchers used algorithmically designed chromatic "patches" to force vision algorithms to misclassify items onto which they were placed (see Brown et al., 2018). These patches can be designed to reliably cause an algorithm to falsely classify any object as being some other arbitrary object (e.g., a toaster) when they are placed in the same field of view.

As investors increasingly use visual data to measure various sustainability dimensions of assets, and use algorithms to analyze that data, they become exposed to this type of manipulation. For instance, slight distortions to satellite images could trick an algorithm into mischaracterizing the extent of pollution or deforestation in an area, or mistake electric or hydrogen-fueled vehicles for ones fueled by gasoline. Further troubling is the pace at which algorithms that can successfully deceive both humans and other algorithms are evolving – e.g., by making very subtle perturbations to pixels or soundbites (see Das et al., 2018; Poursaeed et al., 2018).

ASSESSING VULNERABILITY

In playing data defense against these threats, the question of severity is essential. These threats may be highly probable, but what defenses should be mounted depends on the likely scale of damages these threats can inflict. These scales will vary substantially across investors and depend on their unique portfolios, execution strategies, approaches to accounting for sustainability in investment processes, and data management and governance protocols, among other context-specific factors. In the next section, we cover defensive actions that most investors could deploy to help guard against exploitation. In this section, we focus not on calculating the likely costs of exploitation, but on key issues to address when assessing how vulnerable an organization is to exploitation by means of sustainability data. Furthermore, we concentrate here on assessing vulnerability in data ingestion, rather than from data exhaust. Vulnerabilities stemming from the latter are usually more idiosyncratic across organizations, whereas vulnerabilities in ingestion are often easier to assess systematically. We cover defenses for both in the next section.

In assessing how investors become vulnerable to exploitation when ingesting sustainability data, we focus on two types of *entry points*: the types of decisions that sustainability data enters as an input, and how sustainability data enters the organization itself.

Decision entry points

Very generally, we can distinguish two categories of investment decision that any type of data can inform (not just sustainability data): selection decisions – whether to hold any amount of a given asset or not – and decisions on how to manage a given asset once a decision has been made to own it (such management decisions may include the number of shares to own, or how much of the risk budget should be allocated to the asset). Differences between these two categories make investors vulnerable to exploitation in different ways, because decisions in each tend to be based on distinct types of data.

In general, we note that selection decisions tend to be *less delegated and less discretionary* than management decisions. Selection decisions are often made at higher levels in the organization and are regularly more formulaic. For example, divestment decisions are often made by members of senior management or investment committees, as are rules for what types of asset are prohibited (e.g., the stock of tobacco or oil companies). Likewise, because such decisions are often scrutinized by entities outside the organization, attempts are typically made to make them objective (or at least appear so). Consequently, in sustainable investing, selection decisions are routinely based on discrete variables (e.g., does a company burn coal or not?) and are heavily subject to asymmetries in valence: a single "negative" data point is often sufficient to force a categorical decision to not own an asset, while many "positive" data points may be needed to permit ownership. Collectively, these properties make selection decisions particularly susceptible to exploitation by manipulation.

The degree of this susceptibility is strongly dictated by two features of selection decisions:

- whether binding selection criteria are publicly disclosed (e.g., definitive screens that prevent or require ownership of an asset) and the extent to which these criteria are based on binary variables; and
- how aggregated and filtered sustainability data is by the time it reaches selection decision-makers.

It should be evident that having widespread visibility on what an organization cannot or must invest in exposes it to manipulation. On the other hand, selection decisions will be less vulnerable when they are based on composite variables (i.e., aggregated from several sources) that are verified by multiple individuals internally prior to reaching selection decision-makers. Selection decisions are thus most likely to be manipulated by sustainability data that can reach selection decision-makers directly and in raw form – such as high-impact false news, whether as (e.g.) a deep-faked article, video, or similarly forged data.

Although potentially less sweeping, management decisions (i.e., those occurring after the decision to own an asset has been made, or before any decision to divest outright) can make an investor equally as vulnerable to exploitation. These decisions can also be manipulated by false news or other unfiltered data, but they are typically more responsive to "small" exploitations than selection decisions are. For example, while deep-faked images of a factory producing more pollution or a logging company removing more trees than expected may not force a divestment decision, they could result in a pricing or risk revision that causes an investor to partially sell out of an equity position. These smaller-scale exploitations can be easier to engineer and sustain than those that are needed to force many selection decisions, especially because the data on which they are based will tend to be seen by fewer individuals in an organization before a decision is made (if any individuals even see that data at all – e.g., in instances where management decisions are made algorithmically).

Overall, it is not clear *a priori* whether exploitation through selection decisions or through management decisions is generally more detrimental to investors. Both types of decision are viable entry points for exploitation, and investors should be aware of how they utilize sustainability data in either case. It is clear, however, that to be exploited through data ingestion, corrupted data must enter the organization from the outside.[22] Vulnerability assessments must thereby take into account how sustainability data enters the organization in the first place.

Organizational entry points

"Provenance" is the golden word in assessing how vulnerable an investor is to exploitation through sustainability data. Knowing the lineage of data – in terms of parties that have accessed and changed it up to the point that it entered the organization, and thereafter – is pivotal for accurately assessing vulnerability. There are two dimensions of provenance that we see as integral: *source* (the identity of the last entity that "touched" the data before it entered the organization) and *format* (e.g., raw text, polished numbers taken from a data provider's secure dashboard, or photos scraped from an unsecure internet domain).

Of these dimensions, knowledge of the data's source – and chain of custody for that data after it left its source – has the strongest impact on vulnerability. If it can be known with certainty that a dataset entered the organization directly from a trustworthy source, considerations on the form in which it entered the organization become far less important. In earlier work (see Monk, Prins, and Rook, 2019), the importance of a transparent and credible chain of custody led us to encourage the use of data-vendor platforms as sources of sustainability data (along with other alt-data) – i.e., subscribing to established third-party providers that can be trusted to supply data that has been verified, or at least has a low probability of having been corrupted.

We still believe sourcing sustainability data from trusted platform providers is advisable, but with the added proviso that either:

1. The provider must have a diverse enough supply of data products that public knowledge of the investor being a subscriber to the platform would not allow others to infer key data driving the investor's decisions; or
2. Specifics of what data the platform provider supplies are not accessible by parties that may exploit the investor (e.g., the provider only accepts institutional investors as clients and does not disclose to other entities any specific information on the data it provides).

Since both of these conditions are hard to meet in practice, we caution investors to be wary of what sustainability data they consume from subscription platforms.

Yet, regardless of whether data is sourced from a platform or not, if any of the links in the chain of custody for the data cannot be verified or are not credible, scrutiny of the format in which the data entered the organization becomes a crucial (and often the dominant) concern. More specifically, it becomes necessary to have a crystal-clear record of what steps were taken to verify the authenticity and accuracy of the data after it entered the organization. To this end, we observe that it can be invaluable to have an "approved uses" hierarchy for data that originates outside the organization (whether it be sustainability data or not). As an example, one Canadian pension fund that we have studied (see Monk and Rook, 2019) uses a three-tiered hierarchy, whereby:

- *Unprocessed data* cannot be used for official reporting or making trading decisions, but is usable for research, prototyping, or other ad hoc and exploratory analysis.
- *Unit-approved data* meets requirements placed on it by a specific business unit within the organization, and it can be used for decisions under the control of that unit, but cannot be used for organization-wide decisions.
- *Authenticated data* can be used for all decisions and must have passed strict quality assurance and validation processes.

Hierarchies of this nature help create a balance between the confidence an organization can place in data and the severity of impact from being manipulated through it. By forcing data that informs high-impact decisions to go through stricter validation processes, expected harm from exploitation can be effectively reduced.

We believe the foregoing considerations form a solid starting point for investors to assess how vulnerable their organizations may be to manipulation through any type of data. Yet, being able to assess vulnerability is of little value to an investor if it cannot do anything to defend itself.

PRACTICAL DEFENSES

Although there is no silver bullet for investors to defend against exploitation, there is an emerging suite of practical steps that any investor can take to greatly mitigate the threat of being exploited through data – be it sustainability data or otherwise. These steps should be considered best practice.

The strongest defensive strategies an investor can employ are:

1. Give sustainability data "first-class citizenship" by putting it on equal footing with all other types of investment data – that is, hold it to equal standards of quality, allocate the same data management and data governance resources to it, and take similar steps to guard its identity as would be taken for all other forms of data used in decisions; and
2. Behave as a long-term owner of assets.

The first strategy remedies a deficiency we have repeatedly raised throughout the chapter: treating sustainability data as separate and distinct from other data often leads to it being under-resourced, under-scrutinized, and under-valued.

The second strategy may be more surprising, but is no less effective. Long-term investors are less threatened by exploitation because they operate over more protracted timescales than other investors do. This is not to say that they necessarily move more slowly or are less active than other investors. Instead, it means they do not need to be as rushed or reactive in their decision-making. This reduces the hazard of exploitation on both ends of the holding period: they have more time to deeply study and understand an asset before purchasing it (and so are better positioned to identify how they could face detection or manipulation by owning it); and they face less pressure to exit a position in response to "sudden changes" that might in fact be attempts at exploitation. Long-term investors are also in better positions to own assets more directly (see Monk, Sharma, and Sinclair, 2017) and thus can enjoy less obstructed information channels to assets in their portfolio. For example, they may be able to contact a company's management directly to clarify news that it is acting unsustainably.

Of course, the success of either strategy relies on an investor having some minimum level of capability for its data management and data governance systems (for data in general, not just with sustainability data). Yet, many institutional investors struggle to make such systems performant. We therefore turn to recommend defense strategies that do not rely on general data management and governance capabilities. Our recommendations are structured along the logic that exploitation comes from either detection or manipulation, so that the most efficient and effective defenses are:

- to camouflage what sustainability data the organization uses for its decisions; and
- to camouflage how and when it takes investment actions on sustainability data.

Data camouflage

The cheapest and most effective step an investor can take to camouflage what sustainability data it uses for its investment decisions is to limit disclosure of what sustainability criteria it uses, or to make these criteria not fully specific and non-binding (for example, failing to meet one of more of the criteria would not force an immediate, total exit from a position). Excessive transparency is certainly not the norm for "mainstream" investment strategies – and being excessively transparent is not inherently advantageous. It therefore seems peculiar that excessive transparency remains so popular for sustainable investing.

The next best step an investor can take is to avoid relying on single data sources in any investment decision. Basing decisions on a single data source makes identification of that source easier for would-be exploiters. This dictum to base decisions on multiple sources of sustainability data also helps combat problems of manipulation, as it is more difficult to alter or fabricate data from several sources.

Many of the other practical approaches for an investor to camouflage the sustainability data it uses have a cybersecurity flavor (and are more technical in nature). These include:

- randomizing or masking the IP/TCP addresses that employees use in their online activities;
- using dummy (but secure) email domains that can be used for signup/ login to web services;
- taking steps to minimize or prevent other parties' ability to track geolocation data;
- monitoring and enforcing what terms-of-service employees can agree to for web services; and
- restricting employees' use of personal devices while they are on-site or doing related work.

One final approach to data camouflage of which we have rarely seen is collaboration among institutional investors to *jointly own* sustainability datasets.[23] Pointedly, it can be harder for others to detect what data an investor is using when it has exclusive access to that data. But cultivating such proprietary datasets can be expensive and time-consuming. Since relatively few institutional investors compete directly with one another, it is possible to lower these costs through the joint construction and ownership of sustainability data with peer institutional investors.

Action camouflage

Strategies for data camouflage aim to reduce the threat of investors being exploited by concealing the inputs to their decision-making. A complementary set of defensive strategies – what we call *action camouflage* – instead focuses on reducing exploitation by concealing the outputs from their decisions. As even the best efforts at data camouflage cannot guarantee avoiding detection, we see it as advisable for investors to explore both types of camouflage.

We start our treatment of action camouflage by mentioning a defensive strategy that is not camouflage at all: knowing the counterparty in transactions. Intuitively, having familiarity with a trading partner, and being able to cleanly recognize their motives for trading, can vastly reduce the risk of being exploited – even if the data on which one's trades are being made is identifiable. By and large, it is not easy to know one's counterparty with sufficient detail in mainstream public securities markets. This is an argument against heavy participation in such markets, at least via mainstream exchanges and trading venues. Instead, it suggests that investors may more reliably avoid exploitation by participating primarily in private markets – where counterparties are more likely to be known.

Of course, few investors are likely to be able to play only in private markets. Indeed, most institutional investors are bound to chiefly invest in publicly listed securities for the foreseeable future. Another remedy is therefore to make transactions less predictable. Many approaches exist for doing so. Below, we mention a few that we feel are most practical.

A first strategy is to create lag-time: avoid fast reactions to the arrival of new data by selling or buying only after a sufficient waiting period, and then spread out transactions into small batches. Introducing waiting as a strategy has the side benefit of providing extra time to vet sustainability data, and so potentially detect any attempted corruption of it. Another strategy is to practice some randomization in transactions. For example, vary order types or occasionally place a few "dummy trades" that are withdrawn prior to execution. A further strategy for action camouflage is to split trades across exchanges, or to participate in dark pools.

SUMMARY

Sustainable investing presents immense opportunities for financial markets and their participants, as well as society and the natural world. Yet, historically, its progress has been impeded by a lack of sufficient data. The rise of alternative data is fast helping to remedy this deficiency, but brings with it new responsibilities in how investors handle sustainability-related data. Key among these is ensuring that proper defenses are in place to guard against mistreatment by bad actors who may use sustainability data to profit at investors' expense. We have described the motives and methods that such exploitative activities may take, but have also conveyed the relative straightforwardness of techniques for data defense that investors can use to disarm them. Our treatment of these issues should in no way discourage investors from tapping into the power of alt-data for improving their abilities in sustainable investing. Instead, it should help them do so more effectively, by practicing sound data defense.

NOTES

1 Throughout this chapter, we intend "investors" to mean investment organizations, rather than individuals.
2 This may happen, e.g., when investors try to short stocks whose reputation becomes (temporarily) tarnished by acting unsustainably.
3 Of course, like any other data, alt-data itself should ideally be transparent (e.g., its origins should be clear), and particular alt-datasets should be universally available, especially when

they convey essential ESG information (much like mainstream financial data contained in 10-Ks and 20-Fs does for investment decisions that ignore sustainability). But transparency of data itself is distinct from transparency by an investment organization on what data it uses for making decisions. It is important to note here that, although an organization might not be transparent on what data it uses for its decisions, it can nevertheless be transparent (or at least be able to provide credible/verifiable assurances) on what controls it has on its processes for managing that data: external stakeholders in such organizations need not be totally blind to the organization's data-related activities.

4 Importantly, recognize that as any one alt-dataset becomes more commonly used, it transitions to being mainstream data – and so eventually ceases to be alt-data.

5 Much of the research on the costs to investors of exploitation has been conducted in the context of adversarial trading (e.g., frontrunning). See, for example, Angel, Broms, and Gastineau (2016), Gastineau (2008), Saglam (2018), Van Kervel and Menkveld (2019), Yang and Zhu (2019), and references therein.

6 For brevity, throughout the rest of the chapter, when referring to sustainability-related alt-data, we will use the term "sustainability data."

7 Greenwashing is the act of some entity (usually a corporation) misstating the sustainability of its operations, which may include its production processes, employment practices, or any other environmental or social consequences from how it conducts business. Adversarial trading is the practice of attempting to profit from targeting the trading activities of a specific market participant (rather than market participants generally). It takes many forms, but primarily involves inducing another party to trade when it otherwise would not, or accept worse prices for trades than it otherwise would. For example, an adversarial trader may use techniques to anticipate the execution of a large block-order trade and execute a replica trade before the original is fulfilled, and then reverses that action almost instantly. Doing so creates a near-immediate, low-risk profit for the adversarial trader, while the victim suffers a higher cost of execution.

8 Reverse greenwashing is the act of making an entity look less sustainable (i.e., dirtier) than it actually is. This can be considered "relative greenwashing" when it is applied to a company's competitors, as it makes that company look comparatively more sustainable than it in fact is. In reality, adversarial traders are less likely to use greenwashing to exploit investors than they are to use anticipatory trading based on sustainability data – e.g., try to beat investors to a trade because they know or can guess what sustainability data investors use in making decisions.

9 Examples of features that may outright prevent investment in a company include producing certain types of munitions (such as cluster bombs), or operations in embargoed or sanctioned countries (such as those listed by the United Nations). On the flipside, some investors are required to allocate predetermined portions of their portfolios to owning securities that contribute to the Sustainable Development Goals stipulated by the United Nations General Assembly.

10 Although a growing number of institutional investors treat sustainability as core to their mission and strategies (and thus give it a primary place in their operations and portfolios), this is not yet the norm.

11 Of course, this predicament isn't unique to sustainability data, and likewise exists for all types of data. An important concern to raise here is that data in general introduces special risks to the organization, and it is oftentimes sensible for organizations to consider "data risk" as occupying its own distinct category in their risk management frameworks.

12 Making public announcements (e.g., press releases) on software contracts can also strongly contribute to detection-related exploitation.

13 Purposeful and malicious alteration of data ingested by another party is sometimes called data poisoning. A strong parallel exists between data poisoning and the production of malicious open-source software. It is common practice for organizations to vet open-source libraries before they are approved for any type of use inside the organization, but the degree of vetting aligns with the trustworthiness of a library's source as well as the purposes for which it will be used. Following similar practices is advisable for alt-datasets.

14 This has been the case historically. Below, we describe reasons why this might not remain the case in the future.

15 Of course, also knowing the investor's identity is usually hugely helpful.

16 It is tempting to think an entity's passive footprint is not fully "identifying" without access to at least part of its active footprint. Yet, research shows that even a modest amount of passive data can suffice to de-anonymize users (see, e.g., Perez, Musolesi, and Stringhini, 2018).

17 This use will be non-standard in some circles, as some sources only apply the term to image-based data (e.g., videos and photos). For convenience, we also extend its use to non-image data, such as text.

18 See Goodfellow, Bengio, and Courville (2016).

19 See OpenAI (2019) and Radford et al. (2019).

20 Algorithms for computer vision are widely considered to be more mature than those for natural-language processing and understanding – as measured by how they compare with human performance.

21 See, for example, Schroepfer (2019) and Dufour and Gully (2019).

22 Unless, of course, the malicious actor is an insider within the organization. We omit discussion of such cases here.

23 A notable exception is the platform run by Dutch pension funds APG and PGGM: www.apg.nl/en/article/-Wereldwijd-%20SDI-Asset%20-Owner%20-Platform/1110

REFERENCES

Angel, J., Broms, T. and Gastineau, G. (2016). 'ETF transaction costs are often higher than investors realize', *Journal of Portfolio Management*, 42(3), pp. 65–75.

Brown, T., Mane, D., Roy, A., Abadi, A. and Gilmer, J. (2018). 'Adversarial patch'. Available at: https://arxiv.org/abs/1712.09665 (Accessed: 29 November 2019).

Das, N., Shanbhogue, M., Chen, S.-T., Hohman, F., Li, S., Chen, L., Kounavis, M. and Chau, D. (2018). 'Shield: fast, practical defense and vaccination for deep learning using JPEG compression'. Available at: https://arxiv.org/abs/1802.06816 (Accessed: 29 November 2019).

Dufour, N. and Gully, A. (2019). 'Contributing data to deepfake detection research'. *Google AI Blog*. Available at: https://ai.googleblog.com/2019/09/contributing-data-to-deepfake-detection.html (Accessed: 29 November 2019).

Gastineau, G. (2008). 'The cost of trading transparency: what we know, what we don't know, and how we will know', *Journal of Portfolio Management*, 35(1), pp. 72–81.

Goodfellow, I., Bengio, Y. and Courville, A. (2016). *Deep Learning*. Cambridge, MA: MIT Press.

Goodfellow, I., Pouget-Abadie, J., Mirza, M., Xu, B., Warde-Farley, D., Ozair, S., Courville, A. and Bengio, Y. (2014). 'Generative adversarial networks'. Available at: https://arxiv.org/abs/1406.2661 (Accessed: 29 November 2019).

In, S. Y., Monk, A. and Rook, D. (2019). 'Integrating alternative data (also known as ESG data) in investment decision making', *Global Economic Review*, 48, pp. 237–260.

Monk, A., Prins, M. and Rook, D. (2019). 'Rethinking alternative data in institutional investment', *Journal of Financial Data Science*, 1(1), pp. 14–31.

Monk, A. and Rook, D. (2018). 'The technological investor: deeper innovation through reorientation'. Available at: https://papers.ssrn.com/sol3/papers.cfm?abstract_id=3134078 (Accessed: 29 November 2019).

Monk, A. and Rook, D. (2019). *The Technologized Investor: Innovation through Reorientation*. Palo Alto, CA: Stanford University Press (forthcoming).

Monk, A., Sharma, R. and Sinclair, D. (2017). *Reframing Finance: New Models of Long-Term Investment Management*. Palo Alto, CA: Stanford University Press.

OpenAI. (2019). 'Better language models and their implications'. Available at: https://openai.com/blog/better-language-models/ (Accessed: 29 November 2019).

Perez, B., Musolesi, M. and Stringhini, G. (2018). 'You are your metadata: identification and obfuscation of social media users using metadata information'. Available at: https://arxiv.org/abs/1803.10133 (Accessed: 29 November 2019).

Poursaeed, O., Katsman, I., Gao, B. and Belongie, S. (2018). 'Generative adversarial perturbations'. Available at: https://arxiv.org/abs/1712.02328 (Accessed: 29 November 2019).

Radford, A., Wu, J., Child, R., Luan, D., Amodei, D. and Sutskever, I. (2019). 'Language models are unsupervised multitask learners'. Available at: https://d4mucfpksywv.cloudfront.net/better-language-models/language_models_are_unsupervised_multitask_learners.pdf (Accessed: 29 November 2019).

Saglam, M. (2018). 'Order anticipation around predictable trades', *Financial Management*, XXX, pp. 1–35.

Schroepfer, M. (2019). 'Creating a data set and a challenge for deepfakes'. Available at: https://ai.facebook.com/blog/deepfake-detection-challenge/ (Accessed: 29 November 2019).

Van Kervel, V. and Menkveld, A. (2019). 'High-frequency trading around large institutional orders', *Journal of Finance*, 74(3), pp. 1091–1137.

Vaswani, A., Shazeer, N., Parmar, N., Uszkoreit, J., Jones, L., Gomez, A., Kaiser, L. and Polosukhin, I. (2017). 'Attention is all you need'. Available at: https://arxiv.org/abs/1706.03762 (Accessed: 29 November 2019).

Yang, L. and Zhu, H. (2019). 'Back-running: seeking and hiding fundamental information in order flows', *Review of Financial Studies* (forthcoming). doi:10.1093/rfs/hhz070

PART IV

Accelerating transformational change

15

Investing sustainably

Transforming assets owners from sayers to doers

Keith Ambachtsheer

INTRODUCTION

Terms such as "sustainable finance" and "ESG" have migrated from back-of-fice obscurity in asset owner organizations to front-office prominence. But do these shifts represent true transformational change? Or are they largely cases of "me too-ism"? This chapter addresses these two questions through two related topics: (1) clarifying what "true transformational change" in an asset owner organization really means, and (2) how to best tell the transformational change story to stakeholders and to the wider world.

Two separate expert panels have recently addressed this "transformation to sustainable investing" topic:

1. *A four-member panel commissioned by the Canadian federal government* tabled its final report *Mobilizing Finance for Sustainable Growth* in June 2019 (Government of Canada, 2019). The report makes specific recommendations directly related to the implications of the transformation to sustainable investing for asset owners.
2. *A six-member panel commissioned by the State of New York* tabled its final report titled *Decarbonization Advisory Panel Beliefs and Recommendations* for the US$200 billion NY State Common Fund two months earlier (Decarbonization Advisory Panel, 2019). This report too makes specific recommendations directly related to asset owner transformation to sustainable investing.

On how to tell the transformational change story to stakeholders and the wider world, the work of the International Integrated Reporting Council (IIRC) is very helpful, especially its Integrated Reporting Framework introduced in December 2013 (IIRC, 2013). This chapter makes liberal use of these three cited works in addressing the "what is sustainable investing?" and "how to best tell the transformational change story" topics.

WISDOM FROM TWO EXPERT PANELS

The Canadian panel's broad vision is for the country to be a leader in the global transition to a low-emissions future, and a trusted source of climate-smart solutions, expertise, and investment. The report makes 15 recommendations, six of which relate directly to asset owners:

1. *Implement the TCFD recommendations*: define and pursue a Canadian approach to doing this.
2. *Clarify the scope of "fiduciary duty"*: specifically, what is required from trustee boards related to climate change-related issues?
3. *Foster a knowledgeable financial support ecosystem*: dimensions of such an ecosystem include education, consulting, audit, and disclosure.
4. *Embed climate risk into the supervision of the financial system*: including in monitoring, regulation, and legislation.
5. *Foster transition-oriented and clean-tech financing*: through green bonds, loans, and private equity, and also setting a global standard for such financings.
6. *Integrate "sustainability" into asset management*: this should become "business as usual" rather than seen as an extraneous, non-integrated activity.

The Canadian panel's sixth recommendation is a good transition to the work of the NY State panel. This panel laid out a ten-year transition path to a fully sustainable investment program for the $200 billion NY State Common Retirement Fund (NYSCRF). Its report sets out a sustainable investing paradigm and what it will take to actually implement it.[1] Their recommendations are not only relevant to the NYSCRF, but to any asset owner organization wanting to move to a sustainable investment program.

The NY State Panel report starts by setting out the foundational beliefs on which the panel's recommendations are based. They offer a strong basis for the foundational beliefs of any asset owner organization:

• *Climate change is an existential threat* to global economies, markets, and earth systems. The threat has both physical and transition dimensions.

- *Global warming of ±2°C would cause significant value-destruction* [...] which would become major at +3°C [...] a reality still under-appreciated by the public at large and undervalued in financial markets.
- *The window to ±2°C is closing* as policies are not matching ambitions. Both adaption and mitigation measures should be vigorously pursued. Physical risks are already appearing in certain regions. Transition risks are already appearing in certain industry sectors with high carbon emissions.
- *There is an opportunity side to these dynamics*, for example in such areas as energy, agriculture, real estate, and infrastructure.
- *Organizations with effective modeling and decision-making capabilities* will have comparative advantages in navigating these risks and opportunities.
- *"Back-testing" as a risk mitigation measure may be unhelpful* as climate-related future events are likely to differ from past events.
- *"Soft barriers" are also likely to be unhelpful* as traditional rules about geographical and industry weightings, about benchmarks, and about how investment managers and consultants are used, may stifle the innovative mindsets needed to address future climate-related risks and opportunities.
- *More active oversight and execution capabilities will be required* for asset owners to deal with the realities of climate change and its investment consequences. In short, start where you can, but expand fund capabilities with a genuine sense of urgency.

Taken together, these foundational beliefs lead to the panel's opening "Transition Ambition and First Big Step" recommendation.

The "Transition Ambition and First Big Step" recommendation

To kick-start the fund's journey to sustainability, the panel recommends setting out an explicit time-bound fund transition ambition. Specifically, that all fund investments are "sustainable" by 2030, where "sustainable" means investments that are "consistent with a +2C degree future or lower" (Decarbonization Advisory Panel, 2019, p. 11). Such investments may directly or indirectly work to help create that future or have a neutral effect on its development. To help visualize this, the panel offers a counterfactual: "Unsustainable assets assume expected values that are inconsistent with the physical impacts and transition pathways of whichever warming scenario is assumed. Sustainable assets have integrity against science-based assumptions. Unsustainable assets do not" (Decarbonization Advisory Panel, 2019, p. 11).

In addition to being the basis for a "Minimum Standards Test" for divestment, this "sustainability" definition also leads to the panel's First Big Step recommendation. It is to create an explicit "climate solutions" component of the fund. All investments in this component meet the "sustainability" test. It would act as a leading edge in the drive towards achieving the fund's 2030 100% sustainability ambition. It would also foster the development of the requisite modeling capabilities to test for sustainability. Such capabilities should be able to model corporate value-creation chains from product demand, cost structures, competitive positioning, to sustainable profitability. Organizationally, achieving this Transition Ambition would be led by a Head of Climate Solutions. A key accountability for this position would be to expand the "sustainability" criterion for investments to 100% of the total fund by 2030.

Seven specific investment-related recommendations

There are seven specific recommendations:

- *Establish and employ a "minimum standards test,"* which would serve as the basis on which the fund decides to buy, hold, or sell assets exposed to transition and physical risks. The report devotes a detailed exhibit on the development and uses of the test.
- *Reconsider benchmarks.* Traditional market indexes reflect historical trends without regard for future climate-related impacts. They should be replaced by newly developed sustainability-oriented indexes and best-in-class investment products.
- *Develop expertise in climate-risk modeling.* Most currently available models and databases need upgrading. The fund should build its own capabilities, working with highly qualified partners.
- *Re-audition asset managers and consultants.* Given the panel's transition and related recommendations, do the fund's current managers and consultants have the necessary culture, skills, and experience to be effective partners? If not, it will essential to replace them.[2]
- *Integrate sustainability metrics into compensation structures.* This holds for internal professionals as well as for external asset managers and consultants.
- *Break the soft barriers.* To achieve the Transition Ambition to sustainability, old conventions (e.g., target weightings, performance targets, fee structures) will have to be broken, and replaced by new metrics and criteria.
- *Review staffing requirements.* To successfully manage the transition, the fund will have to materially enhance its management, research, and development capabilities.

From here, the report moves on to make recommendations in the engagement, advocacy, and education areas.

Four specific engagement, advocacy, and education recommendations

There are four specific recommendations:

- *Support forward-thinking companies.* Publicly celebrate corporate leadership in sustainability!
- *Advocate for smart climate finance policies.* This should be done locally, nationally, globally, and include the creation of green investment opportunities.
- *Engage with consequences and collaborate with peers.* Develop and employ the "minimum standards test" as soon as possible in engaging with both investee corporations and with asset managers. Look for and lever collaboration opportunities with like-minded peers, on both advocacy and co-investment opportunities.
- *Educate beneficiaries and staff.* Resources should be devoted to keeping both fund beneficiaries and employees up to date on climate-related developments in general, and on the fund's transition plan and progress towards its achievement in particular.

Taken together, the panel's broad transition recommendation and its 11 specific implementation recommendations add up to a monumental challenge not just for NYSCRF, but for any asset management organization. For example, in an April 2019 Top1000 Funds article about the panel's recommendation, panel member Cary Krosinsky noted: "In general, we find that asset owners are resource-challenged, especially on sustainability issues. This needs to change [...] it is one thing to build a solid plan surrounding issues of sustainability, and another to execute that plan well" (Krosinsky, 2019).

Krosinsky's cautionary note is worth some elaboration. It is not just a matter of reading the 11 recommendations and implementing them. Their effective implementation will require strategic leadership, exceptional integrative thinking capabilities, strong analytical and technical skill sets, and well-structured incentive programs. Many asset owner organizations do not score well in these four effectiveness areas. So implicit in the panel's 11 recommendations is a 12th: ensuring that the organization has the governance, management, and technical skills to implement its 11 recommendations.

THE ORIGINS AND VALUE OF *INTEGRATED REPORTING*

Reflecting on the successful execution of a sustainability plan for asset owners and managers, I recalled former colleague Roger Martin (2007) teaching the power of integrative thinking over a decade ago. He argues that we are born with minds that can hold two conflicting ideas in constructive tension which we can use to think our way through integrating them into a new superior idea. So I welcomed the formation of the International Integrated Reporting Council (IIRC) in 2010. The more I learned about the IIRC initiative, the more I became convinced that it fitted Marshall McLuhan's famous dictum that "the medium is the message."[3] The very act of an organization choosing to tell its value-creating story using the medium of integrated thinking and reporting sends the message to an organization's stakeholders that it cares deeply about creating sustainable value for them.

Here is how the IIRC (2013, p. 2) itself defines Integrated Reporting:

> *Integrated thinking* takes into account the connectivity and interdependence between a range of factors that affect an organization's ability to create value over time. *Integrated Reporting* improves the quality of information available to stakeholders, promotes a more cohesive and efficient approach to reporting, and enhances accountability and stewardship for the broad base of capitals used by the organization.

Based on these definitions, the IIRC issued a report titled *The International <IR> Framework* in December 2013.

In my own writings since then I have argued that the framework is not just helpful for corporations, but for asset owner organizations as well. I noted that initial efforts by asset owner organizations to use the framework showed the potential to materially improve stakeholder communications in a number of ways, but that more work was needed to turn that potential into reality. This chapter identifies what that work is, and offers a roadmap to get it done.

Adapting the framework to an asset owner context – seven guiding principles

The <IR> Framework sets out seven guiding principles in the creation of an <IR> report. Adaptions to asset owner contexts are added in italics:

1. *Strategic focus and future orientation*: explain how organizational strategies will create stakeholder value in the shorter and long terms and the related use of capital resources. *For asset owners, that explanation should start with the purpose of the financial assets under its control, who the key stakeholders are, how risks and rewards are defined and allocated, how intergenerational fairness is monitored, and how in that context micro "value" is best defined and measured. There is also the macro "value" question of how effective asset management functions activate the ability of finance to positively impact the common good (e.g., through its stewardship actions as a PRI signatory and through supporting the UN's Sustainable Development Goals).*[4]

2. *Connectivity of information*: paint a holistic picture of how various factors integrate to create value over time. *For asset owners, such a picture would include an explanation of how the organization's own capital resources (e.g., its financial assets base, its human and intellectual capital, its network capital, its IT capital, and its physical capital) and "common" external capital resources (e.g., air, water) combine to create both micro and macro "value."*

3. *Stakeholder relationships*: describe the stakeholders, their relationships to the organization, and their fiduciary duties to them. *For asset owner organizations, key micro stakeholders likely include some combination of current and future asset beneficiaries, retirees, workers, employers, and taxpayers. At a macro level, it becomes society at large.*

4. *Materiality*: provide information on matters impacting the organization's ability to create value over time. *For asset owners, key success drivers would include political stability, the rule of law, clear organization mandates, good governance, and an absence of wealth-extracting agency issues and costly artificial constraints.*

5. *Conciseness*: use no more words than necessary. *And thus fight natural tendencies towards ever greater detail and complexity.*

6. *Reliability and completeness*: include all material matters with balance and accuracy. *Yes!*

7. *Consistency and comparability*: present information to enhance comparability over time, and to other organizations to the extent possible. *Yes!*

These seven guiding principles should be embodied in seven integrated report content elements.

Adapting the framework to an asset owner context: seven integrated report content elements

Again, adaptations to asset owner contexts are added in italics to the integrated report content descriptions:

1. *Organizational overview and external environment*: what does the organization do, and what are its context and circumstances? *The asset owner organization invests the financial assets entrusted to it to support the organization's obligation to cost-effectively generate a predictable payment stream to current and future asset beneficiaries (e.g., pension plan members, taxpayers, endowment/foundation beneficiaries, etc.) in an inter-generationally fair manner. Further, it does so within the context of its stewardship obligations as a signatory of the PRI's 6 Principles of Responsible Investment and the support of the UN's 17 Sustainable Development Goals (SDGs).*

2. *Governance*: how does the organization's governance structure support value creation over time? *A carefully created selection process ensures the asset owner organization has an ongoing, robust, effective governance process. The board member selection process emphasizes both a sense of public duty and collective skill and experience in such fields as accounting, actuarial practices, business and financial management, information technology, and investment management. Key board accountabilities include CEO hiring and evaluation, risk appetite expression and monitoring, compensation policy, and strategic plan approval and monitoring. The board understands fiduciary duty and supports the organization's mandate to create "value" at both micro and macro levels.*

3. *Business model*: how does the organization create stakeholder value over time? *Asset owner organizations create micro value for their stakeholders in three distinct ways: (1) by having sufficient assets to meet future payment obligations, (2) by matching broad asset risk exposure to the ability and willingness of asset stakeholders to bear it, and (3) by seeking out or creating distinct investment opportunities that generate higher long-term sustainable risk-adjusted rates of return than their passive alternatives.[5] A related question here is the organizational mix of insourcing versus outsourcing. At the macro level, value is created by integrating investment decisions with the organization's PRI stewardship obligations and the 17 SDGs.*

4. *Performance*: what did the organization achieve over the period in the context of its strategic objectives, and what were the impacts on capital resources? *Given all the above, did the asset owner organization meet its payment obligations over the evaluation period? Does it have sufficient assets to meet future payment obligations? Are its asset risk exposures properly set? Are its active investment processes generating excess risk-adjusted rates of return in line with expectations and in line with its stated PRI stewardship obligations? How did the organization's investment decisions impact the 17 UN SDGs?*

5. *Risks and opportunities*: what are the key risks and opportunities and how are they addressed by the organization? *What could happen on the future payment obligations side to make them higher than expected? Lower than expected? What could happen on the asset side to produce returns lower than expected? Higher than expected? What contingencies are in place to deal with these unexpected outcomes? What other risks and opportunities should the asset owner organization consider? For example, in relation to its human and intellectual capital? Its network capital? Its IT capital? Its physical capital? Or its reputation?*

6. *Strategy and resource allocation*: where does the organization want to go, and how is it going to get there? *As an example, is the asset owner organization comfortable with its current governance and business models? With*

its current array of capitals and their quality? With its risk assessment and mitigation procedures? With its relationships and reporting protocols to stakeholders? If not, what improvement actions will be taken?

7. *Outlook*: what challenges and uncertainties does the organization face in achieving its strategic objectives? What are the implications for its business model and future performance? *Given everything that has been addressed in content elements 1–6, these final two questions should almost answer themselves!*

Addressing the elephants in the asset owner board room

Why should every asset owner organization in the world use the Integrated Reporting Framework to tell its value-creation story? Because it forces the leadership of these organizations to constructively address the possible elephants in their board rooms. Here are five:

1. Value-creation in asset owner organizations can take place at two levels: micro and macro. It is not a matter of choosing one over the other, but of integrating both perspectives into a seamless whole.
2. Decisions must be based on the balanced consideration of the interests of *all* organizational stakeholders, not just some.
3. Effective organization governance is a critical success driver. Thus governance effectiveness must be measured and reported.
4. Business model clarity and capital resource adequacy are also critical success drivers. Thus they too must be clearly addressed in integrated reporting.
5. Performance reporting must be directly integrated with the stated internal and external value-creating ambitions of the organization.

It takes a positive, constructive medium to send stakeholders messages about how an asset owner is addressing these five strategic challenges. The <IR> Framework fits the bill.[6]

WAGON TRAINS, <IR>, AND CBUS

Simply believing there is a "better way" of doing things is not enough to bring that "better way" about. Actually creating positive change requires hard work to break through multiple technical and behavioral barriers. So where to start? Ever the master of simplifying complex management problems, Peter Drucker proposed his Wagon Train theory: find out what makes the lead wagons crossing the prairies go faster and share these findings with the follow-on wagons.

Australia's Construction and Building Unions Superannuation Fund (CBUS) qualifies as a lead wagon in Integrated Reporting by virtue of deciding to adopt the framework four years ago. Founded in 1984, CBUS is one of Australia's largest industry super funds with (as of mid-2018) 778,000 members, 136,000 employers, and AUS$47 billion in assets. With an average member age of 39, it is a relatively young fund with significant growth potential in the years ahead.

How does CEO David Atkin view the CBUS decision to adopt <IR> four years ago? He ends his comments in the 2018 annual report with these words: "Finally, it is important to acknowledge that <IR> provides a useful framework to articulate our business model. Now, in our fourth integrated reporting cycle, we are reaping the benefits of a deeper alignment of our business planning with it" (CBUS, 2018, p. 7).

Following the structure of the <IR> Framework, the rest of this chapter summarizes the CBUS value-creation story in six parts: (1) organizational overview, capital resources, and value-creation, (2) governance, (3) business model, (4) performance, (5) risks and opportunities, (6) strategy, resource allocation, and outlook.

Organizational overview, capital resources, and value-creation

An outline of the CBUS organization has already been provided above. The organization deploys six types of capital to create stakeholder value: (1) financial (accumulated retirement savings), (2) manufactured (real estate, IT equipment), (3) human (its people), (4) intellectual (economic, financial, actuarial models), (5) social/relationships (its business and personal networks), (6) natural (land, water, air).

CBUS uses these capitals to address the four desires that it has found matter most to its members and their employers:

1. having enough income in retirement;
2. Looking out for our interests;
3. investing responsibly and sustainably;
4. continuing to manage CBUS as a strong, reliable, innovative organization.

To meet these stakeholder needs, the organization will create value in six specific ways:

1. Design and implement member product and services that meet their expressed needs.
2. Provide advice and assistance to members.
3. Provide advice and solutions to employers.
4. Advocate member and employer interests.
5. Evaluate and manage business partner relationships.
6. Support the UN's 17 SDGs.

The 2018 <IR> annual report tells the story of how CBUS uses its six types of capital to achieve these value-creating goals. Here is a summary of that story.

Governance

The report opens with this statement from the 16-member CBUS board: "Our Board has acknowledged that our Report follows the Integrated Reporting Framework, which allows us to tell our members and other stakeholders how we create value for them" (Construction and Building Unions Superannuation Fund (CBUS), 2018, p. 2). From there it profiles the board in five dimensions: tenure, gender, age, hours of training, and skills/experience. For example, the distribution of board skills/experience is legal – 19%, building/construction – 28%, finance/investment – 19%, property – 16%, and public policy – 19%. The five standing committees are investment, audit and risk, people, member/employer services, and nomination. The performance of these committees and the board as a whole is evaluated on a regular basis with the assistance of an outside third party. There are clear policies on conflicts of interest and board remuneration, gender, and tenure.

The board oversees the development and implementation of the CBUS strategic plan. It sharpens its strategic focus through offsite meetings that cover topics such as retirement readiness and the impacts of changing demographics and technology on the organization and its stakeholders. The board is expanding the responsibilities of its people committee to delve more deeply into and support organizational priorities such as strengthening culture and updating remuneration policy. The investment committee is overseeing the implementation of a new investment model, which includes enhancing the integration of ESG considerations into the investment decision framework.

Business model

To meet the expressed needs and wants of its member and their employers, the CBUS business model has two key components:

1. *Advice/administration services component*: provides retirement-related information, advice, and assistance to members and their employers, and advocates on their behalf. Key elements of this structure include active member engagement and feedback mechanisms, an expanding digital presence (e.g., video account statements, retirement income estimates), a relevant array of insurance products, and a comprehensive employer engagement, support, and advocacy program.
2. *Investment decision-making component*: generates competitive, sustainable net long-term returns within pre-established risk budgets. Key

elements of this structure are taking an integrative total portfolio perspective, innovating through sourcing investments through multiple channels, direct investing, insourcing, and rigorous due diligence processes including such ESG considerations as carbon emissions, sustainable supply chains, gender and cultural diversity, and labor rights, health, and safety.

The report contains a special section titled "Our Approach to Responsible Investing," which explains the CBUS fundamental belief of IR's importance to delivering long-term value for its members who work (or have worked) in the building and construction industries. Explicit reference is made to using the UN's 17 SDGs as criteria for creating a global quality equities strategy, as well as to inform the CBUS voting and engagement intentions. An investment example was Bright Energy (a wind and solar renewable energy company). Two engagement examples were Commonwealth Bank of Australia (money laundering and cultural issues) and Rio Tinto (lack of climate-related disclosures). CBUS believes the "S" in ESG is best tackled through collective action organizations such as the Responsible Investment Association of Australia and the global Workforce Disclosure Initiative.

Performance

The two business model components each have their own performance metrics:

1. *Advice/administration services component*: member satisfaction rating is 86%. Average active member balance is $57,000. Proportion of active members with adequate savings levels is 70%. Proportion of members retained with an income stream account after retirement is 80%. Average income stream member account is $277,000. A project to understand income stream member behavior and sustainability of income in retirement is under way.[7] On the employer side, the satisfaction rating is 92%. Projects to maintain high employer satisfaction ratings and attract new employers are under way. There is a detailed scorecard listing actual member and employer experience metrics vs. targets.

2. *Investment decision-making component*: the ten-year net return on the CBUS default investment option was 7.2% vs. 6.4% for the median industry fund and 5.3% for the median retail fund.[8] Longer and shorter evaluation periods produced similar results. These results were achieved with a below-median equity portfolio carbon footprint (280 vs. 290) and a property portfolio sustainability GRESB[9] score of 97/100, which is 3rd out of 874 global rankings. The report also provides more qualitative performance assessments on SDGs related to gender equality, renewable energy, sustainable infrastructure, and participating in collective national and international ESG/SDG-related initiatives.

External Risks/ Opportunities	Impact on Organization	Internal Risks/ Opportunities
Financial Markets	Meeting member/employer needs	Governance
Information Security	Growth/Sustainability	People/Talent
Legislative/Regulatory	Brand/Reputation	Culture

FIGURE 15.1 CBUS risks and opportunities matrix

CBUS also measures and reports on progress in improving internal business functions such as governance, people management, IT, and finance.

Risks and opportunities

CBUS sees future demographic, political, economic, and environmental developments embodying both risks and opportunities for the organization. Its <IR> Report sets out a risks/opportunities matrix as an organizing framework. Figure 15.1 represents a simplified version of it.

The report provides a detailed strategy matrix setting out CBUS future goals and the plans to achieve them. A key strategy philosophy is to seek out opportunities that (a) will enhance meeting member and employer needs, organization growth/sustainability, and brand/reputation, and (b) to mitigate the risks that would negatively impact these three organizational goals.

Strategy, resource allocation, and outlook

Looking ahead, the report makes two assertions: "CBUS will win [...] 1. By looking after its members and employers better than anyone else, and 2. By being an innovative, long-term, patient investor with a proven track record of superior outcomes" (CBUS, 2018, p. 50). To that end, it will achieve these four goals over the next two years:

1. *Increase active member engagement*: raise the proportion of members at adequate retirement savings levels materially above the current 70%.
2. *Increase retiring member engagement*: raise the proportion of retiring members that stay with the fund through the income stream option materially above the current 80%.

3. *Increase employer engagement*: raise the proportion of industry employers who have chosen CBUS as the super provider for their employees materially above the current 50%.
4. *Provide superior investment results*: by moving in-house investing to 25% of assets, reducing investment costs by 0.15% of assets, continuing to develop our sustainable investment capabilities, and continuing to produce first quartile investment returns.

The report lays out detailed strategies for each of these four goals. The strategies to achieve Goal 4 (produce superior investment results) include enhancing the new investment model on both technical and talent fronts, enhancing the direct investing program (especially in real estate), reducing agency and other friction costs, and creating a climate change roadmap.

BECOMING AN <IR> LEAD WAGON

Can you imagine a world where all asset owners tell their value-creating stories using the <IR> Framework? While none will match the CBUS narrative exactly, all would have important commonalities. All would explain why they exist, how they are governed, their business model for sustainable investing, their results, how they see their prospective risks and opportunities, and what they will do to produce even more sustainable value tomorrow. Is your asset owner organization prepared to join CBUS as a lead wagon on this journey?

NOTES

1　The NY State Expert Panel's report's six authors came together in early 2018 with diverse sets of expertise, work backgrounds, and viewpoints. Their initial mandate was to address the relatively narrow "divestment vs. engagement" issue in a climate change context. As they began to work together, two things happened. First, they realized their report should go well beyond the divestment/engagement issue. Second, what initially appeared to be six differing perspectives eventually integrated into a broad consensus on not only the issues the report should address, but also on the recommendations how to address them.
2　As an example of an asset management organization transitioning to sustainable investing, the panel cites a report by BNP Paribas Asset Management titled "Global Sustainability Strategy."
3　This dictum was the basis of Marshall McLuhan's (1964) book *Understanding Media*.
4　A recent study by Maastricht University Professor Rob Bauer et al. titled "Get Real!" indicated the majority of members of a Dutch pension plan favored the explicit use of sustainable investment practices in managing the plan's financial assets.
5　A recent study by Harvard University Professor George Serafeim titled "Public Sentiment and the Price of Corporate Sustainability" shows that sustainability rankings are increasingly reflected in stock prices, unless overshadowed by negative short-term market sentiment (see Serafeim, 2018). The implication is that to be useful, equity valuation models need to be regularly updated to reflect changing investor behavior.
6　With some modifications, the framework can be equally effectively used by asset management organizations.

7   Given the number one wish of CBUS members is "to have enough income in retirement," this is an important project.
8   CBUS could expand its performance benchmarking activities by comparing a suite of performance metrics vs. those of its national and international peers as it currently does with its property portfolio.
9   GRESB stands for Global Real Estate Sustainability Benchmark.

REFERENCES

Construction and Building Unions Superannuation Fund (CBUS). (2018). *CBUS 2018 Integrated Report: "Built for All of Us"*. Available at: www.cbussuper.com.au/content/dam/cbus/files/governance/reporting/Annual-Integrated-Report-2018.pdf (Accessed: 15 January 2020).

Decarbonization Advisory Panel. (2019). *Decarbonization Advisory Panel Beliefs and Recommendations*. Available at: www.osc.state.ny.us/reports/decarbonization-advisory-panel-report.pdf (Accessed: 15 January 2020).

Government of Canada. (2019). *Final Report of the Expert Panel on Sustainable Finance*. Available at: http://publications.gc.ca/collections/collection_2019/eccc/En4-350-2-2019-eng.pdf (Accessed: 15 January 2020).

International Integrated Reporting Council (IIRC). (2013). *Integrated Reporting Framework*. Available at: https://integratedreporting.org/wp-content/uploads/2013/12/13-12-08-THE-INTERNATIONAL-IR-FRAMEWORK-2-1.pdf (Accessed: 15 January 2020).

Krosinsky, C. (2019). *NY State's commons climate plan*. Available at: www.top1000funds.com/2019/04/ny-state-commons-climate-plan/ (Accessed: 15 January 2020).

Martin, R. (2007). *The Opposable Mind*. Cambridge, MA: Harvard Business School Press.

McLuhan, M. (1964). *Understanding Media*. New York: Mentor.

Serafeim, G. (2018). *Public Sentiment and the Price of Corporate Sustainability*. Available at: www.hbs.edu/faculty/Pages/item.aspx?num=55162 (Accessed: 15 January 2020).

16

Building a balanced and scalable strategic asset allocation to meet financial and ESG impact goals[1]

Karen Karniol-Tambour, Carsten Stendevad, Daniel Hochman, Jacob Davidson, and Brian Kreiter

INTRODUCTION

For decades, Bridgewater has engineered scalable portfolios to help institutional investors achieve their goals. In the past, these goals have typically been financial (e.g. return and risk targets), but now many investors are also seeking to achieve environmental, social, and governance (ESG) impacts through their portfolios. We believe the best way to achieve both financial investment goals and ESG impact goals is through portfolio engineering that incorporates these objectives holistically, beginning with crisply defining an investor's goals, systematically looking across a variety of asset classes to find assets that are aligned to these goals, and then combining those assets to create a portfolio that is designed to achieve the highest possible ratio of return to risk.

In this chapter, we will demonstrate how we would use this approach to build a scalable strategic portfolio that is designed to produce higher risk-adjusted returns over time than traditional strategic asset allocations using assets that further the UN Sustainable Development Goals (SDGs). We have chosen to focus on building a strategic (beta) portfolio because approximately 90% of the risk in typical institutional portfolios is in the strategic

---

1 Bridgewater Associates is a global leader in institutional portfolio management with approximately US$140 billion in assets under management as of June 2020. Founded by Ray Dalio in 1975, Bridgewater is a pioneer in multiple areas of investment, including its fundamental and systematic approach to investing, the separation of alpha and beta, and risk parity. Bridgewater manages portfolios for a wide array of institutional clients globally, including public and corporate pension funds, foreign governments and central banks, university endowments, and charitable foundations.

asset allocation, so engineering a quality strategic asset allocation represents a crucial foundation for investors' financial and impact goals.[2] From an impact perspective, we systematically select assets that are aligned to the UN SDGs at the beginning of the portfolio construction process, leading to a portfolio more aligned to the SDGs than market indices. From a financial perspective, we utilize Bridgewater's time-tested and stress-tested All Weather portfolio construction process to collect market risk premiums efficiently (a roughly 0.6 expected return-to-risk ratio at 10% expected volatility). This approach results in a portfolio that we expect will achieve over 2% higher annualized returns above cash through time than a global 60/40 portfolio, with comparable risk.[3] We break our approach to building this portfolio into three key steps:

1. *Setting clear goals for the portfolio.* To illustrate our approach, we have chosen a representative set of financial and ESG impact goals for our strategic portfolio: the financial goal is to generate positive, consistent returns across a range of economic environments, and the ESG impact goal is to further the UN Sustainable Development Goals. The SDGs are a collection of 17 global goals set by the United Nations General Assembly for the year 2030 that have been ratified by 193 countries. While investors can have many ESG impact goals, we have selected the SDGs because of their wide acceptance by governments and asset owners, their orientation toward positive environmental and social impact, and because the UN has defined indicators that can be used to measure the activities of asset issuers. Because we want to create an allocation that can achieve both financial and ESG impact goals at scale, we will also build the portfolio so that it can be held at institutional sizes.

2. *Selecting assets aligned with the portfolio's goals.* Once we have clearly defined the portfolio's goals, we look across the universe of global assets and systematically select those that are aligned to the UN SDGs and can be held at institutional scale. By systematically selecting assets at the start of the portfolio construction process, we can ensure the assets in the portfolio meet the goals we have set out. It also allows us to re-evaluate which assets meet the portfolio's goals over time as existing markets evolve and new markets become available.

---

2 We believe it is important for investors to separate strategic exposure (beta) from active views (alpha). Please see Appendix A for a discussion of ESG integration as a potential source of alpha.

3 There is no guarantee that expected performance will be achieved. Return expectations do not include any applicable management fees. Global 60/40 portfolio refers to 60% capital weight in world equities and 40% capital weight in world government bonds.

3. *Using assets aligned with the portfolio's goals to build the most efficient strategic portfolio possible.* Having defined a universe of assets that are aligned to our goals, we apply Bridgewater's All Weather portfolio construction framework using these assets. The All Weather framework is based on balancing the macroeconomic drivers of asset returns (i.e. growth and inflation) to create a strategic asset allocation with the highest possible return-to-risk ratio. We've used this framework as an asset manager for over two decades and stress-tested it over 100 years and across many countries. By applying this framework to SDG-aligned assets, we can build a portfolio we expect will achieve a 0.6 return-to-risk ratio through time (compared with a 0.4 expected ratio for a 60/40 portfolio).[4] Importantly, the strong expected performance of this portfolio relative to a 60/40 portfolio is a result of this beta portfolio construction approach, not from our use of SDG-aligned assets (which we do not expect would materially affect the portfolio's performance given our approach).

In the pages that follow, we describe each of these steps in more detail. We hope this example of building a scalable portfolio that is designed to achieve a high risk-adjusted return and further the UN SDGs will be applicable to a wide range of investors. However, we believe the three-step portfolio construction approach illustrated in this chapter can be applied to any set of financial and ESG impact goals that investors might choose.

1. SETTING CLEAR GOALS FOR THE PORTFOLIO

The crucial first step in building any portfolio is for investors to clearly lay out their goals so they can design an asset allocation that best achieves them.

Having worked with investors for decades to design investment portfolios, we believe most investors' financial goals can be best summed up as follows: build a portfolio that will reliably meet required returns, with minimal likelihood of unacceptable outcomes. This means the portfolio must generate positive, consistent returns (high return-to-risk ratio) across a range of economic environments. In recent years, institutional investors have become increasingly focused on incorporating ESG-related issues into the investment process to help them achieve those financial goals – i.e. to reduce their risk or increase their returns. As part of our own investment research process, for example, we have found it critical to study a broad range of topics relating to economic inequality, populism, and issues relating to the transition from

---

4 There is no guarantee that expected performance will be achieved. Return expectations do not include any applicable management fees. Global 60/40 portfolio refers to 60% capital weight in world equities and 40% capital weight in world government bonds.

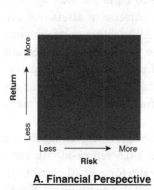

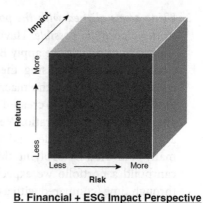

A. Financial Perspective   **B. Financial + ESG Impact Perspective**

FIGURE 16.1 Increasingly, many investors have both financial and ESG impact goals

Source: Bridgewater Associates, LP

fossil fuel to greener types of energy because they are pertinent to how economies and markets work.

Increasingly, however, we see some investors adding an explicit ESG impact dimension to their investment goals in addition to this traditional financial dimension (Figure 16.1). These investors seek to create ESG impact (particularly social and environmental impact) through their asset allocation by directing capital toward issuers that further their ESG impact goals (and away from those who do not).[5] These investors, in other words, face the challenge of optimizing across two types of investment goals – financial and ESG impact. The challenge we set for ourselves in this chapter was to build a strategic asset allocation that could achieve financial investment goals while also directing capital at scale toward entities aligned to investors' ESG impact goals.

In this chapter, we will build a diversified portfolio designed to achieve a set of financial and ESG impact goals we think are shared by many investors:

- ESG Impact Goal: Further the UN Sustainable Development Goals by systematically directing capital toward issuers that are aligned to the SDGs.
- Financial Goal: Generate positive, consistent returns (high return-to-risk ratio) across a range of economic environments.

Finally, we want to make sure investors can apply large amounts of capital toward achieving both of these goals. In order to do this, we will build the portfolio using assets that are liquid enough to be held at institutional sizes.

---

5 Some investors also seek to have environmental and social impact via active ownership, but that is not the focus of this chapter.

2. SELECTING ASSETS ALIGNED WITH
THE PORTFOLIO'S GOALS

Once we've specified the goals of the portfolio, our next step is to define a diverse universe of assets that will allow us to achieve them. In the case of the goals described above, this involves starting with a universe of global assets and systematically selecting assets that:

A.   further the SDGs
B.   can be held at scale

The net of this approach is that the assets in the portfolio are systematically selected based on their alignment with the UN SDGs and their ability to be held at institutional sizes. We discuss both dimensions below.

A. Selecting assets that further the UN SDGs

The UN SDGs represent a broad global framework for social and environmental impact. Although not explicitly designed for investors, the SDGs are emerging as a widely agreed-upon framework for governments and increasingly for asset owners and asset managers. The SDGs are expansive (e.g. "end poverty in all its forms everywhere") and contain specific and measurable indicators defined by the UN (roughly 200) that help investors and researchers to assess whether a given entity is helping to achieve them (see Figure 16.2 overleaf).

Determining asset alignment with the SDGs is an imperfect exercise. There is not one optimal methodology, the SDGs differ in how measurable and relevant they are depending on the asset class or entity, and precisely quantifying the SDG alignment or measuring the impact of a given asset is difficult. Global assessments require large-scale, multivariable analysis, the data quality and availability required for such analysis is imperfect, and no single viewpoint can provide a complete picture of an issuer's SDG alignment. We therefore approach this challenge humbly.

That said, the general process of identifying a "signal" amid the "noise" is a conceptual and analytical challenge that is at the core of Bridgewater's decades of experience doing systematic financial and economic research. We believe we have developed an initial process to define a set of assets that further the SDGs in which we can have confidence. As with any other systematic process we build, we would want to continually improve this process over time as we learn more and better data becomes available. This process is shown in Figure 16.3 and works as follows:

- *We selected high-quality research partners who have developed different methodologies to assess assets based on their alignment to the SDGs.*

Examples of specific Indicators:

Goal 7. Ensure access to affordable, reliable, sustainable and modern energy for all

7.1 By 2030, ensure universal access to affordable, reliable and modern energy services

7.2 By 2030, increase substantially the share of renewable energy in the global energy mix

7.3 By 2030, double the global rate of improvement in energy efficiency

7.a By 2030, enhance international cooperation to facilitate access to clean energy research and technology, including renewable energy, energy efficiency and advanced and cleaner fossil-fuel technology, and promote investment in energy infrastructure and clean energy technology

7.1.1 Proportion of population with access to electricity

7.1.2 Proportion of population with primary reliance on clean fuels and technology

7.2.1 Renewable energy share in the total final energy consumption

7.3.1 Energy intensity measured in terms of primary energy and GDP

7.a.1 Mobilized amount of United States dollars per year starting in 2020 accountable towards the $100 billion commitment

FIGURE 16.2 UN SDGs: high-level goals and indicators

Source: Bridgewater Associates, LP/United Nations (www.un.org/sustainabledevelopment/)

Because we are not experts on SDG assessment, we have partnered with a number of high-quality research organizations with expertise in this field. Different research organizations have different approaches: for example, in the case of equities, some methodologies assess a company by examining the alignment of its products and services with the SDGs (e.g. an oil company vs. a solar energy company), while others look at the sustainability of its business model (e.g. its supply chains or management of human capital). Some processes are fully systematic while others rely on analyst discretion. We deeply studied the different approaches and methodologies of different organizations and selected the ones we thought best captured an issuer's SDG alignment. As the SDG data ecosystem expands and improves, we will continue to assess new and existing data and research and update our process accordingly.

- *We created a systematic selection methodology to combine multiple SDG assessments into one holistic assessment.* As mentioned, there are multiple ways to assess asset issuers against the SDGs and different processes lead to different results. Since no single process can be fully comprehensive, we have built a system that processes the data from the research providers we have chosen and combines the various data elements into a holistic assessment that we believe is more accurate. This assessment separates securities into five categories based on their alignment with the SDGs: highly positive, positive, marginal, adverse, and highly adverse.

- *Once we have assessed the universe of eligible securities, we selected only those that we are confident are aligned to the SDGs.* Our confidence in a quality assessment of SDG alignment is highest when we have a lot of good data that points in the same direction (i.e. a triangulated assessment). We select securities with a positive or highly positive alignment with the SDGs for inclusion in the portfolio.

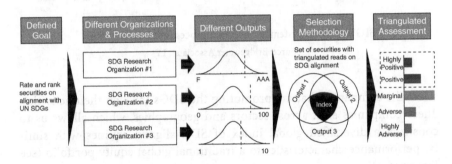

FIGURE 16.3 How our systematic selection process works[6]
Source: Bridgewater Associates, LP

Because no two asset classes are exactly alike, this systematic selection process can work differently depending on the asset class to which it is applied. However, the broad principles of deep research and triangulation apply across all of the assets we assess. By following this triangulation process across a variety of asset classes, we are able to create a universe of assets that are likely to advance the achievement of the UN SDGs. Below, we show how this triangulation process is applied across some of the major asset classes.

Equities: Through our systematic selection process, we assess over 5,000 of the largest publicly traded companies globally representing over US$60 trillion in market capitalization for their alignment with the SDGs. We then

---

6 Diagram of systematic selection process is illustrative and is not meant to reflect actual security selection.

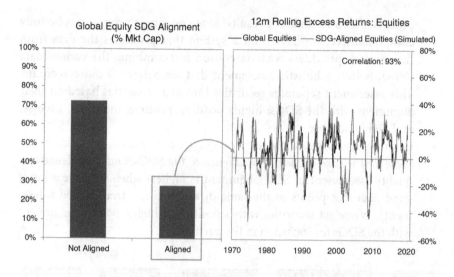

FIGURE 16.4 Systematic selection process applied to equities[7]

Source: Bridgewater Associates, LP

select the companies that are promoting the SDGs through their activities. These companies exist across sectors and geographies, which allows us to construct a diversified global index of SDG-aligned equities with similar performance characteristics to a traditional global equity portfolio (see Figure 16.4).

Government bonds: Through our systematic selection process, we assess over 150 countries for their alignment with the SDGs. While most countries are not aligned to the SDGs at this time, the largest government bond issuers tend to also be those most aligned to the SDGs. This allows us to build a diversified and highly liquid SDG-aligned bond allocation with similar performance characteristics to a traditional global bond allocation (see Figure 16.5).

Other bond issuers: There are many bond issuers who use the money they raise in bond markets to promote sustainable development (see Figure 16.6). For example, there is a large market cap available to investors of bonds issued by multilateral institutions such as the World Bank and the Inter-American Development Bank. These organizations explicitly pursue sustainable development through lending their capital and incorporating it into their mandates.

---

7 Past performance is not indicative of future results. SDG-aligned equities are selected based on proprietary Bridgewater analysis.

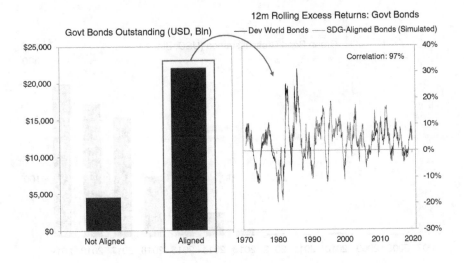

FIGURE 16.5 Systematic selection process applied to government bonds[8]

Source: Bridgewater Associates, LP

Institution	Total
European Investment Bank	577
Kreditanstalt für Wiederaufbau	487
World Bank	185
Asian Development Bank	96
Inter-American Development Bank	92
European Bank for Reconst. & Dev.	37
African Development Bank	30
Council of Europe Development Bank	28
Corp. Andina de Fomento	20
Total	1,553

FIGURE 16.6 Development bank debt outstanding (USD, billion)[9]

Source: Bloomberg, LP

Additionally, there is a growing market for "green" bonds, which raise capital for the purposes of sustainable projects (see Figure 16.7).

Commodities: For investors, commodity futures can be an important part of a portfolio because they provide valuable diversification during times of

---

8 Chart shows estimate of world bonds outstanding at ten-year duration. Dev world bond performance is based on 7.5-year constant duration bonds. Past performance is not indicative of future results. SDG-aligned government bonds are selected based on proprietary Bridgewater analysis.

9 Data as of November 2019.

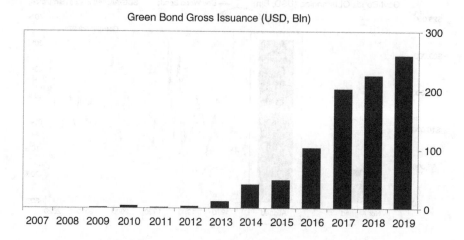

FIGURE 16.7 Green bond issuance (annual, USD billion)[10]

Source: BIS

higher-than-expected inflation (as we explain in more detail in Section 3). This therefore raises the question of how investing in commodity futures relates to the SDGs. In general, we believe the participation of investors is necessary for commodity futures markets to function well, and this participation benefits investors, producers, and end-consumers alike. Investors play two essential roles: (1) by taking the other side of producers' trades, they allow producers to hedge their risks, and (2) their active trading helps set accurate expectations for future prices while also providing liquidity to the market. These activities encourage producers to make upfront investments and to expand production when prices are high, resulting in lower, more stable prices for end-consumers. As a result, we see well-functioning commodity markets as consistent with sustainable development and we would therefore include commodity futures such as agriculture (SDG 2, Zero Hunger) and industrial metals (SDG 9, Industry, Innovation and Infrastructure). Additionally, reducing fossil fuel dependency is consistent with the SDGs (SDG 7, Affordable and Clean Energy; SDG 13, Climate Action) and therefore fossil fuel futures are excluded from this portfolio. Beyond commodity futures, we recognize that many commodity production companies' operations are not sustainable. Importantly, commodity futures are not linked to any individual commodity producer and our systematic selection of equities in this portfolio is designed to exclude equities issued by unsustainable companies.

---

10   Green bond data through 2019.

B. Selecting assets that can be held at institutional scale

In order to design a portfolio that can achieve the financial and ESG impact goals we've outlined at institutional sizes, we need to further systematically filter our asset universe to include only assets that can be held at scale. To do this, we must make sure the assets we select for the portfolio have large market caps, low trading costs, and transparent pricing.

Based on our systematic selection process, we believe this is achievable in public markets. The market cap of public assets that contribute to the UN SDGs is large (over US$40 trillion). For example, based on our estimates, the market cap of SDG-aligned equities and sovereign bonds is approximately US$17 trillion and US$22 trillion respectively. As a result, it is now possible for investors to build an SDG-aligned portfolio at institutional scale.

Below, we show a simplified example of how we would systematically select assets that meet our scalability criteria (large market caps, low trading costs, and transparent pricing) and further the SDGs (Figure 16.8). To choose which government bonds to hold, we start with the universe of all sovereign bonds and sort those bonds across two dimensions: (1) a measure of each sovereign's SDG alignment, and (2) the size of each sovereign's bond market cap. We select only the securities that further the SDGs (moving to the right on the chart) and are accessible at institutional sizes (moving up on the chart).

We believe that including institutional scalability as an explicit factor in our systematic selection process not only makes the portfolio we are designing accessible to institutional investors, but also gives investors the ability to incorporate additional assets into their portfolio over time as

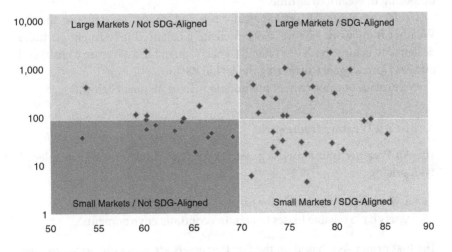

FIGURE 16.8 Sovereign SDG alignment vs. bonds outstanding (USD billion, log scale)

Source: Bridgewater Associates, LP

markets develop. For example, green bonds are an asset class that meets many investors' ESG impact goals and is experiencing rapid growth. In the early 2010s, the green bond market was not developed enough (i.e. relatively small, illiquid, and difficult to trade) for most institutional investors to access. But this market is rapidly evolving, and it is now increasingly investable at institutional sizes. By continuing to assess the universe of global assets using the systematic selection criteria we have outlined, investors can continue to evolve their portfolios to include additional assets as those assets become accessible.

3. USE ASSETS ALIGNED WITH THE PORTFOLIO'S GOALS TO DESIGN THE MOST EFFICIENT STRATEGIC PORTFOLIO POSSIBLE

Having established a sample set of assets that further the SDGs and can be held at scale, the next step is to combine these assets into a portfolio that is designed to achieve the most consistent returns possible from a strategic asset allocation.

We believe the best way to build a strategic portfolio with the highest possible return-to-risk ratio is by balancing the portfolio to the primary drivers of asset class risk: changes in discounted growth and inflation. We do this by applying our All Weather framework for building a balanced portfolio, which was pioneered by Bridgewater in 1996 and stress-tested over 100 years of market history. We believe this approach leads to more consistent returns, minimizing drawdowns and enabling a greater compounding of wealth over time.

Using the assets we systematically selected above, we can use the All Weather framework (Figure 16.9) to create a balanced investment portfolio designed to achieve both our financial goals (a high ratio of return to risk) and our ESG impact goal (furthering the UN SDGs).

We explain our investment methodology in more detail below.

A. The All Weather framework

The All Weather framework is based on just two fundamental principles of asset pricing:

1. Assets outperform cash over time.
2. Assets have reliable biases to certain economic environments.

The first principle is based on the fact that assets are generally priced to offer a higher return than cash over time in order to incentivize investors to part

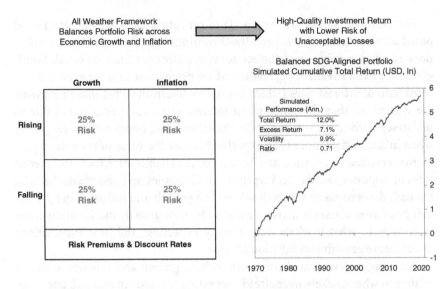

FIGURE 16.9 Applying the All Weather approach to SDG-aligned assets to build a balanced SDG-aligned portfolio[11]

Source: Bridgewater Associates, LP

with the liquidity and safety of their cash (this return above cash is referred to as a "risk premium").

The second principle is based on the fact that any single asset class comes with exposure to economic conditions and, as a result, is biased to do well in some economic environments and poorly in others. These economic biases are a logical result of the nature of an asset's cash flows and what markets are expecting those cash flows to be worth.

For example, stocks give you a claim on future earnings and are priced based on what the market expects those earnings to be through time, so stocks do well when earnings and the economy are stronger than expected. Bonds give you a fixed stream of payments and are priced based on the expected forward path of interest rates (which is used to determine what those payments are worth), so they do better when interest rates unexpectedly fall due to unforeseen economic weakness. On the other hand, bonds tend to do poorly when inflation rises more than expected because the value of their fixed payments is eroded by inflation and because central banks often increase interest rates in response to inflation surprises, which pushes up bond yields. Because the cash flows of assets are so closely tied to growth and inflation, the performance of asset classes is driven primarily by how growth and inflation come in relative to what markets were already expecting, and how expectations about future growth and inflation change.

The insight that what drives assets is how growth and inflation come in relative to what markets were already expecting (i.e. growth and inflation "surprises") is critical, as it means that economic biases have no expected return and just add risk. Equities will outperform not if growth is high, but if growth comes in higher than what markets already expecting. And markets are reasonably efficient at discounting future conditions over time, with no systematic bias to over- or under-discount future growth or inflation, so there is no expected return from being exposed to growth or inflation surprises (Figure 16.10).

Given these principles of asset pricing, the goal of a strategic portfolio becomes clearer: you want to capture the risk premiums that assets offer while minimizing economic biases as much as possible. We do this by balancing risk across assets with opposing economic biases. This way, a surprise in growth or inflation will cause some assets to underperform but will cause others to outperform, and if we've balanced the portfolio well, the overall effect of economic surprises on portfolio volatility should be minimized. What we literally do is construct four sub-portfolios – one designed to outperform in each growth/inflation environment – and spread risk equally across those sub-portfolios. We fill each sub-portfolio with assets biased to do particularly well in that economic environment. This leaves the risk premiums and discount rates across assets as the primary drivers of returns (Figure 16.11).

B. Applying the All Weather framework to assets furthering the UN SDGs

As mentioned, we've been applying this approach to global assets in our All Weather strategy since its inception in 1996. While the asset mix we have designed in this chapter is not the same as what we hold in our global All Weather strategy, the way that these assets respond to economic fundamentals – i.e. their biases to certain economic environments – is the same. Below, we

show the biases of global equities and bonds in terms of their historical performance in different growth and inflation environments, and compare those
biases with the biases of equities and bonds that are systematically selected by
our SDG criteria. As shown, assets that further the SDGs have the same biases
you would logically expect. This makes sense to us because the most important
driver of these biases is the fundamental nature of the asset class's cash flows,

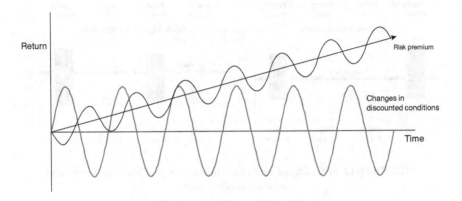

FIGURE 16.10 Two timeless drivers of any beta investment

Note: The positive excess return of assets over time comes from the risk premium. Changes in discounted economic conditions add volatility without adding return. Source: Bridgewater Associates,
LP

	Growth	Inflation
Rising	**25%** Risk	**25%** Risk
Falling	**25%** Risk	**25%** Risk
	Risk Premiums & Discount Rates	

FIGURE 16.11 Balance portfolio risk to growth and inflation

Source: Bridgewater Associates, LP

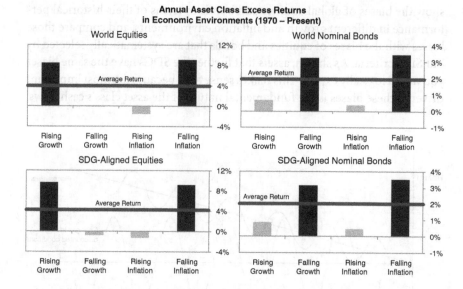

FIGURE 16.12 SDG-aligned assets have the same logical biases to growth and inflation as other assets[12]

Source: Bridgewater Associates, LP

not the particulars of the specific investment. Based on our research, most asset classes – including equities, nominal bonds, inflation-linked bonds, and commodities – have the same economic sensitivities when they are chosen through our systematic selection process (Figure 16.12).

C. Building a balanced portfolio that meets financial and ESG impact goals

Because assets systematically selected by SDG criteria have largely the same properties as global assets, our approach to building the most efficient port-folio using SDG-aligned assets is a straightforward application of the All Weather framework: we start with our systematically selected universe of assets and spread risk equally across assets that tend to do well in each of the four economic environments. We show the allocation of this balanced SDG-aligned portfolio in Figure 16.13.

---

12 Returns shown in excess of cash. A rising (falling) inflation month is defined as a month in which the current rate of inflation is greater (lower) than the 12-month moving average rate of inflation. A rising (falling) growth month is defined as a month in which the current rate of real GDP growth is greater (lower) than the 12-month moving average rate of real GDP growth. SDG-aligned assets are selected based on proprietary Bridgewater analysis.

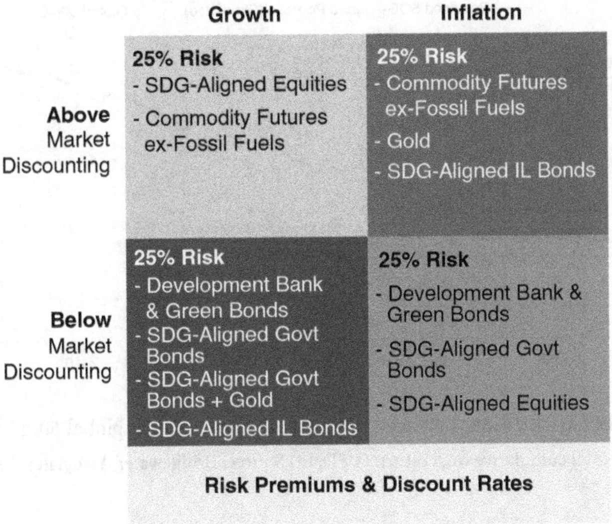

	Growth	Inflation
Above Market Discounting	**25% Risk** - SDG-Aligned Equities - Commodity Futures ex-Fossil Fuels	**25% Risk** - Commodity Futures ex-Fossil Fuels - Gold - SDG-Aligned IL Bonds
Below Market Discounting	**25% Risk** - Development Bank & Green Bonds - SDG-Aligned Govt Bonds - SDG-Aligned Govt Bonds + Gold - SDG-Aligned IL Bonds	**25% Risk** - Development Bank & Green Bonds - SDG-Aligned Govt Bonds - SDG-Aligned Equities

Risk Premiums & Discount Rates

FIGURE 16.13 Balanced SDG-aligned portfolio
Source: Bridgewater Associates, LP

The result is a portfolio designed to meet both the financial and the ESG impact goals we set out to achieve. The assets in the portfolio have all been systematically selected for their alignment with the UN SDGs and have been combined in a way that is designed to generate a significantly more consistent return than any single asset class or concentrated allocation by minimizing the portfolio's vulnerability to any one economic environment.

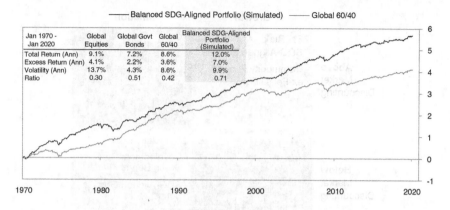

FIGURE 16.14 Balanced SDG-aligned portfolio vs. global 60/40[13]

Note: cumulative total return (USD, ln) Source: Bridgewater Associates, LP

Above, we show the simulated historical investment returns of a balanced SDG-aligned portfolio compared with global equities, global bonds, and a global 60/40 portfolio (Figure 16.14). As you can see, a balanced SDG-aligned allocation would have generated 7% annualized returns in excess of cash at 10% risk since 1970 (slightly above the 0.6 ratio that we expect the strategy will achieve through time). This is a much higher ratio of return to risk than bonds, equities, or a 60/40 portfolio was able to achieve. Notably, a balanced SDG-aligned portfolio would have generated a higher return than global equities with less risk, minimizing drawdowns and allowing for a greater compounding of wealth through time.

13 Global 60/40 refers to 60% capital weight in world equities and 40% capital weight in world government bonds. Excess returns for investments shown above a US cash benchmark. Returns shown gross of any applicable management fees. "Balanced SDG Portfolio" is simulated using the Balanced SDG-Aligned Portfolio Simulation as described in the "Balanced SDG-Aligned Portfolio Simulation Disclosure". It is expected that the simulated performance will periodically change as a function of both refinements to our simulation methodology and the underlying market data. HYPOTHETICAL OR SIMULATED PERFORMANCE RESULTS HAVE CERTAIN INHERENT LIMITATIONS. UNLIKE AN ACTUAL PERFORMANCE RECORD, SIMULATED RESULTS DO NOT REPRESENT ACTUAL TRADING OR THE COSTS OF MANAGING THE PORTFOLIO. ALSO, SINCE THE TRADES HAVE NOT ACTUALLY BEEN EXECUTED, THE RESULTS MAY HAVE UNDER- OR OVER-COMPENSATED FOR THE IMPACT, IF ANY, OF CERTAIN MARKET FACTORS, SUCH AS LACK OF LIQUIDITY. SIMULATED TRADING PROGRAMS IN GENERAL ARE ALSO SUBJECT TO THE FACT THAT THEY ARE DESIGNED WITH THE BENEFIT OF HINDSIGHT. NO REPRESENTATION IS BEING MADE THAT ANY ACCOUNT WILL OR IS LIKELY TO ACHIEVE PROFITS OR LOSSES SIMILAR TO THOSE SHOWN. PAST RESULTS ARE NOT NECESSARILY INDICATIVE OF FUTURE RESULTS. CONFIDENTIAL AND PROPRIETARY. The Balanced SDG-Aligned Portfolio does not represent a product or service that is available for purchase by any investor. Please review the "Important Disclosures and Other Information" located at the end of this chapter.

The strong financial performance of this portfolio relative to a 60/40 portfolio is a result of our beta portfolio construction approach, not from our use of SDG-aligned assets. We do not think that limiting the portfolio to SDG-aligned assets materially affects the portfolio's performance because there are enough available assets to create a diversified portfolio balanced to economic environments. While there is no precision around expected returns and we prefer to be conservative with performance assumptions, we would expect a balanced SDG-aligned portfolio to have a return-to-risk ratio of about 0.6 through time. This is considerably more efficient than a global 60/40 portfolio, which we expect to have a return-to-risk ratio of roughly 0.4.[14]

As we've shown above, engineering a portfolio with these financial characteristics is possible using SDG-aligned assets. Figure 16.15 illustrates that a balanced SDG-aligned portfolio has a higher return-to-risk ratio and greater alignment to the SDGs than a global 60/40 portfolio. This is a demonstration of one way that investors with both financial and ESG impact goals can engineer portfolio solutions that meet their return, risk, and impact targets.

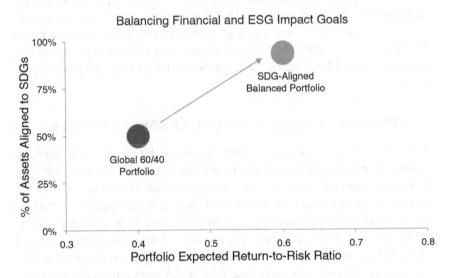

FIGURE 16.15 Balancing financial and ESG impact goals[15]

Source: Bridgewater Associates, LP

14 There is no guarantee expected performance will be achieved. Return expectations do not include any applicable management fees. The Balanced SDG-Aligned Portfolio does not represent a product or service that is available for purchase by any investor.

15 Global 60/40 shown is based on market cap weighted portfolio of world large cap equities and world government bonds. Analysis is based on the systematic selection process described in this chapter. There is no guarantee expected performance will be achieved. Return expectations do not include any applicable management fees.

CONCLUSION

Increasingly, investors are seeking to design strategic portfolios that achieve both financial goals and ESG impact goals. We believe the best way to do so is through the approach outlined in this chapter: using portfolio engineering to incorporate both financial and impact objectives holistically, beginning with a clear definition of investors' goals, systematically selecting assets that are aligned with those goals, and combining those assets using high-quality portfolio construction to create the best possible portfolio.

In this chapter, we have demonstrated how investors can build a scalable strategic portfolio that is designed to meet investors' financial and ESG impact goals. From an impact perspective, the approach we have outlined systematically selects assets that are aligned to the UN SDGs at the beginning of the portfolio construction process to create an asset allocation that is more aligned to the SDGs than market indices. From a financial perspective, this approach uses Bridgewater's time-tested and stress-tested All Weather portfolio construction process to design a portfolio that we expect will outperform traditional asset allocations over time and generate positive, consistent returns (high return-to-risk ratio) across a range of economic environments.[16] This strategic asset allocation therefore can serve as a crucial foundation for investors with financial and ESG impact goals.

APPENDIX A: ESG AS A POTENTIAL SOURCE OF ALPHA

As mentioned, we have focused this chapter on building a beta portfolio because approximately 90% of the typical institutional portfolio's risk is in its strategic asset allocation, meaning changes to that allocation can have the most impact along both financial and ESG impact dimensions. Importantly, our approach to building this strategic portfolio does not assume that achieving investors' ESG impact goals will also help them achieve their financial goals. Rather, we have designed a beta portfolio using assets that further ESG impact goals that we think earns the market risk premium in the most efficient way possible.

However, we often hear investors discussing whether ESG-related criteria (e.g. the sustainability of certain companies) can be used to tactically modify a portfolio in a way that will help them achieve above-market returns (increase return or reduce risk relative to a standard benchmark).

---

16 There is no guarantee expected performance will be achieved.

In other words, these investors are asking whether ESG integration can be a source of alpha.

We believe that good, diversifying alpha of any kind is valuable if you can find it and that understanding any issue that impacts markets – including issues commonly associated with ESG – can be a potential source of alpha. In the research process behind our own alpha strategies, we have sought to deeply understand a wide range of issues that are often associated with ESG (e.g. the economic impact of the decline of coal, the rise of renewable energy, income inequality, and the drivers of sustainable long-term growth across countries and across time) and how they connect to asset markets, because these topics are important for understanding the key drivers of global markets and economies.

However, generating alpha is very difficult. It requires unique insight that is not yet reflected in markets, and there are many talented players constantly competing to find and exploit new alpha opportunities before everyone else. Due to these intense competitive pressures, it makes sense to us that alpha strategies that are based on simple, replicable rules and openly shared in the public domain should be viewed with skepticism. In particular, we would caution against two common mistakes that we see across all alpha styles – including alpha strategies based around ESG – that we think are important for investors to understand and avoid:

1. *Betting on a trend without considering whether that trend is already priced into markets*: For example, an investor might read a report noting the rising popularity of AI and then purchase shares in the leading AI companies. We would be cautious about making this bet based purely on such information. Markets are discounting machines, and for a given AI equity to outperform, it is not enough that AI companies earn higher profits in the coming years; they must do better than markets are already expecting and is already reflected in their price. This requires thoughtful analysis to assess how equity markets are discounting the future, and the discounting in equity markets changes constantly, requiring ongoing evaluation.

   We sometimes see this misconception in the ESG space. We have often heard investors assert that an ESG equity allocation (e.g. an allocation that thematically invests in the most environmentally sustainable companies) will outperform a broad equity index or have higher risk-adjusted returns than a typical equity allocation. Just as in the example above, we would be careful about assuming that markets are not already pricing in the impact of better ESG policies on company profits. Pricing may also differ across ESG issues; for example, a shift to a low-carbon economy may be discounted in the stock prices of the relevant companies, while the falling profitability of companies that fail to meet adequate safety

standards may not be discounted. Most importantly, we would reiter-
ate that beating markets is extremely difficult, and we would apply high
standards to evaluating potential alpha strategies (including ESG alpha
strategies).

2. *Ascribing too much importance to any one pressure, when a range of many
   pressures drives markets*: For example, we see many equity strategies that
   buy equities primarily based on whether the valuation is attractive (i.e.
   the company has a lower-than-average P/E ratio, a higher-than-average
   dividend, and stable earnings). However, there are many, many pressures
   on market pricing at any given time, and no one pressure will exclusively
   drive the price of an asset over time. For example, an equity could indeed
   have an attractive valuation given existing fundamentals, but growth
   could fall, or interest rates could rise, or demand for that company's
   products could drop – all of which could lead to negative returns. An
   alpha strategy based around just a few of those dynamics is unlikely to
   perform well through time. Our time-tested alpha systems have many
   indicators, and we expect to only get our bets right a little more than half
   the time.

   We have seen this misconception crop up in the ESG space as well.
   For example, we see some investors pursuing alpha strategies that are
   primarily based on a small number of ESG dynamics – e.g. selling companies that score poorly on certain ESG issues and buying companies
   that score well. While we believe that a deep understanding of issues
   associated with ESG could provide useful insight to generating alpha, we
   would again be cautious about taking views based on any one dynamic
   alone.

Because alpha is so difficult, we would hold a high bar for assessing any alpha
strategy and would look deeply into its performance and process. The characteristics we would look at to determine if an alpha strategy is likely to be
reliable include:

- *Is the source of alpha both logical and stress-tested across time and
  countries?*
- *Biases and reliability*: In which environments does the alpha perform
  well? In which environments does it perform poorly? Has the true alpha
  been separated from what can be accessed cheaply as a passive investment (i.e. beta)?
- *Length and richness of track record*: Has this source of alpha been tested
  through a variety of challenging economic and market environments?
- *Plausibility*: A return stream that looks too good to be true may really be
  too good to be true.

- *Quality of thinking*: Favor alpha sources that reflect deep investment understanding and are likely to generate unique insights going forward.
- *Transparency and consistency of investment process.*

This is not to say that one should not look to issues associated with ESG as one potential source of alpha. We have been alpha practitioners for 35+ years and would be the first to highlight the beneficial role that alpha can play in a portfolio. And, as mentioned, we incorporate many topics that are associated with ESG in our investment research process. But as alpha practitioners ourselves, we also know first-hand how difficult it is and, as a result, how important it is to rigorously evaluate an alpha strategy before investing.

IMPORTANT DISCLOSURES AND OTHER INFORMATION

This chapter has been prepared solely for informational purposes and is not an offer to buy or sell or a solicitation of an offer to buy or sell any security or to participate in any trading strategy. In the future, Bridgewater may offer a fund or trading strategy that follows a similar investment strategy to the simulated portfolio presented herein. Any such offering will be made pursuant to a definitive offering memorandum (the "OM"), which will contain the terms and risks of making an investment with Bridgewater in the relevant fund and other material information not contained herein and which will supersede this information in its entirety. Investors should not construe the contents of this chapter as legal, tax, accounting, investment, or other advice.

An investment in any Bridgewater fund or strategy involves significant risks and there can be no assurance that any fund or strategy will achieve its investment objective or any targets or that investors will receive any return of their capital. An investment in any Bridgewater fund or strategy is suitable only for sophisticated investors and requires the financial ability and willingness to accept the high risks inherent in such an investment (including the risk of loss of their entire investment) for an indefinite period of time.

Any forward-looking statements contained herein reflect Bridgewater's current judgement and assumptions, which may change in the future, and Bridgewater has no obligation to update or amend such forward-looking statements.

Any tables, graphs, or charts relating to performance, whether hypothetical or simulated, included in this chapter are intended only to illustrate the performance of indices, strategies, or specific accounts for the historical periods shown. When creating such tables, graphs, and charts, Bridgewater may incorporate assumptions on trading, positions, transactions costs, market impact estimations, and the benefit of hindsight. For example, transaction cost estimates used in simulations are based on historical measured costs and/or modelled costs, and attribution is derived from a process of attributing positions held at a point in time to specific market views and is inherently imprecise. Such tables, graphs, and charts are not intended to predict future performance and should not be used as a basis for making any investment decision. Bridgewater has no obligation to update or amend such tables, graphs, or charts.

The material contained herein may exhibit the potential for attractive returns; however, it also involves a corresponding high degree of risk. Targeted performance, whether mathematically based or theoretical, is considered hypothetical and is subject to inherent limitations such as the impact of concurrent economic or geopolitical elements, forces of nature, war, and other factors not addressed in the analysis, such as lack of liquidity. There is no guarantee that the targeted performance for any fund or strategy shown herein can or will be achieved.

Bridgewater research utilizes data and information from public, private, and internal sources, including data from actual Bridgewater trades. None of the information related to a fund or strategy that Bridgewater may provide is intended to form the basis for any investment decision with respect to any retirement plan's assets.

In certain instances amounts and percentages in this chapter are approximate and have been rounded for presentation purposes. Statements in this chapter are made as of the date appearing on this chapter unless otherwise indicated. The delivery of this chapter shall not at any time under any circumstances create an implication that the information contained herein is correct as of any time subsequent to such date. Bridgewater has no obligation to inform recipients of this chapter when information herein becomes stale, deleted, modified, or changed.

BALANCED SDG-ALIGNED PORTFOLIO
SIMULATION DISCLOSURE

The Balanced SDG-Aligned Portfolio is not a simulation of an ESG All Weather strategy product and is not being offered for investment. This is an example of the investment profile of an All Weather strategy simulation that does not include corporate credit, emerging market debt, or fossil fuels (oil, natural gas).

Where shown, all performance of the Balanced SDG-Aligned Portfolio Simulation is based on simulated, hypothetical performance and not the returns of any Bridgewater strategy. Bridgewater's investment selection and trading strategies are systematic and rules-based. However, they are not fully automated and they do include human input. As a result, back-tested returns are designed based on assumptions about how Bridgewater would have implemented such a strategy if one existed at the time. These assumptions are intended to approximate such implementation, but are inherently speculative.

The simulated performance for Balanced SDG-Aligned Portfolio Simulation was derived by applying Bridgewater's current investment systems and portfolio construction logic to historical market returns across the markets selected for the Balanced SDG-Aligned Portfolio Simulation. A list of the markets used appears below. We use actual market returns when available as an input for our hypothetical returns and otherwise use Bridgewater Associates' proprietary estimates, based on other available data and our fundamental understanding of asset classes. In certain cases, market data for an exposure which otherwise would exist in the simulation may be omitted if the relevant data is unavailable, deemed unreliable, immaterial, or accounted for using proxies. Proxies are assets that existed and for which data is available, which Bridgewater believes would approximate returns for an asset that did not exist or for which reliable data is not available. Examples of omitted markets or markets accounted for using proxies include, but are not limited to, certain commodity markets. The mix and weightings of markets traded for Balanced SDG-Aligned Portfolio Simulation are subject to change in the future.

The Balanced SDG-Aligned Portfolio Simulation includes periodic adjustments that are made to the Balanced SDG-Aligned Portfolio Simulation's desired strategic asset allocation and level of risk pursuant to Bridgewater's systematic strategic management process. Such strategic management is based on a systematic process that assesses whether the assumptions underlying the Balanced SDG-Aligned Portfolio (that assets will outperform cash, and that assets can be reasonably balanced against each other) are under threat, and systematically adjusts or reduces exposures accordingly. When applicable, the returns of the Balanced SDG-Aligned Portfolio Simulation reflect adjustments based on this systematic strategic management process.

Simulated asset returns are subject to considerable uncertainty and potential error, as a great deal cannot be known about how assets would have performed in the absence of actual returns. The Balanced SDG-Aligned Portfolio Simulation is an approximation of what we believe an implementation process would be but not an exact replication and may have differences including but not limited to the precise mix of markets used and the weights applied to those markets. It is expected that the simulated performance will periodically change as a function of both refinements to our simulation methodology (including the addition/removal of asset classes) and the underlying market data. There is no guarantee that previous results would not be materially different. Future strategy changes could materially change previous simulated returns in order to reflect the changes accurately across time.

Transaction and maintenance costs are accounted for and are estimates themselves based on historical measured costs and/or modelled costs.

Returns are shown gross of fees as Bridgewater has not yet devised a fee schedule for the Balanced SDG-Aligned Portfolio Simulation. Investment advisory fees are described in Bridgewater's ADV Part 2A. Gross of fees performance (i) excludes the deduction of management fees, and other operating expenses (the "fees and expenses") and (ii) includes the reinvestment of interest, gains, and losses. Including the fees and expenses would lower performance. There is no guarantee regarding Balanced SDG-Aligned Portfolio strategy's ability to perform in absolute returns or relative to any market in the future, during market events not represented, or during market events occurring in the future. Market conditions and events vary considerably, are unpredictable, and can have unforeseen impacts resulting in materially adverse results.

MARKETS INCLUDED IN THE BALANCED SDG-ALIGNED PORTFOLIO SIMULATION

The Balanced SDG-Aligned Portfolio Simulation includes returns from the following markets: global nominal interest rates, global inflation linked bonds, commodities, and developed and emerging market equities that have been selected based on their alignment with the UN Sustainable Development Goals.

17

The imperative of sustainable investing for asset owners

Herman Bril[1,2]

INTRODUCTION: THE VALUE OF MONEY IS CHANGING

Sustainable investment is moving towards the mainstream. First emerging in the 1980s from the efforts of labor unions, churches, and foundations to promote value-based changes and social responsibility, it is now reaching maturity in the global financial system. The IMF (2019) recently devoted an entire chapter of its 2019 Global Financial Stability Report to sustainable finance, incorporating environmental, social, and governance (ESG) considerations with emphasis on the critical impact of climate change on macroeconomic considerations. But despite the evolution from socially responsible investing to sustainable investing, the field lacks clear definition and taxonomy, and there are few agreed standards for reporting and measurement. This has a serious effect on the willingness of asset owners to proactively adopt sustainable investment practices in their investment mandates and operations.

Successful sustainable investment moving forward will require asset owner industry leaders to overcome the confusion and ambiguity in the field and focus on the complex organizational challenges of implementing sustainable investment approach. It is incumbent upon the investment community to provide insight and stimulate debate around the increasing importance of sustainable investing. Quite apart from policymakers, they may hold the key to how to get there.

Understanding asset owners and their relevance in society requires a paradigm shift well beyond just a narrowly defined ESG perspective. Such a shift must focus on how asset owners can apply sustainable investing practices across all dimensions of their investment mandate, investment beliefs and strategy, technology, corporate cultural aspects, and change management. Furthermore, such fundamental change must demonstrate that a holistic approach to understanding sustainable investing, though complex and arduous, is both worthwhile and necessary, its reward a more stable and enduring investment outcome. Implementing sustainable investment practices across an entire portfolio does of course require leadership, a sense of urgency, and intensive dialogue with all stakeholders to secure the best long-term financial, environmental, and societal outcomes. Collectively, asset owners possess immense potential to drive sustainable investment practices. Embracing this practical thought continuum presents a unique opportunity and offers a path to a new horizon for our most trusted institutions and stewards of capital to prepare for the unavoidable realities of the investment landscape of tomorrow.

A short description of asset owners and their relevance

Asset owners, including pension funds, sovereign wealth funds, endowments and foundations, mutual funds and insurance funds, collectively manage USD$131 trillion in assets worldwide (Willis Towers Watson, 2019). They can be defined broadly by three key characteristics. First, they are the trustees[3] (or boards) who work directly for a defined group of beneficiaries in a fiduciary capacity under an arrangement of delegated responsibility. Second, they are linked to a sponsor[4] and constructed as a not-for-profit entity under an implicit societal license to operate. Third, they are purposely designed to delivering mission-specific outcomes to beneficiaries in the form of a financial promise, based on a recurring stream of contributions and investment returns. Pension funds are significant players in the asset owner landscape, with a two-thirds ratio of assets to GDP in the most developed economies. Tasked with securing the financial futures of millions of active participants and retirees, pension funds represent democratization of finance in action and have the greatest potential to generate positive impact for a more prosperous society.

The universal asset owner has a unique role in driving sustainable investing

The origins of these collective savings vehicles lie in co-operatives and mutual insurance schemes, organizations of people who have the same needs (they share actuarial risk, benefit from scale, low costs, etc.). Mutual companies are unique because they were established to serve the insurance needs of policyholders (or members) without also having to meet the investment needs of shareholders. The member is the sole focus of a mutual company. The origins of a mutual company are small, locally based co-operatives, groups which work or act together for common or mutual benefits to strengthen their financial security – purposely built on the sustainable principles born from survival needs. In today's world, these local membership organizations, in the form of defined benefit pension plans, have grown to become global financial superpowers, such as the ABP out of the Netherlands, which manages assets of nearly US$460 billion and has 3 million active and retired participants. These mega financial institutions can be classified as universal asset owners. A universal asset owner is, per Urwin (2011, p.1):

> a large institution investing long-term in widely diversified holdings across multiple industries and asset classes and adapting its investment strategy to these circumstances. For universal owners, overall economic performance will influence the future value of their portfolios more than the performance of individual companies or sectors. This suggests that universal owners will support the goals of sustainable growth and well-functioning financial markets. A universal owner will also view these goals holistically and seek ways to reduce the company level externalities that produce economy-wide efficiency losses.

The logic of this classification is sound. And yet it contains a fundamental paradox: that local membership mutuals can create a global socioeconomic footprint based on their (local) beliefs and preferences, shaped by history and the cultural context of societal influences in their country of origin. Schoenmaker and Schramade (2019), referencing research from Liang and Renneboog (2017), find that legal origin – interpreted as systems of social control of economic life – helps explain cross-country variation in companies' ESG activities. ESG scores are higher in countries operating under civil law than in common law countries. These higher ESG scores reflect social preferences for good corporate behavior and stakeholder orientation. Such social preferences are more embedded in rule-based mechanisms that restrict firm behavior ex-ante and are more prevalent in civil law countries. By contrast, ex-post judicial settlement mechanisms are more important in common law countries. The common law tradition emphasizes shareholder primacy and a private market-oriented strategy of social control, and perhaps because of this emphasis, it is also less stakeholder-oriented (Liang and Renneboog, 2017). This suggests that eliciting the sustainability preferences of members and other stakeholders, in order to foster transparency, is critical to ensuring accountability and reinforcing the license of global asset owners to operate.

As long as nation states align with and support global financial markets – and a majority are powerless to duck this reality – asset owners, and more specifically pension funds, will have immense influence on driving sustainable outcomes in pursuit of their own financial interests. This is consistent with promoting more prosperous societies. But what is prosperity? What is the role of the market? And why might we argue that they are inherent in capitalism?

Capitalism is a complex, evolutionary system

Hanauer and Beinhocker (2014) argue that capitalism is best understood as an evolving system, continually creating and sampling new solutions to address arising challenges. Some solutions are "fitter" than others, and the fittest survive and propagate while the unfit wither. Companies face not only disruptive competition but unpredictability, nonlinearity, and circularity of cause-and-effect relationships within a VUCA world, all of which increase complexity. Robustness and resilience are the first lines of defense. Additionally, companies need to develop coping strategies like adaptation, innovation, mitigation, and cooperation. These are the collective drivers of survivorship and, in essence, the parameters of ever-changing capitalism. The core drivers of this complex process are:

- the creation of long-term economic value based on an idea that solves a problem ("entrepreneurship");
- the avoidance of risks that could compromise long-term economic value ("risk management");
- the belief that externalities are not a free option ("planetary boundaries");
- the belief that resilience, adaptation (innovation and technology), and cooperation drive survivorship and progress ("capitalism"); and
- the underpinning of thriving businesses and the accumulation of solutions to human problems ("humanism").

The economist Joseph Schumpeter called this evolutionary process "creative destruction," and highlights the importance of risk-taking by entrepreneurs (backed by investors) and the need for practical experimentation to evolve. Understanding prosperity as solutions and capitalism as an evolutionary problem-solving system explains why it might be considered the most effective social technology ever devised for creating rising standards of living (Hanauer and Beinhocker, 2014). Nevertheless, the reverse outcome is also possible – as Niall Ferguson mentioned in an interview with *McKinsey Quarterly* (2019):

> capitalism is in a crisis, as usual. Creative destruction creates pain and creates losers. This is the normal state of affairs, and we shouldn't be surprised that it is going on. There will always be people challenging the legitimacy of the system.

Capitalism can't work without well-functioning governments that design rules to enable innovation, empower markets, ensure competition, and address social problems.

What does this mean for asset owners? According to Porter, Serafeim, and Kramer (2019), when investors ignore their social responsibility and fail to recognize the powerful connection between company strategy, social purpose, and economic value, they erode the impact and legitimacy of capitalism as a vehicle for advancing society. It is no wonder that so many have lost faith in capitalism. When economic inequality increases and social needs are greater than ever, ignoring the synergy between corporate success and social progress emboldens critics and puts the future of capitalism at risk.

Porter, Serafeim, and Kramer (2019) ask: how do we bring investors and society together again? Investing in companies that contribute profitably to social progress, and withdrawing capital from those that do not, will create a virtuous cycle in which the improving welfare of customers, employees, and communities generates future growth and expanded opportunities for more citizens. The authors argue – in line with Hanauer and Beinhocker (2014) – that a social need can be tackled with a profitable business model. Thus is the magic of capitalism unleashed. Answers to the many deeply rooted societal problems we face become self-sustaining and scalable. However, a serious flaw in this presumed logical reasoning is that many in the investment community have moved away from fundamental investing and its powerful social purpose, seeing algorithm-driven strategies and trading on market movements as ends in themselves, illuminating the pitfalls of short-termism. In the process, the connection between capital investment and social improvement is lost (Porter, Serafeim, and Kramer, 2019).

A redefined view of capitalism underpins that the value of money can be a catalyst. This supports the premise that the universal asset owner, indeed the aggregate of asset owners, should lead the way in becoming sustainable investors – to pursue their self-interest, and to ensure that capitalism supports more sustainable and prosperous societies, backed by effective policymaking by governmental institutions and regulators.

This holistic world view deviates from the teachings of standard economic thought and traditional finance theory. Moreover, advocating for this narrative in an international context of growing societal discontent and tribal politics is hugely challenging. Then again, this context may also present a unique opportunity; never let a crisis go to waste.

We have seen how sustainable investment might be considered imperative for asset owners. But how can this be operationalized in practice? There are many challenges. The next section will describe how asset owners might evolve to become sustainable investors. The important role of technology and alternative data will then be addressed. Finally, a successful transition depends on change management and corporate culture, which is then outlined.

WHAT DOES IT TAKE TO BECOME A
SUSTAINABLE INVESTOR?

Put simply: more than one can imagine. This section will begin with an outline of the importance of governance and effective boards. This in turn is closely related to fiduciary duty, which defines the legal boundaries for boards (and trustees). We will then discuss the purpose of organizations, their missions and visions, and how sustainable investing might be integrated into them. Next, we will see how investment beliefs and strategy are formulated. Finally, we will examine negative screening, divestment, and the need for a forward-looking climate strategy.

Good governance and effective boards are critical to success

The effect of good governance on investment management and performance cannot be understated. Naturally, then, it's in styles of governance that we can locate the greatest (untapped) potential for an asset owner to set sustainable investment goals. Several key factors contribute to good governance within pension funds, including appropriate governance structures; well-defined accountabilities, policies, and procedures; and suitable processes for the selection and operation of governing bodies and managing institutions. Not surprisingly, good governance requires leadership by professional executives with the expertise and integrity required to navigate a fund's direction and to withstand pressures from multiple constituencies (Rajkumar and Dorfman, 2011). Having a governing board set sustainable investment goals in alignment with greater organizational policies endows its leaders with greater authority to execute and achieve optimal outcomes.

The primary roles of a pension fund's board are to define its goals, set policy, organize the investment process, and monitor and calibrate choices to adapt to any changing circumstances (Koedijk, Slager, and van Dam, 2019). An efficient board has a positive influence on long-term outcomes and, thus, the fund's license to operate. The board has an important but challenging role, as fiduciary, to act in the best interest of its participants. This includes formulating an investment policy statement (IPS), which describes the governance, strategy, risk management, metrics, and targets, as well as reporting to stakeholders, often in a highly regulated jurisdiction. In defining the IPS, the board is a servant to many masters: it must satisfy the demands and objectives of the sponsor; the sometimes-unclear preferences of the participants and beneficiaries; and the political and regulatory environment. Because of their sheer size and impact, asset owners are exposed to reputational risk, shifting norms in society, and sometimes find themselves under pressure from special interest groups (NGOs) or political pressure. Implicitly, they must act as a prudent societal fiduciary based on a principle of "doing no harm." This is not an easy task for the average trustee, often a layman working part-time and without recompense (for example, non-executive board members representing the various constituents), surrounded by lawyers and professional investment advisors from the private sector – not always themselves aligned – and, of course, operating within a complex legal and regulatory environment.

How can a board integrate into its agenda a sustainable investment framework? The impetus to do so may come from sponsors, participants, consultants, regulators, NGOs, investment managers, peers in the industry, or – ideally – leadership from within a well-informed board itself.

Part of the problem is one of definition. "Sustainable investment" has heretofore been rather loosely pinned down. Indeed, the financial services industry has spawned a slew of terms that may confuse rather than clarify investment objects and outcomes insofar as they pertain to sustainable investments. The IMF recognized this lack of clarity as a roadblock in its October 2019 Global Financial Stability Review, recommending "standardization of ESG investment terminology … [to] support market development, address greenwashing concerns and reduce reputational risk." The Institute of International Finance (IIF, 2019) has since created a working group for simplifying sustainable investment terminology, proposing three categories for discussion: "exclusion," "inclusion," and "impactful" (see Appendix 1 outlining the proposed standardized terms).

While ensuring that sustainable investment makes it onto the agenda is the first step, defining it clearly is just as important – and as difficult. As a board, though, it's understanding your role and duty that is the critical step in successful implementation.

Fiduciary responsibility – know thyself

Boards are bound by fiduciary duty to act in the best interests of their beneficiaries. The interaction of this legal principle with proposed sustainable investment policies is a source of lively debate within the pension fund industry. Fiduciary duties exist to ensure that those who manage other people's money act in their beneficiaries' best interests, rather than serving their own self-interests. How fiduciary duty is defined thus has profound implications. Some institutional investors previously believed that ESG issues were not relevant to portfolio value and were therefore not consistent with their fiduciary duties. This assumption is no longer supported. In 2015 former US Vice President Al Gore introduced the "Fiduciary Duty in the 21st Century program," whose final instalment, published in October 2019, affirmed that fiduciary duty must incorporate ESG issues into investment analysis and decision-making processes. Investors who fail to incorporate ESG issues are not only failing their fiduciary duty but are increasingly likely to be subject to future legal obstacles.

Of course, common sense would argue that all material factors potentially impacting investment returns should be incorporated into investment decisions. However, the legislative and legal challenge is how to properly define such measures without incorporating all of the more contentious political objectives pushed by NGOs. One positive development is that credit rating agencies are now incorporating ESG considerations in their ratings, including analytics to assess the many risks that are likely to result from climate change. This alone perhaps demonstrates how entwined ESG issues have become with mainstream finance principles. For pension funds, the objective is to integrate sustainable investing by considering material ESG factors while remaining entirely consistent with their fiduciary responsibility to meet long-term investment objectives.

Understanding the importance of governance and an effective board to implementing necessary change is a prerequisite for transitioning asset owners to a more optimal footing. The integration of the concept of sustainable investing into our understanding of fiduciary duty has an inevitable impact on the asset owner's purpose.

Purpose – mission and vision determine the investment mandate

A deep understanding of an organization's purpose defines the role of the asset owner in society. It answers the question of why asset owners have an integral role in driving sustainable investing, as outlined in the introduction.

Following through on the financial promises to asset owners' members, and thus guaranteeing financial security to beneficiaries, is a social good. To do so, as we have seen, trustees should account for material ESG considerations when investing and deploying assets. But the question remains: what role do values and ethics play for the asset owner? Should they care about a more prosperous society, or simply be long-term money-producing machines? Are they future takers or future makers?

This chapter's premise is that today's savers are tomorrow's pensioners; all seek financial security and a more prosperous society. These days, though, our collective well-being and survival depend on the maintenance not only of physical and financial capital but also of natural, human, and social capital (Mayer, 2018). This conceptual framework was globally formulated and agreed upon by the United Nations with the inception of the Sustainable Development Goals in September 2015. Subsequently, following the Conference of Parties' agreement on a global climate deal in Paris in December 2015, world leaders quantified their commitment to our well-being by pledging to prevent an increase in average global temperatures of more than 2 degrees Celsius above pre-industrial levels.

Pension funds, which are key players in financial democratization, can – and should – be future makers, simply by virtue of the fact that positive financial and societal outcomes are central to their fiduciary responsibility.

It is critical for the sponsor, board, and constituency of pension plans to discuss their objectives. But this discussion is not a simple one. While it is of necessity deeply intertwined with fiduciary duty and investment beliefs, encompassing standard financial theory and neoclassical economic thought, to further complicate matters, the debate around purpose is merging more and more with questions of "political economy."[5] This opens the door to complex, often divergent, sometimes irrational views. A once commonsensical, centrist discussion has allowed itself to become a political battleground. This has only become more the case in the years since the Global Financial Crisis of 2008, and the "Wall Street" bailouts that followed in its wake. Main Street was – and in some places remains – disillusioned. The cultural, financial, educational, and political divides between rural and urban communities are stark. Despite numerous economic and technological advancements which have boosted GDP and reduced unemployment, market dynamics have also generated greater inequality, and it is common knowledge that the American Dream is available only to a happy few. Hence, the political backlash of both sides of the aisle.

These economic and social challenges must be digested by boards when defining their organizational purpose, mission, and vision. Board leadership is defined by the ability to address these matters within the context of their fiduciary duty. Leadership requires defining principles, clear communication channels, and the ability to build bridges and promote consensus in order to define a path to greater societal and better environmental outcomes. Given that pension funds are, primarily, the collective savings vehicles for "Main Street" workers, they can play an important role in producing a more equitable society and livable planet while in the same time acting in their financial self-interest.

A clear purpose helps asset owners to form the principles for their investment beliefs and strategy, as we shall see in the next section. These principles form an important step in the journey toward implementing sustainable investing. They require a grounded, real-world view of financial markets, of the role of ESG screening, and of the issue of divesting and designing forward-looking climate change-based solutions for institutional investment strategies.

Investment beliefs and strategy – in the eye of the beholder

According to Koedijk, Slager, and van Dam (2019), investment beliefs are an effective governance guide for boards or investment committees when making investments. Beliefs can guide and discipline investment decisions. A good set of beliefs must be firmly rooted in theory, practice, and experience, and some are more evidence-based than others. Either way, beliefs guide choices for years to come. An effective approach to sustainable investment would be undergirded by a belief that portfolios that have integrated material ESG metrics into their investment decision-making process – and have supported them through an active engagement (stewardship) strategy – could provide returns superior to those of conventional portfolios, while exhibiting lower risk over the long term. The low risk point is critical because investing is not just about making the highest returns; it is about avoiding large losses and protecting downside risk capture. The power of compounding returns increases dramatically if the tail events are reduced.

Investment belief is not an exact science. It is a social construct based on history, finance theory, statistical models, sound judgment, and experience. It is not static, and it evolves over time, based on new and developing academic and practitioner insights. The next section will critically review modern economics.

The emancipation of the homo economicus into the homo pancasilaus[6]

The dominance of traditional homo economicus management and investment thinking has been very linear and often simplistic, based on neoclassical economic ideology, overly reliant on mathematics and Gaussian models grounded in unrealistic rational assumptions. At the heart of modern macroeconomics is the same illusion that uncertainty can be confined to the mathematical manipulation of known probabilities. To understand and weather booms and slumps requires a different approach to thinking about uncertainty (King, 2016).

The reliance on such an approach has persisted because most investment professionals were trained, like good neoclassical economists, to believe in the model of the rational "economic person." Standard economics, taught at all the leading universities, places human cognition and motivation in a "black box," using models that assume that people consider all possible costs and benefits from a self-interested perspective and then make a thoughtful and rational decision. This school of thinking ignores psychological and social influences on behavior. Individuals are not calculating automatons, as explained by Yannis Papadogiannis (2014) in his book *The Rise and Fall of Homo Economicus: The myth of the rational human and the chaotic reality*. Rather, people are malleable and emotional actors whose decision-making is influenced by contextual cues, local social networks, social norms, and shared mental models. Despite the repeated inability of economic forecasting models to predict accurately, there is a persistent belief that there is, if only we could find it, a "model" of the economy that will produce forecasts that are exactly right (King, 2016). The Global Financial Crisis exposed the fallibility of traditional theories of economic thought, and its aftermath renewed interest in heterodox schools of economic thought, including behavioral, complexity, evolutionary, ecological, and geographical. The first step to overturning conventional wisdom, when conventional wisdom is wrong, is to look at the world around you. See the world as it is, not as others wish it to be (Thaler, 2015).

The Institute for New Economic Thinking (INET) at Oxford University was founded in 2012 in the wake of the Global Financial Crisis to promote innovative, policy-relevant economic research that might explore different economic views. The traditional efficient market hypothesis is under attack and at risk of being replaced by more evidence-based, multi-disciplinary approaches. Andrew Lo, author of the adaptive markets theory, writes that, "Markets do look efficient under certain circumstances, namely, when investors have had a chance to adapt to existing business conditions, and those conditions remain relatively stable over a long period" (Lo, 2017, p. 3). But as explained earlier in this chapter, a VUCA world in transition is not particularly stable, and the fact that integrating material ESG considerations as standard in active portfolio management is not yet mainstream presents an opportunity. Combined with active engagement or stewardship, investment managers have the opportunity, through incorporating ESG considerations, to create portfolios with enhanced risk-and-return profiles compared with traditionally managed or passive portfolios over the long term.

Formulating investment beliefs also requires a discussion of organizational values (moral, faith-based, and ethical) and purpose as the basis for exclusion, or (negative) screening (e.g., actively avoid certain investments). We will discuss this in more detail in the next section.

To screen or not to screen – and the dilemma of fossil fuel divestments

Should asset owners exclude certain investments? This is another complex discussion that calls into question not only fiduciary duty but also the efficacy of applying negative screening on moral, ethical, or values-based grounds.

For example, should asset owners ban investments in tobacco companies, or controversial weapon manufacturers? More recently, some financial institutions have started to put coal – and, in some cases, all fossil fuels – on their exclusion list due to their impact on global carbon emissions. This is often triggered by pressure from NGOs. But despite such action, the initial effects of exclusion and divestment are limited (Schoenmaker and Schramade, 2019).

The "exclusion" decision depends on many factors, including the license to operate, the values of the sponsor or the beneficiaries, investment beliefs, active vs. passive investment style, social norms, and, in some cases, legal or political considerations. It requires an intensive dialogue with all stakeholders. Asset owners vary in their exclusionary approach and often combine such policies with an ESG integration policy, supported by active engagement. The most contentious discussion is about straightforward fossil fuel divestments. But divestments can be designed in more refined ways.

As this book demonstrates elsewhere, climate risk is by far the biggest systemic risk that asset owners face. The financial risks associated with climate change can be divided into two broad categories: (1) those associated with effective policies and other public and private efforts to contain climate change (transition risk or mitigation risk associated with a transition to a low(er) carbon future); and (2) those associated with a failure to address climate change effectively (i.e., the physical risk associated with adaptation to a high(er) carbon future). Mitigation risk is the price of success in the fight against global warming; physical risk is the price of failure (Citi, 2019).

Looking at the current climate trajectory, it seems likely that asset owners will first be financially impacted by more physical risk – the first corporate bankruptcy (PG&E) was recorded in 2019[7] – and this will be the catalyst for transition risk. Trends often need a crisis to bring them to the forefront of people's minds. That's one of the lessons of history: trends, if they unfold over decades, don't necessarily produce big political outcomes; there needs to be some kind of catalyst (McKinsey Quarterly, 2019). Unfortunately, humans seem to need a more urgent crisis to change behavior, to adapt, mitigate, innovate, and cooperate their way out of trouble. Irrespective of which kind of financial risk comes first, asset owners will be impacted negatively by both transition and physical risks and therefore must address the investment implications of these risks in order to preserve accumulated pension capital and sustain stable returns. While technical discussions of externalities and policy development dominate the sustainability debate, the real transition challenge is developing integrated thinking and implementing effective transition management (Schoenmaker and Schramade, 2019).

The world needs to transition to a decarbonized economy by 2050 to offset the impact of climate risk on society. Are low-carbon portfolios the solution for asset owners? Not necessarily, as divesting high-emitting carbon companies from your portfolio and transferring those shares to other investors is hardly a structural solution. This may lead to short-term negative-return consequences and does not prevent physical risk exposure. The sobering message is that every single investment needs to stem from top–down and bottom–up analysis, together with a deep ESG materiality analysis. This goes way beyond incorporating just an ESG rating from a provider. Headline scores have been widely adopted because they are easy to consume, but an effective approach requires developing strategy-specific frameworks that disaggregate materiality within the context of financial analysis, as explained in the next section, which is about technology and alternative data.

The most effective investment approach is investing in emission reduction to increase profitability – especially investing in companies that are high emitters but have already started down the path towards a low-carbon economy. Recent work by Entelligent (2018)[8] concludes that the highest emitters with defined and committed climate-transition strategies present the greatest opportunity for global carbon reduction. Watching how emitters adapt to both the transition and physical risk is the key to unlocking the financial markets and the innovation necessary to adapt to environmental threats. Today, firms working towards carbon-reduction targets are providing more than anecdotal evidence that they are helping drive innovation, reducing costs and boosting profits, all while gaining a long-term competitive advantage and safeguarding their future profitability. The relationship between carbon reduction and corporate financial performance has been subject to extensive empirical enquiry, all of which supports sustainable investing. Carbon-efficient firms tend to be "quality firms" in terms of financial characteristics and corporate governance. Corporate social performance is also found to be positively associated with future financial performance. Poor environmental performance is negatively correlated with the intangible asset value of firms (Entelligent, 2018).

Linking climate-mitigation investment strategies back to the earlier analysis, in particular the concept of capitalism as an evolutionary system that solves problems, can help us to determine the future fitness of a company during transition periods. This overarching conceptual framework is the basis for developing a so-called "soft" divestment strategy. Coping with climate change requires decarbonization of the entire economy to stay well below 2 degrees Celsius. This transition will require multiple decades, for reasons including the fact that countries are at such wildly contrasting stages of economic development; the access to energy of those at the Base of the Pyramid;[9] the status of alternative solutions and financial recourses; and demographic trends.

The objective of a soft divestment strategy is to identify winners – companies that are strategically preparing and investing in the transition, and that understand physical risk (sustainability change agents) – versus the possible losers – companies that are ignoring these long-term systemic changes. Actively overweighting investments in winners and underweighting losers (up to no exposure at all) in relation to a global equity benchmark is a rational and systematic way to deal with the complexity of transition risk, which is non-linear, multi-period and uncertain. This dynamic coping approach compensates for unpredictable future climate states, but also addresses the demand for innovation and breakthroughs in clean technology. Coping strategies are especially important in financial markets because these strategies are a link between the present and the future (King, 2016). As an investment strategy towards a given sector, this is a dynamic, flexible alternative to a static "hard divestment" approach. It can also be designed as a sector-neutral strategy and with a relatively low tracking error (a measure of active portfolio risk vs. the benchmark).

The perceived signaling advantages of a hard divestment approach can be replaced by an active engagement and stewardship strategy that promotes incremental change. The soft divestment approach is also more politically attuned to today's pressure on multilateralism and the rise of tribal populism. A soft divestment strategy does not punish emerging markets or create international political backlash, and is, in addition, fully compliant with an asset owner's fiduciary duty. The message and strategy is consistent with the objective of the universal asset owner: they are a long-term investor who invests in companies with a defined future-fitness profile that aligns with a best-in-class sustainability strategy and thus ensures a greater probability for long-term profitability.

Climate change requires a forward-looking approach

The future is inherently uncertain and scientific models cannot predict the future perfectly. Hence, climate change modeling requires multiple plausible assumptions and scenario analysis to understand a variety of possible future states. Given the mounting evidence of growing climate risks to human survival and the health and functioning of our society, investors need to identify the financial risks from climate change that are unique to their portfolio and create their own beliefs and strategies to protect assets. Investors will therefore need more advanced systems to integrate energy economics, alternative climate scenarios, and traditional financial data in their evaluations of return and risk exposures vis-à-vis climate change and the attendant transformations in our energy systems. Asset owners often lack internal expertise and require strategic partnerships with leading providers of predictive climate analytics to enhance their sustainable investment approach, or to build internal capabilities. Active strategies need highly sophisticated climate- and energy-simulation models to assess companies' ability to adapt to various carbon-emission scenarios.

It is necessary to distinguish between a forward-looking climate approach and traditional ESG applications of a carbon footprint analysis in constructing soft divestment portfolios. A forward-looking climate approach integrates energy economics and alternative climate scenarios with traditional financial data to evaluate return and risk exposures related to (extreme) climate change scenarios. This approach provides a predictive, company-level dataset on transition risk, with climate forecasting built on carbon budgets, policy projections, technological diversions towards alternative sources of energy, and projected energy pathways as a key starting input. The output is a dynamic quarterly adjusted security-level risk-measure and -ranking system to integrate into portfolio construction. This approach complements traditional carbon footprint analysis, which aggregates plant-level and indirect emissions from self-reported Scope 1 and Scope 2 data[10] to measure an asset's carbon footprint or the footprint of the entire portfolio. The two approaches will allow investors to evaluate both a company's impact on the environment as well as impact of environmental changes on the company. The power of a forward-looking climate approach is that it uses a series of climate risk assessment scores (E-Scores[11]) in a global and data-driven model to apply the standards used in a predictive model. This methodology uses projections from global energy and climate models for multiple climate scenarios and translates these projections down to the asset level as a guidance system that can be performance-tested by using conventional back-testing methods.

The transition risk computed using E-Scores is a result of macroeconomic realization of a company's exposures towards multiple climate scenario analyses that capture current energy transitions and future energy transition trajectories at company or asset level. This differs from more traditional ESG approaches and practices that use an ex-post carbon footprint risk analysis to show the realized carbon footprints of the company/asset, which in turn gives a static picture that is used to construct a "low-carbon" portfolio typically designed to track to a given equity index.

The integration of both approaches is important to evaluate the overall sustainability of the asset. Carbon footprint analysis provides knowledge on where an asset is on the carbon meter today, whereas a forward-looking climate E-Score provides guidance on which direction an asset is moving by tracking its energy transition trajectory.

Recent climate-investment research from Entelligent (2018) indicates that, despite limitations of data available in the market today, companies with a better E-Score are more likely to have:

- a superior environmental score that offers consistent global coverage compared with scores computed using traditional, bottom–up ESG methodology;
- lower direct (Scope 1) carbon emissions; and
- emerging environmental corporate leaders.

Integrating a forward-looking climate approach using E-Score values can help investors evaluate the climate change transition risk and achieve greater climate sustainability in their investment portfolios. They can also be designed to outperform an equity index without compromising risk factors.

After outlining the importance of investment beliefs in this section, it becomes clear that implementing a sustainable investment strategy requires a dynamic approach to addressing investment climate risk through innovative technology, alternative data, and expertise.

TECHNOLOGY AND ALTERNATIVE DATA ARE GAME CHANGERS

Stories are powerful and memorable, but, as Thaler (2015) tells us, an individual anecdote can only serve as an illustration. To really convince skeptics, we need to change the way we tell stories. We need data. Lots of it.

Investment managers require new technology and alternative data to make better and more informed investment decisions to further improve risk/ return characteristics of actively managed portfolios. The greatest challenge lies in the practical implementation and application of data itself. ESG integration requires dynamic and innovative tools that materially co-integrate alternative datasets that are not conventionally used for supporting investment decision-making. When used effectively, advances in technology and nonfinancial data will continue to enable greater systematic ESG integration and improve transparency.

Significantly, recent advances in data formulation such as AI, big data, and machine learning are and will continue to have a substantial impact on the investment management industry. The datafication of society will give sophisticated investors much deeper insight in value drivers, externalities, trends, and risks, based on actual evidence-based behavior of corporates and consumers. This technology can also be used to measure the Sustainable Development Goals (SDG) footprint of a company. Although still in the early stages of development, prospective advances such as natural language processing (NLP) have the potential to disintermediate data ownership and create more accurate and accessible ways of assessing the future fitness of a company. These assessments can then be used to further enhance asset owners' engagement strategies and improve the quality of ESG ratings.

Sustainable investing requires access to alternative raw data from multiple sources rather than just aggregate ESG ratings. These larger, more diverse datasets can then be used to construct internal proprietary ESG technology and dashboards which will more efficiently distil underlying material ESG data by separating noise from signal.

The effect will be cumulative and will offer a clear advantage over conventional portfolio management approaches. Giving portfolio managers more robust screening capabilities and predictive efficacy, such as fast- and slow-moving ESG signals, systematically combining financial metrics and alternative data, and implementing a soft divestment approach will create multiple layers of confidence, which will in turn increase the likelihood of a portfolio's risk and return profile improving over multiple market cycles.

One challenging aspect to implementing more innovative technological solutions in this space is that many asset owners outsource most of their assets to investment managers or passive index trackers. This creates an additional layer of complexity when it comes to building internal capabilities, know-how, technology, and integrated data competency. As a result, best-in-class sustainable asset owners typically manage the majority of their assets internally. This is also more cost-effective and creates and fosters a culture of innovation and excellence.

CORPORATE CULTURE AND CHANGE MANAGEMENT – THE SOFT SIDE IS THE HARDEST PART

Culture in financial institutions is a nebulous concept that means different things to different people. Because of its fuzziness, it tends to be overlooked (Thakor, 2016). As a result, implementing a sustainable investing concept is far easier said than done.

Implementation is technically complex and can expose entrenched biases and beliefs, and political and cultural differences. The way people analyze and interpret the world and look at experimental data is intimately entwined with their existing, preconceived understanding of how the world works, which Thomas Kuhn (1970) called incommensurability. In other words, in economics it is quite common for people to agree about the data but disagree entirely about what it means (Cooper, 2014). To make matters even more difficult, ESG data and the resulting ratings are still confusing – sometimes contradictory, with a low correlation between providers, and with no firm, agreed standards. Furthermore, asset owners have to deal with multiple stakeholders at various levels, taking into account regulatory and legal considerations. As mentioned earlier, even defining sustainable investing is not straightforward. Collectively, the complex interactions of expertise, beliefs, and organizational behavior and forces can easily lead to procrastination and paralysis.

Harnett (2018, p. 2) thoroughly researched the following relevant question: "now that ESG information is more widely available, why has this not catalyzed a greater shift towards Responsible Investment (RI) integration in mainstream investment decisions?" She finds that, while RI is increasingly being adopted within more mainstream investment firms, it is not always fully integrated throughout the firm, and uptake varies geographically based on exposure to networks of information, knowledge-sharing, and institutional, organizational, and individual norms. More specifically, she notes that learning, language, and leadership within the institutional investment industry hinder the mainstreaming of RI knowledge and practice, and that

ESG information is a necessary but not sufficient element in the comprehensive development and implementation of RI strategies. Because of persistent skepticism among many mainstream investors as to the financial materiality of ESG factors, she says RI can be seen as a moral decision to which you must sign up. It is easy to understand why the mainstreaming of RI has not gathered greater pace.

Implementing sustainable investing, for most asset owners, is a journey that begins with small steps. Integrating sustainable investing within asset organizations requires visionary leadership. Those leaders must establish a high-performance culture with an emphasis on passion for further development and innovation. Boards should continually push themselves out of their comfort zones and recruit leaders who can successfully set the tone from the top, a tone that fosters a culture that prizes open-mindedness, that produces creative solutions and constant adaptation, and that permits failing quickly. Creating an environment where an organization can learn and explore, build partnerships (e.g., PRI), and test new technologies and alternative data sources will help build knowledge and capabilities and be a positive catalyst for change. Unfortunately, the asset owner industry, which has been focused on the efficiency for the better part of a century, is now faced with the challenge of figuring out how to be innovative, which seemingly goes against the DNA of many of these organizations (Clark and Monk, 2017).

According to Thaler (2015), capable leaders must create environments in which employees feel that making evidence-based decisions will always be rewarded, no matter what outcome occurs. The ideal organizational environment encourages everyone to observe, collect data, and speak up. Unfortunately, this sort of culture is unfamiliar to most asset owners. Groupthink, political pressure, bureaucracy, limited resources, fixated investment beliefs, and a culture of silos – and sometimes resistance – create deeply embedded routines that have to be overcome. Gillian Tett (2015, p. x) notes in her research:

> almost everywhere I looked in the financial crisis it seemed that tunnel vision and tribalism had contributed to the disaster. People were trapped inside their little specialist departments, social groups, teams of pockets of knowledge, or put differently, inside their silos.

Corporate culture is a tremendously important factor in determining success in a change intervention.

The competing values framework is a helpful approach for characterizing organizational culture in simple, easy-to-communicate terms (see Figure 17.1; Thakor, 2016).

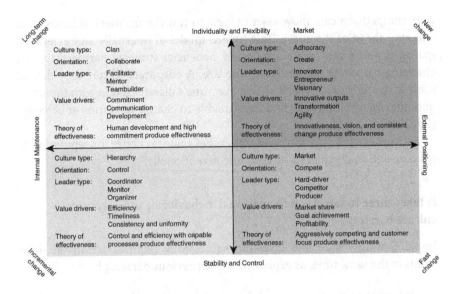

FIGURE 17.1 The competing values framework

Source: Reproduced from Anjan Thakor, "Corporate Culture in Banking," Federal Reserve Bank of New York *Economic Policy Review,* vol. 22, no. 1 (2016), available at www.newyorkfed.org/research/epr/2016/epr_2016-thakor-corporate-culture

This framework enables any organization to assess its current culture as well as its preferred culture. It is not uncommon for asset owners to be more inclined towards "incremental change" – and "stability and control" – as depicted in Figure 17.1, because pension funds are organizations focusing on the long term and responsible for billions of dollars. But also, because there are fewer pressures on institutional investors to change and innovate than there are on their private, commercial counterparts. Most asset owners have a legal right to represent the interest of "captive" beneficiaries. The large majority of pension funds have made no meaningful changes to the way they do business in decades, for they are often embedded in particular economic and political environments that seem to constrain rather than encourage evolution (Clark and Monk, 2017).

The natural trajectory would be to transition from "incremental change" to "long-term change" before the organization is ready to deal with "new change," as shown in Figure 17.1. This is where an external asset manager may have the edge over an asset owner managing in-house assets. It is relatively easier for commercial investment managers to operate in the "new change" quadrant. Therefore, if structured properly, a mix of internally and externally managed assets can create knowledge diffusion, while value-added peer-to-peer competition can allow asset owners to test the frontiers of innovation and stay ahead of the curve. This hybrid model of internally and externally managed assets can create a mutually beneficial strategic partnership. But changing corporate culture is no sinecure. A corporate culture may defend itself so strongly that, despite almost everyone's dissatisfaction with the status quo, the organization may find itself unable to change its norms of behavior (Lo, 2016).

As Keynes said, "worldly wisdom teaches that it is better for reputation to fail conventionally than to succeed unconventionally."

It takes three to tango – informational, behavioral, and corporate culture barriers

Implementing sustainable investing successfully requires action on three fronts at the same time, as explained in the previous paragraph:

- informational – this is about data, tools, metrics, scientific evidence, and knowledge;
- behavioral – cognitive biases and psychological underpinnings; and
- corporate culture – the purpose, values, and culture of the organization.

In their research on the behavioral barriers to taking institutional action on climate change, Guyatt and Poulter (2019) found evidence of cognitive biases and psychological underpinnings, namely myopia, herding, and reliance on heuristics and rules of thumb. Cognitive dissonance, narrow framing, loss aversion, status quo bias, and overconfidence were also factors. The study revealed, among other things, that: (a) leaders displayed a surprisingly broad success rate across all types of behavioral barriers and were more than happy to live with the discomfort and potential reputational, career, and other risks; (b) the challenges with taking action on climate change were not purely related to lack of data or availability of models; and (c) external pressure from stakeholders can be effective at overcoming behavioral barriers by helping key decision-makers to prioritize climate change.

Other recent research (Willis Towers Watson, 2019) showed that governance and cultural considerations need to be revisited. The Thinking Ahead Institute identified two principal challenges to organizations that are failing to adapt. The first was to reset their purpose, mission, and vision (business model). For this, their strategy and culture must change, and they must develop a more coherent view of their core stakeholders and their needs. The second was to strengthen their governance and leadership (operating model). The relative influence of asset owners compared with asset managers is set to rise, in part through building bigger teams with stronger leadership, but also through the streamlining of governance, particularly in delegations, partners, and processes.

Change is neither easy nor obvious. Most of us live in accordance with norms that we abhor. We may not think about them; they are part of the furniture. Nevertheless, we abhor them. The problem is that a norm cannot be changed unilaterally. To be sure, we can defy it, but defiance comes at a cost, and it may end up entrenching rather than undermining existing norms. What is needed is a movement, initiated and championed by those who say that they disapprove of or want to change the norm. Success will be achieved when a tipping point is reached (Sunstein, 2019).

CONCLUDING REMARKS – CALL FOR ACTION

The value of money is changing. As we have seen in this chapter, asset owners can play a unique role in promoting sustainable investing in pursuit of both financial self-interest and a more prosperous society at large. But of course, the road to hell is paved with good intentions. Transforming an organization and surmounting barriers is easier said than done. Asset owners tend to have three key resources within the organization: human capital, systems, and processes. The fund's level of sophistication in these three areas will tend to drive the organization's decisions about assets, access, and execution (Clark and Monk, 2017). Leading institutions are paving the way, but others have held back. One common reason is that they believe sustainable investing ordinarily produces lower returns than conventional strategies, despite research findings to the contrary (Bernow, Klempner, and Magnin, 2017). But make no mistake, it is urgent that asset owners step up to the plate because "past performance is no guarantee of future results," and both society and the planet find themselves increasingly beleaguered.

The world is at a crossroads; long-held paradigms are shifting. Globalization is contracting. Trade wars are back in vogue. Chimerica is unraveling. Meanwhile, protests are taking place all over the world; so-called strongman populism is flourishing; and multilateralism is in retreat. Increasingly, it seems we are living in a G-Zero world (Bremmer, 2013). At the same time, the world is facing increasing pressure from climate change, which is affecting food, energy, and water, all of which intersect critically with geopolitics. Technology is disrupting manufacturing; corporations are digitizing their processes. Social media connects people but is also enabling echo-chamber tribalism and disrupting the normal functioning of democracy. Economies are being propped up by free money infusion from central banks who seem to offer the only game in town (El-Erian, 2016).

Sound hopeless? Have faith in history. Nothing is more consistent in world history than the adoption by successful rebels of the methods they were accustomed to condemn in the forces they deposed. Social evolution is preceded mostly by economic, political, intellectual, and moral innovation. New situations require novel responses; development requires experiment and innovation (Durant and Durant, 2010). The only constant in life is change. Non-equilibrium is the natural state of the economy, and therefore it is always open to change. There are two main reasons for this: fundamental (or Knightian) uncertainty, and technological innovation (Arthur, 2014).

Simply put, we face an unprecedented systemic threat. Anthropogenic climate change is a global and long-term threat. It does not require a model to reason that polluting or altering our environment significantly could put us in uncharted territory, with no statistical precedent and potentially cataclysmic consequences. According to Norman et al. (2015), the popular belief that uncertainty undermines the case for taking seriously the "climate crisis" that scientists tell us we face is the opposite of the truth. Properly understood, as driving the case for precaution, uncertainty radically underscores that case, and may even constitute it.

We know what we must do. Let's get started.

Appendix 1

TABLE 17.1
Proposed standardized terminology

Proposed standardized term	Exclusion investments	Inclusion investments	Impactful investments	Philanthropic investments
Simplified explanation	Actively avoid investing in unsustainable corporates and countries	Actively invest in sustainable corporates and countries	Seek to have a direct, positive impact on society and/or the environment with your money, while also targeting market or better financial returns	Seek to have a direct, positive impact on society and/or the environment with your money, and willing to earn sub-market financial returns to do this
Financial performance	Market/ market minus	Market/market plus	Market/market plus	Market minus
Environmental and/or social impact of investment	None	Indirect	Direct	Direct
Measurement of direct impact of investment			Yes	Optional
Measurement of indirect impact of investment		Optional	No	Optional
Current terms used	Best-in-class screening	Aligned	Active ownership	Blended finance
terms currently used capriciously that need to be used in a single category	Biblical investing	B-Corporation (B-Corp)	v	Blue bonds
		Best-in-class screening	Company activism	Community investing
	Clean investing		Company engagement	
	Divestment	Climate bonds	Company executive	Development finance institute bonds / DFI bonds
	Ethical investing	Environmental, social, and governance investing (ESG)	Collaboration	Development impact bonds
	Ethically minded investing	ESG corporate bonds		Humanitarian impact bonds

(Continued)

TABLE 17.1 (Cont.)

Exclusion investments	Inclusion investments	Impactful investments	Philanthropic investments
Exclusionary screening	ESG equity themes	Corporate activism	**Impact**
Faith-based investing	ESG focused	Corporate engagement	Impact bonds
Impact	**ESG integration**	Development finance institute bonds / DFI bonds	Impact capitalism
Impact investing (II)	ESG investing	SDG engagement	Impact economy
Jewish investing	ESG thematic investing	**Impact**	**Impact investing (II)**
Negative screening	**Ethical investing**	**Impact investing (II)**	Social bonds
Norms-based screening	**Ethically minded investing**	Multilateral development bank bonds / MDS bonds	Social enterprise
Positive screening	Focused integration	Shareholder action	Social entrepreneurs
Screening investing	Gender-lens investing	**Triple bottom line**	Social finance
Shariah investing	Gender-smart investing		Social impact bonds
Values-based investing	Green bonds		Social impact investing
	Green investing		Social investing
	High ESG rating equities		Sustainable finance
	Impact investing (II)		**Triple bottom line**
	Improving ESG equities		Universal ownership
	Integration		
	Long-term investment themes		
	Mission-aligned investing		
	Positive screening		
	Responsible investing		
	Screening investing		

Socially responsible investing (SRI)

Socially conscious investing

SRI equity themes

Sustainability indices

Sustainability-themed investing

Sustainability themes

Sustainable bonds

Sustainable thematic investing

Tactical ESG

Thematic investing

Values-based investing

Source: Reproduced by permission from the Institute of International Finance (IIF), "The Case for Simplifying Sustainable Investment Terminology," a discussion paper prepared by IIF and informed by discussions of the IIF Sustainable Finance Working Group, p. 5. © 2019 The Institute of International Finance.

NOTES

1 The views expressed herein are those of the author and do not necessarily reflect the views of the United Nations.

2 Acknowledgement: I would like to thank Tom Stoner and Adam Phillips for their very helpful contributions to this chapter.

3 A trustee of a retirement plan is the entity or group of individuals (sometimes one individual) which holds the assets of the plan in trust. They are responsible for the oversight and investment of pension fund assets. Trustees are the primary stewards of the plan's assets and are the ultimate decision-makers in relation to the investments of the assets. They have a fiduciary responsibility to invest plan assets prudently, impartially, and cost-effectively in accordance with governing laws and documents, and, most importantly, with loyalty toward, that is, solely in the best interest of, plan participants and their beneficiaries (Croft and Malhotra, 2016).

4 A plan sponsor is a designated party – usually a company or employer – that sets up a retirement plan for the benefit of an organization's employees.

5 Political economy originated in moral philosophy and included the topic of distribution of national income and wealth. Today, the term "economics" usually refers to the narrow study of the economy absent other political and social considerations.

6 Homo pancasilaus has a number of indicators which characterizes human personality: divinity, humanity, unity, society, and justice (Sitorus, Triyuwono, and Kamayanti, 2017).

7 See: www.wsj.com/articles/pg-e-wildfires-and-the-first-climate-change-bankruptcy-11547820006

8 See: www.entelligent.com

9 There are some 4.5 billion people in the base of the pyramid (BoP) as customers. These people live primarily in Asia, Africa and South America. The BoP is defined as people who earn less than $8 per day.

10 The GHG Protocol Standard classifies a company's GHG emissions into three "scopes." Scope 1 emissions are direct emissions from owned or controlled sources; Scope 2 emissions are indirect emissions from the generation of purchased energy.

11 E-Score™, developed and trade marked by Entelligent, is a measure of company/issuance fitness with respect to uncertainty over a wide range of potential climate change scenarios.

REFERENCES

Arthur, B. (2014). *Complexity and the economy*. Oxford: Oxford University Press.

Bernow, S., Klempner, B. & Magnin, C. (2017). From 'Why' to 'Why Not': Sustainable Investing as the New Normal. [Online] *McKinsey & Company*. Available at: www.mckinsey.com/industries/private-equity-and-principal-investors/our-insights/from-why-to-why-not-sustainable-investing-as-the-new-normal (Accessed: 23 November 2019).

Bremmer, I. (2013). *Every nation for itself*. New York: Portfolio/Penguin.

Citi. (2019). *Managing the Financial Risk of Climate Change*. Available at: www.citivelocity.com/citigps/managing-financial-risks-climate-change/ (Accessed: 6 January 2020).

Clark, G. & Monk, A. (2017). *Institutional investors in global markets*. Oxford: Oxford University Press.

Cooper, G. (2014). *Money, blood and revolution*. Petersfield: Harriman House.

Croft, T. & Malhotra, A. (2016). *The responsible investor handbook*. Sheffield: Greenleaf.

Durant, A. & Durant, W. (2010). *The lessons of history*. New York: Simon & Schuster.

El-Erian, M. (2016). *The only game in town: central banks, instability, and avoiding the next collapse*. New York: Random House.

Entelligent. (2018). *Developing prudent investment strategies to address climate change risk and opportunities*. Boulder, CO: Entelligent.

Guyatt, D. & Poulter, J. (2019). *Institutional investors and the behavioral barriers to taking action on climate change*. San Francisco: ClimateWork Foundation.

Hanauer, N. & Beinhocker, E. (2014). Capitalism Redefined. [Online] *Democracy Journal*. Available at: https://democracyjournal.org/magazine/31/capitalism-redefined/?page=all (Accessed: 6 January 2020).

Harnett, E. (2018). *Responsible Investment and ESG: An Economic Geography*. Doctoral Dissertation, Hilda's College, University of Oxford.

Institute of International Finance (IIF). (2019). *The Case for Simplifying Sustainable Investment Terminology.* [online] Available at: www.iif.com/Publications/ID/3633/The-Case-for-Simplifying-Sustainable-Investment-Terminology (Accessed: 24 November 2019).

International Monetary Fund (IMF). (2019). Global Financial Stability Report, October 2019: Lower for Longer (Chapter 6: Sustainable Finance). Available at: www.elibrary.imf.org/view/IMF082/26206-9781498324021/26206-9781498324021/ch06.xml?lang=en (Accessed: 24 November 2019).

King, M. (2016). *The end of alchemy*. London: Little Brown Book Group.

Koedijk, K., Slager, A. & van Dam, J. (2019). *Achieving investment excellence*. Chichester: John Wiley & Sons.

Kuhn, T. (1970). *The structure of scientific revolutions*. Chicago, IL: University of Chicago Press.

Liang, H. & Renneboog, L. (2017). 'On The Foundations Of Corporate Social Responsibility'. *The Journal of Finance*, 72(2), pp. 853–910.

Lo, A. (2016). 'The Gordon Gekko Effect: The Role of Culture in the Financial Industry'. *Economic Policy Review, Federal Reserve Bank of New York*, 22(1), pp. 17–42.

Lo, A. (2017). *Adaptive markets*. Princeton, NJ: Princeton University Press.

Mayer, C. (2018). *Prosperity*. Oxford: Oxford University Press.

McKinsey Quarterly. (2019). *Don't be the villain': Niall Ferguson looks forward and back at capitalism in crisis. [Video]* Available at: www.mckinsey.com/featured-insights/long-term-capitalism/dont-be-the-villain-niall-ferguson-looks-forward-and-back-at-capitalism-in-crisis (Accessed: 24 November 2019).

Norman, J., Read, R., Bar-Yam, Y. & Taleb, N. (2015). *Climate models and precautionary measures. Issues in Science and Technology.* [online] Available at: https://necsi.edu/climate-models-and-precautionary-measures (Accessed: 24 November 2019).

Papadogiannis, Y. (2014). *The rise and fall of homo economicus*. North Charleston, SC: CreateSpace Independent Publishing Platform.

Porter, M., Serafeim, G. & Kramer, M. (2019). *Where ESG Fails*. [Online] *Institutional Investor*. Available at: www.institutionalinvestor.com/article/b1hm5ghqtxj9s7/Where-ESG-Fails (Accessed: 10 January 2020).

Rajkumar, S. & Dorfman, M. (2011). *Governance and investment of public pension assets*. Washington, DC: World Bank.

Schoenmaker, D. & Schramade, W. (2019). *Principles of sustainable finance*. Oxford: Oxford University Press.

Sitorus, J., Triyuwono, I. & Kamayanti, A. (2017). 'Homo Economicus Vis A Vis Homo Pancasilaus: A Fight against Positive Accounting Theory'. *Pertanika Journal of Social Sciences & Humanities*, 25, pp. 311–320.

Sunstein, C. (2019). *How change happens*. Cambridge, MA: MIT Press.

Tett, G. (2015). *The silo effect*. New York: Simon & Schuster.

Thakor, A. (2016). 'Corporate Culture in Banking'. *Economic Policy Review, Federal Reserve Bank of New York*, 22(1), pp. 5–16.

Thaler, R. (2015). *Misbehaving*. London: Random House.

Urwin, R. (2011). 'Pension Funds as Universal Owners: Opportunity Beckons and Leadership Calls'. *Rotman International Journal of Pension Management*, 4(1), pp. 26–33.

Willis Towers Watson. (2019). *The Thinking Ahead Institute's Asset Owner 100.* [online] Available at: www.thinkingaheadinstitute.org/en/Library/Public/Research-and-Ideas/2019/11/AO100_2019_Survey (Accessed: 17 November 2019).

18

Sustainable investing

Shaping the future of theory and practice

Herman Bril, Georg Kell, and Andreas Rasche

THREE THEMES SHAPING SUSTAINABLE INVESTING

What can we take away from the diverse contributions and insights brought together in this book? The aim of this book is to bring together practitioner and academic voices to reflect on the current state of sustainable investing as well as possible paths to a new horizon (see Chapter 1). Instead of summarizing the contribution of each chapter, we identify three high-level themes that cut across a number of chapters. We use these three themes to discuss the past, present, and future of sustainable investing. We do not argue that these three themes reflect a comprehensive summary of the chapters. Rather, our aim is to highlight those topics that underlie the discussions in this book, either explicitly or implicitly. We believe that the three themes are important pillars when shaping the future of sustainable investing, both in theory and in practice.

ACCELERATING CHANGE

One of the most striking insights gained from the diverse contributions in this book is that the theories and practices that underpinned the industrial era are no longer sufficient to navigate the future (see, e.g., Chapters 2, 3, and 7). This realization is fueled by the accelerating change we can observe across different domains. Technological advances are disrupting existing structures of the economy and are giving rise to novel questions about social welfare, employment, social justice, and governance. At the same time the impact of economic activities on nature and the basic conditions for human life are increasingly forcing us to establish a fundamentally new relationship with the natural environment. To quote former UN Secretary-General Kofi Annan: "The speed of markets clearly outpaces the ability of societies and their political systems to adjust to them, let alone to guide the course they take" (United Nations, 1999).

One would hope that societies everywhere would reboot, pause, and adjust in order to find new ways of employing the unprecedented resources at our disposal to tackle both ecological and social challenges at hand. We could easily green all the world's deserts, restore natural habitats, and create socially meaningful employment for everybody. But alas, homo sapiens still has a long way to go to achieve enlightenment. Myths of the past still give meaning to people's lives and the blanket of civilization is as razor thin today as it was one hundred years ago, despite the many lessons that history has taught us. Here and there we can observe sincere efforts to adjust to a new era. Efforts by some Scandinavian countries (Strand and Freeman, 2015) and the recently introduced European Green Deal (European Commission, 2020) are such efforts that have the potential to renew the bargain between markets and societies while responding to ecological and social imperatives ahead of us.

But foreign policy and international relations between the biggest powers have yet to align around a common purpose fit for the new era. Ancient power concepts still dominate political decision-making and the notion of planetary public goods has yet to be developed. Worse, the dark forces of nationalism, ethnic chauvinism, and populism are gaining momentum and are tapping into ancient fears and fueling divides. Clearly, the current state of affairs points towards greater divergences and tensions rather than alignments. As the impact of climate change will eventually force governments to take much bolder steps, we can only hope that societies everywhere and their political systems and representatives will realize that old thinking and power concepts are no longer useful. The case for planetary stewardship will eventually emerge and reshape relationships between nations and cultures. The question is when and under what circumstances such insights will at last take hold and how big the price we will have to pay to learn will be.

In the meantime, business and investors are facing uncertainties but also have the extraordinary opportunity to shape the transition. Making markets future-fit lies within reach. It is clear what needs to be done, and the means to do so are mostly available already. Corporations and investors can now be at the forefront of environmental stewardship by forming a strong ethical foundation and a clear purpose that serves private and public interests. They can build social trust with strong values that are understood everywhere. Thanks to digitalization and new insights from climate science, investors can now steer capital away from harmful economic activities towards sustainable activities.

Financial systems can integrate nontraditional factors into their valuation. The data and artificial intelligence (AI) revolution will accelerate this trend, and as investors increasingly are rewarding good ESG practices of corporations, a new powerful market-led driver is at work (see Chapter 12 by Omar Selim).

As the realization that old dogmas and theories are no longer sufficient to build the future we want is settling in, there is now a premium on innovation and the ability to bring together expertise from different fields to find future-proof solutions. For example, economists have to learn how to interpret findings of climate science and investors need to develop capacities to translate relevant social-economic implications into investment decision-making. The rapidly changing framework conditions clearly put a premium on the ability to integrate diverse observations into meaningful assumptions about future risks and returns and by doing so ultimately change valuations and cost of capital. Ultimately, price signals need to change to reflect a new balance between ecology, society, and profits.

SUSTAINABLE INVESTMENT – MUCH BROADER THAN NARROW ESG RATINGS

Another key takeaway of this book is that sustainable investment by itself is really a paradigm shift in traditional investment thinking. Not in the sense of why we invest in the first place, which is essentially to generate the required future returns to secure future financial outcomes on behalf of the beneficiaries. It's how we invest and how the value of money is changing. How do we value expected future cash flows in different macro-economic, monetary policy, fiscal, geopolitical, social, environmental, technological, and demographic scenarios?

Radical uncertainty is what we are facing in a VUCA world (see Chapter 1), and that means that our best bet is to become Darwinian thinkers and always aim for future fitness. Both in the way we build our global investment portfolios and how we assess companies to invest in. Robustness, resilience, and coping strategies are the winning attributes in an unpredictable world. Strategic sustainability and risk management are completely intertwined and best understood in an evolutionary perspective.

This means rethinking capitalism, taking into account planetary boundaries (Chapter 6), new economic thinking, and the role of societal fairness. To make it even more challenging, we need to be able to manage multiple time horizons to survive in the short term while focusing on the long term. This requires a clear sense of purpose, building strong institutions, fit-for-purpose governance, and Level 5[1] leadership (Collins, 2011).

The investment industry has an important role to play in this paradigm shift toward sustainable investment. The recent announcement from

BlackRock (one of the world's biggest asset managers) to fully embrace sustainable investment is a game-changer towards mainstreaming (BlackRock, 2020). The IMF also reported for the first time about sustainable investment in its Global Outlook. Financial regulators are also debating their role and possible actions regarding climate change. *The Green Swan* (Bolton et al., 2020), published by the Bank for International Settlements, argued that climate change is a systematic risk; hence regulators have a role to play. The most exposed financial institutions are perhaps insurance companies. They face not only transition risk, physical risk on both the asset and liability side of the balance sheet, but also health care and mortality risk. This is not something to worry about in the future; it is happening today. Uninsurable risk will become a major issue for people in certain areas, with negative knock-on effects on regional concentrated insurance companies' business models.

Most traditional asset owners still believe in the 60% equity and 40% bonds asset allocation portfolio, often with a material home bias (too much invested in their own country) and implemented using passive index trackers. Without question, this was an extremely successful approach over the last decade, post-global financial crisis. However, it's highly unlikely that this will be a successful strategy in the next decades. Recent successful performance makes it hard to change the strategy towards sustainable investing and building a more future-proof portfolio. The easy way is to stay the course and fail conventionally. Change is perceived riskier and scarier. Relying on historical statistical data and using "mean-variance optimization" techniques to calculate the "efficient" portfolio is the standard textbook approach backed by Nobel laureate economists and investment consultants. Can't go wrong, right? Time will tell, but be prepared for a different outcome, as explained in Chapter 16. McKinsey Global Institute (2020) published a report, *Climate Risk and Response: Physical hazards and socioeconomic impacts*, and concluded that the socioeconomic impacts of climate change will likely be nonlinear as system thresholds are breached and have knock-on effects; and could be substantial as a changing climate affects human beings, as well as physical and natural capital.

The purpose of this book is to promote debate, exchange ideas, provide a deeper understanding of how financial institutions, companies, regulators, and governments can embrace sustainable investment, and find a collective *path to a new horizon*. We have enough scientifically supported understanding of the risks we are facing, even though we cannot quantify it fully in our models as described in Chapter 13 by Helga Birgden. Strategic risk management is to avoid financial or societal outcomes we cannot bear, irrespective of the (unknown) probabilities. Sustainable investing is an imperative, as explained by Herman Bril in Chapter 17.

KNOWING AND BELIEVING

The different contributions in this volume show: we already know a lot about sustainable investing. The field has matured in impressive ways during recent years. While early debates focused on practices like positive and negative screenings, the integration of ESG issues into mainstream finance has proven that knowledge development in this field cannot rest on the assumption that "financial" and "non-financial" decision-making can be neatly separated. Both are inextricably intertwined. Of course, there are areas about which we could (and should) know more. Together, the contributors to this book high-lighted three areas in particular.

First, we still have no solid theoretical foundation for discussing sustainable investing. As debated in Chapters 1 and 2, well-known conceptual frame-works, like the efficient market hypothesis, do not hold anymore and need to be revised and updated. Theoretical advancements not only have to consider new insights on human behavior, but they also have to consider the changing conditions that markets themselves are facing (e.g., fast-paced technological transformations and geopolitical uncertainty). How can we think of finan-cial regulation under conditions of increasing complexity and uncertainty? In which ways do changing environmental conditions impact financial inno-vation? How can we ensure a high level of robustness of the financial system despite accelerating environmental change?

Second, despite the enormous growth of ESG-related data, there are still significant challenges in (a) improving the quality and comparability of this data and (b) linking it to robust financial decision-making. Different chapters in this volume have highlighted the need to enhance the quality of ESG data (see, e.g., Chapter 9). Advancing knowledge in this direction is not purely an academic effort; it also requires political will and improved coordination among investors, regulators, and corporations. What level of standardization do we need for ESG data? How can we achieve such standardization? Will such standardization *ipso facto* improve the comparability of ESG data across regions and sectors? How can we ensure that such data is not manipulated or misused?

Finally, a number of contributions have emphasized that sustainable investing is as much about investor behavior as it is about corporate behavior (see e.g., Chapters 9, 10, and 11). For instance, short-termism is as much a problem in the investment world as it is a problem in the corporate world; of course, because both worlds are heavily interconnected. We need more knowledge about how ESG integration and corporate practices, such as inte-grated reporting, mutually enhance each other. We also need to know more about how corporate governance and sustainable investing can (and should) interact. How do we ensure that boards have sufficient knowledge about the risks and opportunities attached to ESG issues? How do we align formal governance processes and more informal values attached to corporations' culture so that ESG issues are integrated into decision-making at all levels?

Creating more knowledge clearly is one thing, believing in it another. Knowledge creates an awareness of information. Believing requires us to actually trust knowledge, to have faith in it, and to act accordingly. We can absorb enormous amounts of knowledge about sustainable investing. Yet, to create the transformative changes that are required to address some of the grand challenges ahead of us we need to start believing in this very knowledge. Believing requires us to connect sustainable investing to our own base of values. Values are, as Mark Moody-Stuart (Chapter 11) observes, the guiding principles of our actions; they guide how we act as employees and employers, mothers and fathers, investors and investees. Believing in sustainable investing is not a religious act. It simply means to change how we engage with the world around us; it requires us to be open to learning and to rethink conventional mental models that guide our thinking (e.g., about how to value assets). Taken together, advancing our knowledge of and beliefs in sustainable investing can create powerful responses to the sustainability challenges of our time.

Narrative economics, the study of the spread of narratives that impact economic behavior, can improve our ability to anticipate and prepare for economic events. It can also help us structure economic institutions and policy. An economic narrative is a "contagious story that has the potential to change how people make economic decisions" (Shiller, 2019, p. 3). Moving from knowing to believing and acting requires that we create powerful "ESG stories." This book is full of such stories, and hopefully these narratives will shape how people make *different* decisions.

NOTE

1   Level 5 leaders display a powerful mixture of personal humility and indomitable will. They're incredibly ambitious, but their ambition is first and foremost for the cause, for the organization and its purpose, not themselves.

REFERENCES

BlackRock. (2020). A Fundamental Reshaping of Finance. Available at: www.blackrock.com/dk/individuel/larry-fink-ceo-letter (Accessed: 28 January 2020).

Bolton, P., Despres, M., Awazu, L., Da, P., Samama, F., & Svartzman, R. (2020). *The Green Swan: Central Banking and Financial Stability in the Age of Climate Chnage*. Basel: Bank for International Settlements (BIS).

Collins, J. C. (2011). *Good to Great: Why Some Companies Make the Leap ... and Others Don't*. New York: Harper Business.

European Commission. (2020). What Is the European Green Deal? Available at: https://ec.europa.eu/commission/presscorner/detail/en/fs_19_6714 (Accessed: 28 January 2020).

McKinsey Global Institute. (2020). *Climate Risk and Response: Physical Hazards and Socioeconomic Impacts*. Available at: www.mckinsey.com/business-functions/sustainability/our-insights/climate-risk-and-response-physical-hazards-and-socioeconomic-impacts (Accessed: 28 January 2020).

Shiller, R. (2019). *Narrative Economics*. Princeton, NJ: Princeton University Press.

Strand, R., & Freeman, R. (2015). Scandinavian Cooperative Advantage: The Theory and Practice of Stakeholder Engagement in Scandinavia. *Journal of Business Ethics, 127*(1), 65–85.

United Nations. (1999). *Secretary-General Proposes Global Compact on Human Rights, Labour, Environment, in Address to World Economic Forum in Davos* (Press Release, SG/SM/6881). New York: United Nations.

Index

Locators in *italics* refer to figures and those in **bold** to tables, though where concurrent with related text these are not distinguished from principal locators.